Calculus

A

Calculus

J. Hunter
In association with
The Scottish Mathematics Group

Blackie Glasgow and London
Chambers Edinburgh and London

Blackie & Son Limited Bishopbriggs, Glasgow
450/452 Edgware Road, London W2 1EG

W. & R. Chambers Limited 11 Thistle Street, Edinburgh 2

First published 1972
Reprinted 1977
Reprinted 1980

Educational edition

Blackie 0 216 89481 6
Chambers 0 550 75893 3

Net edition

Blackie 0 216 89794 7
Chambers 0 550 75993 X

Printed in Great Britain by Robert MacLehose & Co. Ltd, Renfrew

Preface

The aim of this text on CALCULUS is to present with modern notation and language a book which bridges the gap from sixth-form work at schools to first-year work at colleges and universities. The book arose in the first place as a text to cover the calculus content of Paper II of the Scottish Sixth-Year Studies Examination in Mathematics and as a natural sequel to the work on calculus in Books 8 and 9 of *Modern Mathematics for Schools* (Blackie/Chambers), written by the Scottish Mathematics Group. It is hoped that the book will also be useful for study at the Advanced Level of the General Certificate of Education and for certain courses in colleges of education and universities. As indicated, the work can be used in different ways; for schools almost all of the proofs of results can be omitted (if this is considered desirable) and the ideas introduced and consolidated by means of examples, and, of course, only those topics need be covered which are required for a particular syllabus; for colleges and universities a deeper and more ambitious programme can be used—in all cases the exercises at the ends of the chapters, in which the problems are listed in the order in which the topics are covered, should be regarded as an integral part of the text.

The list overleaf headed "Some basic notation used in this book" indicates some of the prerequisites for a modern treatment of calculus. Since these topics are essential for many other branches of mathematics and its applications, it is suggested that they should be covered, as far as possible, before embarking on a systematic study of calculus. In this sense, part of Chapters 1 to 5 of *Algebra and Number Systems* (mentioned at the end of the list) (or equivalent) should be regarded as part of the present text. Some work on analytical geometry is also necessary and can be found in Part 1 of *Analytic Geometry and Vectors* by J. Hunter (Blackie/Chambers, 1972).

Calculus is an extremely difficult subject to cover at this level, since adequate proofs of results very often depend on work in analysis that can be appreciated by the bulk of students only at a slightly more mature stage. Nevertheless it is important to stress that at this level a point has been reached at the top of the school work in mathematics where intuition by itself is no longer adequate, although still important, and where purely formal manipulation begins to require logical justification. The treatments given of limits and convergence of series are restricted to the minimum necessary for their main contexts in Chapters 1 and 7, respectively. As indicated in Chapter 1 the algebra of limits is more important for differentiation than facility in evaluating complicated artificial limits and in Chapter 7, in the treatment of power-series expansions, little on convergence is required when an approach through Taylor's finite formula is used.

The considerable emphasis placed on the notation and results for functions has many advantages: e.g. it is helpful to picture the chain rule in the form

$$\frac{d}{dx}f(\cdots) = f'(\cdots)\frac{d}{dx}(\cdots),$$

where f' is the derived function of f, and *any* differentiable expression $g(x)$ for which f is differentiable at $g(x)$ can be inserted inside the brackets; also knowledge of bijections and inverse functions is essential to appreciate the justification for the use of the formula $dx/dy = 1/(dy/dx)$. Although the overall treatment given of the subject is still far from logically complete, it is hoped that the presentation will lead on to the next mathematical stage when analysis will be introduced.

Notation

Some basic notation used in this book

Sets

$\in$: belongs to.

$\notin$: does not belong to.

$\subseteq$: is a subset of, or, is contained in.

$\cup$: union.

$\cap$: intersection.

$\emptyset$: the empty set.

$A - B$: the set of those elements of A not in B.

$\mathbf{R}$: the set of all real numbers.

$\mathbf{R}^+ = \{x \in \mathbf{R} : x \geqslant 0\}$; $\mathbf{R}^- = \{x \in \mathbf{R} : x \leqslant 0\}$.

$\mathbf{N} = \{1, 2, 3, \cdots\}$, the set of positive integers.

$\mathbf{Z} = \{0, \pm 1, \pm 2, \cdots\}$, the set of all integers.

$\mathbf{Z}^+ = \{0, 1, 2, \cdots\}$, the set of non-negative integers.

$\mathbf{Q} = \left\{\frac{m}{n} : m, n \in \mathbf{Z}, n \neq 0\right\}$, the set of rational numbers.

$[a, b] = \{x \in \mathbf{R} : a \leqslant x \leqslant b\}$, finite closed interval with end points a, b.

$[a, b) = \{x \in \mathbf{R} : a \leqslant x < b\}$; $(a, b] = \{x \in \mathbf{R} : a < x \leqslant b\}$.

$(a, b) = \{x \in \mathbf{R} : a < x < b\}$, finite open interval with end points a, b.

$[a, \infty) = \{x \in \mathbf{R} : a \leqslant x\}$; $(a, \infty) = \{x \in \mathbf{R} : a < x\}$
$(-\infty, b] = \{x \in \mathbf{R} : x \leqslant b\}$; $(-\infty, b) = \{x \in \mathbf{R} : x < b\}$ } infinite intervals.

$\mathbf{R}^n = \{(x_1, x_2, \cdots, x_n) : x_i \in \mathbf{R}\ (i = 1, \cdots, n)\}$.

Mappings

$f : S \to T$: mapping f from set S to set T, by which $s \in S$ is mapped to its image $f(s) \in T$.

S, T are called the **domain** and **codomain**, respectively, of f.

$f(S) = \{t \in T : t = f(s) \text{ for some } s \in S\}$ is called the **image** of f.

$\{(s, f(s)) : s \in S\}$: the **graph** of f.

$f : S \to T$ is a **real function** when $S \subseteq \mathbf{R}$ and $T \subseteq \mathbf{R}$.

$f : S \to T$ is an **injection** (an injective or $|-|$ mapping) if

$$f(s_1) = f(s_2) \Rightarrow s_1 = s_2 .$$

$f : S \to T$ is a **surjection** (a surjective or onto mapping) if $f(S) = T$, i.e. every member of T is an image under f.

$f : S \to T$ is a **bijection** (a bijective mapping) if it is *both* injective and surjective.

A *bijection* $f : S \to T$ has an **inverse mapping** $f^{-1} : T \to S$ such that

$$t = f(s) \Leftrightarrow s = f^{-1}(t).$$

$f \circ g : S \to U$: **composition** of $g : S \to T$ and $f : T \to U$ defined by

$$(f \circ g)(s) = f(g(s)) \ \forall s \in S.$$

$f_1 : S_1 \to T_1$ is a **restriction** of $f : S \to T$ if

$$S_1 \subseteq S,\ T_1 \subseteq T \text{ and } f_1(s) = f(s) \ \forall s \in S_1.$$

Logic

$\exists$: there exists.

$\forall$: for all.

$\Rightarrow$: implies.

$\Leftrightarrow$: is equivalent to.

Standard ideas of direct proof, indirect proof by contradiction, counterexamples and proof by induction will be assumed.

Number systems

Properties of the relations $<, \leqslant, >, \geqslant$ on $\mathbf{R}$ will be assumed.

$$|x| = \begin{cases} x, & x \geqslant 0 \\ -x, & x < 0 \end{cases} : \textbf{absolute value of } x \in \mathbf{R}.$$

Note: $\sqrt{(a^2)} = |a| \ (a \in \mathbf{R})$, $|a+b| \leqslant |a| + |b|$, etc.

[These notations and their associated properties, which are assumed where necessary in this book, are developed in Chapters 1 to 5 of *Algebra and Number Systems* by J. Hunter, D. Monk, W. T. Blackburn and D. Donald (Blackie/Chambers, 1971).]

Contents

Differentiation

I

1. Introduction

It will be assumed that the reader has already been introduced to the basic ideas of calculus, and, in particular, of differentiation. Nevertheless we shall give a brief survey of this work. By examining a variety of illustrations involving rates of change such as velocity and acceleration in mechanics, rate of radioactive decay, rate of discharge of electricity through some form of electrical equipment, rate of economic growth, etc., we are led to the consideration of a mathematical model which covers all such situations. This model deals with **real functions**, i.e. mappings from the set of real numbers **R** (or subsets of **R**) to **R**, and with the existence of tangent lines to the graph of such a mapping. It will be assumed that the reader knows the basic notation, definitions and results associated with such mappings [see, for example, Chapter 3 of *Algebra and Number Systems* by Hunter, Monk, Blackburn and Donald (Blackie/Chambers, 1971)] and is familiar with the necessary basic properties of the set of real numbers.

The elementary real functions of calculus can be classified as follows.

(1) The **zero function:** its domain is **R**, its image is $\{0\}$, and its graph is the x-axis, $y = 0$.

(2) Polynomials: a **real (non-zero) polynomial function** f is defined by a formula of the form

$$f(x) = a_n x^n + a_{n-1} x^{n-1} + \cdots + a_1 x + a_0, \tag{1.1}$$

where $n \geqslant 0$ and $a_0, a_1, \cdots, a_n$ are real numbers with $a_n \neq 0$.

The function f is said to be of **degree** n, and $f(x)$, given by (1.1), is called a **real polynomial** of **degree** n. A polynomial function has domain **R**.

If $n = 0$, i.e. if $f(x) = a_0 \; \forall x \in \mathbf{R}$, then f is called the **constant function** with value a_0. The graph of this function is the line $y = a_0$ parallel to the x-axis.

It is often convenient when dealing with polynomials to call the zero function the zero polynomial.

If $n = 1$, i.e. if $f(x) = a_1 x + a_0 \ \forall\, x \in \mathbf{R}$, then f is called a **linear function**; its graph is the line $y = a_1 x + a_0$.

If $n = 2$, i.e. if $f(x) = a_2 x^2 + a_1 x + a_0 \ \forall\, x \in \mathbf{R}$, then f is called a **quadratic function**; its graph is the parabola $y = a_2 x^2 + a_1 x + a_0$.

For $n = 3, 4, \cdots$, the polynomial is called **cubic**, **quartic**, etc.

(3) Rational functions: such a function f is defined by a formula of the form

$$f(x) = \frac{\text{a polynomial}}{\text{a polynomial}}, \text{ e.g. } f(x) = \frac{a_n x^n + \cdots + a_1 x + a_0}{b_m x^m + \cdots + b_1 x + b_0},$$

where the coefficients $a_0, \cdots, a_n$ and $b_0, \cdots, b_m$ are real numbers with $a_n \neq 0$, $b_m \neq 0$, and where we can assume that the numerator and denominator have no common polynomial factor of degree $\geqslant 1$. The domain of definition of f is $\mathbf{R} - \{\text{real zeros of the denominator}\}$; for example,

$$\frac{x}{x^2 - 1} \text{ has domain } \mathbf{R} - \{1, -1\}.$$

(4) $x^{m/n}$, $n \in \mathbf{N}$, $m \in \mathbf{Z}$ (i.e. rational powers of x): $x^{m/n}$ is defined to be $(x^{1/n})^m$, where $x^{1/n} = \sqrt[n]{x}$, the unique real root of the equation $z^n = x$, with the convention that the root is non-negative when n is *even* and $x \geqslant 0$.

(5) The **trigonometric functions:** these are the **sine**, **cosine** and **tangent** functions and their reciprocals **cosecant, secant** and **cotangent** defined as follows.

$\sin : \mathbf{R} \to \mathbf{R}$ defined by: $\sin x = \sin$ (angle of measure x radians) $\forall x \in \mathbf{R}$;
$\cos : \mathbf{R} \to \mathbf{R}$ defined by: $\cos x = \cos$ (angle of measure x radians) $\forall x \in \mathbf{R}$;

Each of these functions has image $[-1, 1]$; their graphs and basic properties should be revised.

$$\tan : \mathbf{R} - \{\tfrac{1}{2}(2n+1)\pi : n \in \mathbf{Z}\} \to \mathbf{R} \text{ defined by } \tan x = \frac{\sin x}{\cos x};$$

$$\operatorname{cosec} : \mathbf{R} - \{n\pi : n \in \mathbf{Z}\} \to \mathbf{R} \text{ defined by } \operatorname{cosec} x = \frac{1}{\sin x};$$

$$\sec : \mathbf{R} - \{\tfrac{1}{2}(2n+1)\pi : n \in \mathbf{Z}\} \to \mathbf{R} \text{ defined by } \sec x = \frac{1}{\cos x};$$

$$\cot : \mathbf{R} - \{n\pi : n \in \mathbf{Z}\} \to \mathbf{R} \text{ defined by } \cot x = \frac{1}{\tan x} = \frac{\cos x}{\sin x}.$$

The functions tan and cot have image **R** and the functions cosec and sec have image $\mathbf{R}-(-1, 1)$. The usual elementary results for the trigonometric functions will be assumed. The graphs of cosec, sec and cot should be drawn, noting that these functions are the reciprocals of sin, cos and tan respectively.

Note. The trigonometric function $f: \mathbf{R} \to \mathbf{R}$ defined by

$$f(x) = \sin x^\circ = \sin \text{ (angle of measure } x \text{ degrees)}$$

is related to the above sine function by the fact that

$$\sin x^\circ = \sin (\tfrac{1}{180}\pi x \text{ radians}) = \sin (\tfrac{1}{180}\pi x)\,.$$

Similarly for the other trigonometric functions. These functions involving degrees seldom arise in applications and have more complicated derivatives than the above functions.

(6) The **logarithmic**, **exponential**, and **hyperbolic functions**; we shall define these functions later.

Any real function which can be defined in terms of the functions listed under (1), $\cdots$, (6), possibly using composition of functions and inverse functions, is called an **elementary function**. Elementary calculus is concerned with the derivatives and integrals of such functions.

2. Differentiation, the tangent problem

We start with a real function f and its graph $y = f(x)$. If D is the domain of f and $x \in D$, then x is called an **interior point** of D if there is an open interval $(x-\delta, x+\delta)$, $(\delta > 0)$, with centre at x, which is entirely contained in D. Such an interval will be called a **neighbourhood** of x.

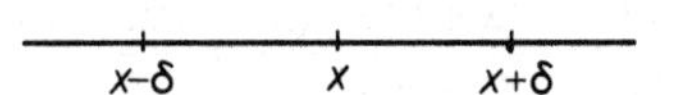

In the first place we consider such interior points and raise the question of whether a tangent line exists at the corresponding point $P(x, f(x))$ on the graph $y = f(x)$ of f. It is natural to consider the

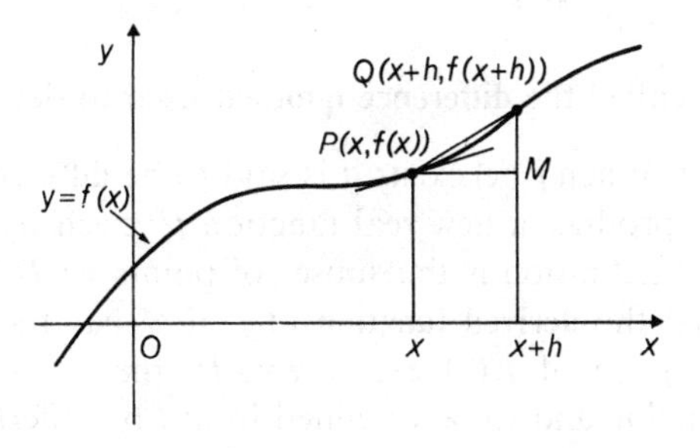

gradient m_{PQ} of the chord PQ joining P to a neighbouring point $Q(x+h, f(x+h))$ on the graph (here, either $h > 0$ or $h < 0$, but $h \neq 0$), and to try to determine what happens to this gradient the closer Q is to P. For a tangent direction at P with gradient L to exist it would be natural to expect the following statement to be true:

"$\exists$ a fixed real number L such that $|m_{PQ} - L|$ can be made as small as we please by taking $|h|$ sufficiently small, but $\neq 0$." (2.1)

[$|x|$ denotes, as usual, the absolute value of the real number x, so that $|x| = x$ when $x \geqslant 0$ and $|x| = -x$ when $x < 0$].

Statement (2.1) can be expressed in symbols as follows:

"Given $\varepsilon > 0$, $\exists \delta > 0$ such that

$$0 < |h| < \delta \Rightarrow |m_{PQ} - L| < \varepsilon.\text{"} \tag{2.2}$$

When (2.1) (and so (2.2)) holds, we write:

$$m_{PQ} \text{ tends to } L \text{ as } h \text{ tends to } 0,$$

and

$$m_{PQ} \to L \text{ as } h \to 0, \quad \text{or} \quad \lim_{h \to 0} m_{PQ} = L,$$

where "lim" is an abbreviation of "limit". Then the number L is the gradient of the tangent at $P(x, f(x))$ to the graph $y = f(x)$.

In fact, in order to stress that L depends on f and on x, we denote it by $f'(x)$, and call it, when it exists, the **derivative** of f at x. Since

$$m_{PQ} = \frac{MQ}{PM} = \frac{f(x+h) - f(x)}{(x+h) - x} = \frac{f(x+h) - f(x)}{h},$$

we thus have:

$$\lim_{h \to 0} \frac{f(x+h) - f(x)}{h} = f'(x). \tag{2.3}$$

$\dfrac{f(x+h) - f(x)}{h}$ is called the **difference quotient** used to determine whether $f'(x)$ exists or not. When $f'(x)$ exists, f is said to be **differentiable** at x. By forming $f'(x)$ we produce a new real function f' given by equation (2.3) whose domain of definition is the subset of points $x \in D$ for which $f'(x)$ exists; f' is called the **derived function** of f. If f' has the same domain of definition as f, i.e. if $f'(x)$ exists $\forall x \in D$, then f is said to be a **differentiable function** and to be obtained from f by **differentiation.**

If $f'(a)$ exists, then the tangent at the point $P(a, f(a))$ on the graph $y = f(x)$ has equation

$$y - f(a) = f'(a)(x-a).$$

Left and right derivatives

In forming $f'(x)$ we considered both $h > 0$ and $h < 0$. If we restrict the discussion to values of $h > 0$, i.e. try to form

$$\lim_{\substack{h\to 0\\(h>0)}} \frac{f(x+h)-f(x)}{h},$$

then, if this limit exists, it is called the **right derivative** of f at x.

Similarly,

$$\lim_{\substack{h\to 0\\(h<0)}} \frac{f(x+h)-f(x)}{h},$$

if it exists, is called the **left derivative** of f at x.

It is intuitively obvious that $f'(x)$ exists if and only if both the left and right derivatives of f at x exist and are equal.

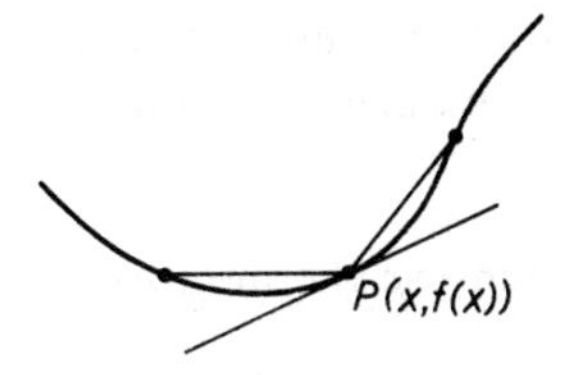

Example 1. If $f(x) = x^2+1$, does $f'(x)$ exist?

Here

$$\frac{1}{h}\{f(x+h)-f(x)\} = \frac{1}{h}\{(x+h)^2+1-x^2-1\} = 2x+h \; (h \neq 0).$$

Thus $$\left|\frac{f(x+h)-f(x)}{h} - 2x\right| = |h| < \varepsilon \text{ whenever } 0 < |h| < \varepsilon.$$

It follows that

$$\frac{f(x+h)-f(x)}{h} \to 2x \quad \text{as} \quad h \to 0.$$

Consequently $f'(x)$ exists for each $x \in \mathbf{R}$ and $f'(x) = 2x$.

In this case f is a differentiable function.

Example 2. If $f(x) = |x|$, does $f'(0)$ exist?

Here $f(0) = 0$ and

$$\frac{f(0+h)-f(0)}{h} = \frac{|h|-0}{h} = \frac{|h|}{h} = \begin{cases} 1 (h > 0), \\ -1 (h < 0). \end{cases}$$

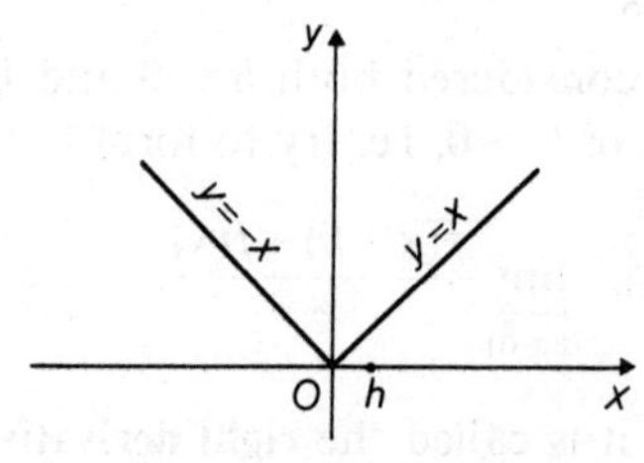

Hence
$$\lim_{\substack{h \to 0 \\ (h>0)}} \frac{f(0+h)-f(0)}{h}$$

exists and is 1, so that f has a right derivative 1 at $x = 0$.

Also
$$\lim_{\substack{h \to 0 \\ (h<0)}} \frac{f(0+h)-f(0)}{h}$$

exists and is -1, so that f has a left derivative -1 at $x = 0$. Since these right and left derivatives are different, it follows that $f'(0)$ does not exist.

Differential notation

Instead of $f'(x)$ we often use the notation

$$\frac{df}{dx} \quad \text{for} \quad \lim_{h \to 0} \frac{f(x+h)-f(x)}{h},$$

if this exists. The notation is used especially when the increment notation Δx is used instead of h (change in the value of x); the corresponding change in the value of f is denoted by Δf, so that

$$\Delta f = f(x+\Delta x) - f(x) \quad \text{and} \quad \frac{df}{dx} = \lim_{\Delta x \to 0} \frac{\Delta f}{\Delta x}.$$

In many cases, particularly when dealing with graphs, it is convenient to write: if $y = f(x)$, then $\dfrac{dy}{dx} = f'(x)$.

Differentials

Although the notation $\dfrac{df}{dx}\left(\text{and } \dfrac{dy}{dx}\right)$ has to be interpreted as a notation for the real number $f'(x)$ and not as a ratio $df:dx$, nevertheless we can in fact define two real numbers dx and df such that $df/dx = f'(x)$.

In the diagram, P is the point $(x, f(x))$ and Q the point $(x+\Delta x, f(x+\Delta x))$, $\Delta x \neq 0$, on the curve $y=f(x)$, and the ordinate through Q

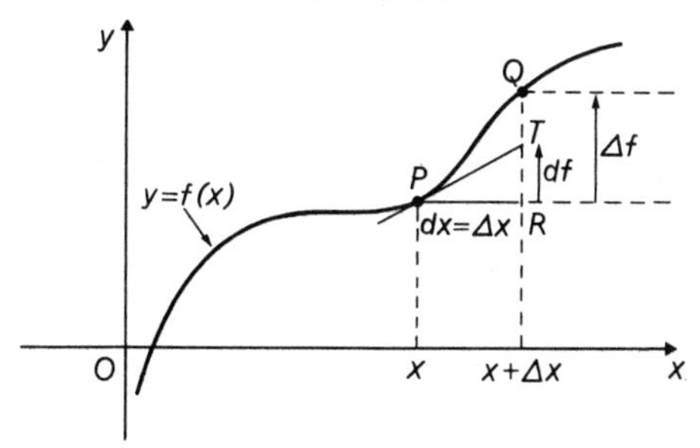

meets the tangent at P in T and the line through P parallel to the x-axis in R. Then $\Delta f = RQ$ and $\Delta x = PR$. Also, if we denote RT by df, then

$$f'(x) = \tan \angle RPT = \frac{RT}{PR} = \frac{df}{\Delta x}, \quad \text{so that} \quad df = f'(x)\Delta x.$$

To obtain a more symmetric notation we write dx for Δx, so that $df = f'(x)dx$ and $df/dx = f'(x)(dx \neq 0)$. For each real number dx a corresponding real number df exists given by $df = f'(x)dx$ (putting $df = 0$ when $dx = 0$); df is called the **differential of** f **at** x. We often use dy as an alternative notation for df.

When $|dx|$ is small, df is an approximation to Δf; for,

$$\frac{\Delta f - df}{dx} = \frac{\Delta f}{\Delta x} - f'(x) \qquad (dx = \Delta x \neq 0)$$

$$\to f'(x) - f'(x) = 0 \quad \text{as} \quad \Delta x \to 0.$$

It follows that $f(x+\Delta x) - f(x) \doteqdot f'(x)\Delta x$ for small $|\Delta x|$, where $\doteqdot$ means "is approximately equal to".

3. Evaluation of particular derivatives, the algebra of derivatives

Since a derivative was defined as a limit, it is not surprising that, in order to establish properties of derivatives, we need properties of limits. In stating these properties we use a notation which can be used in contexts other than that of differentiation; we write

$$\lim_{x \to a} f(x) = L \tag{3.1}$$

when f is defined on a neighbourhood of $a \in \mathbf{R}$, *except possibly at a itself*, and $|f(x)-L|$ can be made as small as we please by taking x close enough to a *but not equal to a*. In symbols, (3.1) means: given $\varepsilon > 0$, $\exists \delta > 0$ such that

$$0 < |x-a| < \delta \Rightarrow |f(x)-L| < \varepsilon. \tag{3.2}$$

The properties of limits that we need for calculus can be listed as follows:

(1) If f is a constant function, say $f(x) = c \ \forall x \in \mathbf{R}$, then $\lim_{x \to a} f(x) = c$.

(2) If f is the identity function on $\mathbf{R}$, so that $f(x) = x \ \forall x \in \mathbf{R}$, then $\lim_{x \to a} f(x) = \lim_{x \to a} x = a$.

If $\lim_{x \to a} f(x)$ *and* $\lim_{x \to a} g(x)$ *exist*, we have:

(3) $\lim_{x \to a} \{f(x)+g(x)\}$ exists and $= \lim_{x \to a} f(x) + \lim_{x \to a} g(x)$;

(4) $\lim_{x \to a} \{f(x)-g(x)\}$ exists and $= \lim_{x \to a} f(x) - \lim_{x \to a} g(x)$;

(5) for each $c \in \mathbf{R}$, $\lim_{x \to a} cf(x)$ exists and $= c \lim_{x \to a} f(x)$;

(6) $\lim_{x \to a} \{f(x)g(x)\}$ exists and $= \lim_{x \to a} f(x) . \lim_{x \to a} g(x)$;

(7) $\lim_{x \to a} \dfrac{f(x)}{g(x)}$ exists and $= \dfrac{\lim_{x \to a} f(x)}{\lim_{x \to a} g(x)}$, provided $\lim_{x \to a} g(x) \neq 0$;

(8) if $f(x) \leqslant g(x)$ on a neighbourhood of a, then $\lim_{x \to a} f(x) \leqslant \lim_{x \to a} g(x)$;

(9) if $\lim_{x \to a} f(x) = \lim_{x \to a} g(x)$ and if $f(x) \leqslant h(x) \leqslant g(x)$ on a neighbourhood of a, then $\lim_{x \to a} h(x)$ exists, and $= \lim_{x \to a} f(x)$.

These properties are proved by using the definition (3.2); some of the proofs are easy and some are quite difficult. All of the properties are plausible and will be assumed without proof.

Example 1 [illustrating the use of properties of limits for derivatives].

If $f(x) = \dfrac{1}{x}$ $(x \neq 0)$, determine $f'(x)$.

Here

$$\frac{f(x+h)-f(x)}{h} = \frac{1}{h}\left\{\frac{1}{x+h} - \frac{1}{x}\right\} = \frac{x-x-h}{hx(x+h)} = \frac{-1}{x(x+h)} \ (h \neq 0),$$

and

$$\lim_{h\to 0}\frac{f(x+h)-f(x)}{h}=\frac{\lim_{h\to 0}(-1)}{\lim_{h\to 0}x\,.\,\{\lim_{h\to 0}x+\lim_{h\to 0}h\}},\text{ using properties (3), (6), (7),}$$

$$=\frac{-1}{x\{x+0\}}=-\frac{1}{x^2},\text{ using properties (1) and (2).}$$

Thus, if $f(x)=\frac{1}{x}\ (x\neq 0)$, then $f'(x)=-\frac{1}{x^2}$.

The following theorem contains the two simplest results on derivatives.

Theorem 1.1

(i) *If* $f(x)=c\ \forall\, x\in\mathbf{R}$, *then* $f'(x)=0\ \forall\, x\in\mathbf{R}$.

(ii) *If* $f(x)=x^n$, *where* $n\in\mathbf{N}$, *then* $f'(x)=nx^{n-1}\ \forall\, x\in\mathbf{R}$.

Proof of (i). Here

$$\frac{f(x+h)-f(x)}{h}=\frac{c-c}{h}=0\ \forall\, h\neq 0;$$

hence $f'(x)$ exists $\forall\, x\in\mathbf{R}$ and $f'(x)=0$. [It follows that the derived function of a constant function is the zero function.]

Proof of (ii). In this case,

$$\frac{f(x+h)-f(x)}{h}=\frac{1}{h}\{(x+h)^n-x^n\}$$

$$=\frac{1}{h}\left\{\left(x^n+\binom{n}{1}x^{n-1}h+\binom{n}{2}x^{n-2}h^2+\cdots+h^n\right)-x^n\right\},$$

using the binomial theorem,

$$=nx^{n-1}+\binom{n}{2}x^{n-2}h+\cdots+h^{n-1}\quad (h\neq 0).$$

Thus, using properties of limits,

$$\lim_{h\to 0}\frac{f(x+h)-f(x)}{h}=nx^{n-1}+\binom{n}{2}x^{n-2}.0+0+\cdots+0=nx^{n-1}.$$

Hence, if $f(x)=x^n$, where $n\in\mathbf{N}$, then $f'(x)=nx^{n-1}$.

Note. Later in this section (see Example 4) we show that if $\alpha\in\mathbf{Q}$, and if $f(x) = x^\alpha$, then $f'(x) = \alpha x^{\alpha-1}$, whenever $f'(x)$ exists. Later still we shall define x^α for any $\alpha \in \mathbf{R}$ and show that $\frac{d}{dx}(x^\alpha) = \alpha x^{\alpha-1}$.

Continuity of a real function

A real function f is said to be **continuous** at $x \in \mathbf{R}$ if $f(x)$ exists (i.e. x is in the domain of f), f is defined on a neighbourhood of x, and if $|f(x+h)-f(x)|$ can be made as small as we please by taking $|h|$ sufficiently small, i.e. if $\lim_{h\to 0} f(x+h) = f(x)$.

A function which is continuous at each point of an interval is said to be **continuous on the interval**. A function continuous at each point of its domain is called a **continuous function**.

Using properties (1), $\cdots$, (7) of limits we see that the constant functions and the identity function are continuous functions and that, if f and g are continuous at x, so are the functions $f+g$, $f-g$, cf, fg and $\frac{f}{g}$ defined by $(f+g)(x) = f(x)+g(x)$, $(f-g)(x) = f(x)-g(x)$, $(cf)(x) = cf(x)$, $(fg)(x) = f(x)g(x)$, $\frac{f}{g}(x) = \frac{f(x)}{g(x)}$ (provided $g(x) \neq 0$); so also is $f \circ g$, assuming that f is defined on a neighbourhood of $g(x)$, where $(f \circ g)(x) = f(g(x))$.

Since, for $n \in \mathbf{N}$, $x^n = x.x.\cdots.x$ (n of these) and since the identity function is continuous, it follows that f, defined by $f(x) = x^n$ ($n \in \mathbf{N}$) is a continuous function. We can now readily deduce that every polynomial and every rational function is continuous.

Another intuitive property of continuity that we shall require, and which can be proved from the definition of a limit, is that, if f is continuous at x and $f(x) \neq 0$, then there exists a neighbourhood of x on which f is non-zero.

The relation between differentiability and continuity is as indicated in the following theorem.

Theorem 1.2

If f is differentiable at x, then f is continuous at x.

Proof.
$$f(x+h) = f(x)+h.\frac{f(x+h)-f(x)}{h} \qquad (h \neq 0)$$
$$\to f(x)+0.f'(x) \quad \text{as} \quad h \to 0.$$

Thus $\lim_{h\to 0} f(x+h) = f(x)$, so that f is continuous at x.

Note. The converse of Theorem **1.2** is not true; for example, if $f(x) = |x|$, then f is continuous at $x = 0$ but not differentiable at $x = 0$.

The algebra of derivatives

I. *If f is differentiable at x and if c is a constant real number, then cf is differentiable at x and $(cf)'(x) = cf'(x)$.*

Proof. $\dfrac{(cf)(x+h)-cf(x)}{h} = c\left\{\dfrac{f(x+h)-f(x)}{h}\right\} \to cf'(x)$ as $h \to 0$, and the result follows.

II. *If f and g are differentiable at x, then $f+g$ is differentiable at x and $(f+g)'(x) = f'(x)+g'(x)$.*

Proof.

$$\begin{aligned}\frac{(f+g)(x+h)-(f+g)(x)}{h} &= \frac{1}{h}[\{f(x+h)+g(x+h)\}-\{f(x)+g(x)\}]\\ &= \frac{f(x+h)-f(x)}{h}+\frac{g(x+h)-g(x)}{h}\\ &\to f'(x)+g'(x) \quad \text{as} \quad h \to 0,\end{aligned}$$

and this proves the result.

Similarly, $f-g$ *is differentiable at x and $(f-g)'(x) = f'(x)-g'(x)$.*

III [The product rule]. *If f and g are differentiable at x, then fg is differentiable at x and $(fg)'(x) = f'(x)g(x)+f(x)g'(x)$.*

Proof.

$$\begin{aligned}\frac{(fg)(x+h)-(fg)(x)}{h} &= \frac{f(x+h)g(x+h)-f(x)g(x)}{h}\\ &= \frac{1}{h}[\{f(x+h)-f(x)\}g(x+h)+f(x)\{g(x+h)-g(x)\}]\\ &= \frac{f(x+h)-f(x)}{h}g(x+h)+f(x)\frac{g(x+h)-g(x)}{h}\\ &\to f'(x)g(x)+f(x)g'(x) \quad \text{as} \quad h \to 0\end{aligned}$$

(using the continuity of g at x), and this establishes the result.

In differential notation, $\dfrac{d}{dx}\{f(x)g(x)\} = \dfrac{df}{dx}g(x)+f(x)\dfrac{dg}{dx}$.

IV [The reciprocal rule]. *If g is differentiable at x and $g(x) \neq 0$, then $\frac{1}{g}$ is differentiable at x and* $\left(\frac{1}{g}\right)'(x) = -\frac{1}{[g(x)]^2}g'(x)$.

$\left[\text{Note that } \frac{1}{g}(x) = \frac{1}{g(x)}.\right]$

Proof.

$$\frac{\frac{1}{g}(x+h)-\frac{1}{g}(x)}{h} = \frac{1}{h}\left\{\frac{1}{g(x+h)}-\frac{1}{g(x)}\right\} = -\frac{1}{g(x)g(x+h)}\frac{g(x+h)-g(x)}{h}$$

$$\to -\frac{1}{[g(x)]^2}g'(x) \quad \text{as} \quad h \to 0,$$

and the result follows.

In differential notation, $\frac{d}{dx}\left(\frac{1}{g(x)}\right) = -\frac{1}{[g(x)]^2}\frac{dg}{dx}$.

V [The quotient rule]. *If f and g are differentiable at x and if $g(x) \neq 0$, then $\frac{f}{g}$ is differentiable at x and* $\left(\frac{f}{g}\right)'(x) = \frac{g(x)f'(x)-f(x)g'(x)}{[g(x)]^2}$.

Proof. $\left(\frac{f}{g}\right)(x) = \frac{f(x)}{g(x)} = f(x).\frac{1}{g(x)}$. From **III** and **IV** it follows that

$$\left(\frac{f}{g}\right)'(x) \text{ exists and } = f'(x)\frac{1}{g(x)}+f(x)\left\{-\frac{1}{[g(x)]^2}g'(x)\right\}$$

$$= \frac{g(x)f'(x)-f(x)g'(x)}{[g(x)]^2}.$$

Again it is useful to write out the rule in differential notation.

Note. Using the algebra of derivatives and the derivatives of c and x^n ($n \in \mathbf{N}$), we can now differentiate all polynomials and rational functions. In differentiating such functions it is often advisable to use differential notation.

Example 2. Differentiate (i) $(x^6+x^4+7)(3-4x^3-2x^5)$, (ii) $\frac{x^3}{x^2-x-5}$.

(i) $\frac{d}{dx}\{(x^6+x^4+7)(3-4x^3-2x^5)\} = (6x^5+4x^3)(3-4x^3-2x^5)$
$\qquad +(x^6+x^4+7)(-12x^2-10x^4)$;

(ii) $$\frac{d}{dx}\left\{\frac{x^3}{x^2-x-5}\right\} = \frac{(x^2-x-5)3x^2-x^3(2x-1)}{(x^2-x-5)^2}$$
$$= \frac{x^2(x^2-2x-15)}{(x^2-x-5)^2} = \frac{x(x-5)(x+3)}{(x^2-x-5)^2}.$$

Example 3. *If* $f(x) = \dfrac{1}{x^n} = x^{-n} (n \in \mathbf{N})$, *then* $f'(x) = (-n)x^{-n-1} = \dfrac{(-n)}{x^{n+1}}$.

Proof.
$$f'(x) = -\frac{1}{(x^n)^2}\frac{d}{dx}(x^n), \quad \text{using } \mathbf{IV},$$
$$= -\frac{nx^{n-1}}{x^{2n}} = (-n)x^{-n-1} = \frac{(-n)}{x^{n+1}}.$$

The final basic rule for differentiation involves the composition function $f \circ g$ [defined by $(f \circ g)(x) = f(g(x))$] of two real functions f, g.

VI [The chain rule]. *If* g *is differentiable at* x *and* f *is differentiable at* $g(x)$, *then* $f \circ g$ *is differentiable at* x *and*

$$(f \circ g)'(x) = f'(g(x))g'(x).$$

Proof.
$$\frac{(f \circ g)(x+h)-(f \circ g)(x)}{h} = \frac{f(g(x+h))-f(g(x))}{h}. \tag{3.3}$$

To simplify notation we write $u = g(x)$ and $k = g(x+h)-g(x)$. By the continuity at x of g, $k \to 0$ as $h \to 0$. Since $g(x+h) = u+k$, the right-hand side of (3.3) is

$$\frac{f(u+k)-f(u)}{h}. \tag{3.4}$$

Since

$$\lim_{k \to 0} \frac{f(u+k)-f(u)}{k} = f'(u),$$

it follows that, if

$$\phi(k) = \frac{f(u+k)-f(u)}{k} - f'(u) \quad (k \neq 0), \quad \text{then} \quad \lim_{k \to 0} \phi(k) = 0.$$

Now, *for* $k \neq 0$,
$$f(u+k)-f(u) = kf'(u)+k\phi(k). \tag{3.5}$$

If we define $\phi(0)$ to be 0, then (3.5) holds for $k = 0$ and so $\forall k$.

Combining (3.3), (3.4) and (3.5) we have

$$\frac{(f\circ g)(x+h)-(f\circ g)(x)}{h}=\frac{kf'(u)+k\phi(k)}{h}$$

$$=f'(u)\frac{g(x+h)-g(x)}{h}+\frac{g(x+h)-g(x)}{h}\phi(k)$$

$$\to f'(u)g'(x)+g'(x).0 \quad \text{as} \quad h\to 0 \quad (\text{then } k\to 0).$$

Thus $(f\circ g)'(x)$ exists and $=f'(g(x))g'(x)$.

Notes 1. If $F=f\circ g$, then $F(x)=f(g(x))$ and $F'(x)=f'(g(x))\cdot g'(x)$.

2. $(f\circ g)'=(f'\circ g)g'$.

3. We often write $\dfrac{d}{dx}(f\circ g)=\dfrac{df}{du}\dfrac{du}{dx}$, where $u=g(x)$, or, if $y=f(g(x))$, then $\dfrac{dy}{dx}=\dfrac{df}{du}\dfrac{du}{dx}$, where $u=g(x)$, or, simply, $\dfrac{dy}{dx}=\dfrac{dy}{du}\dfrac{du}{dx}$.

4. If $F(x)=f(g(h(x)))$, then $F'(x)=f'(g(h(x)))g'(h(x))h'(x)$.

5. In practice, in forming $\dfrac{d}{dx}f(g(x))$, it is advisable to think of the derivative as $f'(\quad)\cdot\dfrac{d}{dx}(\quad)$, where $g(x)$ is placed inside the brackets $(\quad)$. For example $\dfrac{d}{dx}(\quad)^n=n(\quad)^{n-1}\dfrac{d}{dx}(\quad)$, quite independently of the differentiable expression $g(x)$ inside the brackets $(\quad)$; e.g. for any $n\in\mathbf{N}$,

$$\frac{d}{dx}(x^2-2)^n=n(x^2-2)^{n-1}\frac{d}{dx}(x^2-2),$$

$$\frac{d}{dx}(3-5x^4)^n=n(3-5x^4)^{n-1}\frac{d}{dx}(3-5x^4), \quad \text{and so on.}$$

Example 4. *If* $f(x)=x^{p/q}$, *where* $p\in\mathbf{Z}$ *and* $q\in\mathbf{N}$, *then* $f'(x)=\dfrac{p}{q}x^{p/q-1}$.

Proof. $[f(x)]^q=x^p$, and, differentiating with respect to x,

$$q[f(x)]^{q-1}f'(x)=px^{p-1},$$

so that

$$q[f(x)]^q f'(x)=px^{p-1}.x^{p/q},$$

from which we obtain

$$f'(x) = \frac{px^{p-1}x^{p/q}}{qx^p} = \frac{p}{q}x^{p/q-1}.$$

[Note that we have assumed in Example 4 that $f'(x)$ exists.]

Note. From Theorem **1.1** and Examples 3 and 4 we have now shown by stages that, if $\alpha \in \mathbf{Q}$, then $\frac{d}{dx}(x^\alpha) = \alpha x^{\alpha-1}$, when this exists.

Example 5. Find the equation of the tangent at the point A (1, 2) on the curve $y = x\sqrt{(1+3x^2)}$ and find the x-coordinate of the point at which this tangent meets the curve again.

$$\frac{dy}{dx} = \sqrt{(1+3x^2)} + \frac{x\,.\,6x}{2\sqrt{(1+3x^2)}} = \frac{1+6x^2}{\sqrt{(1+3x^2)}} = \frac{7}{2} \quad \text{at} \quad x = 1.$$

Thus the tangent at A has equation $y-2 = \frac{7}{2}(x-1)$, i.e. $y = \frac{1}{2}(7x-3)$. The tangent meets the curve where

$$\tfrac{1}{2}(7x-3) = x\sqrt{(1+3x^2)}. \qquad (3.6)$$

From (3.6), $$4x^4-15x^2+14x-3 = 0,$$

so that $$(x^2-2x+1)(4x^2+8x-3) = 0,$$

on noting (since the tangent "touches" the curve at $x = 1$) that $(x-1)^2$ must be a factor of the polynomial. It follows that the x-coordinate of any point at which the tangent meets the curve again must be a root of the equation $4x^2+8x-3 = 0$. These roots are $-1 \pm \frac{1}{2}\sqrt{7}$ and only $-1-\frac{1}{2}\sqrt{7}$ satisfies (3.6).

[The other root satisfies $\frac{1}{2}(7x-3) = -x\sqrt{(1+3x^2)}$.]

Functions defined implicitly

Consider the equation

$$y^2 = x. \qquad (3.7)$$

The graph of the equation is the parabola indicated. The upper half of

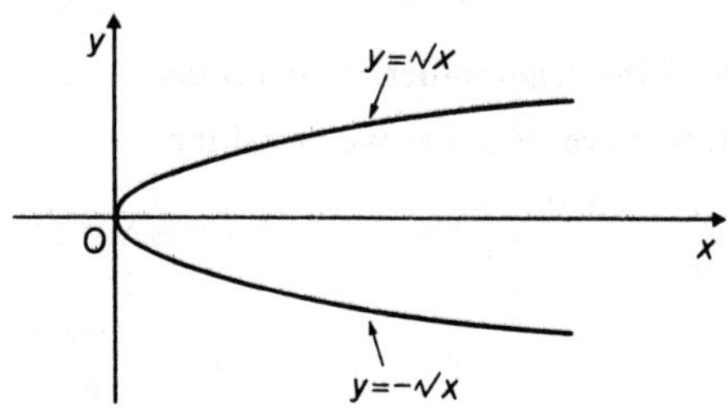

the graph gives rise to a function $f:\mathbf{R}^+ \to \mathbf{R}^+$ given by $f(x) = \sqrt{x}\ \forall x \in \mathbf{R}^+$, and the lower half of the graph gives rise to a function $g:\mathbf{R}^+ \to \mathbf{R}^-$ defined by $g(x) = -\sqrt{x}\ \forall x \in \mathbf{R}^+$. For $x > 0$, $f'(x) = 1/2\sqrt{x}$ and $g'(x) = -1/2\sqrt{x}$. When we say that equation (3.7) defines *y as a differentiable function of x*, we mean that we have chosen either $f(x)$ or $g(x)$ for y and the domains on which each is differentiable. Using the chain rule we can differentiate (3.7) with respect to x to obtain

$$2y\frac{dy}{dx} = 1, \quad \text{i.e.} \quad \frac{dy}{dx} = \frac{1}{2y} \quad (y \neq 0).$$

In this way we obtain the gradient of the tangent at a point on the parabola without solving for y in terms of x. The differentiable functions involved are said to be **defined implicitly**, since no *explicit* formula has been used for any such function.

In many cases, as in the following example, no explicit formula is possible in terms of elementary functions.

Example 6. Assuming that the equation

$$xy^5 + 3x^2y^2 - 2 = 0 \tag{3.8}$$

defines y implicitly as a differentiable function of x, find the equation of the tangent at the point $A(1, -1)$ on the curve represented by (3.8). [We are assuming that (3.8) defines a function differentiable at $x = 1$ and such that $y = -1$ when $x = 1$.]

From (3.8),
$$\frac{d}{dx}(xy^5 + 3x^2y^2 - 2) = 0,$$

and so
$$y^5 + x5y^4\frac{dy}{dx} + 6xy^2 + 3x^2 2y\frac{dy}{dx} = 0,$$

i.e.
$$xy(5y^3 + 6x)\frac{dy}{dx} = -(y^5 + 6xy^2).$$

When $x = 1$ and $y = -1$ we obtain $\dfrac{dy}{dx} = 5$, and the required tangent has equation $y + 1 = 5(x-1)$, i.e. $y = 5x - 6$.

4. Differentiation of the trigonometric functions

To find the derivative of $\sin x$, we consider

$$\frac{\sin(x+h) - \sin x}{h} = \frac{1}{h}\{(\sin x \cos h + \cos x \sin h) - \sin x\}$$

$$= \cos x\frac{\sin h}{h} - \sin x\frac{1 - \cos h}{h}.$$

It follows that, if $\lim\limits_{h\to 0}\dfrac{\sin h}{h}$ and $\lim\limits_{h\to 0}\dfrac{1-\cos h}{h}$ exist and can be evaluated, then we can determine $\dfrac{d}{dx}(\sin x)$. Before investigating these two limits we first show that sin and cos are continuous at $h = 0$, i.e. that

$$\lim_{h\to 0}\sin h = \sin 0 = 0 \quad \text{and} \quad \lim_{h\to 0}\cos h = \cos 0 = 1. \tag{4.1}$$

If $0 < h < \frac{1}{2}\pi$, $\angle COB = h$, BC is the arc shown of the circle, centre O and radius 1, and BA is perpendicular to OC, then

$$\sin h = \frac{|AB|}{|OB|} = |AB|. \qquad [|AB| \text{ denotes the length of } AB.]$$

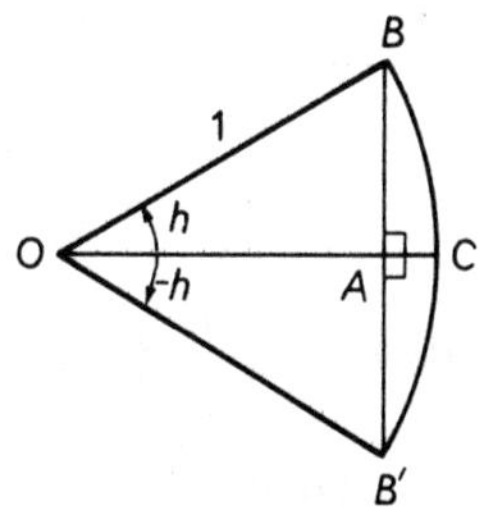

Since $|AB| < \text{arc } BC$, it follows that $0 < \sin h < h$. Also, from the symmetry of the complete figure drawn, $0 < |\sin(-h)| < |-h|$. Hence, if $0 < |h| < \frac{1}{2}\pi$, then $0 < |\sin h| < |h|$. Consequently, $|\sin h| < \varepsilon$ whenever $|h| < \varepsilon$, so that $\lim\limits_{h\to 0}\sin h = 0 = \sin 0$, and sin is continuous at $h = 0$.

Also $1-\cos h = 2\sin^2\frac{1}{2}h \to 2.0^2 = 0$ as $h \to 0$, so that $\lim\limits_{h\to 0}\cos h = 1 = \cos 0$, and cos is continuous at $h = 0$.

We now prove that

$$\text{(i)}\ \lim_{h\to 0}\frac{\sin h}{h} = 1, \qquad \text{(ii)}\ \lim_{h\to 0}\frac{1-\cos h}{h} = 0. \tag{4.2}$$

Proof of (i). As in the above discussion, since we are dealing with $h \to 0$ we can suppose that $|h| < \frac{1}{2}\pi$.

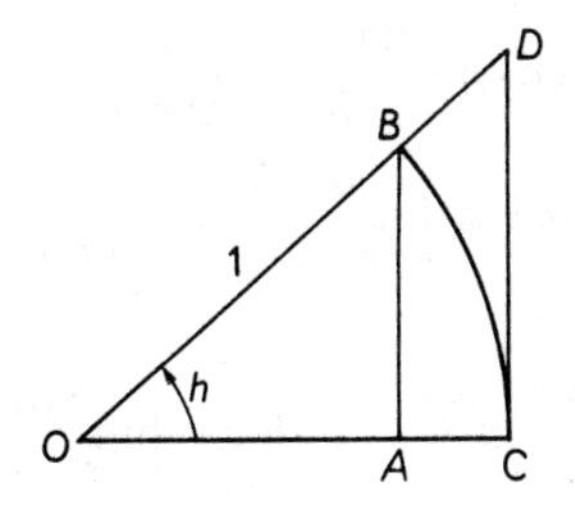

Case $h > 0$. We take the upper part of the figure used above and let CD be the tangent at C to the circle. Then

$$\sin h = \frac{|AB|}{|OB|} = |AB|, \cos h = \frac{|OA|}{|OB|} = |OA|,$$

and
$$\tan h = \frac{|CD|}{|OC|} = |CD|.$$

Now,

area of triangle $OAB <$ area of sector $OCB <$ area of triangle OCD,

and so
$$\tfrac{1}{2}|OA||AB| < \frac{h}{2\pi}\pi . 1^2 < \tfrac{1}{2}|OC||CD|,$$

$$\tfrac{1}{2}\cos h \sin h < \tfrac{1}{2}h < \tfrac{1}{2}\frac{\sin h}{\cos h},$$

$$\frac{\sin h}{h} < \frac{1}{\cos h} \quad \text{and} \quad \cos h < \frac{\sin h}{h} \quad (\text{since } h > 0, \cos h > 0),$$

giving
$$\cos h < \frac{\sin h}{h} < \frac{1}{\cos h}. \tag{4.3}$$

Case $h < 0$. If $h = -k$, then $k > 0$, and, by (4.3),

$$\cos k < \frac{\sin k}{k} < \frac{1}{\cos k}.$$

Consequently,
$$\cos(-h) < \frac{\sin(-h)}{(-h)} < \frac{1}{\cos(-h)},$$

so that
$$\cos h < \frac{\sin h}{h} < \frac{1}{\cos h},$$

on noting that $\cos(-h) = \cos h$ and $\sin(-h) = -\sin h$.

It follows that, if $0 < |h| < \tfrac{1}{2}\pi$, then

$$\cos h < \frac{\sin h}{h} < \frac{1}{\cos h}.$$

Thus
$$\lim_{h\to 0} \cos h \leqslant \lim_{h\to 0} \frac{\sin h}{h} \leqslant \frac{1}{\lim_{h\to 0} \cos h},$$

and, by (4.1),

$$1 \leqslant \lim_{h\to 0} \frac{\sin h}{h} \leqslant 1, \quad \text{so that} \quad \lim_{h\to 0} \frac{\sin h}{h} = 1.$$

Proof of (ii).

$$\frac{1-\cos h}{h} = \frac{2\sin^2 \frac{1}{2}h}{h} = \tfrac{1}{2}h \, . \frac{\sin \frac{1}{2}h}{\frac{1}{2}h} \, . \frac{\sin \frac{1}{2}h}{\frac{1}{2}h}$$

$$\to \tfrac{1}{2} . 0 . 1 . 1 \quad \text{(by (i))} \quad \text{as} \quad h \to 0,$$

so that
$$\lim_{h \to 0} \frac{1-\cos h}{h} = 0.$$

Theorem 1.3

$$(1)\ \frac{d}{dx}(\sin x) = \cos x, \qquad (2)\ \frac{d}{dx}(\cos x) = -\sin x. \qquad (4.4)$$

Proof of (1).

$$\frac{\sin(x+h)-\sin x}{h} = \frac{1}{h}\{(\sin x \cos h + \cos x \sin h) - \sin x\}$$

$$= \cos x \frac{\sin h}{h} - \sin x \frac{1-\cos h}{h}$$

$$\to \cos x \, . \, 1 - \sin x \, . \, 0 \quad \text{as} \quad h \to 0,$$

and so
$$\frac{d}{dx}(\sin x) = \cos x.$$

Proof of (2).

$$\frac{\cos(x+h)-\cos x}{h} = \frac{1}{h}\{(\cos x \cos h - \sin x \sin h) - \cos x\}$$

$$= (-\sin x)\frac{\sin h}{h} - \cos x \frac{1-\cos h}{h}$$

$$\to -\sin x \, . \, 1 - \cos x \, . \, 0 \quad \text{as} \quad h \to 0,$$

and so
$$\frac{d}{dx}(\cos x) = -\sin x.$$

[*Alternative proof of* (2):

$$\frac{d}{dx}(\cos x) = \frac{d}{dx}\{\sin(x+\tfrac{1}{2}\pi)\} = \cos(x+\tfrac{1}{2}\pi)\frac{d}{dx}(x+\tfrac{1}{2}\pi)$$

$$= -\sin x \, . \, 1 = -\sin x.$$]

Note. Since sin and cos are differentiable functions they are continuous functions.

Using (4.4) and the algebra of derivatives we can now differentiate the other trigonometric functions. We obtain the following list:

(1) $\dfrac{d}{dx}(\sin x) = \cos x,$ (2) $\dfrac{d}{dx}(\cos x) = -\sin x,$

(3) $\dfrac{d}{dx}(\tan x) = \sec^2 x,$ (4) $\dfrac{d}{dx}(\sec x) = \sec x \tan x,$

(5) $\dfrac{d}{dx}(\operatorname{cosec} x) = -\operatorname{cosec} x \cot x,$ (6) $\dfrac{d}{dx}(\cot x) = -\operatorname{cosec}^2 x;$

for, noting that $\cos^2 x + \sin^2 x = 1$,

$$\frac{d}{dx}(\tan x) = \frac{d}{dx}\left(\frac{\sin x}{\cos x}\right) = \frac{\cos x(\cos x) - \sin x(-\sin x)}{\cos^2 x} = \frac{1}{\cos^2 x} = \sec^2 x;$$

$$\frac{d}{dx}(\sec x) = \frac{d}{dx}\left(\frac{1}{\cos x}\right) = -\frac{1}{\cos^2 x}(-\sin x) = \frac{\sin x}{\cos^2 x} = \sec x \tan x;$$

$$\frac{d}{dx}(\operatorname{cosec} x) = \frac{d}{dx}\left(\frac{1}{\sin x}\right) = -\frac{1}{\sin^2 x}(\cos x) = -\frac{\cos x}{\sin^2 x} = -\operatorname{cosec} x \cot x;$$

$$\frac{d}{dx}(\cot x) = \frac{d}{dx}\left(\frac{\cos x}{\sin x}\right) = \frac{\sin x(-\sin x) - \cos x(\cos x)}{\sin^2 x} = -\frac{1}{\sin^2 x}$$
$$= -\operatorname{cosec}^2 x.$$

Example 1. Differentiate

(i) $\cos^3 x \cos 3x$, (ii) $\cos(\sin \sqrt{x})$, (iii) $\sec x \tan x$.

(i) $$\frac{d}{dx}(\cos^3 x \cos 3x) = -3\cos^2 x \sin x \cos 3x + \cos^3 x \,.(-3\sin 3x)$$
$$= -3\cos^2 x(\sin 3x \cos x + \cos 3x \sin x)$$
$$= -3\cos^2 x \sin 4x;$$

(ii) $$\frac{d}{dx}\{\cos(\sin\sqrt{x})\} = -\sin(\sin\sqrt{x})\frac{d}{dx}(\sin\sqrt{x})$$
$$= -\sin(\sin\sqrt{x})\cos\sqrt{x}\frac{d}{dx}(\sqrt{x})$$
$$= -\frac{1}{2\sqrt{x}}\sin(\sin\sqrt{x})\cos\sqrt{x};$$

(iii) $$\frac{d}{dx}(\sec x \tan x) = (\sec x \tan x)\tan x + \sec x\,(\sec^2 x)$$
$$= \sec x(1+2\tan^2 x),$$
on noting that $\sec^2 x = 1+\tan^2 x$.

Example 2. Find the equation of the tangent at the point given by $x = \frac{1}{4}\pi$ on the curve $y = \sin^2 x$.

$$\frac{dy}{dx} = 2\sin x\cos x = 1 \quad \text{at} \quad x = \tfrac{1}{4}\pi.$$

Since the point has coordinates $(\frac{1}{4}\pi, \frac{1}{2})$, the tangent has equation $y-\frac{1}{2} = x-\frac{1}{4}\pi$, i.e. $y = x+\frac{1}{2}-\frac{1}{4}\pi$.

5. Higher derivatives

Suppose that a function f is differentiable on an interval; its derived function f' is also defined on this interval. If f' is also differentiable, then its derived function is denoted by f'' and called the **second derived function of** f; its value at x is denoted by $f''(x)$ or $\dfrac{d^2f}{dx^2}$ and called the **second derivative of** f **at** x. To avoid continual use of the word "function" we shall often call f' and f'' the first and second derivatives, respectively, of f.

Similarly we can form the following derivatives, if they exist: f''', the **third derivative of** f, $f'''(x)$ or $\dfrac{d^3f}{dx^3}$ denoting its value at x; $f^{(\mathrm{IV})}$, the **fourth derivative of** f, $f^{(\mathrm{IV})}(x)$ or $\dfrac{d^4f}{dx^4}$ denoting its value at x; ...

$f^{(n)}$, the nth **derivative of** f, $f^{(n)}(x)$ or $\dfrac{d^nf}{dx^n}$ denoting its value at x.

$f^{(n)}$ $(n \geqslant 2)$ are called the **higher derivatives of** f of **orders** $n = 2, 3, \cdots$. It is often convenient to denote f and $f(x)$ by $f^{(0)}$ and $f^{(0)}(x)$.

Example 1. If $f(x) = \dfrac{2x}{x^2+1}$, find $f''(x)$.

$$f'(x) = 2.\frac{x^2+1-2x^2}{(x^2+1)^2} = 2\frac{1-x^2}{(x^2+1)^2}.$$

$$f''(x) = 2\left\{\frac{-2x}{(x^2+1)^2} - \frac{2(1-x^2).2x}{(x^2+1)^3}\right\}$$

$$= \frac{-4x}{(x^2+1)^3}\{x^2+1+2-2x^2\} = \frac{4x(x^2-3)}{(x^2+1)^3}.$$

Example 2. Find the nth derivative at x of

$$\text{(i) } \frac{1}{x-1}, \qquad \text{(ii) } \frac{1}{x^2-1}, \qquad \text{(iii) } \sin x, \qquad \text{(iv) } \cos x.$$

(i) If

$$f(x) = \frac{1}{x-1},\ f'(x) = \frac{(-1)}{(x-1)^2},\ f''(x) = \frac{(-1)^2 . 1 . 2}{(x-1)^3},\ f'''(x) = \frac{(-1)^3\, 3!}{(x-1)^4};$$

we can now show, by induction, that $f^{(n)}(x) = \dfrac{(-1)^n\, n!}{(x-1)^{n+1}} \forall\, n \geqslant 1$.

(ii) When we have noted that $\dfrac{1}{x^2-1} = \dfrac{1}{2}.\dfrac{1}{x-1} - \dfrac{1}{2}.\dfrac{1}{x+1}$, we can proceed to deal, as in (i), with the separate terms $\dfrac{1}{x-1}$ and $\dfrac{1}{x+1}$.

(iii) If $f(x) = \sin x$, then $f'(x) = \cos x = \sin (x + \frac{1}{2}\pi)$;

$$f''(x) = \cos (x + \tfrac{1}{2}\pi) = \sin (x + \tfrac{1}{2} . 2\pi);$$

$$f'''(x) = \cos (x + \tfrac{1}{2} . 2\pi) = \sin (x + \tfrac{1}{2} . 3\pi).$$

This suggests that

$$f^{(n)}(x) = \sin (x + \tfrac{1}{2}n\pi) \quad (n = 1, 2, 3, \cdots). \tag{5.1}$$

We prove (5.1) by induction. The statement involved is true for $n = 1$. Assume that it is true for $n = k \geqslant 1$, so that $f^{(k)}(x) = \sin (x + \frac{1}{2}k\pi)$. Then $f^{(k+1)}(x) = \cos (x + \frac{1}{2}k\pi) = \sin (x + \frac{1}{2}k\pi + \frac{1}{2}\pi) = \sin (x + \frac{1}{2}(k+1)\pi)$, so that the statement is also true for $n = k+1$. The result (5.1) now follows by induction.

(iv) Prove similarly that, $\forall\, n \geqslant 1, \dfrac{d^n}{dx^n}(\cos x) = \cos (x + \frac{1}{2}n\pi)$.

Example 3. Verify that

$$y = \sin\left(\frac{1}{\sqrt{x}}\right) + \cos\left(\frac{1}{\sqrt{x}}\right)$$

satisfies the "differential equation"

$$4x^3 \frac{d^2y}{dx^2} + 6x^2 \frac{dy}{dx} + y = 0.$$

$$\frac{dy}{dx} = \cos\left(\frac{1}{\sqrt{x}}\right)\left(\frac{-1}{2x^{3/2}}\right) - \sin\left(\frac{1}{\sqrt{x}}\right)\left(\frac{-1}{2x^{3/2}}\right). \tag{5.2}$$

$$\frac{d^2y}{dx^2} = \left\{\cos\left(\frac{1}{\sqrt{x}}\right) - \sin\left(\frac{1}{\sqrt{x}}\right)\right\}\frac{3}{4x^{5/2}} - \left\{\sin\left(\frac{1}{\sqrt{x}}\right) + \cos\left(\frac{1}{\sqrt{x}}\right)\right\}\frac{1}{4x^3},$$

and, by using (5.2) and the expression for y,

$$4x^3\frac{d^2y}{dx^2} = -2x^{3/2}\frac{dy}{dx}.3x^{1/2} - y, \quad \text{so that} \quad 4x^3\frac{d^2y}{dx^2} + 6x^2\frac{dy}{dx} + y = 0.$$

6. Rates of change

We start with a function f differentiable at x. If x is changed to $x+h$, then $f(x)$ changes to $f(x+h)$. The *average change* in the value of the function f over the interval determined by x and $x+h$ is

$$\frac{f(x+h)-f(x)}{(x+h)-x} = \frac{f(x+h)-f(x)}{h},$$

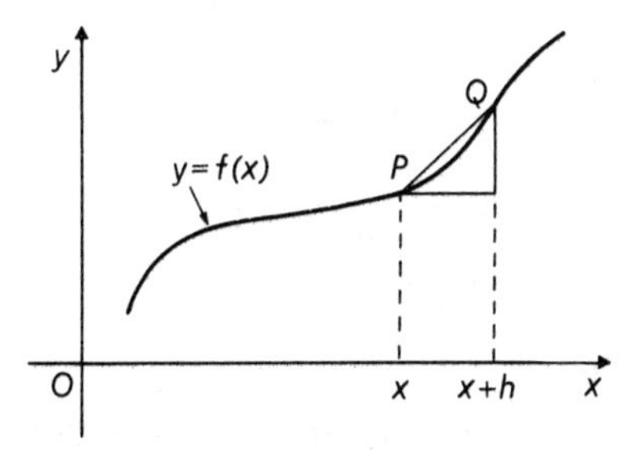

and $\lim\limits_{h\to 0}\dfrac{f(x+h)-f(x)}{h}$ is called **the rate of change of f at** x. Thus this rate of change is simply $f'(x)$, i.e. $\dfrac{df}{dx}$ in differential notation.

In mechanics, if x denotes the position at time t of a particle moving along a straight line, then the *velocity* and *acceleration* of the particle are, respectively, $\dfrac{dx}{dt}$ (the rate of change of x with respect to t) and $\dfrac{d^2x}{dt^2}$ (the rate of change of velocity with respect to t). If x is measured in metres and t in seconds, then $\dfrac{dx}{dt}$ is in metres per second (m/s) and $\dfrac{d^2x}{dt^2}$ in metres per second^2 (m/s^2).

For a particle moving in the x, y-plane whose position at time t is (x, y) the velocity and acceleration are given by the vectors $\boldsymbol{v}$, $\boldsymbol{\alpha}$, where

$$\boldsymbol{v} = \left(\frac{dx}{dt}, \frac{dy}{dt}\right) \quad \text{and} \quad \boldsymbol{\alpha} = \left(\frac{d^2x}{dt^2}, \frac{d^2y}{dt^2}\right),$$

the components of the vectors being the components in the x- and y-directions.

For a particle moving in x, y, z-space the corresponding vectors are

$$\boldsymbol{v} = \left(\frac{dx}{dt}, \frac{dy}{dt}, \frac{dz}{dt}\right) \quad \text{and} \quad \boldsymbol{\alpha} = \left(\frac{d^2x}{dt^2}, \frac{d^2y}{dt^2}, \frac{d^2z}{dt^2}\right).$$

Example 1. A particle is moving on the x-axis so that at time t (seconds) its position x in metres relative to the origin is given by $x = t^3+3t$. Find its velocity and acceleration at time $t = 2$.

$\frac{dx}{dt} = 3t^2+3$, $\frac{d^2x}{dt^2} = 6t$, so that, at $t = 2$, the velocity is 15 m/s and the acceleration is 12 m/s^2.

Example 2. A sphere is expanding in such a way that its radius is increasing at the rate of 1 cm/s. How fast is its volume expanding when its radius is 12 cm?

If r denotes the radius and V the volume, then $V = \frac{4}{3}\pi r^3$. We are given that $\frac{dr}{dt} = 1$ and we require $\frac{dV}{dt}$ when $r = 12$. Now $\frac{dV}{dt} = 4\pi r^2 \frac{dr}{dt} = 4\pi r^2 = 4\pi \, . \, 12^2 = 576\pi$ (when $r = 12$).

7. Partial differentiation

In physics, the volume of a quantity of gas depends on pressure, temperature and possibly other variables. In an experiment we may be interested in the change of volume when only the pressure is allowed to vary. The mathematical model for such a situation involves a function of several variables and the rate at which this function changes when only one of the variables changes.

Suppose that f is a mapping from $\mathbf{R}^n = \mathbf{R} \times \mathbf{R} \times \cdots \times \mathbf{R}$ (n of these) to $\mathbf{R}$, the value of f at the point $(x_1, x_2, \cdots, x_n) \in \mathbf{R}^n$ being denoted by $f(x_1, x_2, \cdots, x_n)$, so that f is a function of the n variables $x_1, x_2, \cdots, x_n$. If

$$\lim_{h \to 0} \frac{f(x_1+h, x_2, \cdots, x_n) - f(x_1, x_2, \cdots, x_n)}{h}$$

exists, then it is called the **partial derivative of** f (at the point $(x_1, x_2, \cdots, x_n)$) **with respect to** x_1 and denoted by $f_1(x_1, \cdots, x_n)$, or $f_{x_1}(x_1, \cdots, x_n)$ or $\frac{\partial f}{\partial x_1}$ (read as "partial df by dx_1"). The derivative is formed with $x_2, \cdots, x_n$ fixed and only x_1 varying.

Similarly, we can form the other partial derivatives of f, namely

$$\frac{\partial f}{\partial x_2}, \cdots, \frac{\partial f}{\partial x_n}.$$

Since the limit process involved is the same as that for differentiation of functions of one variable, the standard derived functions and rules for differentiation go over to partial differentiation; e.g.

$$\frac{\partial}{\partial x}\{f(x, y).g(x, y)\} = \frac{\partial f}{\partial x}.g(x, y)+f(x, y).\frac{\partial g}{\partial x} \quad (x, y \text{ being the variables}),$$

$$\frac{\partial}{\partial y}\sin(x-2y) = \cos(x-2y)\frac{\partial}{\partial y}(x-2y) = -2\cos(x-2y),$$

$$\frac{\partial}{\partial x_1}f(g(x_1, x_2, \cdots, x_n)) = f'(g(x_1, x_2, \cdots, x_n)).\frac{\partial g}{\partial x_1} \quad \text{(chain rule).}$$

Example 1. If
$$u = \frac{x-2y+3z}{\sqrt{(x^3+z^3)}},$$
show that
$$x\frac{\partial u}{\partial x}+y\frac{\partial u}{\partial y}+z\frac{\partial u}{\partial z} = -\frac{1}{2}u.$$

$$\frac{\partial u}{\partial x} = \frac{1}{\sqrt{(x^3+z^3)}}-\frac{3}{2}\frac{x^2(x-2y+3z)}{(x^3+z^3)^{3/2}},$$

$$\frac{\partial u}{\partial y} = \frac{-2}{\sqrt{(x^3+z^3)}},$$

$$\frac{\partial u}{\partial z} = \frac{3}{\sqrt{(x^3+z^3)}}-\frac{3}{2}\frac{z^2(x-2y+3z)}{(x^3+z^3)^{3/2}}.$$

Thus
$$x\frac{\partial u}{\partial x}+y\frac{\partial u}{\partial y}+z\frac{\partial u}{\partial z} = \frac{x-2y+3z}{\sqrt{(x^3+z^3)}}-\frac{3}{2}\frac{(x^3+z^3)(x-2y+3z)}{(x^3+z^3)^{3/2}}$$
$$= -\frac{1}{2}\frac{x-2y+3z}{\sqrt{(x^3+z^3)}} = -\frac{1}{2}u.$$

Example 2. If $V = \sin(2+x^2y)$, verify that $\frac{\partial}{\partial x}\left(\frac{\partial V}{\partial y}\right) = \frac{\partial}{\partial y}\left(\frac{\partial V}{\partial x}\right)$.

$$\frac{\partial V}{\partial x} = 2xy\cos(2+x^2y), \quad \frac{\partial}{\partial y}\left(\frac{\partial V}{\partial x}\right) = 2x\cos(2+x^2y)-2x^3y\sin(2+x^2y),$$

$$\frac{\partial V}{\partial y} = x^2\cos(2+x^2y), \quad \frac{\partial}{\partial x}\left(\frac{\partial V}{\partial y}\right) = 2x\cos(2+x^2y)-2x^3y\sin(2+x^2y),$$

and a glance shows that

$$\frac{\partial}{\partial x}\left(\frac{\partial V}{\partial y}\right) = \frac{\partial}{\partial y}\left(\frac{\partial V}{\partial x}\right).$$

Higher-order derivatives

$\dfrac{\partial}{\partial x_i}\left(\dfrac{\partial f}{\partial x_i}\right)$, if it exists, is denoted by $\dfrac{\partial^2 f}{\partial x_i^2}$ $(i = 1, 2, \cdots)$;

$\dfrac{\partial}{\partial x_i}\left(\dfrac{\partial f}{\partial x_j}\right)$, if it exists, is denoted by $\dfrac{\partial^2 f}{\partial x_i \partial x_j}$ $(i, j = 1, 2, \cdots)$;

$\dfrac{\partial}{\partial x_i}\left(\dfrac{\partial^2 f}{\partial x_i^2}\right)$, if it exists, is denoted by $\dfrac{\partial^3 f}{\partial x_i^3}$ $(i = 1, 2, \cdots)$;

$\dfrac{\partial}{\partial x_i}\left(\dfrac{\partial^2 f}{\partial x_j \partial x_k}\right)$, if it exists, is denoted by $\dfrac{\partial^3 f}{\partial x_i \partial x_j \partial x_k}$ $(i, j, k = 1, 2, \cdots)$;

and similarly for higher-order derivatives.

As suggested in Example 2, the following result holds for all "well behaved" functions:

$$\frac{\partial}{\partial x_i}\left(\frac{\partial f}{\partial x_j}\right) = \frac{\partial}{\partial x_j}\left(\frac{\partial f}{\partial x_i}\right), \qquad \text{i.e.} \quad \frac{\partial^2 f}{\partial x_i \partial x_j} = \frac{\partial^2 f}{\partial x_j \partial x_i}.$$

This is called the **commutative property** of partial differentiation. It implies that the order in which a prescribed number of partial differentiations is carried out does not matter.

Example 3. If $V = \dfrac{1}{\sqrt{(x^2+y^2+z^2)}}$, verify that V satisfies the "partial differential equation"

$$\frac{\partial^2 V}{\partial x^2} + \frac{\partial^2 V}{\partial y^2} + \frac{\partial^2 V}{\partial z^2} = 0. \tag{7.1}$$

[V is the potential at the point (x, y, z) in space due to a unit point charge at the origin; equation (7.1) is called Laplace's equation.]

$$\frac{\partial V}{\partial x} = \frac{-x}{(x^2+y^2+z^2)^{3/2}}; \qquad \frac{\partial^2 V}{\partial x^2} = \frac{-1}{(x^2+y^2+z^2)^{3/2}} + \frac{3x^2}{(x^2+y^2+z^2)^{5/2}}.$$

The corresponding equations for $\dfrac{\partial^2 V}{\partial y^2}$ and $\dfrac{\partial^2 V}{\partial z^2}$ can be written down from considerations of symmetry, and

$$\frac{\partial^2 V}{\partial x^2}+\frac{\partial^2 V}{\partial y^2}+\frac{\partial^2 V}{\partial z^2} = \frac{-3}{(x^2+y^2+z^2)^{3/2}}+\frac{3(x^2+y^2+z^2)}{(x^2+y^2+z^2)^{5/2}}$$

$$= \frac{-3+3}{(x^2+y^2+z^2)^{3/2}} = 0.$$

Example 4. Show that, if $z = x\sin\left(\frac{1}{y}-\frac{1}{x}\right)$, then z satisfies the partial differential equation

$$x^2y^2\frac{\partial^2 z}{\partial x\partial y} - xy^2\frac{\partial z}{\partial y} = z.$$

$$\frac{\partial z}{\partial y} = x\cos\left(\frac{1}{y}-\frac{1}{x}\right).\left(\frac{-1}{y^2}\right);$$

$$\frac{\partial^2 z}{\partial x\partial y} = -\frac{1}{y^2}\cos\left(\frac{1}{y}-\frac{1}{x}\right)-\frac{x}{y^2}\left(-\sin\left(\frac{1}{y}-\frac{1}{x}\right)\right).\frac{1}{x^2},$$

and so
$$\frac{\partial z}{\partial y} = -\frac{x}{y^2}\cos\left(\frac{1}{y}-\frac{1}{x}\right),$$

$$\frac{\partial^2 z}{\partial x\partial y} = -\frac{1}{y^2}\cos\left(\frac{1}{y}-\frac{1}{x}\right)+\frac{1}{xy^2}\sin\left(\frac{1}{y}-\frac{1}{x}\right).$$

Thus
$$x^2y^2\frac{\partial^2 z}{\partial x\partial y} - xy^2\frac{\partial z}{\partial y} = \begin{cases} -x^2\cos\left(\frac{1}{y}-\frac{1}{x}\right)+x\sin\left(\frac{1}{y}-\frac{1}{x}\right) \\ +x^2\cos\left(\frac{1}{y}-\frac{1}{x}\right) \end{cases}$$

$$= x\sin\left(\frac{1}{y}-\frac{1}{x}\right) = z.$$

Example 5. If z is defined as a function of x and y with derivatives $\frac{\partial z}{\partial x}$ and $\frac{\partial z}{\partial y}$ by the equation

$$ax^3+by^3+cz^3+3xyz = 0, \tag{7.2}$$

a, b, c being constants, show that

$$x\frac{\partial z}{\partial x}+y\frac{\partial z}{\partial y} = z.$$

Differentiating (7.2) partially with respect to x, we have:

$$3ax^2+3cz^2\frac{\partial z}{\partial x}+3yz+3xy\frac{\partial z}{\partial x}=0, \qquad \text{so that} \quad \frac{\partial z}{\partial x}=-\frac{ax^2+yz}{cz^2+xy},$$

$(cz^2+xy\neq 0)$. Similarly, differentiating (7.2) partially with respect to y, we obtain (provided that $cz^2+xy\neq 0$):

$$\frac{\partial z}{\partial y}=-\frac{by^2+xz}{cz^2+xy}.$$

Hence
$$x\frac{\partial z}{\partial x}+y\frac{\partial z}{\partial y}=-\frac{ax^3+by^3+2xyz}{cz^2+xy}$$

$$=\frac{cz^3+xyz}{cz^2+xy}, \qquad \text{using (7.2)},$$

$$=z.$$

Example 6. If f is a twice-differentiable function of a single variable with first- and second-order derived functions f' and f'' and if

$$u=f(x^2+2xy),$$

find an expression for $\dfrac{\partial^2 u}{\partial x^2}$.

By the chain rule, $\dfrac{\partial u}{\partial x}=f'(x^2+2xy)\dfrac{\partial}{\partial x}(x^2+2xy)$

$$=2(x+y)f'(x^2+2xy).$$

Hence
$$\frac{\partial^2 u}{\partial x^2}=2f'(x^2+2xy)+2(x+y)f''(x^2+2xy)\frac{\partial}{\partial x}(x^2+2xy)$$

$$=2f'(x^2+2xy)+4(x+y)^2f''(x^2+2xy). \tag{7.3}$$

Exercise. Verify this result (7.3) for $f=\sin$.

Example 7. If f and g are twice-differentiable functions of a single variable and if $V=f(x+at)+g(x-at)$, where a is a constant, show that

$$\frac{\partial^2 V}{\partial t^2}=a^2\frac{\partial^2 V}{\partial x^2}. \tag{7.4}$$

[Equation (7.4) is called the *wave equation* in 1-dimensional space; it holds for all waves travelling along the x-axis, x denoting position at time t.]

$$\frac{\partial V}{\partial t} = f'(x+at)\frac{\partial}{\partial t}(x+at)+g'(x-at)\frac{\partial}{\partial t}(x-at)$$
$$= af'(x+at)-ag'(x-at),$$

and
$$\frac{\partial^2 V}{\partial t^2} = af''(x+at)\frac{\partial}{\partial t}(x+at)-ag''(x-at)\frac{\partial}{\partial t}(x-at)$$
$$= a^2\{f''(x+at)+g''(x-at)\}. \tag{7.5}$$

Also,
$$\frac{\partial V}{\partial x} = f'(x+at)\frac{\partial}{\partial x}(x+at)+g'(x-at)\frac{\partial}{\partial x}(x-at)$$
$$= f'(x+at)+g'(x-at),$$

and
$$\frac{\partial^2 V}{\partial x^2} = f''(x+at)\frac{\partial}{\partial x}(x+at)+g''(x-at)\frac{\partial}{\partial x}(x-at)$$
$$= f''(x+at)+g''(x-at). \tag{7.6}$$

Clearly the result (7.4) follows from (7.5) and (7.6).

Exercise. Verify (7.4) when $f = \sin$ and $g = \cos$.

Note. We have verified that V, a sum of two arbitrary functions f, g of $x+at$ and $x-at$, respectively, is a solution of the partial differential equation (7.4). It can be shown that V is the general solution of (7.4) (i.e. contains all "well-behaved" solutions).

EXERCISE 1

1. Starting from the definition of a derivative, find the derived functions of the functions f, g defined on $\mathbf{R}-\{-\frac{1}{3}\}$ by

$$\text{(i) } f(x) = \frac{1}{3x+1}, \qquad \text{(ii) } g(x) = \frac{1}{(3x+1)^2}.$$

2. Discuss for each of the following functions f the existence of right and left derivatives at $x = 0$ and determine whether $f'(0)$ exists.

$$\text{(i) } f(x) = \begin{cases} x^2 & \text{when } x \geqslant 0, \\ 0 & \text{when } x < 0, \end{cases} \qquad \text{(ii) } f(x) = \begin{cases} x^2 & \text{when } x \geqslant 0, \\ x & \text{when } x < 0, \end{cases}$$

$$\text{(iii) } f(x) = x+|x|,\ \forall x \in \mathbf{R}, \qquad \text{(iv) } f(x) = \begin{cases} 2x & \text{when } x \geqslant 0, \\ x+a|x| & \text{when } x < 0. \end{cases}$$

In the case of (iv) show that there is one possible constant a for which $f'(0)$ exists.

3. Differentiate with respect to x:

(i) $\dfrac{x}{(1+x)^2}$, (ii) $\dfrac{3x+4}{x^2+1}$, (iii) $\dfrac{x}{x^2+1}$,

(iv) $\dfrac{2x+1}{x(x^2+1)}$, (v) $\dfrac{5x-1}{x^2-x+1}$, (vi) $\left(\dfrac{1+x}{1-x}\right)^5$,

(vii) $\dfrac{x^3}{(x^2-3)^3}$, (viii) $\dfrac{1}{1-\sqrt{x}}$, (ix) $\dfrac{1+\sqrt{x}}{1-\sqrt{x}}$,

(x) $\dfrac{x}{\sqrt{(1+x^2)}}$, (xi) $\dfrac{x+1}{\sqrt{(2x^2+x-3)}}$, (xii) $x^3\sqrt{(1+x^2)}$,

(xiii) $(x+1)^{1/3}(x+3)^{7/3}$, (xiv) $x^3(a^2+x^2)^{5/2}$ $(a \neq 0)$, (xv) $\cos^2 x+\sin 3x$,

(xvi) $\dfrac{\sin x}{2+\cos x}$, (xvii) $\dfrac{\sin x}{\sin x+\cos x}$, (xviii) $\sin^3 x\cos 3x$,

(xix) $\sin\left(\dfrac{1}{x}+\cos x\right)$, (xx) $\dfrac{\cos^5 x}{\sin 5x}$, (xxi) $\cos(\sin 4x)$,

(xxii) $\dfrac{\sin x}{\sqrt{(5-4\cos x)}}$, (xxiii) $\sin x\sqrt{(\cos 2x)}$, (xxiv) $x\tan 2x$,

(xxv) $\sqrt{(\sec x^2)}$, (xxvi) $\sqrt{\{\sin(1-2x)\}}$, (xxvii) $(\sqrt{\cos 6x})\operatorname{cosec}^3 x$,

(xxviii) $\sin\{x(1-2x)^{1/3}\}$, (xxix) $\cot\sqrt{(x^3-3x)}$, (xxx) $\sqrt{(\sec^3 x\sec 3x)}$,

(xxxi) $\tan(\cos x^{1/3})$, (xxxii) $\cot(\tan x^{5/4})$.

4. Find the equation of the tangent to each of the following curves at the point given:

(i) $y = x^8$ at the point $(1, 1)$,
(ii) $y = x^3-5x$ at the point $(2, -2)$,
(iii) $y = x^{2/3}$ at the point $(-8, 4)$,

(iv) $y = \dfrac{x}{x^2+3}$ at the point given by $x = 1$,

(v) $y = \sin x$ at $x = \frac{1}{3}\pi$,
(vi) $y = \cot \pi x$ at $x = \frac{1}{6}$.

5. Find the nth derivatives of

(i) $\dfrac{1}{2x-1}$, (ii) $\dfrac{1}{4x^2-1}$, (iii) $\sin 2x$.

6. Find the equation of the tangent to the curve

$$y = \frac{1}{x^2+x-2}$$

at its point of intersection with the y-axis, and find the coordinates of the point at which this tangent meets the curve again.

7. Find the equation of the tangent at the point $(1, 4)$ on the curve $y = x^4 - 2x^3 + 5$, and the coordinates of the other point in which the tangent meets the curve.

8. Find the equations of the tangent and normal at the point $P(\frac{1}{2}t_1{}^2, t_1)$ $(t_1 \neq 0)$ on the parabola $y^2 = 2x$ and the coordinates of the point in which the normal at P meets the curve again.

9. Show that the line $y = -x$ is a tangent to the curve $y = x^3 - 6x^2 + 8x$, and find the point of contact. Does this line intersect the curve at any other point?

10. If $f(x) = \dfrac{\cos x}{\sin x + \cos x}$, find the values of x in the interval $[0, 2\pi]$ for which $f''(x) = 0$.

11. (i) Verify that $y = x \sin x$ is a solution of the differential equation

$$x^2 \frac{d^2y}{dx^2} - 2x\frac{dy}{dx} + (x^2+2)y = 0.$$

(ii) If $y = A\cos 2x + B\sin 2x$, where A and B are constants, find a differential equation, involving y and $\dfrac{d^2y}{dx^2}$, which y satisfies for any real numbers A, B.

12. If $(x+y)^3 - 5x + y = 1$ defines y as a differentiable function of x, find $\dfrac{dy}{dx}$ in terms of x and y. Find the equation of the tangent to the given curve at the point at which it meets the line $x+y = 1$.

13. If $(x+y)^4 = 4xy$, show that $\dfrac{dy}{dx} = \dfrac{y(3x-y)}{x(x-3y)}$.

14. Find the equation of the tangent at the point $(2a, 4a)$ on the curve $x^3 + y^3 = 9axy$, where a is a non-zero constant, and find the coordinates of the point where this tangent meets the curve again.

15. If the equation $2x^2 + 6xy + 4y^2 = 3$ defines y as a twice-differentiable function of x, express $\dfrac{dy}{dx}$ in terms of x and y, and show that

$$\frac{d^2y}{dx^2} = \frac{3}{(3x+4y)^3}.$$

16. If the equation $y^4 = 4xy + 3$ defines y as a twice-differentiable function of x, find $\dfrac{dy}{dx}$ in terms of x and y, and show that

$$\frac{d^2y}{dx^2} = \frac{3(1-y^4)}{2(y^3-x)^3}.$$

17. (i) Show that the rate of change of the area of a circle with respect to the radius equals in magnitude the circumference. Find also the magnitude of the rate of change of the area with respect to the circumference.

(ii) Show that the rate of change of the volume of a sphere with respect to the radius equals in magnitude the surface area. Find also the magnitude of the rate of change of the volume with respect to the surface area.

18. Assuming that a raindrop is a perfect sphere and that through condensation it accumulates moisture at a rate equal to twice its surface area, show that its radius increases at a constant rate.

19. A particle is moving on the x-axis so that at time t (seconds) its position (in metres) from the origin O is given by $x = 16t^6 - 3t$. Find the acceleration and position of the particle at the instant at which the velocity is zero.

20. A point moves on the parabola with equation $y = 2x^2 + 3x$. Find the point on the curve at which the rate of change of the y-coordinate is 7 times the rate of change of the x-coordinate.

21. At time t a stone is at a point P at height y above a point A on the ground. If $y = a - \frac{1}{2}gt^2$, where a, g are constants, and if AP subtends on angle θ at a point O on the ground 10 units of distance from A, find the rate at which θ is changing when the stone strikes the ground.

22. A tank shaped as a right-circular cone is standing vertically with its open flat top upwards, and water is flowing into the tank at the rate of 1 cubic metre/minute. If the radius of the flat top is 3 metres and the height of the cone is 10 metres, find the rate at which the water level is rising when the depth of water (at its deepest point) is 2 metres.

23. Find the first-order partial derivatives with respect to each of the variables of the function f defined by

$$f(r, \theta, z) = \frac{r(2 - \cos 2\theta)}{r^2 + z^2}.$$

24. (i) If $u = \dfrac{x+y}{\sqrt{x} + \sqrt{y}}$, show that $x\dfrac{\partial u}{\partial x} + y\dfrac{\partial u}{\partial y} = \frac{1}{2}u$.

(ii) If $v = \dfrac{x+3y}{\sqrt{(x^3 - 2y^3)}}$, show that $x\dfrac{\partial v}{\partial x} + y\dfrac{\partial v}{\partial y} = -\frac{1}{2}v$.

25. Verify that $V = \sqrt{(y - x^2)}$ is a solution of the partial differential equation

$$4y\frac{\partial^2 V}{\partial y^2} - \frac{\partial^2 V}{\partial x^2} = 0.$$

26. If $f: \mathbf{R}^2 - \{(0, 0)\} \to \mathbf{R}$ is defined by

$$f(x, y) = \frac{xy}{(x^2 + y^2)^2}, \quad \text{show that} \quad \frac{\partial^2 f}{\partial x^2} + \frac{\partial^2 f}{\partial y^2} = 0.$$

27. If $w = \sin(x+ct)+\cos(2x+2ct)$, where c is a non-zero constant, show that

$$\frac{\partial^2 w}{\partial t^2} = c^2 \frac{\partial^2 w}{\partial x^2}.$$

28. Verify that $V = \dfrac{1}{\sqrt{\{(x-a)^2+(y-b)^2+(z-c)^2\}}}$, where a, b, c are constants, is a solution of the equation

$$\frac{\partial^2 V}{\partial x^2}+\frac{\partial^2 V}{\partial y^2}+\frac{\partial^2 V}{\partial z^2} = 0.$$

29. If f is a differentiable function of a single variable, show that

$$z = -\frac{x}{y}\cos(xy)+f\left(\frac{x}{y}\right)$$

is a solution of the equation

$$x\frac{\partial z}{\partial x}+y\frac{\partial z}{\partial y} = 2x^2\sin(xy).$$

30. If z is defined as a function of x and y with derivatives $\dfrac{\partial z}{\partial x}$ and $\dfrac{\partial z}{\partial y}$ by the equation $ax^4+by^4+cz^4+4xyz^2 = 0$, a, b, c being constants, show that

$$x\frac{\partial z}{\partial x}+y\frac{\partial z}{\partial y} = z.$$

31. Show that $z = xy\, g\left(\dfrac{x-y}{xy}\right)$, where g is a differentiable function of a single variable, is a solution of the equation

$$x^2\frac{\partial z}{\partial x}+y^2\frac{\partial z}{\partial y} = (x+y)z.$$

32. Show that $V = f(x^2-y^2)+g\left(\dfrac{y}{x}\right)$, where f and g are twice-differentiable functions of a single variable, is a solution of the equation

$$xy\left(\frac{\partial^2 V}{\partial x^2}+\frac{\partial^2 V}{\partial y^2}\right)+(x^2+y^2)\frac{\partial^2 V}{\partial x\partial y}+y\frac{\partial V}{\partial x}+x\frac{\partial V}{\partial y} = 0.$$

Increasing and decreasing functions, critical points, maxima and minima

1. Increasing and decreasing functions

We consider a real function f and suppose that I is an interval on which f is defined.

The function f is said to be **increasing on** or **over** I if

$$x_1 \leqslant x_2 \Rightarrow f(x_1) \leqslant f(x_2),$$

for each such pair of points x_1, x_2 in I; f is said to be **decreasing on** I if

$$x_1 \leqslant x_2 \Rightarrow f(x_1) \geqslant f(x_2).$$

Also, we say that f is **strictly increasing on** I if

$$x_1 < x_2 \Rightarrow f(x_1) < f(x_2),$$

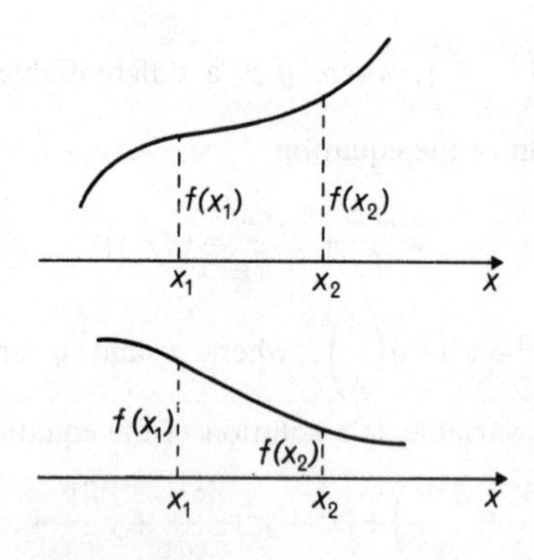

and that f is **strictly decreasing on** I if

$$x_1 < x_2 \Rightarrow f(x_1) > f(x_2).$$

Example 1. (i) The function f given by $f(x) = 2x$ is increasing on **R** since $x_1 \leqslant x_2 \Rightarrow 2x_1 \leqslant 2x_2$ for any such real numbers x_1, x_2. In fact, it is clear that f is strictly increasing on **R**. The graph of f is the line $y = 2x$.

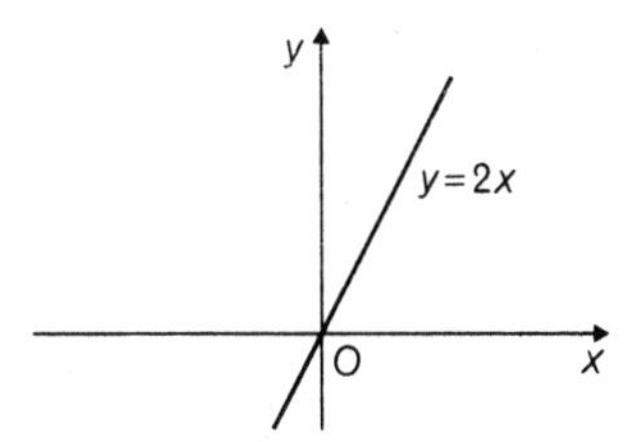

(ii) The function f given by $f(x) = x^2$ is strictly increasing on $\mathbf{R}^+ = \{x \in \mathbf{R} : x \geqslant 0\}$ and strictly decreasing on $\mathbf{R}^- = \{x \in \mathbf{R} : x \leqslant 0\}$; for, if $x_1, x_2 \in \mathbf{R}^+$ and $x_1 < x_2$, then $x_1{}^2 < x_2{}^2$, but, if $x_1, x_2 \in \mathbf{R}^-$ and $x_1 < x_2$, then $x_1{}^2 > x_2{}^2$.

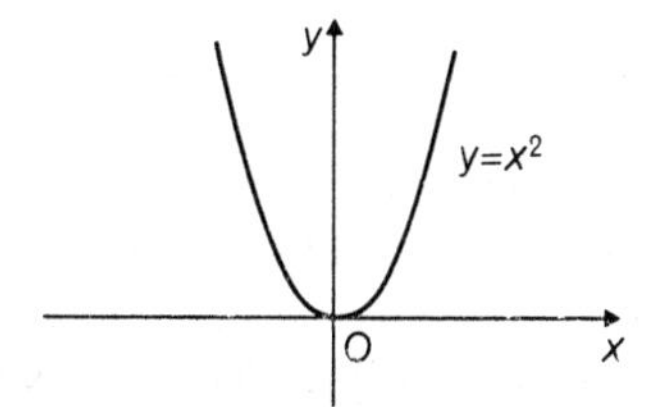

(iii) The function f given by $f(x) = \sin x$ is strictly increasing on the interval $[-\frac{1}{2}\pi, \frac{1}{2}\pi]$ and strictly decreasing on the interval $[\frac{1}{2}\pi, \frac{3}{2}\pi]$.

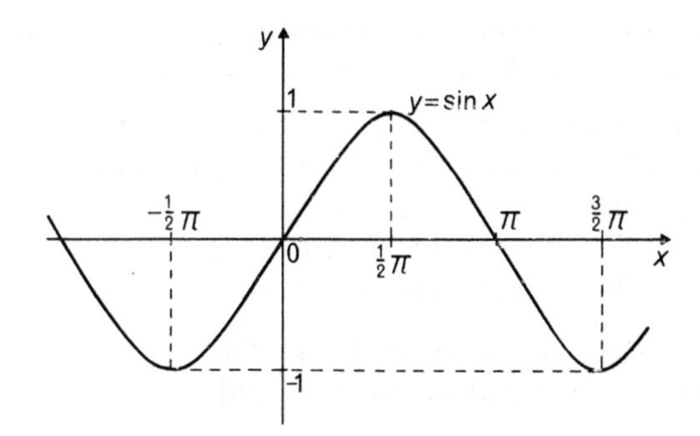

In the case of a differentiable function f it is natural to try to determine how the derived function f' can be used in dealing with intervals of increase or decrease of f. The discussion will make use of the following important result in calculus.

Theorem 2.1 (The Mean Value Theorem)

If f is a function which is continuous on the closed interval $a \leqslant x \leqslant b$

and differentiable on the open interval $a < x < b$, then there is a real number c such that $a < c < b$ and

$$f'(c) = \frac{f(b)-f(a)}{b-a},$$

i.e. *the gradient of the tangent at the point $C(c, f(c))$ on the graph of f is parallel to the chord AB, where A is the point $(a, f(a))$ and $B(b, f(b))$ on the graph.*

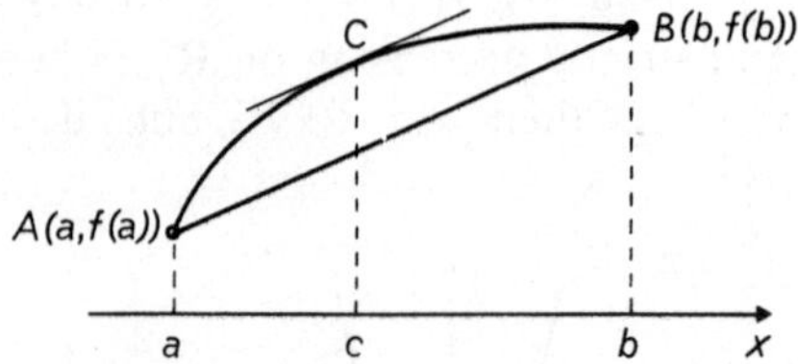

The result is intuitively obvious from a diagram, but the proof requires more analysis than is reasonable in a book at this level.

The special case of Theorem 2.1 in which $f(a) = 0 = f(b)$ and $f'(c) = 0$, where $a < c < b$, is usually called **Rolle's theorem**.

Our first application of the Mean Value Theorem is to provide a proof of the following theorem.

Theorem 2.2

If f is a function which is continuous on some interval I and differentiable on the open interval, (a, b) say, determined by I, then

(i) *if $f'(x) = 0$ $\forall x \in (a, b)$, f is a constant function on I;*
(ii) *if $f'(x) > 0$ $\forall x \in (a, b)$, f is strictly increasing on I;*
(iii) *if $f'(x) < 0$ $\forall x \in (a, b)$, f is strictly decreasing on I;*
(iv) *if $f'(x) \geqslant 0$ $\forall x \in (a, b)$, f is increasing on I;*
(v) *if $f'(x) \leqslant 0$ $\forall x \in (a, b)$, f is decreasing on I.*

Proof. Suppose that x_1, x_2 are in I and that $x_1 < x_2$; by the Mean Value Theorem, $\exists c$ such that $x_1 < c < x_2$ and

$$f'(c) = \frac{f(x_2)-f(x_1)}{x_2-x_1},$$

i.e. $$f(x_2)-f(x_1) = (x_2-x_1)f'(c). \tag{1.1}$$

Case (i): Here $f'(c) = 0$, and so, from (1.1), $f(x_2) = f(x_1)$. Similarly, if $x_3 < x_1$, we obtain: $f(x_1) = f(x_3)$. Keeping x_1 fixed it follows that $f(x) = f(x_1)$ $\forall x \in I$, so that f is constant on I.

Case (ii): Here $f'(c) > 0$, and so, from (1.1), $f(x_2) > f(x_1)$ since

$x_2 - x_1 > 0$. Thus, on I, $x_1 < x_2 \Rightarrow f(x_1) < f(x_2)$, i.e. f is strictly increasing on I.

Case (iii): Here $f'(c) < 0$, and so, from (1.1), $f(x_2) < f(x_1)$ since $x_2 - x_1 > 0$. Thus, on I, $x_1 < x_2 \Rightarrow f(x_1) > f(x_2)$, i.e. f is strictly decreasing on I.

The proofs of (iv) and (v) are similar to those of (ii) and (iii).

Example 2. Determine the intervals of increase and of decrease for the following differentiable (and so continuous) real functions:

(i) f defined on $\mathbf{R}$ by $f(x) = x^2 + 6x$;

(ii) g defined on $\mathbf{R}$ by $g(x) = x^4 - 8x^2 + 1$;

(iii) h defined on $\mathbf{R} - \{-3, 1\}$ by $h(x) = \dfrac{1}{(x+3)(x-1)^2}$.

By Theorem 2.2 it is enough to consider the sign of the derivatives.

(i) Here $f'(x) = 2x + 6 = 2(x+3)$. Thus $f'(x) > 0$ for $x > -3$ and $f'(x) < 0$ for $x < -3$. It follows that f is strictly increasing on $[-3, \infty)$ and strictly decreasing on $(-\infty, -3]$.

(ii) Here $g'(x) = 4x^3 - 16x = 4x(x^2 - 4) = 4x(x+2)(x-2)$. In a case like this it is useful to draw up a table of sign.

x:	→	-2	→	0	→	2	→
x:	−	−	−	0	+	+	+
x^2-4:	+	0	−	−	−	0	+
$g'(x)$:	−	0	+	0	−	0	+

It follows that $g'(x) > 0$ for $-2 < x < 0$ and for $x > 2$ and that $g'(x) < 0$ for $x < -2$ and for $0 < x < 2$. Consequently g is strictly increasing on $[-2, 0]$ and on $[2, \infty)$ and strictly decreasing on $(-\infty, -2]$ and on $[0, 2]$.

(iii) In this case, check that

$$h'(x) = \frac{-(3x+5)}{(x+3)^2(x-1)^3}.$$

The corresponding table of sign is as follows:

x:	→	-3	→	$-\frac{5}{3}$	→	1	→
$-(3x+5)$:	+	+	+	0	−	−	−
$(x+3)^2$:	+	0	+	+	+	+	+
$(x-1)^3$:	−	−	−	−	−	0	+
$h'(x)$:	−	∞	−	0	+	∞	−

[The infinite symbol ∞ merely indicates that $h'(x)$ is not defined at the points involved.]

It follows that $h'(x) > 0$ for $-\frac{5}{3} < x < 1$ and that $h'(x) < 0$ for $x < -3$, for $-3 < x < -\frac{5}{3}$ and for $x > 1$. Consequently h is strictly increasing on $[-\frac{5}{3}, 1)$ and strictly decreasing on $(-\infty, -3)$, on $(-3, -\frac{5}{3}]$ and on $(1, \infty)$. [Note that h is defined at $x = -\frac{5}{3}$, but not at $x = -3$ or $x = 1$.]

Example 3. Show that, $\forall x \in \mathbf{R}^+$, $\sin x \leqslant x$.

Writing $f(x) = x - \sin x$, we have to show that $f(x) \geqslant 0$ on $\mathbf{R}^+$.

Now $f'(x) = 1 - \cos x \geqslant 0$ $\forall x \in \mathbf{R}$ (since $\cos x \leqslant 1$). Thus f is increasing on $\mathbf{R}$. In particular, $f(x) \geqslant f(0)$ $\forall x \geqslant 0$; but $f(0) = 0$, and so, $x - \sin x \geqslant 0$ $\forall x \in \mathbf{R}^+$. From this the required result follows.

Using part (i) of Theorem 2.2 we can establish at this stage the following result which will be used later in dealing with anti-differentiation.

Theorem 2.3

If f and g are functions differentiable on an interval I and such that $f'(x) = g'(x)$ $\forall x \in I$, then $\exists C \in \mathbf{R}$ (C a constant) such that

$$f(x) = g(x) + C, \quad \forall x \in I.$$

Proof. If $h = f - g$, then $h(x) = f(x) - g(x)$, and

$$h'(x) = f'(x) - g'(x) = 0 \quad \forall x \in I.$$

It follows from the facts given that h satisfies the conditions involved in part (i) of Theorem 2.2 and so h has a constant value, C say, on I. Thus $f(x) - g(x) = C$, $\forall x \in I$, and the required result follows.

2. Critical points

It was clear from the functions considered in Example 2 of Section **1** that, in dealing with the rate of change of a *differentiable* function f, the real numbers x for which $f'(x) = 0$ play an important role. A point $(c, f(c))$ on the graph $y = f(x)$ (of such a function f) such that $f'(c) = 0$ is called a **critical point** of f. For simplicity we say that $x = c$ gives a critical point or that c is a critical point of f; $f(c)$ is called a **critical value** of f. At a critical point the tangent is parallel to the x-axis; for this reason the term **stationary point** is often used instead of critical point.

The possible behaviour of f in a neighbourhood of a critical point c of f ($f'(c) = 0$) is indicated in the following diagrams.

(i) $f'(x) = 0$ **on a neighbourhood of** c.

Here f is constant on the neighbourhood and has the value $f(c)$; the graph there is part of the line $y = f(c)$.

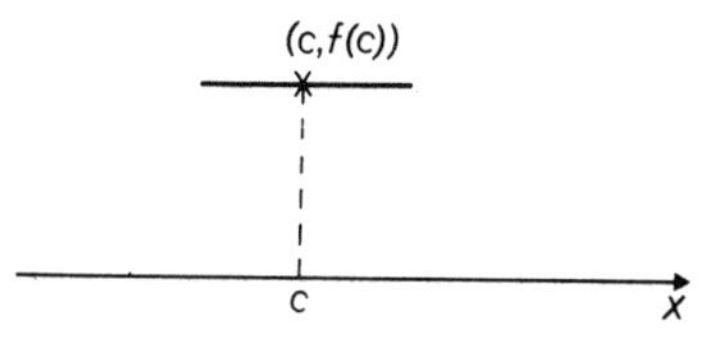

(ii) $f'(x) < 0$ **to left of** $x = c$ **and** $f'(x) > 0$ **to right of** $x = c$.

In this case the shape of the graph near the point $(c, f(c))$ is as shown. $f(c)$ is called a **local minimum value** of f or a **minimum turning value** of f, attained at the **local minimum point** $x = c$.

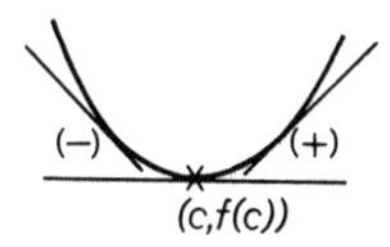

For a general function f, *not necessarily differentiable*, $x = c$ is called a **local minimum point** of f if $\exists$ a neighbourhood N of c such that

$$f(x) > f(c) \ \forall x \in N - \{c\}.$$

(iii) $f'(x) > 0$ **to left of** $x = c$ **and** $f'(x) < 0$ **to right of** $x = c$.

Here $f(c)$ is called a **local maximum value** of f or a **maximum turning value** of f, attained at the **local maximum point** $x = c$.

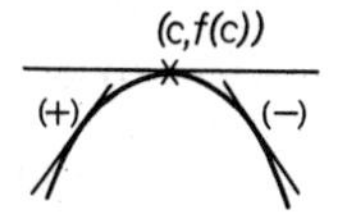

For a function f, *not necessarily differentiable*, $x = c$ is called a **local maximum point** of f if $\exists$ a neighbourhood N of c such that

$$f(x) < f(c) \ \forall x \in N - \{c\}.$$

(iv) $f'(x) > 0$ **to left and to right of** $x = c$.

Such a point is called a **horizontal point of inflexion** (*H.P.I.*) **on a**

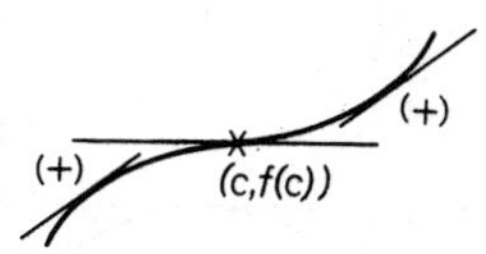

rising curve. We shall consider points of inflexion in more detail in the next chapter.

(v) $f'(x) < 0$ **to left and to right of** $x = c$.

Such a point is called a **horizontal point of inflexion** (*H.P.I.*) **on a falling curve.**

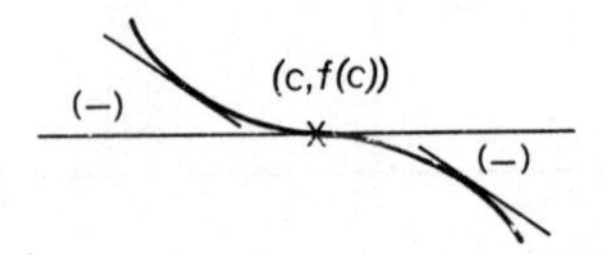

Two other cases which can arise with elementary functions but are not as important as the cases (i), ⋯, (v) are:

(vi) $f'(x) = 0$ **to left and** > 0 **(or** < 0**) to right of** $x = c$,

and

(vii) $f'(x) = 0$ **to right and** > 0 **(or** < 0**) to left of** $x = c$.

Example 1. If $f(x) = \begin{cases} x^2 & \text{when} \quad x \geqslant 0 \\ 0 & \text{when} \quad x < 0 \end{cases}$, evaluate $f'(0)$ and sketch the graph in a neighbourhood of $x = 0$. [Note that this example illustrates case (vi).]

Example 2. Determine the nature of each of the critical points of the following functions:

(i) f defined on $\mathbf{R}$ by $f(x) = x^5 - 15x^3 + 2$;

(ii) g defined on $\mathbf{R} - \{0\}$ by $g(x) = \dfrac{x^2 - 2}{x^4}$.

(i) $f'(x) = 5x^4 - 45x^2 = 5x^2(x^2 - 9) = 5x^2(x+3)(x-3)$.

Thus the critical points are $x = 0$, -3 and 3 and the critical values of f are $f(0) = 2$, $f(-3) = 164$ and $f(3) = -160$.

To determine the nature of each point we can draw up tables as follows in each of which a neighbourhood is considered (from left to right).

$x = 0$

x:	→	0	→
x^2:	+	0	+
$x^2 - 9$:	−	−	−
$f'(x)$:	−	0	−

$f(x)$:

H.P.I. (0, 2) on a falling curve.

$x = -3$

x:	→	−3	→
x^2:	+	+	+
$x+3$:	−	0	+
$x-3$:	−	−	−
$f'(x)$:	+	0	−

$f(x)$:

Local maximum at point (−3, 164)

$x = 3$

x:	→	3	→
x^2:	+	+	+
$x+3$:	+	+	+
$x-3$:	−	0	+
$f'(x)$:	−	0	+

$f(x)$:

Local minimum at point (3, −160)

$$\text{(ii) } f(x)=\frac{1}{x^2}-\frac{2}{x^4};\quad f'(x)=\frac{2}{x^5}(4-x^2)=\frac{2}{x^5}(2+x)(2-x).$$

The critical points are $x = -2$ and $x = 2$, and the critical values of f are

$$f(-2)=\tfrac{1}{8} \quad\text{and}\quad f(2)=\tfrac{1}{8}.$$

$x = -2$

x:	$\to$	-2	$\to$
$2+x$:	$-$	0	$+$
$2-x$:	$+$	$+$	$+$
$2/x^5$:	$-$	$-$	$-$
$f'(x)$:	$+$	0	$-$
$f(x)$:		$\times$	

Local maximum at point $(-2, \frac{1}{8})$

$x = 2$

x:	$\to$	2	$\to$
$2+x$:	$+$	$+$	$+$
$2-x$:	$+$	0	$-$
$2/x^5$:	$+$	$+$	$+$
$f'(x)$:	$+$	0	$-$
$f(x)$:		$\times$	

Local maximum at point $(2, \frac{1}{8})$.

3. Maxima and minima

We suppose that f is a given real function and that D is a subset of **R** on which f is defined. If $\exists c \in D$ such that

$$f(c) \geqslant f(x), \quad \forall x \in D,$$

then $f(c)$ is called the **maximum value of f on D**; it is attained at the point $x = c$ and possibly at other points of D. If $\exists d \in D$ such that

$$f(d) \leqslant f(x), \quad \forall x \in D,$$

then $f(d)$ is called the **minimum value of f on D**; it is attained at the point $x = d$ and possibly at other points of D.

If D is the maximal domain of f we usually call $f(c)$ and $f(d)$ (if they exist) simply the **maximum** and **minimum values of** f.

Example 1. (i) $f(x) = \sin x$.

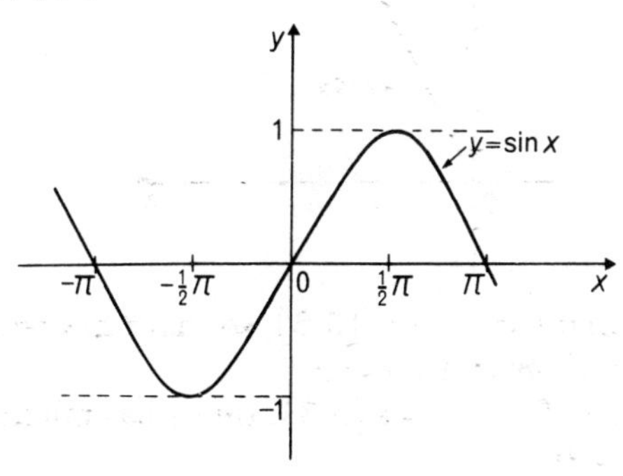

Since $\sin \frac{1}{2}\pi = 1$ and $\sin x \leqslant 1$ $\forall x \in \mathbf{R}$, it follows that 1 is the maximum value of $\sin x$ on $\mathbf{R}$; it is attained at the points $x = (2n+\frac{1}{2})\pi$, $n \in \mathbf{Z}$.

Similarly, since $\sin(-\frac{1}{2}\pi) = -1$ and $\sin x \geqslant -1$ $\forall x \in \mathbf{R}$, -1 is the minimum value of $\sin x$ on $\mathbf{R}$; it is attained at the points $x = (2n-\frac{1}{2})\pi$, $n \in \mathbf{Z}$.

(ii) $f(x) = x^2 - 2x - 3$.

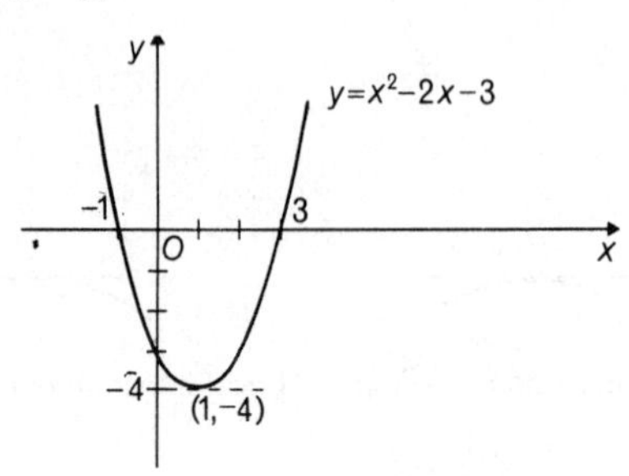

Here $f(x) = (x-1)^2 - 4 \geqslant -4$ $\forall x \in \mathbf{R}$, and $= -4 \Leftrightarrow x = 1$. Thus this quadratic function has minimum value -4 (on $\mathbf{R}$), attained only at $x = 1$.

For any given large positive real number M we can find $x \in \mathbf{R}$ such that $x^2 - 2x - 3 > M$. It follows that f, given by $f(x) = x^2 - 2x - 3$, has no maximum value on $\mathbf{R}$; in this case we often write

$$x^2 - 2x - 3 \to \infty \text{ as } x \to \infty \quad \text{and} \quad x^2 - 2x - 3 \to \infty \text{ as } x \to -\infty$$

to mean that $f(x)$ is unbounded (and positive) as x increases through positive values and as x decreases through negative values.

(iii) $f(x) = 2x$ on $[0, 3]$.

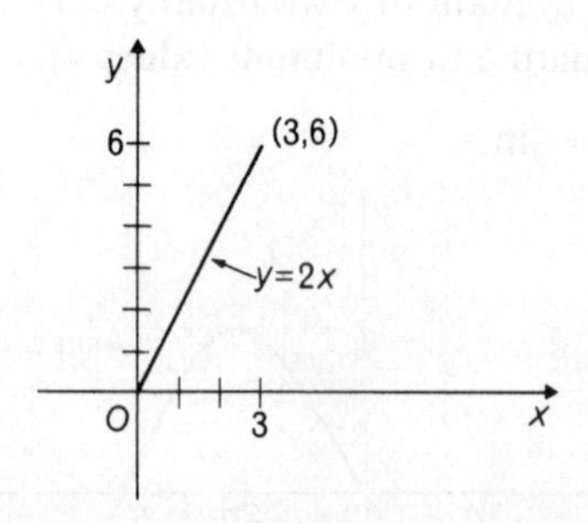

Here $f(3) = 6$ and $6 \geqslant 2x$ $\forall x \in [0, 3]$, so that f has maximum value 6 on the interval $[0, 3]$, given by $x = 3$.

Also $f(0) = 0$ and $0 \leqslant 2x$ $\forall x \in [0, 3]$; thus f has minimum value 0 on $[0, 3]$, given by $x = 0$.

(iv) $f(x) = 2x$ on $[0, 3)$.

In this case f has no maximum value on $[0, 3)$, but it has minimum value 0 on $[0, 3)$, given by $x = 0$.

(v) $f(x) = 2x$ on $(0, 3)$.

Here f has no maximum value or minimum value on the interval.

(vi) $f(x) = \frac{1}{x}$ on $\mathbf{R} - \{0\}$.

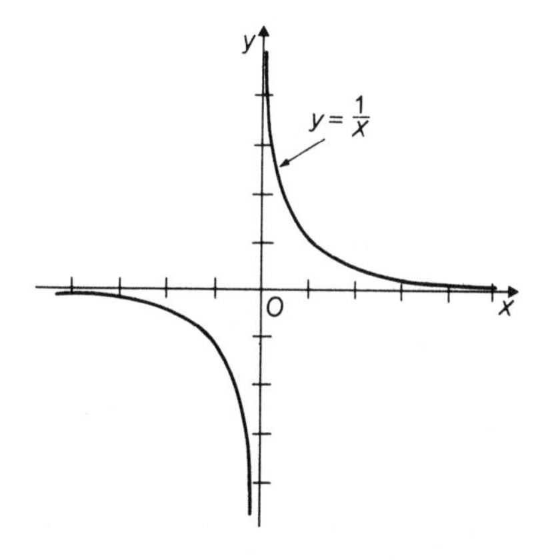

This function, whose graph is the rectangular hyperbola $y = 1/x$, has no maximum value or minimum value on $\mathbf{R} - \{0\}$ since its value is unbounded ($\to \infty$) when $x \to 0$ through positive values, and unbounded (but negative, i.e. $\to -\infty$) when $x \to 0$ through negative values.

From these six illustrations we see that a differentiable function may not have a maximum value or a minimum value and that, when such a value exists, it may or may not occur at a critical point of the function.

The following theorem, which will not be proved, shows that *continuity* is a sufficient condition to ensure the existence of a maximum value and a minimum value of a function on a *closed* interval.

Theorem 2.4

If the function f is continuous on the closed interval $[a, b]$, then f has a maximum value and also a minimum value on $[a, b]$.

We now show, in the case of a function *differentiable* on an *open* interval, that a maximum value and a minimum value can occur *only at critical points.*

Theorem 2.5

Let f be a function which is defined and differentiable on the open interval (a, b); if f has a maximum value on (a, b) attained at $x = c$ (so that $f(c) \geqslant f(x)\ \forall x \in (a, b)$), then $f'(c) = 0$, i.e. c is a critical point of f.

Proof. If $c+h \in (a, b)$, with $h > 0$,

then $$f(c+h) \leqslant f(c).$$

Thus $$f(c+h) - f(c) \leqslant 0,$$

and $$\frac{f(c+h)-f(c)}{h} \leqslant 0 \quad (\text{since } h > 0).$$

Consequently $$\lim_{\substack{h\to 0\\(h>0)}} \frac{f(c+h)-f(c)}{h} \leqslant 0, \quad \text{so that } f'(c) \leqslant 0, \tag{3.1}$$

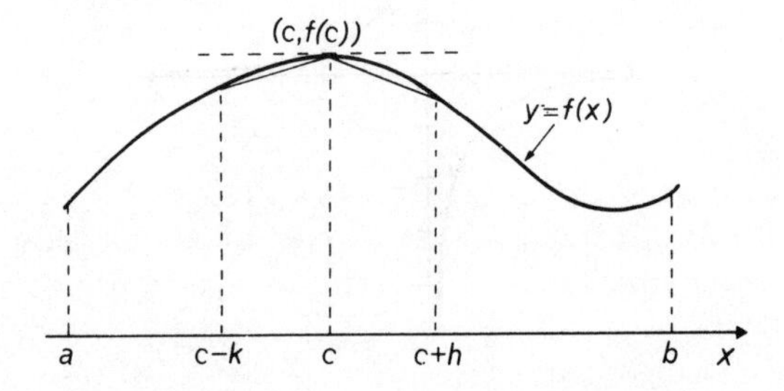

since $f'(c)$ exists (the left and right derivatives at c being $f'(c)$).

If now $c-k \in (a, b)$, with $k > 0$, then $f(c-k) - f(c) \leqslant 0$. In this case,

$$\frac{f(c-k)-f(c)}{(-k)} \geqslant 0 \quad (\text{since } k > 0).$$

Hence, writing h for $-k$, we deduce that

$$\lim_{\substack{h\to 0\\(h<0)}} \frac{f(c+h)-f(c)}{h} \geqslant 0, \quad \text{so that } f'(c) \geqslant 0. \tag{3.2}$$

From (3.1) and (3.2) the required result, that $f'(c) = 0$, follows.

Corollary. By a similar argument we can replace in Theorem 2.5 the word *maximum* by *minimum* and $\geqslant$ by $\leqslant$.

Combining Theorems 2.4 and 2.5 we obtain the following useful result.

Theorem 2.6

Let f be a function which is continuous on the closed interval $[a, b]$ and differentiable on the open interval (a, b); then the maximum value of f on $[a, b]$ is $\max(f(a), f(b), f(c))$, *where $f(c)$ is the largest critical value of f on (a, b) and the minimum value of f on $[a, b]$ is* $\min(f(a), f(b), f(c_1))$, *where $f(c_1)$ is the smallest critical value of f on (a, b).*

Note. $\max(f(a), f(b), f(c))$ denotes the largest of the three real numbers $f(a), f(b), f(c)$ and $\min(f(a), f(b), f(c))$ denotes the smallest.

From Theorem 2.6 it follows that, in dealing with the maximum and minimum values of such functions on a closed interval, we have to consider the end points and the critical points of the function which lie in the interval.

Example 2. Find the maximum and minimum values of the function f defined by the following formula on the given closed interval:

$$f(x) = 5x^6 + 6x^5 - 15x^4 + 4 \text{ on } [-1, 2].$$

$$f'(x) = 30x^5 + 30x^4 - 60x^3 = 30x^3(x^2 + x - 2) = 30x^3(x+2)(x-1).$$

Thus the critical points of f are $x = 0, -2$ and 1; of these $x = 0$ and 1 are in the given interval $[-1, 2]$. Thus the maximum value of f on $[-1, 2]$ is $\max(f(-1), f(0), f(1), f(2))$, i.e. $\max(-12, 4, 0, 276)$, and so is $f(2) = 276$ attained at the end point $x = 2$. Also the minimum value of f on $[-1, 2]$ is $f(-1) = -12$ attained at the other end point $x = -1$.
The maximum value of this function f on the interval $[-3, 0]$ is $\max(f(-3, f(-2), f(0))$, i.e. $\max(976, -108, 4)$, and so is $f(-3)$ attained at the end point $x = -3$; also the minimum value of f on $[-3, 0]$ is $f(-2) = -108$ attained at the critical point $x = -2$. [Clearly $x = -2$ is a local minimum point of f.]

Example 3. If the tangent at the point given by $x = a$ $(a > 0)$ on the curve $y = x^2 - 3$ meets the x, y-axes at the points P, Q respectively, show that the area Δ of triangle OPQ, where O is the origin, is given by

$$\Delta = \frac{(3 + a^2)^2}{4a},$$

and find the value of a for which this area is a minimum.

Here $$\frac{dy}{dx} = 2x = 2a$$

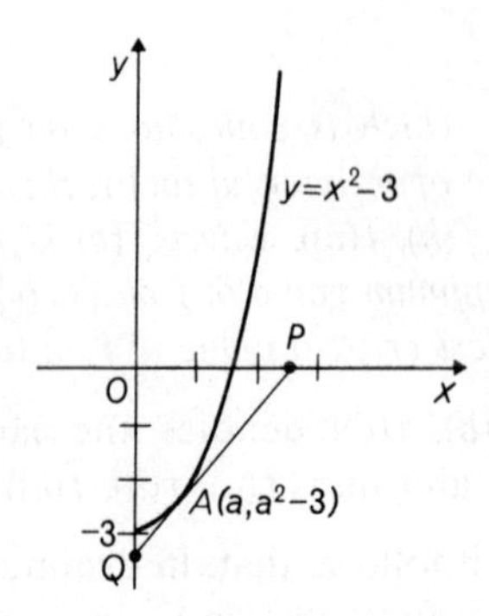

at the point $A(a, a^2-3)$. The tangent at A has equation

$$y-(a^2-3) = 2a(x-a),$$

i.e.
$$y-2ax = -3-a^2.$$

Thus P is the point $\left(\dfrac{3+a^2}{2a}, 0\right)$ and $Q(0, -(3+a^2))$,

so that
$$\Delta = \tfrac{1}{2}|OP||OQ| = \frac{(3+a^2)^2}{4a}.$$

Our problem is to find the minimum value on the interval $a > 0$ of the differentiable function defined by the formula

$$\Delta = \frac{1}{4a}(a^4+6a^2+9) = \frac{1}{4}\left(a^3+6a+\frac{9}{a}\right).$$

In this case Theorem 2.6 does not apply since the interval is not closed.

Now $\dfrac{d\Delta}{da} = \dfrac{1}{4}\left(3a^2+6-\dfrac{9}{a^2}\right) = \dfrac{3}{4a^2}(a^4+2a^2-3) = \dfrac{3}{4a^2}(a^2-1)(a^2+3).$

The only critical point in the interval $a > 0$ is $a = 1$. For $0 < a < 1$,

$$\frac{d\Delta}{da} < 0,$$

and so Δ is strictly decreasing on the interval $(0, 1]$; also for $a > 1$,

$$\frac{d\Delta}{da} > 0,$$

and so Δ is strictly increasing on the interval $[1, \infty)$. It follows that $a = 1$ gives the minimum value of Δ on $a > 0$, this value being 4.

[Δ has no maximum value on $a > 0$ since $\Delta \to \infty$ when $a \to \infty$.]

Example 4. Two corridors of widths 16 metres and 2 metres meet as shown in the diagram at right angles. Find the length of the longest (thin) ladder held horizontally but with its plane vertical that can be taken round the corner.

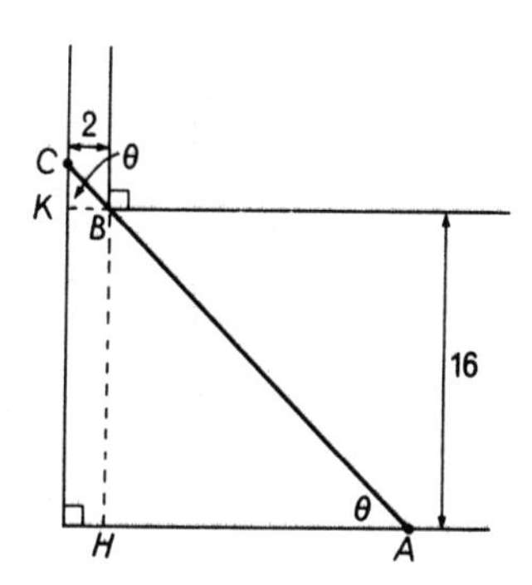

In negotiating the corner the ladder will occupy positions such as ABC. Thus the answer to the problem is the minimum possible length of AC. In a practical problem of this type we produce a mathematical model introducing any variables required.

If θ is the radian measure of the angles shown, then, from the diagram,

$$\frac{|BH|}{|AB|} = \sin\theta \quad \text{and} \quad \frac{|BK|}{|BC|} = \cos\theta,$$

so that
$$|AB| = \frac{16}{\sin\theta} \quad \text{and} \quad |BC| = \frac{2}{\cos\theta}.$$

Thus
$$|AC| = \frac{16}{\sin\theta} + \frac{2}{\cos\theta}, \quad 0 < \theta < \tfrac{1}{2}\pi.$$

Now
$$\frac{d}{d\theta}(|AC|) = -\frac{16\cos\theta}{\sin^2\theta} + \frac{2\sin\theta}{\cos^2\theta} = \frac{2\cos\theta}{\sin^2\theta}(\tan^3\theta - 8)$$

$$= \frac{2\cos\theta}{\sin^2\theta}(\tan\theta - 2)(\tan^2\theta + 2\tan\theta + 4).$$

The only critical point in $(0, \frac{1}{2}\pi)$ is α where $\tan\alpha = 2$. For $0 < \theta < \alpha$, we have $\tan\theta < 2$ and so $\frac{d}{d\theta}(|AC|) < 0$; for $\alpha < \theta < \frac{1}{2}\pi$, we have $\tan\theta > 2$ and so $\frac{d}{d\theta}(|AC|) > 0$. Consequently $|AC|$ is strictly decreasing on $(0, \alpha]$

and strictly increasing on $[\alpha, \frac{1}{2}\pi)$, so that $\theta = \alpha$ gives the minimum value of $|AC|$ on $(0, \frac{1}{2}\pi)$.

Now $$\sin\alpha = \frac{2}{\sqrt{5}} \quad \text{and} \quad \cos\alpha = \frac{1}{\sqrt{5}};$$

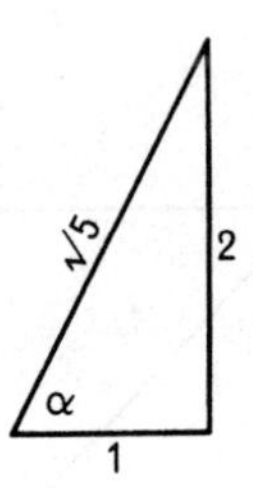

thus $|AC|$ has minimum value

$$\frac{16}{\sin\alpha} + \frac{2}{\cos\alpha} = 10\sqrt{5} \doteqdot 22{\cdot}36,$$

and this gives the length in metres of the longest ladder that could be taken round the corner in the manner indicated.

Example 5. V is the sum of the volumes of two cubes of sides x and y such that the sum of the surface areas of the two cubes is 12. Find the dimensions of the cubes for which V is a minimum.

$$V = x^3 + y^3 \quad \text{and} \quad 6x^2 + 6y^2 = 12, \quad \text{i.e. } x^2 + y^2 = 2.$$

Thus $$V = x^3 + (2 - x^2)^{3/2}, \quad \text{and} \quad 0 \leqslant x \leqslant \sqrt{2}.$$

$$\frac{dV}{dx} = 3x^2 - 3x(2-x^2)^{1/2} = \frac{3x\{x^2 - (2-x^2)\}}{x + (2-x^2)^{1/2}} = \frac{6x(x^2-1)}{x+(2-x^2)^{1/2}}.$$

It follows that the only critical point of V in $(0, \sqrt{2})$ is $x = 1$. Consequently the minimum value of V is the least of the values of V at $x = 1$, $x = 0$ and $x = \sqrt{2}$ (using Theorem **2.6**), i.e. of 2, $2\sqrt{2}$ and $2\sqrt{2}$, respectively. Thus V is a minimum when $x = 1$ and so $y = 1$.

EXERCISE 2

1. Find the intervals of increase and of decrease (if any) of the differentiable real functions defined by the following formulae:

(i) $f(x) = 3x - x^3$, (ii) $f(x) = x^5 + x^3 + x$, (iii) $f(x) = 3 + 8x^2 - x^4$,

(iv) $f(x) = \dfrac{x^2}{(x-1)^3}$, (v) $f(x) = \dfrac{x}{(x-1)(x+2)}$, (vi) $f(x) = \dfrac{1}{x(x-2)^2}$,

(vii) $f(x)=\dfrac{x}{x^4+3}$, (viii) $f(x)=\left(\dfrac{x-1}{x+1}\right)^3$, (ix) $f(x)=\dfrac{x}{\sqrt{(x^3+4)}}$,

(x) $f(x)=\dfrac{x+1}{(x-4)^2x^{1/3}}$, (xi) $f(x)=2x+\cos x$, (xii) $f(x)=x+2\sin x$.

2. Determine the nature of each of the critical values (if any) of the real functions given in Problem **1**.

3. Find the coordinates and determine the nature of each of the critical points of the following curves (graphs of functions):

(i) $y=x^4+4x^3$, (ii) $y=x(x^4-5)$, (iii) $y=3x^4-8x^3+6x^2$,

(iv) $y=\dfrac{x^2}{1-x}$, (v) $y=\dfrac{x^5}{(x+2)^2}$, (vi) $y=\dfrac{x}{(x^2-1)^{1/3}}$,

(vii) $y=x-2\cos x$, (viii) $y=\sin^2 x$, (ix) $y=2x-\tan x$,
taking (vii) and (viii) on the interval $[-\pi, \pi]$ and (ix) on the interval $(-\frac{1}{2}\pi, \frac{1}{2}\pi)$.

4. Find in the interval $[0, \pi]$ the critical points of the curve

$$y=\sin x+\tfrac{1}{2}\sin 2x+\tfrac{1}{3}\sin 3x,$$

and determine the nature of each.

5. Find the constant a such that the curve

$$y=x^2+\frac{a}{x}$$

has a local minimum point at $x=2$.

6. If the curve $y=x^3+ax^2+bx$ has critical points at $x=1$ and $x=3$ determine the constants a and b, and find the nature of each of the critical points.

7. By considering $f(x)=\cos x-1+\frac{1}{2}x^2$, show that, $\forall x \geqslant 0$, $\cos x \geqslant 1-\frac{1}{2}x^2$. Deduce that, $\forall x \in \mathbf{R}$, $\cos x \geqslant 1-\frac{1}{2}x^2$.

8. (i) If $f(x)=\dfrac{1}{1-x^2}$, show that, $\forall x \in (0, 1)$, $f(x)>1$.

(ii) If $g(x)=\dfrac{1}{(1+4x)(1-x)^4}$, show that, $\forall x \in (0, 1)$, $g(x)>1$.

9. If $f(x)=\sin x - x\cos x$, show that, $\forall x \in [0, \pi]$, $0 \leqslant f(x) \leqslant \pi$.

10. If $n \in \mathbf{N}$, show that, $\forall x \geqslant 0$,

(i) $(1+x)^n \geqslant 1+nx$, (ii) $(1+x)^n \geqslant 1+nx+\frac{1}{2}n(n-1)x^2$.

11. Give in each of the cases (i)–(iv) an example of a real function which has, on the open interval (0, 1), (i) a maximum and a minimum, (ii) a maximum but no minimum, (iii) a minimum but no maximum, (iv) neither a maximum nor a minimum.

12. Find the maximum and minimum values of the functions defined by the following formulae on the given closed intervals:

(i) $f(x) = 3-2x-x^2$ on $[-2, 1]$;
(ii) $f(x) = x^3-3x^2+4$ on $[-3, 5]$;
(iii) $f(x) = 3x^4-4x^3-54x^2+108x$ on $[-4, 2]$;
(iv) $f(x) = \dfrac{3x+4}{x^2+1}$ on $[-1, 2]$;
(v) $f(x) = \cos^3 x$ on $[0, 2\pi]$;
(vi) $f(x) = \cos 2x + \sin 2x$ on $[0, \pi]$.

13. If $f(x) = \dfrac{x}{(x+1)(x+4)}$, determine whether f has a maximum value or a minimum value on the interval $(-1, 3)$.

14. Find the coordinates of the point on the parabola $y = x^2$ which is closest to the point $A\ (3, 0)$.

15. Find the equation of the normal to the parabola $y^2 = 2x$ at the point $P(\frac{1}{2}t_1{}^2, t_1)(t_1 \neq 0)$. If the normal meets the parabola again at Q, find the value of t_1 for which the length $|PQ|$ is a minimum.

16. Of all rectangles with given area, find
(i) the one with the smallest perimeter,
(ii) the one with the shortest diagonal.

17. Find the rectangle of greatest or least perimeter which can be inscribed in a circle of radius a.

18. A right circular cone has height 12 cm and radius of base 3 cm. Find the dimensions of the cylinder of largest volume contained inside the cone and having the same axis as it.

19. A right circular cone is circumscribed about a sphere of radius a in such a way that the sphere touches the base of the cone as well as the curved surface. Show that, if the vertical height of the cone is x, the radius of the base is

$$a\sqrt{\left(\frac{x}{x-2a}\right)}.$$

Hence prove that the cone of minimum volume containing a given sphere has twice the volume of the sphere.

20. A container in the shape of a circular cylinder is to have a given volume V. Show that the total surface area is least possible when the height of the cylinder is twice the radius of the base and find this area.

21. A prism of constant volume 2 cubic units has equilateral triangles as ends and rectangles as faces. Find the length of side of the triangular ends when the surface area of the prism is a minimum.

If, as an additional condition, the length of side of the triangular ends lies in the interval $[1, 3]$, find the largest possible surface area of the prism.

22. An open rectangular box consisting of a square base and four rectangular sides is to be constructed so that the sides and base have thickness 0·5 cm and the internal capacity of the box is 500 cubic centimetres. If the internal dimensions of the box are x, x and y cm, show that the volume of material required is $V\,\text{cm}^3$ where $V=(y+\frac{1}{2})(x+1)^2-500$, and find the values of x and y for which this volume is least.

Curves and curve sketching

1. Concavity of a curve

In this chapter we introduce and investigate some further properties of graphs and then, using some or all of the information that has been obtained for such curves, we consider the important and interesting subject of curve sketching.

So far, for a differentiable function f we have seen that a knowledge of $f'(x)$ gives information about the increase and decrease of f. When $f''(x)$ also exists we obtain information about the increase and decrease of f'; it is natural to investigate what additional information this gives about f and its graph.

Let a be a point of an open interval on which f, f' and f'' exist; we start with the following assumption:

$$f''(x) > 0 \ \forall x \in N, \quad \textit{where } N \textit{ is a neighbourhood of } a. \tag{1.1}$$

It follows from Theorem **2.2** of Chapter 2 that f' is strictly increasing on N, so that $f'(x) < f'(a)$ for x near a to the left and $f'(x) > f'(a)$ for x near a to the right. Since exactly one of the conditions (i) $f'(a) > 0$, (ii) $f'(a) = 0$, (iii) $f'(a) < 0$ holds, it follows that there are three possible types of behaviour of the graph $y = f(x)$ on N as illustrated in the following diagrams:

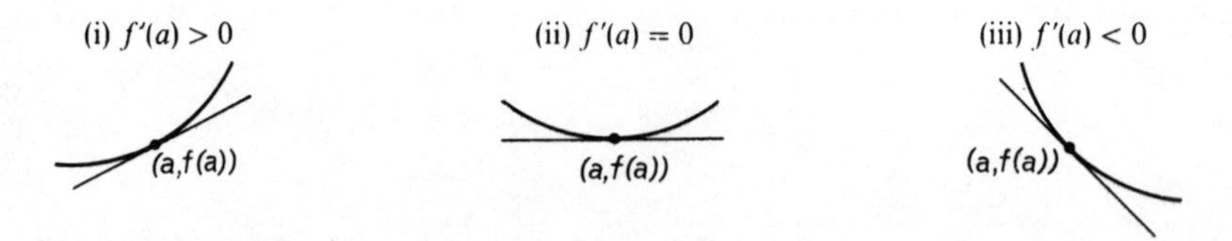

In each case the curve is **concave up** on N, i.e. "opens upwards" on N. Consequently we have the following result:

$$f''(x) > 0 \textit{ on a neighbourhood } N \textit{ of } a \Rightarrow y = f(x) \textit{ is concave up on } N. \tag{1.2}$$

From (1.2) we obtain the following result:

$$\left.\begin{array}{l} f''(a) > 0, \\ f'' \text{ continuous at } a \end{array}\right\} \Rightarrow y = f(x) \textit{ is concave up on a neighbourhood of } a; \tag{1.3}$$

for, the given conditions in the implication (1.3) imply that there is a neighbourhood N of a on which $f''(x)$ is positive.

Note. For the local minimum case illustrated in (ii) we can prove the following simpler result in which only $f''(a)$ is needed and not information about f'' on a neighbourhood of a.

$$\left.\begin{array}{l} f'(a) = 0 \\ f''(a) > 0 \end{array}\right\} \Rightarrow x = a \textit{ gives a local minimum value of } f. \tag{1.4}$$

Proof. Since

$$\lim_{h \to 0} \frac{1}{h}\{f'(a+h) - f'(a)\} = f''(a) > 0,$$

it follows that we can find $\delta > 0$ such that

$$\left|\frac{1}{h}\{f'(a+h) - f'(a)\} - f''(a)\right| < f''(a)$$

for all h satisfying $0 < |h| < \delta$. On examining the expression inside the modulus sign $|\quad|$ and on noting that $-f''(a) < 0$, we deduce that, for $0 < |h| < \delta$,

$$\frac{1}{h}\{f'(a+h) - f'(a)\} > 0.$$

Since $f'(a) = 0$, it follows that

$$\frac{1}{h} f'(a+h) > 0;$$

consequently $f'(a+h) > 0$ for $h > 0$ and $f'(a+h) < 0$ for $h < 0$ (where $0 < |h| < \delta$). Thus f is strictly decreasing to the left of a and strictly increasing to the right of a, so that $f(a) < f(x)$ for all x $(\neq a)$ on a neighbourhood of a. Hence $f(a)$ is a local minimum value of f.

Suppose now that, instead of (1.1), we make the following assumption:

$$f''(x) < 0 \ \forall x \in N, \textit{ where } N \textit{ is a neighbourhood of } a. \tag{1.5}$$

In this case f' is strictly decreasing on N and again there are three possible cases.

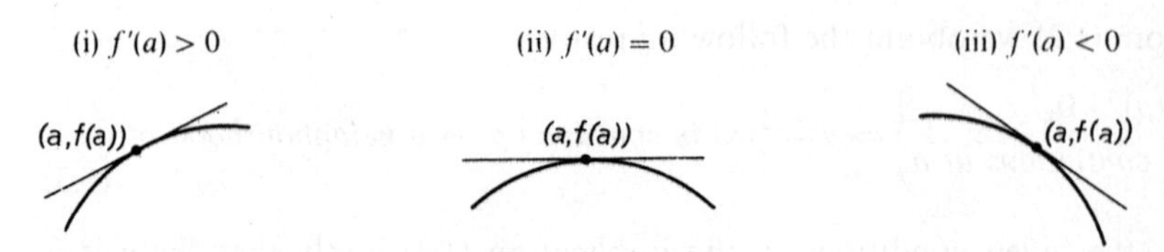

In each case the curve is **concave down** on N, i.e. "opens downwards" on N. Consequently we have the following result:

$$f''(x) < 0 \textit{ on a neighbourhood } N \textit{ of } a \Rightarrow y = f(x) \textit{ is concave down on } N. \qquad (1.6)$$

Also, corresponding to (1.3), the following result holds:

$$\left.\begin{array}{l} f''(a) < 0 \\ f'' \textit{ continuous at } a \end{array}\right\} \Rightarrow y = f(x) \textit{ is concave down on a neighbourhood of } a. \qquad (1.7)$$

For the local maximum case illustrated in (ii) we obtain the following result, similar to (1.4) and established by a similar proof:

$$\left.\begin{array}{l} f'(a) = 0 \\ f''(a) < 0 \end{array}\right\} \Rightarrow x = a \textit{ gives a local maximum value of } f. \qquad (1.8)$$

Note. If $x = a$ is a critical point of f, then, provided $f''(a)$ exists and can easily be evaluated, it is often simpler to use (1.4) and (1.8) in determining the nature of the point rather than the sign of $f'(x)$ on a neighbourhood of a.

Example. Discuss the concavity of the curve

$$y = 3x^4 - 4x^3 - 1.$$

$$\frac{dy}{dx} = 12x^3 - 12x^2; \quad \frac{d^2y}{dx^2} = 12(3x^2 - 2x) = 36x(x - \tfrac{2}{3}).$$

It follows that $\dfrac{d^2y}{dx^2} > 0$ for $x > \frac{2}{3}$ or $x < 0$

and that $\dfrac{d^2y}{dx^2} < 0$ for $0 < x < \frac{2}{3}$.

Consequently the curve is concave up on the intervals $(\frac{2}{3}, \infty)$ and $(-\infty, 0)$ and concave down on the interval $(0, \frac{2}{3})$.

The critical points of the curve are $x = 0$ and $x = 1$.

At $x = 1$, $y = -2$ and $\dfrac{d^2y}{dx^2} = 12 > 0$,

so that, by (1.4), $(1, -2)$ is a local minimum point on the curve.

At $$x = 0,\ y = -1 \text{ and } \frac{d^2y}{dx^2} = 0;$$

in this case results (1.4) and (1.8) are not helpful, but the nature of the point $(0, -1)$ can be obtained by considering $\frac{dy}{dx}$ on a neighbourhood of $x = 0$. Check that $(0, -1)$ is a horizontal point of inflexion.

2. Points of inflexion on a curve

We have already met in Chapter 2 horizontal points of inflexion,

where the tangent is parallel to the x-axis and concavity changes from *up* (indicated by $+$) to *down* (indicated by $-$) or from *down* to *up*. We now extend these ideas with the following definition.

A **point of inflexion** (*P.I.*) **on a curve** is a point on the curve at which the direction of concavity changes from up on the left to down on the right, or vice versa.

Suppose now that $x = a$ is a *P.I.* on the curve $y = f(x)$ and that f'' exists and is continuous at $x = a$. Then, by (1.3), $f''(a) \not> 0$, and, by (1.7), $f''(a) \not< 0$; consequently $f''(a) = 0$, so that $x = a$ is a root of the equation $f''(x) = 0$.

Notes 1. Some curves have points of inflexion where $f''(x)$ does not exist; for example

$$y = x^{1/3} \quad \text{at} \quad x = 0 \text{ (i.e. } x = y^3).$$

In this case we can say that "$f'(0) = \infty$ and $f''(0) = \infty$".

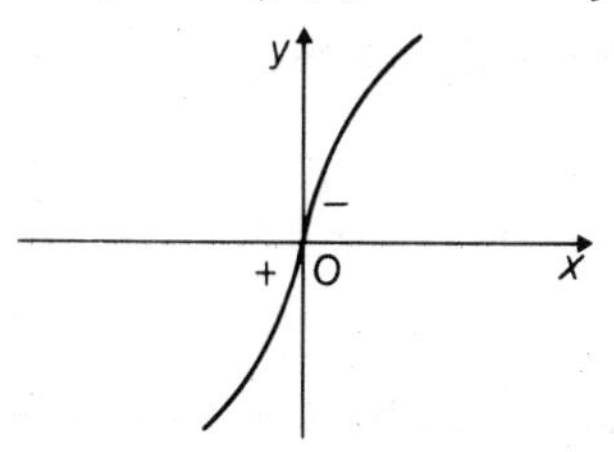

2. The condition $f''(x) = 0$ (when f'' is continuous) for a *P.I.* on the curve $y = f(x)$ is only a *necessary condition*. It is *not sufficient*, i.e. we can have $f''(a) = 0$ without $x = a$ giving a *P.I.*

For example, $\quad y = x^4 \quad \text{at} \quad x = 0.$

Here
$$\frac{dy}{dx} = 4x^3, \frac{d^2y}{dx^2} = 12x^2$$

and both are 0 at $x = 0$; it is easy to check that $x = 0$ gives a local minimum point.

3. If $x = a$ is a *P.I.* on a curve $y = f(x)$, where f'' is continuous at $x = a$, then the shape of the curve in a neighbourhood of the point $(a, f(a))$ can be determined by evaluating $f'(a)$ and by drawing up a table of sign for $f''(x)$ on a neighbourhood of $x = a$.

Example 1. If $f'(x) = (x-1)^4(x-8)^3$, find the x-coordinates of the points of inflexion on the graph of f and determine the shape of the graph in a neighbourhood of each point.

Check that
$$\begin{aligned} f''(x) &= 7(x-1)^3(x-8)^2(x-5) \\ &= 0 \Leftrightarrow x = 1, 5 \text{ or } 8. \end{aligned}$$

In this case a table of sign for $f''(x)$ can be used.

x :	→	1	→	5	→	8	→
$(x-1)^3$:	−	0	+	+	+	+	+
$(x-8)^2$:	+	+	+	+	+	0	+
$(x-5)$:	−	−	−	0	+	+	+
$f''(x)$:	+	0	−	0	+	0	+
$f'(x)$:		0		−		0	

(x = 1) (x = 5) (x = 8 gives a local minimum point)

The points of inflexion are given by $x = 1$ and $x = 5$.

Example 2. Find the critical point and the point of inflexion on the curve $y = x^2 - \dfrac{2}{x}$, and determine the shape of the curve in a neighbourhood of each point.

$$\frac{dy}{dx} = 2x + \frac{2}{x^2} \quad \text{and} \quad \frac{d^2y}{dx^2} = 2 - \frac{4}{x^3}.$$

$$\frac{dy}{dx} = \frac{2}{x^2}(x^3+1) = \frac{2}{x^2}(x+1)(x^2-x+1),$$

and the only real root of the equation

$$\frac{dy}{dx} = 0 \quad \text{is} \quad x = -1,$$

giving a critical point $(-1, 3)$. Since

$$\frac{d^2y}{dx^2} = 6 > 0 \quad \text{when} \quad x = -1,$$

this critical point is a local minimum point.

$$\frac{d^2y}{dx^2} = \frac{2}{x^3}(x^3-2) = \frac{2}{x^3}(x-2^{1/3})(x^2+2^{1/3}x+2^{2/3}),$$

and the only real root of the equation

$$\frac{d^2y}{dx^2} = 0 \quad \text{is} \quad x = 2^{1/3},$$

giving the point $(2^{1/3}, 0)$.

Using the table of sign indicated we see that $(2^{1/3}, 0)$ is a *P.I.*, the shape being as shown.

x:	$\rightarrow$	$2^{1/3}$	$\rightarrow$
x^3-2:	$-$	0	$+$
x^3:	$+$	$+$	$+$
$\frac{d^2y}{dx^2}$:	$-$	0	$+$
$\frac{dy}{dx}$:		$+$	

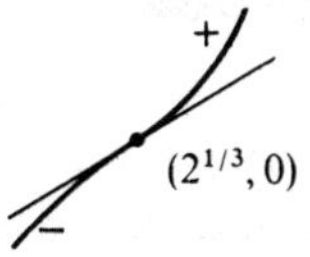

$(2^{1/3}, 0)$

3. Asymptotes of a curve

A line l is called an **asymptote of a curve** C if there is an unbounded part C_1 of C such that the perpendicular distance to l from a point P of $C_1 \to 0$ as $|OP| \to \infty$, where O is the origin.

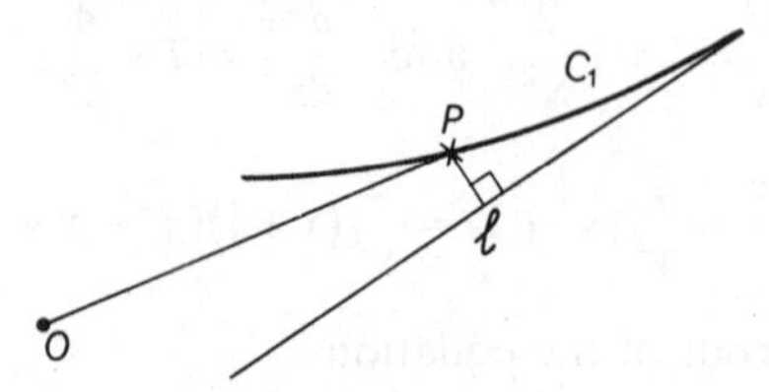

I. Vertical asymptotes. For the graph $y = f(x)$ of a rational function f, vertical asymptotes and the approaches to these are most easily obtained from a table of sign for $f(x)$. We illustrate this with the curve

$$y = \frac{x+2}{x^2(x^2-1)} = \frac{x+2}{x^2(x+1)(x-1)}.$$

On noting that the zeros of numerator and denominator in increasing order are $x = -2, -1, 0, 1$, we have the following table of sign.

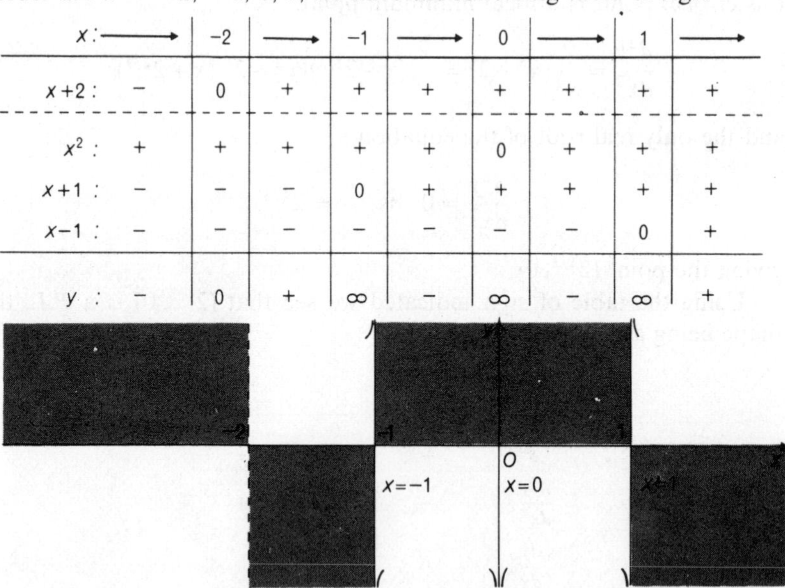

x:	→	-2	→	-1	→	0	→	1	→
$x+2$:	−	0	+	+	+	+	+	+	+
x^2:	+	+	+	+	+	0	+	+	+
$x+1$:	−	−	−	0	+	+	+	+	+
$x-1$:	−	−	−	−	−	−	−	0	+
y:	−	0	+	∞	−	∞	−	∞	+

It follows that the lines $x = -1$, $x = 0$ and $x = 1$ (arising from zeros of the denominator) are vertical asymptotes and that the approach to each is as shown. For example, for $x = 1$, y is positive to the right of $x = 1$ and so $y \to +\infty$ as $x \to 1$ from the right; also y is negative to the left of $x = 1$ and so $y \to -\infty$ as $x \to 1$ from the left. The shading indicates regions in which the curve does not lie.

II. Non-vertical asymptotes. Here, if the graph is $y = f(x)$ and $y = mx + c$ is an asymptote, we aim at expressing $f(x)$ as

$$f(x) = mx + c + \frac{a}{x} + \frac{b}{x^2} + \frac{d}{x^3} + \cdots \tag{3.1}$$

for points on the unbounded part of the graph which is asymptotic to the line $y = mx + c$.

If $a \neq 0$, the approach of the graph to the asymptote is given by the fact that

$$y \doteqdot mx + c + \frac{a}{x}$$

for large $|x|$ (where $\doteqdot$ means "is approximately equal to").

If $a = 0$, $b \neq 0$, the approach is given by

$$y \doteqdot mx + c + \frac{b}{x^2},$$

for large $|x|$; and so on.

Example 1. Find the asymptote of each of the curves

$$\text{(i)}\ y = \frac{x^3}{x^2+1}, \qquad \text{(ii)}\ y = \frac{x^3}{x^2+x+1}$$

and the approach to each asymptote.

In each case the denominator has no real zeros and so neither curve has a vertical asymptote.

(i) Keeping (3.1) in mind we express $\dfrac{x^3}{x^2+1}$ in descending powers of x. This can be achieved by dividing the numerator by the denominator using long division, or by using a binomial expansion, if possible.

$$\begin{array}{r|l}
 & x - \frac{1}{x} + \frac{1}{x^3} \cdots \\
\hline
x^2+1 & x^3 \\
 & \underline{x^3 + x} \\
 & -x \\
 & \underline{-x - \frac{1}{x}} \\
 & \frac{1}{x} \\
 & \underline{\frac{1}{x} + \frac{1}{x^3}}
\end{array}$$

By long division, we see that, for large $|x|$,

$$y \doteqdot x - \frac{1}{x}.$$

Thus $y = x$ is an asymptote.

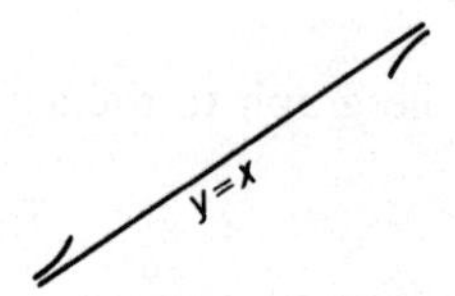

If $x > 0$ (x large), then $y_{(\text{curve})} < y_{(\text{line})}$, and so the curve approaches the asymptote from below; if $x < 0$ ($|x|$ large), then $y_{(\text{curve})} > y_{(\text{line})}$, and so the curve approaches the asymptote from above.

[Alternatively, $\dfrac{x^3}{x^2+1} = x\left(1+\dfrac{1}{x^2}\right)^{-1} = x\left(1-\dfrac{1}{x^2}+\dfrac{1}{x^4}-\dots\right)$

$$= x - \frac{1}{x} + \frac{1}{x^3} - \cdots \ (|x| \text{ large}).]$$

(ii) In this case, using long division,

$$y \doteqdot x - 1 + \frac{1}{x^2} \quad \text{for large } |x|.$$

$$\begin{array}{r|l}
 & x - 1 + \dfrac{1}{x^2} \\
\hline
x^2+x+1 & x^3 \\
 & \underline{x^3+x^2+x} \\
 & \quad -x^2-x \\
 & \quad \underline{-x^2-x-1} \\
 & \qquad\qquad 1 \\
 & \qquad\qquad \underline{1+\dfrac{1}{x}+\dfrac{1}{x^2}} \\
 & \qquad\qquad \dots
\end{array}$$

Thus $y = x - 1$ is an asymptote of the curve, and the approach is as shown.

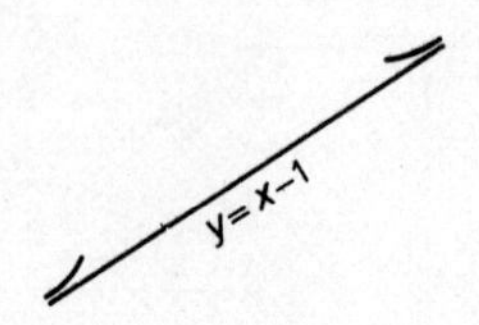

III. Shape of a curve at infinity. In dealing with graphs of rational functions the following observations are often useful. If

$$y = a_n x^n + a_{n-1} x^{n-1} + \cdots + a_1 x + a_0,$$

then
$$y = a_n x^n \left(1 + \frac{a_{n-1}}{a_n} \cdot \frac{1}{x} + \cdots + \frac{a_0}{a_n} \cdot \frac{1}{x^n}\right),$$

so that $y/a_n x^n \to 1$ as $|x| \to \infty$. We write $y \sim a_n x^n$ and say that y is **asymptotic to** $a_n x^n$ as $|x| \to \infty$ or that y **behaves like** $a_n x^n$ as $|x| \to \infty$.

Example 2. Discuss the shape at infinity of the curve

$$y = \frac{x^4}{x^2+1}$$

Here
$$y = \frac{x^4}{x^2+1} = \frac{x^2}{1+\dfrac{1}{x^2}} \sim x^2 \quad \text{as} \quad |x| \to \infty.$$

In fact we can obtain more accurate information by noting that

$$y = x^2 - 1 + \frac{1}{x^2} + \cdots \quad \text{for large } |x|.$$

Thus the curve is asymptotic to the parabola $y = x^2 - 1$ with approach as indicated.

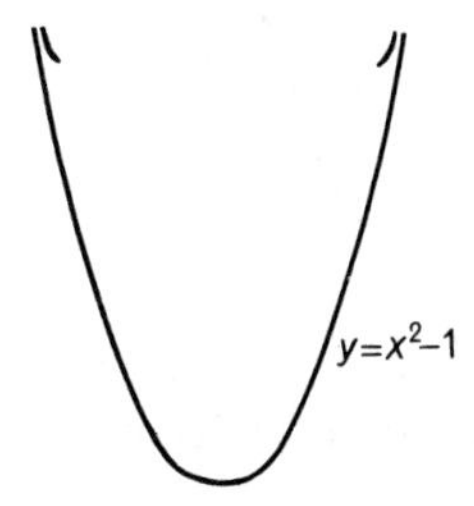

4. Symmetry of curves

A graph $y = f(x)$ of a real function f has the y-axis as an axis of symmetry if, whenever $(x, f(x))$ lies on the graph so does $(-x, f(x))$, i.e. if $f(-x) = f(x)$ for all x in the domain of f. A function which satisfies this latter condition is called an **even function.** Examples of even functions are the functions defined by the formulae

$$f(x) = 2,\ x^2,\ x^{2n} (n \in \mathbf{N}),\ x^6 - 4x^4 + 1,\ \frac{1}{x^2},\ \frac{1}{x^2-2},\ \cos x,\ \sec x.$$

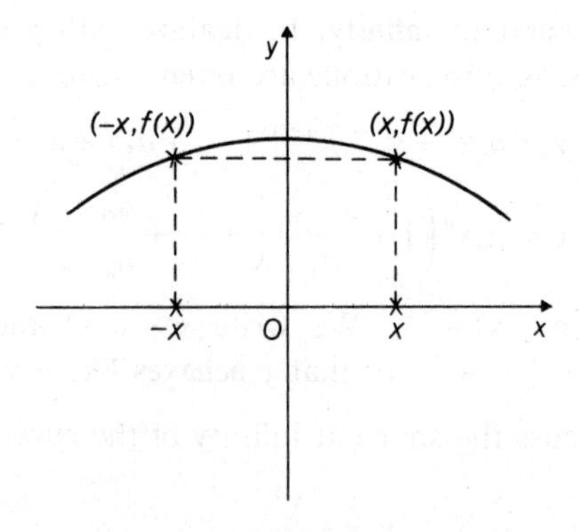

From the definition of an even function it is clear that the domain S of such a real function is symmetrical about zero in the sense that $x \in S \Rightarrow -x \in S$. Check this for each of the above functions.

The graph $y = f(x)$ is symmetrical with respect to the origin, i.e. has half-turn symmetry about the origin, if, whenever $(x, f(x))$ lies on the graph so does $(-x, -f(x))$, i.e. if $f(-x) = -f(x)$ for all x in the domain

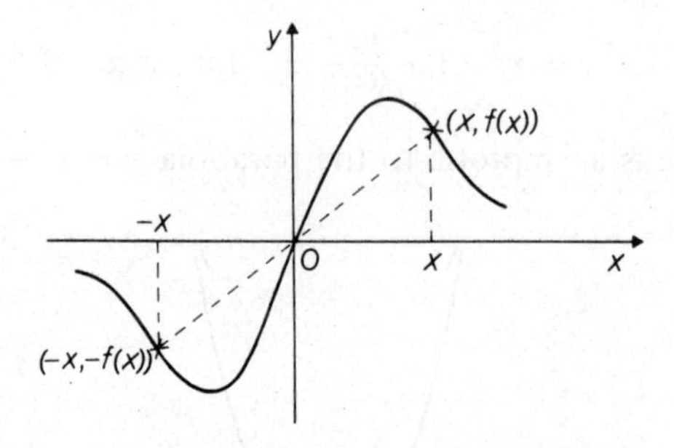

of f. A function which satisfies this latter condition is called an **odd function**. Some examples of odd functions are the functions defined by the formulae

$$f(x) = x,\ x^3,\ x^{2n-1} (n \in \mathbf{N}),\ x^7 - 8x^3 + 5x,\ \frac{1}{x},\ \frac{1}{x^3 - x},$$
$$\sin x,\ \operatorname{cosec} x,\ \tan x,\ \cot x.$$

The domain of an odd function is symmetrical about zero. Also, if an odd function f is defined for $x = 0$, then $f(0) = 0$; for, $f(-x) = -f(x)$ with $x = 0$ gives $2f(0) = 0$ and so $f(0) = 0$.

Which of the above odd functions are defined at $x = 0$?

A curve has the x-axis as an axis of symmetry if, whenever a point (x, y) lies on the curve so does the point $(x, -y)$. Such a curve is not the

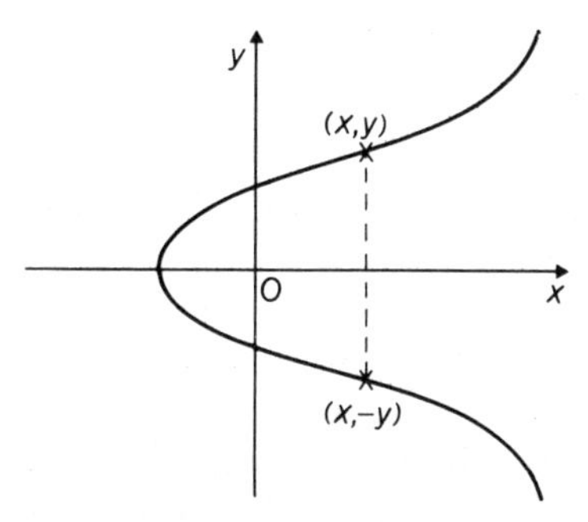

graph of a function, but may be the union of the graphs of two or more easily defined functions; e.g. the parabola $y^2 = x$ is

$$\{(x, \sqrt{x}) : x \geqslant 0\} \cup \{(x, -\sqrt{x}) : x \geqslant 0\}$$

and so is the union of the graphs of the real functions f, g defined on $\mathbf{R}^+$ by $f(x) = \sqrt{x}$ and $g(x) = -\sqrt{x}$.

A curve defined by an equation of the form $y^2 = f(x)$ is symmetrical about the x-axis, since $y^2 = f(x) \Rightarrow (\pm y)^2 = f(x)$. In sketching such a curve it is clearly enough to consider the graph $y = \sqrt{(f(x))}$ since the other half of the curve is its reflection $y = -\sqrt{(f(x))}$ in the x-axis.

5. Curve sketching

In sketching curves we shall constantly use the following result, called the **intermediate-value theorem**.

Theorem 3.1. *Suppose that the real function f is continuous on the closed interval $[a, b]$ and that α is any real number between $f(a)$ and $f(b)$; then $\alpha = f(c)$ for some $c \in [a, b]$.*

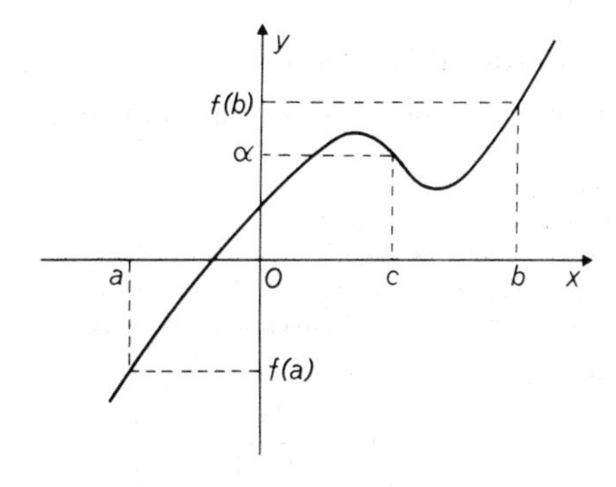

A proof requires deeper properties of **R** than we have available, but the result is intuitively obvious from a diagram. It is clear that the c in the statement of the result is not necessarily unique. The result implies that a continuous function takes every value between any two of its values. We note also that if $\alpha \neq f(a)$ and $\alpha \neq f(b)$, then $c \in (a, b)$.

Example 1. Show that the equation $x^3+x-1=0$ has a real root in the interval (0, 1).

The equation $x^3+x-1=0$ gives the x-coordinates of points in which the graph $y=f(x)$, where $f(x)=x^3+x-1$, meets the x-axis. Since $f(0)=-1$, $f(1)=1$ and $-1<0<1$, $\exists c \in (0, 1)$ such that $0=f(c)=c^3+c-1$. The fact that this root c is the only root of the equation in the interval (0, 1) can be established by considering $f'(x)$. Since $f'(x)=3x^2+1>0\ \forall x \in \mathbf{R}$, it follows that f is a strictly increasing function. Thus c is unique and in fact is the only real root of the equation $x^3+x-1=0$; for, $f(x)<f(0)=-1$ for $x<0$ and $f(x)>f(1)=1$ for $x>1$.

Example 2. Show that every real polynomial equation of *odd* degree has at least one real root.

Such an equation can be expressed in the form

$$x^{2n-1}+a_{2n-2}x^{2n-2}+\cdots+a_1x+a_0=0, \tag{5.1}$$

i.e. $f(x)=0$, say, for some $n \in \mathbf{N}$ and gives the x-coordinates of points in which the graph $y=f(x)$ meets the x-axis. Since $y \sim x^{2n-1}$ as $|x| \to \infty$, it follows that $y \to +\infty$ as $x \to \infty$ and $y \to -\infty$ as $x \to -\infty$. Consequently there are real numbers a and b such that $f(a)<0$ and $f(b)>0$. By the intermediate-value theorem it follows that $\exists c \in (a, b)$ such that $f(c)=0$, and this proves the result.

The equation $x^2+1=0$ shows that the corresponding statement for real polynomial equations of *even* degree is not true.

Sketching graphs of rational functions

It is useful to obtain some or all of the following information:

(1) symmetry,
(2) critical points,
(3) regions of increase and decrease,
(4) asymptotes or asymptotic behaviour,
(5) points of inflexion and concavity,
(6) special points (intersections with axes, asymptotes, etc.).

Example 3. Sketch the curve

$$y=\frac{2x}{x^2+1}. \tag{5.2}$$

(1) If $\quad f(x)=\dfrac{2x}{x^2+1},\quad$ then $\quad f(-x)=-f(x),$

so that f is an odd function and the curve (5.2) has half-turn symmetry about the origin.

$$(2) \qquad \frac{dy}{dx} = \frac{2(1-x^2)}{(x^2+1)^2} = \frac{2(1+x)(1-x)}{(x^2+1)^2} = 0 \Leftrightarrow x = -1 \text{ or } 1.$$

Thus there are two critical points $(-1, -1)$ and $(1, 1)$.

x:	$\rightarrow$	-1	$\rightarrow$
$1+x$:	$-$	0	$+$
$\frac{2(1-x)}{(x^2+1)^2}$	$+$	$+$	$+$
$\frac{dy}{dx}$:	$-$	0	$+$

shape: \ ___ / i.e.

$(-1, -1)$ is a local minimum point

x:	$\rightarrow$	1	$\rightarrow$
$1-x$:	$+$	0	$-$
$\frac{2(1+x)}{(x^2+1)^2}$:	$+$	$+$	$+$
$\frac{dy}{dx}$:	$+$	0	$-$

shape: / ‾‾‾ \, i.e.

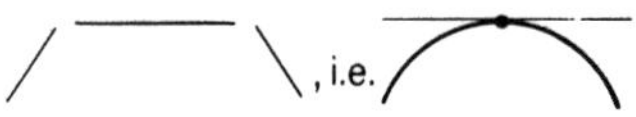

$(1, 1)$ is a local maximum point

[We could deduce the existence of one point from the other by the symmetry about the origin.]

(3) $\frac{dy}{dx} > 0$ when $1-x^2 > 0$, i.e. $-1 < x < 1$;
then the curve is rising;

$\frac{dy}{dx} < 0$ when $1-x^2 < 0$, i.e. $x > 1$ or $x < -1$;
then the curve is falling.

(4) Since $x^2+1 = 0$ has no real root, there is no vertical asymptote.

$$y \doteqdot \frac{2}{x} \quad \text{as} \quad |x| \to \infty;$$

thus $y = 0$ is an asymptote with approach as shown.

$$\begin{array}{r|l} & \frac{2}{x} - \frac{2}{x^3} \\ \hline x^2+1 & 2x \\ & 2x + \frac{2}{x} \\ \hline & \quad -\frac{2}{x} \end{array}$$

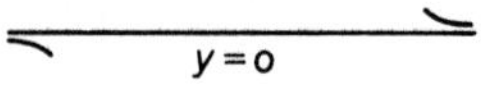

$y = 0$

(5) Check that $$\frac{d^2y}{dx^2} = \frac{4x(x^2-3)}{(x^2+1)^3} = \frac{4x(x+\sqrt{3})(x-\sqrt{3})}{(x^2+1)^3}$$
$$= 0 \Leftrightarrow x = -\sqrt{3},\ 0,\ \sqrt{3}.$$

We examine a neighbourhood of each of the three points
$$(0, 0),\ (-\sqrt{3}, -\tfrac{1}{2}\sqrt{3}),\ (\sqrt{3}, \tfrac{1}{2}\sqrt{3}).$$

x:	$\to$	0	$\to$
$4x$:	$-$	0	$+$
$\frac{x^2-3}{(x^2+1)^3}$:	$-$	$-$	$-$
$\frac{d^2y}{dx^2}$:	$+$	0	$-$
$\frac{dy}{dx}$:		2	

x:	$\to$	$-\sqrt{3}$	$\to$
$x+\sqrt{3}$:	$-$	0	$+$
$\frac{4x(x-\sqrt{3})}{(x^2+1)^3}$:	$+$	$+$	$+$
$\frac{d^2y}{dx^2}$:	$-$	0	$+$
$\frac{dy}{dx}$:		$-\frac{1}{4}$	

x:	$\to$	$\sqrt{3}$	$\to$
$x-\sqrt{3}$:	$-$	0	$+$
$\frac{4x(x+\sqrt{3})}{(x^2+1)^3}$:	$+$	$+$	$+$
$\frac{d^2y}{dx^2}$:	$-$	0	$+$
$\frac{dy}{dx}$:		$-\frac{1}{4}$	

(0, 0) is a *P.I.* $(-\sqrt{3}, -\frac{1}{2}\sqrt{3})$ is a *P.I.* $(\sqrt{3}, \frac{1}{2}\sqrt{3})$ is a *P.I.*

(6) The curve meets the x- and y-axes, i.e. $y = 0$ and $x = 0$, only at the origin.

Sketch of curve $$y = \frac{2x}{x^2+1}:$$

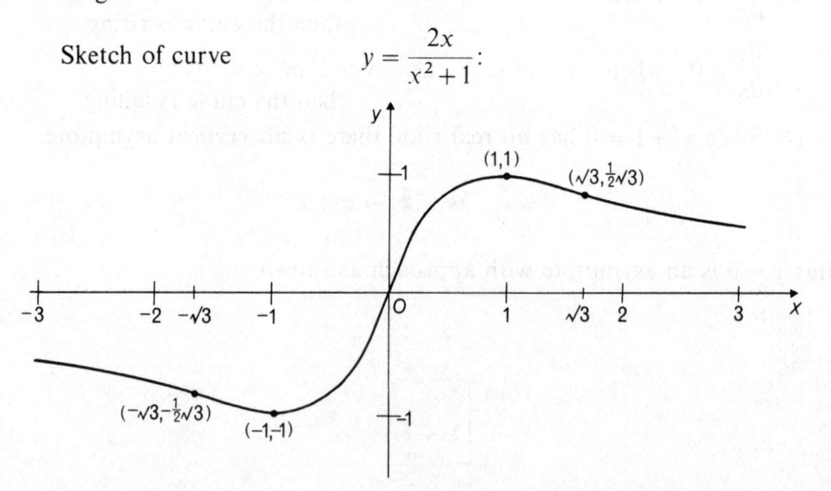

Example 4. Indicate in a rough sketch the shape of the curve
$$y = \frac{1}{8}(x-1)^8 - 3(x-1)^7 + \frac{49}{2}(x-1)^6 - \frac{343}{5}(x-1)^5.$$

This rather complicated equation is the graph of a function f satisfying $f'(x) = (x-1)^4(x-8)^3$, the condition used in Example 1 of Section **2** of this chapter. It was shown in Section **2** that $x = 8$ gives a local minimum point, i.e. $(8, -20\,588{\cdot}6)$, $x = 1$ gives a horizontal point of inflexion, i.e. $(1, 0)$, and $x = 5$ gives a point of inflexion on a falling curve, i.e. $(5, -10\,854{\cdot}4)$. Also $y \sim \frac{1}{8}(x-1)^8$ as $|x| \to \infty$, so that $y \to \infty$ as $x \to \infty$ and as $x \to -\infty$. Since $f'(x) > 0$ for $x > 8$, the function f is strictly increasing on $[8, \infty)$ and crosses the x-axis at exactly one point for $x > 8$; check that this point lies in the interval $(10, 11)$. Since $f'(x) < 0$ for $x < 8$ $(x \neq 1)$ and $f'(1)$ exists and is 0, f is strictly decreasing on $(-\infty, 8]$. Since the y-coordinate of the point given by $x = 8$ is so large numerically, it is enough to give a rough indication of the graph, not drawn to scale. The point of intersection with the y-axis is $(0, 96{\cdot}2)$, coordinates being rounded off to one decimal place where necessary.

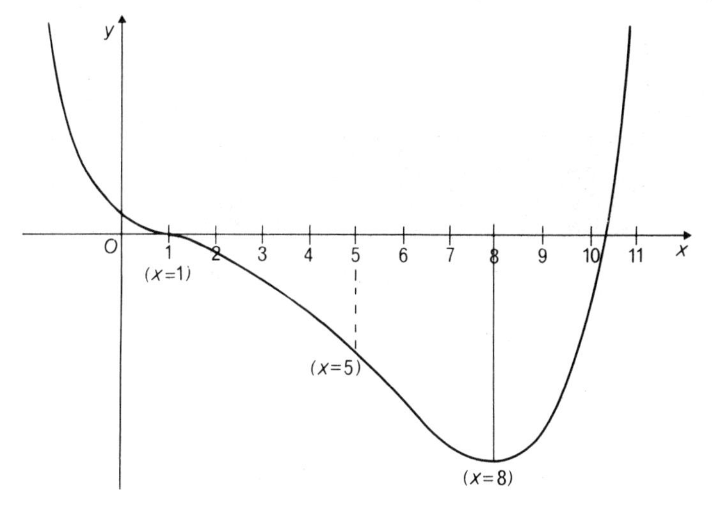

The function defined in Example 4 has image $[f(8), \infty)$, and $f(8)$ is the minimum value of f.

Example 5. Sketch the curve

$$y = \frac{x^2(x+9)}{x^2-1},$$

without discussing concavity or points of inflexion.

Check that

$$\frac{dy}{dx} = \frac{x(x^3-3x-18)}{(x^2-1)^2} = \frac{x(x-3)(x^2+3x+6)}{(x^2-1)^2},$$

and that the critical points of the curve are (0, 0), a local maximum point, and (3, 13·5), a local minimum point.

A table of sign for $y = \dfrac{x^2(x+9)}{(x+1)(x-1)}$ is as follows:

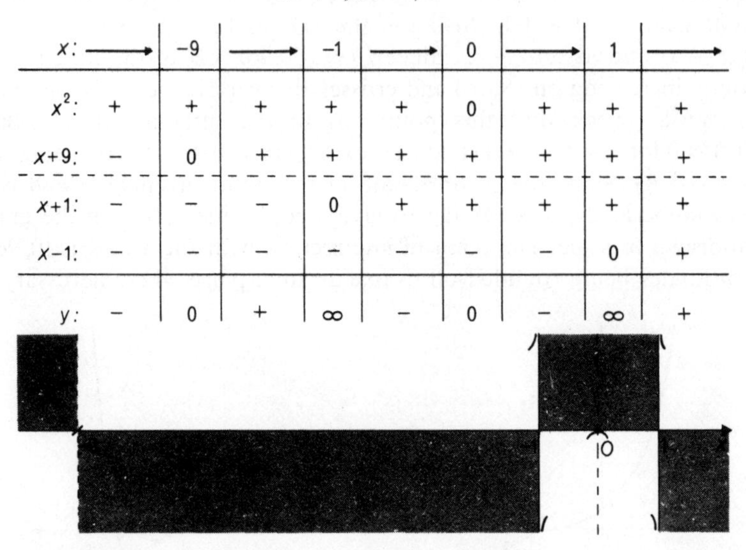

x:	→	−9	→	−1	→	0	→	1	→
x^2:	+	+	+	+	+	0	+	+	+
$x+9$:	−	0	+	+	+	+	+	+	+
$x+1$:	−	−	−	0	+	+	+	+	+
$x-1$:	−	−	−	−	−	−	−	0	+
y:	−	0	+	∞	−	0	−	∞	+

Thus $x = -1$ and $x = 1$ are vertical asymptotes with approaches as shown.

Using long division,

$$y \doteqdot x+9+\frac{1}{x} \quad \text{for large } |x|.$$

Thus $y = x+9$ is an asymptote with approach as indicated.

$$\begin{array}{r|l} & x+9+\frac{1}{x}+\cdots \\ \hline x^2-1 & x^3+9x^2 \\ & x^3 \qquad -x \\ \hline & \quad 9x^2+x \\ & \quad 9x^2 \qquad -9 \\ \hline & \qquad\quad x+9 \end{array}$$

y=x+9

The curve meets the x-axis at the points $(0,0)$ and $(-9,0)$ and the y-axis only at $(0,0)$; it crosses the asymptote $y=x+9$ at the point $(-9,0)$.

Sketch of curve $\quad y=\dfrac{x^2(x+9)}{x^2-1}$:

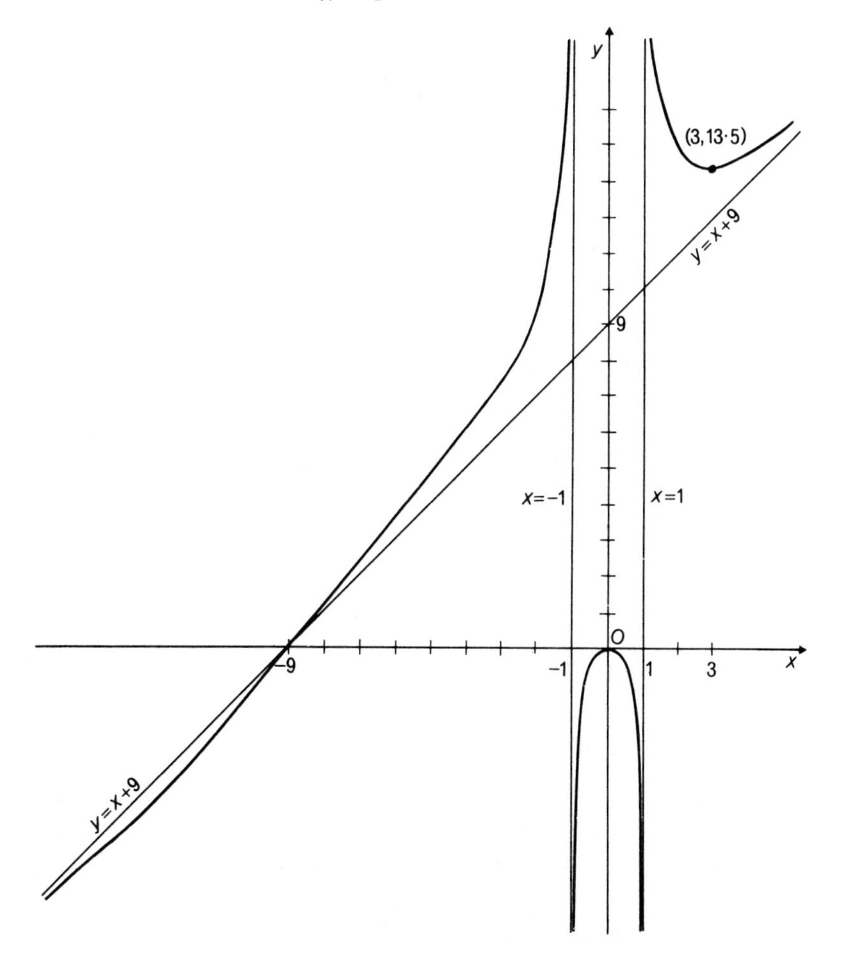

Note. On the same diagram a rough sketch of the graph of the reciprocal function, i.e. of the curve

$$y=\frac{x^2-1}{x^2(x+9)},$$

can easily be obtained by using the following facts:

(i) A zero of $f(x)$ gives rise to a vertical asymptote of

$$y = \frac{1}{f(x)},$$

and vice-versa. [In the case of Example 5, the zeros of f are $x = -9, 0$ and the vertical asymptotes are $x = -1, 1$; correspondingly the zeros of $1/f$ are $x = -1, 1$ and the vertical asymptotes are $x = -9, 0$.]

(ii) A local maximum (or minimum) point $(a, f(a))$ of f gives rise to a local minimum (or maximum) point $(a, 1/f(a))$ of $1/f$ (when $f(a) \neq 0$).

(iii) If $|f(x)| \to \infty$ as $|x| \to \infty$, then $1/f(x) \to 0$ as $|x| \to \infty$. [In the case of Example 5, this shows that $y = 0$ is an asymptote of the reciprocal graph with approach as shown:

$y=0$

(iv) $x = a$ gives a point of intersection of $y = f(x)$ and $y = 1/f(x)$ if and only if $f(a) = 1/f(a)$, i.e. if and only if $f(a) = \pm 1$.

Exercise. From a sketch of $y = \dfrac{x^2(x+9)}{x^2-1}$

deduce a sketch of

$$y = \frac{x^2-1}{x^2(x+9)};$$

deduce also sketches of $\quad y = -\dfrac{x^2(x+9)}{x^2-1}$ and $y = -\dfrac{x^2-1}{x^2(x+9)}$.

Example 6. Sketch the curve

$$y^2 = 1 - x^3.$$

This curve is symmetrical about the x-axis and exists for $x \leqslant 1$. It consists of the graph $y = \sqrt{(1-x^3)}$ and its reflection $y = -\sqrt{(1-x^3)}$ in the x-axis.

For $\quad y = \sqrt{(1-x^3)}, \ \dfrac{dy}{dx} = -\dfrac{3x^2}{2\sqrt{(1-x^3)}} = 0 \Leftrightarrow x = 0;$

this gives as critical point the horizontal point of inflexion $(0, 1)$. Also

$$\frac{dy}{dx} \to \infty \quad \text{as} \quad x \to 1 \ (x < 1),$$

so that the tangent at the point (1, 0) is parallel to the y-axis.

$$y^2 \sim -x^3 \quad \text{as} \quad x \to -\infty,$$

and the curve is as shown.

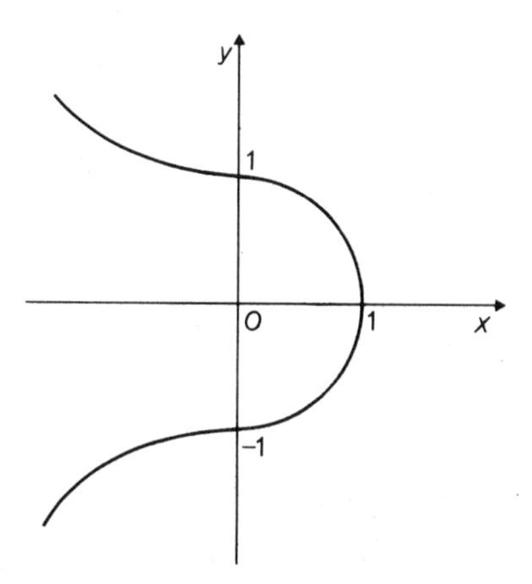

6. Curves using implicit functions

In Section **3** of Chapter 1 we met the idea of a function being defined implicitly by an equation, e.g.

$$xy^5 + 3x^2y^2 - 2 = 0.$$

Although it is often very difficult to obtain a sketch of such a curve, the calculus techniques available can supply a lot of information. The following examples with their solutions illustrate these methods.

Example 1. Show that the point $(-\frac{1}{2}, 1)$ is a point of inflexion on the curve

$$y^4 = 4xy + 3, \tag{6.1}$$

and determine the shape of the curve in a neighbourhood of the point.

Since $x = -\frac{1}{2}$, $y = 1$ satisfy equation (6.1), the point $(-\frac{1}{2}, 1)$ lies on the curve.

Using (6.1), we obtain $\dfrac{dy}{dx} = \dfrac{y}{y^3 - x}$ and $\dfrac{d^2y}{dx^2} = \dfrac{3(1-y^4)}{2(y^3-x)^3}$.

At $(-\frac{1}{2}, 1)$, $\dfrac{dy}{dx} = \dfrac{2}{3} > 0$, and $\dfrac{d^2y}{dx^2} = 0$.

Thus, as x increases on a neighbourhood of $x = -\frac{1}{2}$ so does y and we can draw up a table of sign as follows for $\dfrac{d^2y}{dx^2}$:

x:	$\rightarrow$	$-\frac{1}{2}$	$\rightarrow$
y:	$\rightarrow$	1	$\rightarrow$
$3(1-y^4)$:	+	0	−
$2(y^3-x)^3$:	+	+	+
$\dfrac{d^2y}{dx^2}$:	+	0	−
$\dfrac{dy}{dx}$:		+	
shape:	+	$(-\frac{1}{2},1)$	−

The point is a point of inflexion since concavity changes direction there; the shape is as indicated on noting the sign of $\dfrac{dy}{dx}$ at the point and the directions of concavity on a neighbourhood of the point.

Example 2. Assuming that the equation

$$\sin x+\cos y = x+y \tag{6.2}$$

defines y as a differentiable function of x, express $\dfrac{dy}{dx}$ in terms of x and y. Show that the curve has a critical point in the interval $-\frac{1}{2}\pi \leqslant x \leqslant \frac{1}{2}\pi$ and determine the nature of the point.

Differentiating (6.2) with respect to x, we have

$$\cos x-\sin y\frac{dy}{dx} = 1+\frac{dy}{dx}, \quad \text{so that} \quad \frac{dy}{dx} = \frac{\cos x-1}{1+\sin y} \quad (\sin y \neq -1).$$

Thus $\dfrac{dy}{dx} = 0$ when $\cos x = 1$, i.e. when $x = 0$ in $[-\frac{1}{2}\pi, \frac{1}{2}\pi]$. From (6.2), $x = 0$ implies that $\cos y = y$. Using rough sketches of the graphs

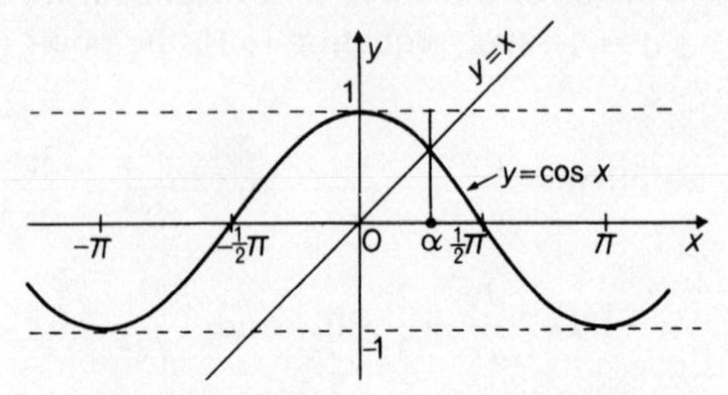

$y = \cos x$ and $y = x$, we see that there is a unique root α of the "transcendental" equation $\cos x = x$ (so that $\cos\alpha = \alpha$), and that $0 < \alpha < \frac{1}{2}\pi$. To determine the nature of the critical point $(0, \alpha)$ we draw up a table of sign for $\dfrac{dy}{dx}$ on a neighbourhood of $x = 0$; since $0 < \alpha < \frac{1}{2}\pi$, we can suppose that $1+\sin y > 0$ on this neighbourhood.

x:	$\rightarrow$	0	$\rightarrow$
$\cos x - 1$:	$-$	0	$-$
$1+\sin y$:	$+$	$+$	$+$
$\dfrac{dy}{dx}$:	$-$	0	$-$
shape:			, i.e (0,α)

Thus $(0, \alpha)$ is a horizontal point of inflexion.

7. Curves by parametric equations.

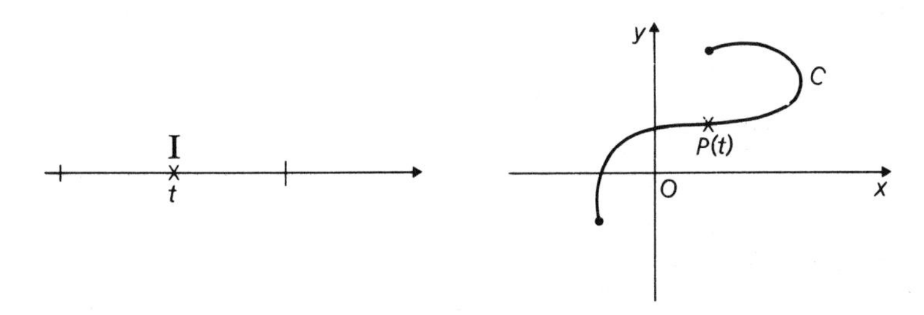

We suppose that C is a curve in the x, y-plane.

If there is a subset I of $\mathbf{R}$ (usually an interval) and a *surjective* (i.e. *onto*) mapping $f: I \rightarrow C$, then we say that f gives a **parametric representation** of the curve C; then, for each $t \in I$, $\exists$ a unique point $P(t) \in C$; t is called a **parameter** for C and $P(t)$, the point given by parameter t. When f is *bijective* (i.e. $|-|$ and onto) each point $P \in C$ has a *unique* parameter.

Usually in a parametrization of C the point $P(t)$ is determined by specifying its x and y coordinates in terms of given functions of t. If the values of these functions at t are denoted by $x(t)$ and $y(t)$ we say that C has parametric equations

$$x = x(t), \quad y = y(t) \quad (t \in I).$$

Then C is the set of points $\{(x(t), y(t)) : t \in I\}$ and a point belongs to C if and only if its coordinates can be expressed in the form $(x(t), y(t))$ for some $t \in I$. Since $\{(x(t), y(t)): t \in I\} = \{(x(u), y(u)): u \in I\}$, the notation used for the parameter does not matter; we often call the parameter a **"dummy variable"**.

Examples:

	x, y-equation	parametric coordinates	parametric equations
(1)	line $y = x$	$\{(t, t): t \in \mathbf{R}\}$	$x = t,\ y = t\ (t \in \mathbf{R})$
(2)	line $x = 1$	$\{(1, t): t \in \mathbf{R}\}$	$x = 1,\ y = t\ (t \in \mathbf{R})$
(3)	parabola $y^2 = 4ax$	$\{(at^2, 2at): t \in \mathbf{R}\}$	$x = at^2,\ y = 2at\ (t \in \mathbf{R})$
(4)	upper-half parabola $y = \sqrt{(4ax)}\ (a > 0)$	$\{(at^2, 2at): t \in \mathbf{R}^+\}$	$x = at^2,\ y = 2at\ (t \in \mathbf{R}^+)$
(5)	circle $x^2 + y^2 = 1$	$\{(\cos t, \sin t): 0 \leqslant t < 2\pi\}$ $= \{(\cos \theta, \sin \theta): 0 \leqslant \theta \leqslant 2\pi\}$	$x = \cos t,\ y = \sin t\ (t \in [0, 2\pi))$ $x = \cos \theta,\ y = \sin \theta\ (\theta \in [0, 2\pi])$
		[Here $\theta = 0$ and $\theta = 2\pi$ both give point $(1, 0)$.]	
(6)	ellipse $\dfrac{x^2}{a^2} + \dfrac{y^2}{b^2} = 1$	$\{(a \cos \theta, b \sin \theta): 0 \leqslant \theta < 2\pi\}$	$x = a \cos \theta,\ y = b \sin \theta\ (\theta \in [0, 2\pi))$
(7)	hyperbola $xy = c^2$	$\left\{\left(ct, \dfrac{c}{t}\right): t \in \mathbf{R} - \{0\}\right\}$	$x = ct,\ y = \dfrac{c}{t}\ (t \neq 0)$
(8)	hyperbola $\dfrac{x^2}{a^2} - \dfrac{y^2}{b^2} = 1$ (right-hand branch)	$\{(a \sec \theta, b \tan \theta): -\frac{1}{2}\pi < \theta < \frac{1}{2}\pi\}$ $(a > 0, b > 0)$	$x = a \sec \theta,\ y = b \tan \theta\ (\theta \in (-\frac{1}{2}\pi, \frac{1}{2}\pi))$

Expressions for $\dfrac{dy}{dx}$ and $\dfrac{d^2y}{dx^2}$ in terms of a parameter t

We assume that a curve C has parametric equations $x = x(t)$, $y = y(t)$ $(t \in I)$ where $x(t)$ and $y(t)$ are differentiable expressions in t, and that y is a differentiable expression in x. Using the chain rule,

$$\frac{dy}{dt} = \frac{dy}{dx}\frac{dx}{dt}, \quad \text{so that} \quad \frac{dy}{dx} = \frac{\dfrac{dy}{dt}}{\dfrac{dx}{dt}} \quad \left(\text{provided } \frac{dx}{dt} \neq 0\right).$$

Using the "fluctional" notation $\dot{x}$ for $\dfrac{dx}{dt}$, $\dot{y}$ for $\dfrac{dy}{dt}$ we have:

$$\frac{dy}{dx} = \frac{\dot{y}}{\dot{x}} \quad (\dot{x} \neq 0). \tag{7.1}$$

When second-order derivatives also exist we can find an expression for $\dfrac{d^2y}{dx^2}$ as follows: From (7.1),

$$\frac{d}{dt}\left(\frac{dy}{dx}\right) = \frac{d}{dt}\left(\frac{\dot{y}}{\dot{x}}\right), \quad \text{so that} \quad \frac{d}{dx}\left(\frac{dy}{dx}\right)\cdot\frac{dx}{dt} = \frac{d}{dt}\left(\frac{\dot{y}}{\dot{x}}\right),$$

and hence
$$\frac{d^2y}{dx^2} = \frac{1}{\dot{x}}\frac{d}{dt}\left(\frac{\dot{y}}{\dot{x}}\right), \tag{7.2}$$

which gives
$$\frac{d^2y}{dx^2} = \frac{\dot{x}\ddot{y} - \ddot{x}\dot{y}}{\dot{x}^3} \quad (\dot{x} \neq 0), \tag{7.3}$$

where
$$\ddot{x} = \frac{d^2x}{dt^2} \quad \text{and} \quad \ddot{y} = \frac{d^2y}{dt^2}.$$

In practice it is usually better to obtain $\dfrac{d^2y}{dx^2}$ from (7.2) rather than (7.3).

Example 1. Find the coordinates of the points on the curve

$$x = 1 - t^2, \; y = t^3 + t \quad (t \in \mathbf{R})$$

at which the gradient is 2.

Here $\dot{x} = -2t$, $\dot{y} = 3t^2 + 1$, and $\dfrac{dy}{dx} = \dfrac{\dot{y}}{\dot{x}} = -\dfrac{3t^2+1}{2t}$ $(t \neq 0)$.

Thus $\dfrac{dy}{dx} = 2 \Leftrightarrow -\dfrac{3t^2+1}{2t} = 2 \Leftrightarrow 3t^2 + 4t + 1 = 0 \Leftrightarrow t = -1$ or $-\frac{1}{3}$;

$t = -1$ gives the point $(0, -2)$, $t = -\frac{1}{3}$ gives the point $(\frac{8}{9}, -\frac{10}{27})$, and these are the points on the curve at which the gradient is 2.

Example 2. Find the equation of the tangent to the curve

$$x = t^2, \; y = t^3 + \tfrac{1}{3}t^2 \quad (t \in \mathbf{R})$$

at the point P with parameter $t = t_1$ $(\neq 0)$, and show that this tangent meets the curve again only at the point Q with parameter $t = -\frac{1}{2}t_1$. Find the critical point on the curve and determine its nature. Discuss the concavity of the curve and sketch the curve.

Here $\dot{x} = 2t$, $\dot{y} = 3t^2 + \frac{2}{3}t$, and $\dfrac{dy}{dx} = \dfrac{\dot{y}}{\dot{x}} = \frac{3}{2}t + \frac{1}{3}(t \neq 0)$.

The gradient at P is $\frac{3}{2}t_1+\frac{1}{3}$ and P has coordinates $(t_1{}^2, t_1{}^3+\frac{1}{3}t_1{}^2)$. The tangent at P has equation

$$y-(t_1{}^3+\tfrac{1}{3}t_1{}^2) = (\tfrac{3}{2}t_1+\tfrac{1}{3})(x-t_1{}^2),$$

i.e.

$$y-(\tfrac{3}{2}t_1+\tfrac{1}{3})x+\tfrac{1}{2}t_1{}^3 = 0. \tag{7.4}$$

This tangent meets the curve at points with parameters t given by

$$t^3+\tfrac{1}{3}t^2-(\tfrac{3}{2}t_1+\tfrac{1}{3})t^2+\tfrac{1}{2}t_1{}^3 = 0,$$

(obtained by inserting $x = t^2$, $y = t^3+\frac{1}{3}t^2$ in (7.4)), and so by

$$t^3-\tfrac{3}{2}t_1t^2+\tfrac{1}{2}t_1{}^3 = 0. \tag{7.5}$$

On remembering that the tangent *touches* the curve at P, so that

$$(t-t_1)^2 = t^2-2t_1t+t_1{}^2$$

is a factor of the left-hand side of (7.5), it is easy to check that (7.5) is

$$(t-t_1)^2(t+\tfrac{1}{2}t_1) = 0,$$

and so that the tangent meets the curve again only at the point Q with parameter $t = -\frac{1}{2}t_1$.

Now
$$\frac{dy}{dx} = 0 \Leftrightarrow t = -\tfrac{2}{9},$$

so that $A(\frac{4}{81}, \frac{4}{729})$ is the only critical point of the curve.

$$\frac{d^2y}{dx^2} = \frac{1}{\dot{x}}\frac{d}{dt}\left(\frac{\dot{y}}{\dot{x}}\right) = \frac{1}{2t}\frac{d}{dt}(\tfrac{3}{2}t+\tfrac{1}{3}) = \frac{3}{4t} \quad (t \neq 0).$$

At A, $\dfrac{d^2y}{dx^2} = -\frac{27}{8} < 0$; thus A is a local maximum point on the curve.

The nature of A can also be obtained from a table of sign for $\dfrac{dy}{dx}$:

$$\frac{dy}{dx} = \tfrac{3}{2}(t+\tfrac{2}{9});$$

t:	$\rightarrow$	$-\frac{2}{9}$	$\rightarrow$
$\dfrac{dy}{dx}$:	$-$	0	$+$
$x = t^2$:	$(>\frac{4}{81})$	$\frac{4}{81}$	$(<\frac{4}{81})$

We note that, since $\dot{x} = 2t$ is negative on a neighbourhood of A, x decreases as t increases on a neighbourhood of A. Thus the shape of the curve there is given by the following table:

x:	$\rightarrow$	$\frac{4}{81}$	$\rightarrow$
$\frac{dy}{dx}$:	$+$	0	$-$
shape:	/	—	\

Again we see that A is a local maximum point on the curve.

Since $\dfrac{d^2y}{dx^2} = \dfrac{3}{4t}$, it follows that the curve is concave up for $t > 0$ and concave down for $t < 0$; $t = 0$ gives the origin $(0, 0)$.

To sketch this particular curve it is helpful to obtain its x, y-equation by eliminating t from the equations $x = t^2$, $y = t^3 + \frac{1}{3}t^2$. Since $y = tx + \frac{1}{3}x$, we have: $(y - \frac{1}{3}x)^2 = t^2x^2$, and the curve has x, y-equation

$$(y - \tfrac{1}{3}x)^2 = x^3. \tag{7.6}$$

From (7.6), $\quad y = \frac{1}{3}x + x^{3/2} \quad$ or $\quad y = \frac{1}{3}x - x^{3/2} \quad (x \geqslant 0).$

On $y = \frac{1}{3}x + x^{3/2}$, $\dfrac{dy}{dx} = \frac{1}{3} + \frac{3}{2}x^{1/2}$ and this $\rightarrow \frac{1}{3}$ as $x \rightarrow 0$.

On $y = \frac{1}{3}x - x^{3/2}$, $\dfrac{dy}{dx} = \frac{1}{3} - \frac{3}{2}x^{1/2}$ and this $\rightarrow \frac{1}{3}$ as $x \rightarrow 0$.

Also the curve behaves like $y = x^{3/2}$ as $x \rightarrow \infty$ on $y = \frac{1}{3}x + x^{3/2}$, and behaves like $y = -x^{3/2}$ as $x \rightarrow \infty$ on $y = \frac{1}{3}x - x^{3/2}$ The curve meets the x-axis, i.e. $y = 0$, where $t = 0$ and $t = -\frac{1}{3}$, i.e. where $x = 0$ and $x = \frac{1}{9}$.

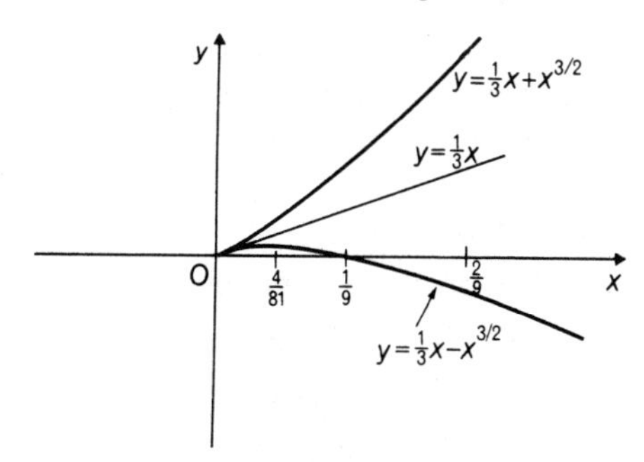

A point on a curve like the origin O for this curve is called a **cusp**; it is a point at which two distinct **branches** of the curve have the same tangent.

Example 3. Show that $\theta = \frac{1}{3}\pi$ gives a point of inflexion on the curve

$$x = \tan\theta,\ y = \sin\theta\cos\theta,\ -\tfrac{1}{2}\pi < \theta < \tfrac{1}{2}\pi,$$

and determine the shape of the curve in a neighbourhood of the point.

$$\dot{x} = \sec^2\theta,\ \dot{y} = \cos^2\theta - \sin^2\theta = \cos 2\theta, \text{ and so } \frac{dy}{dx} = \cos^2\theta\cos 2\theta;$$

also
$$\begin{aligned}\frac{d^2y}{dx^2} &= \frac{1}{\dot{x}}\frac{d}{d\theta}\left(\frac{\dot{y}}{\dot{x}}\right)\\ &= \cos^2\theta.(-2\cos\theta\sin\theta\cos 2\theta - 2\cos^2\theta\sin 2\theta)\\ &= -2\cos^3\theta\sin 3\theta.\end{aligned}$$

For $\theta = \frac{1}{3}\pi,\ \dfrac{d^2y}{dx^2} = 0,\ \dfrac{dy}{dx} = -\frac{1}{8},\ x = \sqrt{3}$ and $y = \frac{1}{4}\sqrt{3}$;

also $\dot{x} = 4\,(>0)$, so that x increases as θ increases on a neighbourhood of $\theta = \frac{1}{3}\pi$. A table of sign for $\dfrac{d^2y}{dx^2}$ on this neighbourhood is:

θ:	$\rightarrow$	$\frac{1}{3}\pi$	$\rightarrow$
x:	$\rightarrow$	$\sqrt{3}$	$\rightarrow$
$\sin 3\theta$:	$+$	0	$-$
$-2\cos^3\theta$:	$-$	$-$	$-$
$\dfrac{d^2y}{dx^2}$:	$-$	0	$+$
$\dfrac{dy}{dx}$:		$-\frac{1}{8}$	
shape:	$-$		$+$

The point is a point of inflexion since concavity changes direction there, and the shape of the curve in a neighbourhood of the point is as shown.

8. Curves by polar coordinates (r, θ)

A point $P(x, y) \neq O$ has polar coordinates (r, θ) as indicated. Usually we take $r > 0$ and $0 \leqslant \theta < 2\pi$; also we say that $r = 0$ gives the origin O.

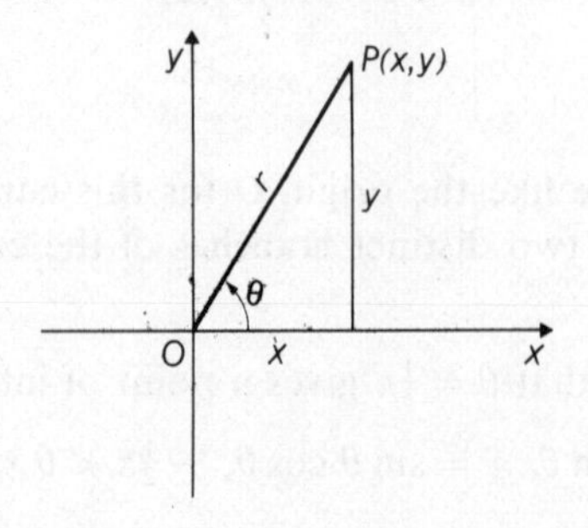

The relations between the (x, y)- and (r, θ)-coordinates are $x = r\cos\theta$, $y = r\sin\theta$. Now $r^2 = x^2+y^2$, so that

$$r = \sqrt{(x^2+y^2)}\ (>0),\ \cos\theta = \frac{x}{\sqrt{(x^2+y^2)}},\ \text{and}\ \sin\theta = \frac{y}{\sqrt{(x^2+y^2)}}.$$

A curve is usually given in terms of polar coordinates by an equation of the form $r = f(\theta)$, where f is some function. Then

$$x = f(\theta)\cos\theta,\quad y = f(\theta)\sin\theta$$

are parametric equations in θ for the curve, and the methods of Section 7 can be used to determine properties of the curve.

We list x, y-equations and corresponding polar equations for some simple curves:

x, y-equation	polar equation
(i) circle $x^2+y^2 = 1$	$r = 1$
(ii) half line $y = x,\ x > 0$	$\theta = \frac{1}{4}\pi$
(iii) line $x = 1$	$r = \sec\theta,\ -\frac{1}{2}\pi < \theta < \frac{1}{2}\pi$
(iv) line $y = 1$	$r = \operatorname{cosec}\theta,\ 0 < \theta < \pi$
(v) circle $x^2+y^2-2ax = 0\quad (a > 0)$	$r = 2a\cos\theta,\ -\frac{1}{2}\pi < \theta \leqslant \frac{1}{2}\pi$ $[r = 0,\ \theta = \frac{1}{2}\pi$ gives $O]$
(vi) circle $x^2+y^2-2by = 0\quad (b > 0)$	$r = 2b\sin\theta,\ 0 \leqslant \theta < \pi$ $[r = 0,\ \theta = 0$ gives $O]$

In sketching a curve $r = f(\theta)$ useful information can often be obtained by applying the formula

$$\cot\psi = \frac{1}{r}\frac{dr}{d\theta}, \tag{8.1}$$

where ψ is an angle which the tangent at $P(r, \theta)$ on the curve makes with the radius vector $\overrightarrow{OP}$.

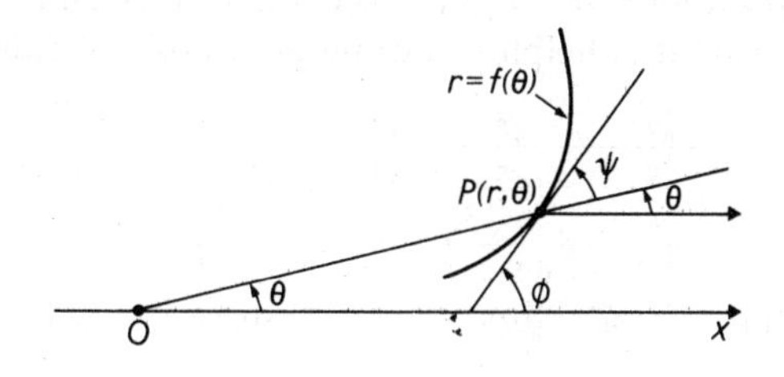

Proof of (8.1).

$$\cot\psi = \cot(\phi-\theta), \quad \text{where} \quad \tan\phi = \frac{dy}{dx} = \frac{\dfrac{dy}{d\theta}}{\dfrac{dx}{d\theta}},$$

$$= \frac{1}{\tan(\phi-\theta)}$$

$$= \frac{1+\tan\phi\tan\theta}{\tan\phi-\tan\theta}$$

$$= \frac{\dfrac{dx}{d\theta}\cos\theta+\dfrac{dy}{d\theta}\sin\theta}{\dfrac{dy}{d\theta}\cos\theta-\dfrac{dx}{d\theta}\sin\theta}$$

$$= \frac{\left(\dfrac{dr}{d\theta}\cos\theta-r\sin\theta\right)\cos\theta+\left(\dfrac{dr}{d\theta}\sin\theta+r\cos\theta\right)\sin\theta}{\left(\dfrac{dr}{d\theta}\sin\theta+r\cos\theta\right)\cos\theta-\left(\dfrac{dr}{d\theta}\cos\theta-r\sin\theta\right)\sin\theta}$$

$$= \frac{\dfrac{dr}{d\theta}(\cos^2\theta+\sin^2\theta)}{r(\cos^2\theta+\sin^2\theta)} = \frac{1}{r}\frac{dr}{d\theta}.$$

Example 1. Sketch the curve $r = a\sqrt{(\sin 2\theta)}$, $a > 0$.

The curve exists where $\sin 2\theta \geqslant 0$, i.e. for $0 \leqslant \theta \leqslant \frac{1}{2}\pi$ and for $\pi \leqslant \theta \leqslant \frac{3}{2}\pi$, in $[0, 2\pi)$.

For this curve,

$$\cot\psi = \frac{1}{r}\frac{dr}{d\theta} = \frac{1}{a\sqrt{(\sin 2\theta)}}\cdot\frac{a\cos 2\theta}{\sqrt{(\sin 2\theta)}} = \cot 2\theta, \quad \text{so that} \quad \psi = 2\theta.$$

Since $\sin 2(\pi+\theta) = \sin 2\theta$ the part of the curve for $\pi \leqslant \theta \leqslant \frac{3}{2}\pi$ is the part for $0 \leqslant \theta \leqslant \frac{1}{2}\pi$ rotated through an angle π; consequently, because of this half-turn symmetry about the origin, it is enough to consider $0 \leqslant \theta \leqslant \frac{1}{2}\pi$. In sketching this part it is helpful to draw up a table of values.

θ	0	$\frac{1}{12}\pi$	$\frac{1}{8}\pi$	$\frac{1}{6}\pi$	$\frac{1}{4}\pi$	$\frac{1}{3}\pi$	$\frac{3}{8}\pi$	$\frac{5}{12}\pi$	$\frac{1}{2}\pi$
ψ	0	$\frac{1}{6}\pi$	$\frac{1}{4}\pi$	$\frac{1}{3}\pi$	$\frac{1}{2}\pi$	$\frac{2}{3}\pi$	$\frac{3}{4}\pi$	$\frac{5}{6}\pi$	π
r	0	$\dfrac{a}{\sqrt{2}}$ $=0{\cdot}71a$	$\dfrac{a}{\sqrt[4]{2}}$ $=0{\cdot}84a$	$a\sqrt{\left(\dfrac{\sqrt{3}}{2}\right)}$ $=0{\cdot}93a$	a	$a\sqrt{\left(\dfrac{\sqrt{3}}{2}\right)}$ $=0{\cdot}93a$	$\dfrac{a}{\sqrt[4]{2}}$ $=0{\cdot}84a$	$\dfrac{a}{\sqrt{2}}$ $=0{\cdot}71a$	0

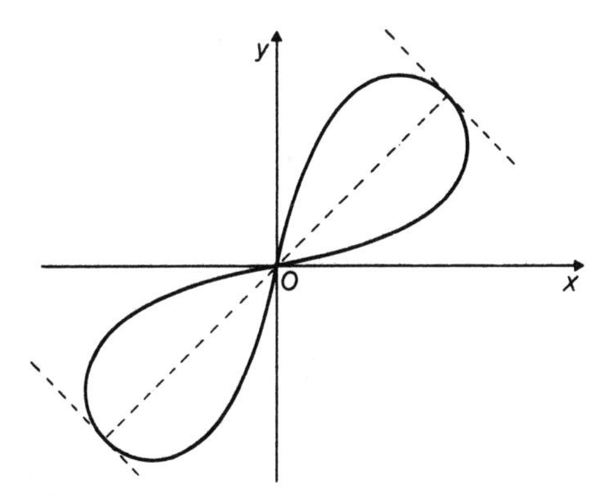

Example 2. Sketch the curve

$$r = 1+\cos\theta = 2\cos^2 \tfrac{1}{2}\theta, \quad -\pi \leqslant \theta \leqslant \pi.$$

Since $\cos(-\theta) = \cos\theta$, it is enough to consider $0 \leqslant \theta \leqslant \pi$, the other half of the curve being the reflection of this part in the x-axis.

Check that $\psi = \frac{1}{2}(\pi+\theta)$; draw up a table of values for $0 \leqslant \theta \leqslant \pi$ and check that the curve, called a **cardioid**, has the following shape:

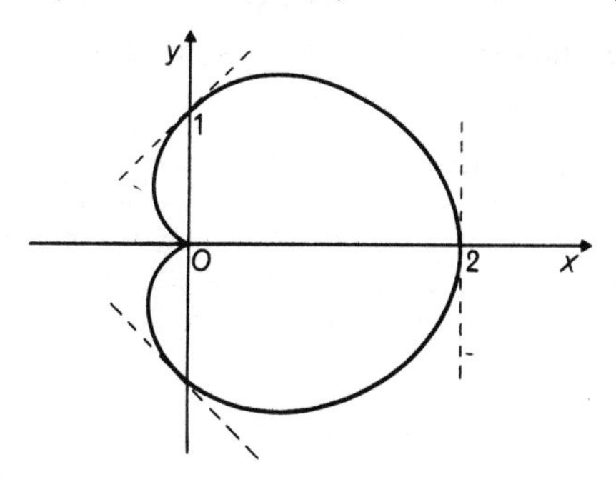

EXERCISE 3

1. Discuss the concavity of the following curves; find the points of inflexion (if any) of the curves and determine the shape of each curve in a neighbourhood of each of the points of inflexion:

(i) $y = 3x-x^3$, (ii) $y = x^4+4x^3$, (iii) $y = x^5+x^3+x$,

(iv) $y = 3x^4-8x^3+6x^2$, (v) $y = \dfrac{x^2}{1-x}$, (vi) $y = \dfrac{x}{x^4+3}$,

(vii) $y = 2x+\cos x$, (viii) $y = x+2\sin x$, (ix) $y = 2x-\tan x$,

taking (vii) on $[-\pi, \pi]$, (viii) on $[-\frac{1}{2}\pi, \frac{3}{2}\pi]$ and (ix) on $(-\frac{1}{2}\pi, \frac{1}{2}\pi)$.

2. Each of the following curves has equation of the form $y = f(x)$. Find the critical points and asymptotes of each curve, and for (i), (ii) and (iii) the points of inflexion. Sketch each curve and deduce rough sketches of the curves

$$y = \frac{1}{f(x)} \quad \text{and} \quad y = -\frac{1}{f(x)}.$$

(i) $y = \dfrac{4x}{3x^2+1}$, (ii) $y = \dfrac{x}{(1+x)^2}$, (iii) $y = \dfrac{x^3}{x^2-3}$,

(iv) $y = x + \dfrac{4}{x^2}$, (v) $y = \dfrac{x^2}{x^3+1}$, (vi) $y = x + \dfrac{4}{x+2}$,

(vii) $y = \dfrac{(x-2)^2}{x(x-3)}$, (viii) $y = \dfrac{(x-2)^2(x+3)}{3-x}$, (ix) $y = \dfrac{2x^2+13x+15}{(x-1)(x^2-1)}$.

3. Discuss the critical points of the curve $y = f(x)$ where

$$f(x) = 12x^5 - 15x^4 - 20x^3 + 30x^2 + 2,$$

and determine the x-coordinates of the points of inflexion. Sketch the curve. What information can you obtain about real roots of the equation $f(x) = 0$?

4. Prove that the x-coordinates of points of inflexion of the curve

$$y = \frac{1-x}{1+x^2}$$

are roots of the equation $x^3 - 3x^2 - 3x + 1 = 0$, and deduce that there are three points of inflexion.

5. Sketch the curves with equations

(i) $y^2 = x(3-x^2)$, (ii) $y^2 = x(x^2-3)$, (iii) $y^2 = x(3-x)^2$,
(iv) $y = x \sin x$, (v) $y = x \cos x$, (vi) $y^2 = x^2 \sin^2 x$.

[*Hint* for (iv): $|x \sin x| \leqslant |x|$; $x \sin x = x \Leftrightarrow \sin x = 1$, and $x \sin x = -x \Leftrightarrow \sin x = -1$; $y = x \sin x$ is bounded by the lines $y = \pm x$.]

6. Show that any critical points of a differentiable function defined by the equation $x^2 + xy + y^2 = 27$ lie on the line $y + 2x = 0$, and find the coordinates of the possible points.

7. Given that the equation $\sin x + \cos y = y$ defines y as a differentiable function of x, express $\dfrac{dy}{dx}$ in terms of x and y. Hence show that y has a critical value at $x = \frac{1}{2}\pi$ and determine the nature of this critical value.

8. For the curve $y^4 = 4xy + 3$, show that

$$\frac{d^2y}{dx^2} = \frac{3(1-y^4)}{2(y^3-x)^3}.$$

Find the points of inflexion on the curve and the shape of the curve in a neighbourhood of each point.

9. Find the equation of the tangent to each of the following curves at the point given:

(i) $x = t^3$, $y = t^4 + 1$ at the point $t = 3$;
(ii) $x = t^2 - 2t$, $y = 1 - t^4$ at the point $t = -1$;
(iii) $x = \sin t$, $y = \cos 2t (-\frac{1}{2}\pi \leqslant t \leqslant \frac{1}{2}\pi)$ at the point $t = \frac{1}{6}\pi$.

10. The curves in this question refer to (i), (ii), (iii) of question **9**.

(a) Find the point on curve (i) at which the tangent is parallel to the line $3y = 4x$.
(b) Find the points on curve (ii) at which the gradient is -16.
(c) Find the point on curve (iii) at which the gradient is $2\sqrt{2}$.

11. Find an x, y-equation for each of the curves (i), (ii) and (iii) of question **9**.

12. Show that there are four points on the curve

$$x = \frac{t^3}{t^2+1}, \quad y = \frac{t}{t^2+1}$$

at which the gradient is equal to $-\frac{1}{10}$.

13. Find the equation of the tangent at the point with parameter $t = 2$ on the curve

$$x = \frac{4t}{t^3+1}, \quad y = \frac{t^2}{t^3+1} \quad (t \neq -1).$$

Find the parameter of the other point at which the tangent meets the curve.

14. For the curve $x = \frac{1}{3}t^3$, $y = 1 + \frac{1}{2}t^2$, find the equation of the tangent at the point with parameter t_0 ($\neq 0$), and find the coordinates of the point at which the tangent meets the curve again. Show in a diagram the shape of the curve in a neighbourhood of the point given by $t = 0$.

15. For the curve $x = 3t - t^3$, $y = 1 - t^2$, find $\dfrac{dy}{dx}$ and $\dfrac{d^2y}{dx^2}$ in terms of t. Draw up a table of sign for $\dfrac{dy}{dx}$; find the nature of the critical point and find the points of intersection with the x- and y-axes. Sketch the curve. Obtain the equation of the normal to the curve at the point with parameter t, and hence find all the points on the curve at which the normal passes through the origin.

16. For the curve

$$x = \tan\theta, \quad y = \sin 2\theta \quad (-\tfrac{1}{2}\pi < \theta < \tfrac{1}{2}\pi),$$

find $\dfrac{d^2y}{dx^2}$ in terms of θ. Find the points of inflexion on the curve and the shape of the curve in a neighbourhood of each point.

17. For the curve $x = t^2 + t$, $y = 3 - t^3$, show that

$$\frac{d^2y}{dx^2} = -\frac{6t(t+1)}{(2t+1)^3} \quad (t \neq -\tfrac{1}{2}).$$

Find the shape of the curve in a neighbourhood of each of its points of inflexion, and sketch the curve.

18. Sketch the curve $x = \cos^3 t$, $y = \sin^3 t$, $0 \leqslant t \leqslant 2\pi$, called the *astroid*.
Show that the point on the part of the curve in the first quadrant which is closest to the point $A(\frac{1}{2}, 0)$ has parameter t where $\cos t = \frac{1}{8}\{1+\sqrt{(33)}\}$.

19. Find an equation in polar coordinates for each of the following curves:
(i) $x^2+y^2 = a^2$ $(a > 0)$, (ii) $y+x = 0$, $x < 0$, (iii) $x+1 = 0$,
(iv) $y^2 = x$, (v) $(x^2+y^2)^2 = 2xy$, (vi) $(x^2+y^2)^3 = x^2-y^2$.

20. Sketch the curves given by the following equations in polar coordinates:
(i) $r = 3$, (ii) $r = 3\cos\theta$, (iii) $r = 3\sec\theta$,
(iv) $r = 2\sin\theta - 1$, (v) $r^2 = a^2\cos 2\theta$ $(a > 0)$, (vi) $r = 3\tan\theta$.

Determine an equation in x, y-coordinates for each of the curves.

Inverse functions

1. Real functions with inverses

For this work we shall assume the relevant definitions and notation used in Chapter 3 of *Algebra and Number Systems* by Hunter, Monk, Blackburn and Donald (Blackie/Chambers, 1971). If f is a bijection $f: S \to T$ (i.e. a $|-|$ and onto mapping from a set S to a set T), then $\exists$ a unique bijection $f^{-1}: T \to S$ such that, if $f(s) = t$, then $f^{-1}(t) = s$; f^{-1} is called the inverse mapping of f.

If f is a real function, so that S and T are subsets of $\mathbf{R}$, it is of interest to find a condition on f which ensures that f is a bijection and so has an inverse real function. Our intuitive picture involves solving $y = f(x)$ to give $x = f^{-1}(y)$; when can we do this in a meaningful way and, if f is differentiable, is f^{-1} also differentiable and how are the derivatives of f and f^{-1} related? The main tool for tackling the problem is provided by the following result.

Theorem 4.1

If a surjective (i.e. *onto*) *real function* $f: S \to T$ *is either strictly increasing on S or strictly decreasing on S, then f is a bijection, and so has an inverse.*

Proof. Since f is surjective (onto) we have merely to show that it is injective (i.e. $|-|$), i.e. that $f(x_1) = f(x_2) \Rightarrow x_1 = x_2$.

Suppose that f is strictly increasing on S: Take x_1, x_2 in S such that $f(x_1) = f(x_2)$. Now either $x_1 < x_2$ or $x_2 < x_1$ or $x_1 = x_2$. But, since f is increasing,

$$x_1 < x_2 \Rightarrow f(x_1) < f(x_2), \quad \text{and} \quad x_2 < x_1 \Rightarrow f(x_2) < f(x_1).$$

Hence $f(x_1) = f(x_2) \Rightarrow x_1 = x_2$ and so f is injective. Thus f is bijective, and so has an inverse.

By a similar argument the same conclusion follows from the assumption that f is *strictly decreasing on S.*

In Theorem **2.2** of Chapter 2 we saw that, for a differentiable function f, the sign of $f'(x)$ is related to the question of whether f is increasing or decreasing. In fact if we tie Theorems **2.2** and **4.1** together we obtain at once the following useful result.

Theorem 4.2

If f is continuous on an interval S and differentiable on the open interval determined by S, and if $f'(x) > 0$ on this open interval, then f^{-1} exists as a mapping from $f(S)$ to S, where $f(S)$ is the image of S by f.

Similarly, the same statement holds with $f'(x) > 0$ replaced by $f'(x) < 0$.

Graphically this result means that from a part of the graph of f on which f is either strictly increasing or strictly decreasing we can define an inverse.

Example 1. Consider f defined on $\mathbf{R}^+$ by $f(x) = x^2 + 1$.

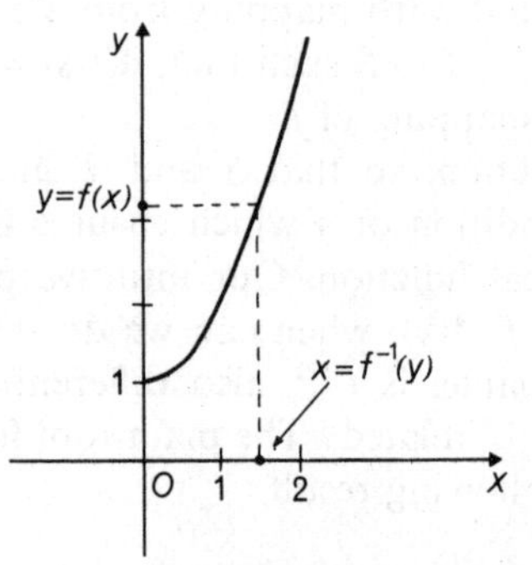

Here $f'(x) = 2x > 0$ on $x > 0$, so that f is strictly increasing on $\mathbf{R}^+$. The image of f is $f(\mathbf{R}^+) = [1, \infty)$, i.e. it is $T = \{y \in \mathbf{R} : y \geqslant 1\}$. $f: \mathbf{R}^+ \to T$ has an inverse $f^{-1}: T \to \mathbf{R}^+$, such that

$$f(x) = y \Leftrightarrow f^{-1}(y) = x \quad (x \in \mathbf{R}^+, y \in T).$$

Thus to find $f^{-1}(y)$ we have to solve $y = x^2 + 1$ for x, noting that $x \geqslant 0$;

$$y = x^2 + 1 \text{ with } x \geqslant 0 \Leftrightarrow y - 1 = x^2 \text{ with } x \geqslant 0$$
$$\Leftrightarrow x = \sqrt{(y-1)}.$$

Hence f^{-1} is defined by the formula: $f^{-1}(y) = \sqrt{(y-1)}$, $\forall y \geqslant 1$. With the usual notation x for the variable we thus have:

$$f^{-1}(x) = \sqrt{(x-1)}, \ \forall x \geqslant 1.$$

Note. The graphs $y = f(x)$ and $y = f^{-1}(x)$ are reflections of each other in the line $y = x$; for, if (x, y) is on the graph of f, so that $y = f(x)$, then (y, x) is on the graph of f^{-1} since $x = f^{-1}(y)$.

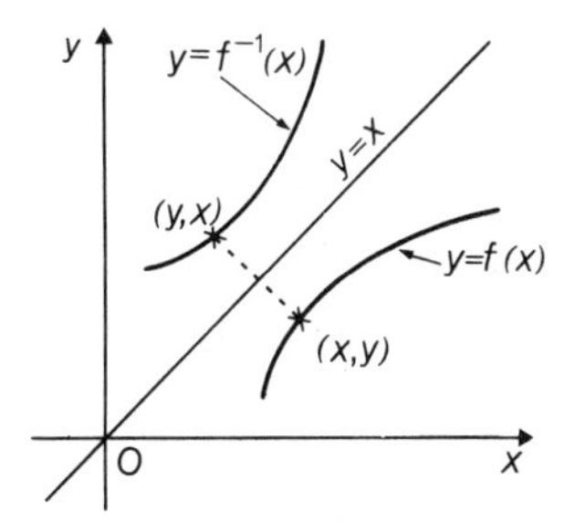

In Example 1 it was possible to obtain easily a formula for the inverse function. We now discuss an example in which we can show that an inverse exists, but cannot easily obtain a formula for the inverse.

Example 2. Show that the restriction of the real function f defined by $f(x) = x^3-3x+1$ to the set $S = \{x \in \mathbf{R} : x \geqslant 1\}$ is a bijection from $S \to f(S)$ and describe the inverse of this restriction.

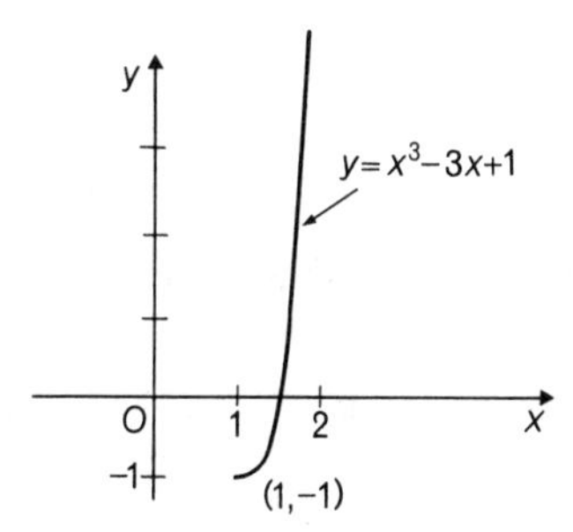

For simplicity we denote the restriction also by f.

$$f'(x) = 3(x^2-1) > 0 \text{ for } x > 1,$$

and so f is strictly increasing on S. Since $f(1) = -1$ and $f(x) \to \infty$ as $x \to \infty$, it follows that the image $f(S)$ of f is $T = [-1, \infty)$. The graph of f on S is as shown, noting that $f'(1) = 0$. $f: S \to T$ is a bijection and $f^{-1}: T \to S$ is such that: if $y \in T$, then $f^{-1}(y) = x$, where $y = f(x) = x^3-3x+1$ $(x \geqslant 1)$. For example, $f^{-1}(-1) = 1$, since $f(1) = -1$; $f^{-1}(3) = 2$ since $f(2) = 3$; $f^{-1}(19) = 3$ since $f(3) = 19$.

What is $f^{-1}(-\frac{1}{8})$? This number is $x(\geqslant 1)$ where $x^3-3x+1 = -\frac{1}{8}$, i.e. $8x^3-24x+9 = 0$, i.e. $(2x-3)(4x^2+6x-3) = 0$, and so $f^{-1}(-\frac{1}{8}) = \frac{3}{2}$ since $4x^2+6x-3 = 0$ has no root $\geqslant 1$.

Example 3. [x^n and $x^{1/n}$, n a positive integer; we separate the cases n even and n odd.]

(i) $f(x) = x^{2m}$, $m \in \mathbf{N}$: here $f'(x) = 2mx^{2m-1} > 0$ $\forall x > 0$.

Hence f is strictly increasing on $\mathbf{R}^+$ and the restriction of f as a mapping $\mathbf{R}^+ \to \mathbf{R}^+$ (noting that $f(0) = 0$) is a bijection with inverse $f^{-1}: \mathbf{R}^+ \to \mathbf{R}^+$ given by

$$f^{-1}(y) = y^{1/2m} \ \forall y \in \mathbf{R}^+ \quad [y = x^{2m} \Leftrightarrow x = y^{1/2m} (x \geqslant 0)],$$

i.e., in x notation, $f^{-1}(x) = x^{1/2m} \ \forall x \in \mathbf{R}^+$.

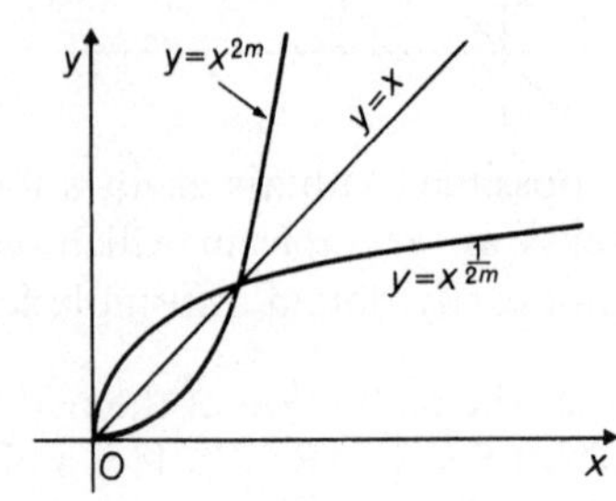

The graphs $y = x^{2m}$ and $y = x^{1/2m}$ $(x \geqslant 0)$ are reflections of each other in the line $y = x$.

(ii) $f(x) = x^{2m-1}$, $m \in \mathbf{N}$: here $f'(x) = (2m-1)x^{2m-2} \geqslant 0 \ \forall x \in \mathbf{R}$ and $= 0 \Leftrightarrow x = 0$ $(m > 1)$.

Hence f is strictly increasing on $\mathbf{R}$ and so f is a bijection with inverse $f^{-1}: \mathbf{R} \to \mathbf{R}$ given by

$$f^{-1}(y) = y^{1/(2m-1)} \ \forall y \in \mathbf{R} \ [y = x^{2m-1} \Leftrightarrow x = y^{1/(2m-1)}],$$

i.e., in x notation,

$$f^{-1}(x) = x^{1/(2m-1)} \ \forall x \in \mathbf{R}.$$

Again the graphs of f and f^{-1} are reflections of each other in the line $y = x$.

2. Derivatives of inverse functions

We start with a differentiable bijection f and show in the following result that its inverse is also differentiable and that the two derivatives are closely related.

Theorem 4.3

Suppose that the real differentiable function $f: S \to T$ has an inverse $g: T \to S$. If $f(x) = y$, so that $x = g(y)$ and if $f'(x) \neq 0$, then g is differentiable at y and

$$g'(y) = \frac{1}{f'(x)} = \frac{1}{f'(g(y))}.$$

Proof. We take $y+k$ in T, $k \neq 0$ and form

$$\frac{1}{k}\{g(y+k)-g(y)\}.$$

Since f is bijective, there is a unique number $x+h$ in S $(h \neq 0)$ such that

$$y+k = f(x+h), \quad \text{and so} \quad x+h = g(y+k).$$

Then

$$k = f(x+h)-y = f(x+h)-f(x), \quad \text{and} \quad h = g(y+k)-x = g(y+k)-g(y).$$

Hence
$$\frac{g(y+k)-g(y)}{k} = \frac{h}{f(x+h)-f(x)} = \frac{1}{\dfrac{f(x+h)-f(x)}{h}}.$$

Since h is uniquely determined by k, it follows that, as $k \to 0$, then $h \to 0$. [This says that g is continuous.] Thus

$$\lim_{k\to 0} \frac{g(y+k)-g(y)}{k} = \frac{1}{\lim\limits_{h\to 0} \dfrac{f(x+h)-f(x)}{h}} = \frac{1}{f'(x)},$$

so that $g'(y)$ exists and

$$g'(y) = \frac{1}{f'(x)} = \frac{1}{f'(g(y))}. \tag{2.1}$$

Differential notation

Writing $\frac{dy}{dx} = f'(x)$, we often denote $g'(y)$ by $\frac{dx}{dy}$ and write

$$\frac{dx}{dy} = \frac{1}{\dfrac{dy}{dx}};$$

but this notation should be used only when we know that $y = f(x)$ can be solved to give $x = f^{-1}(y)$.

In practice, *assuming that g is differentiable*, we can proceed as follows: Differentiating $y = f(x)$ with respect to x we have

$$\frac{dy}{dx} = f'(x),$$

and so
$$g'(y) = \frac{dx}{dy} = \frac{1}{\dfrac{dy}{dx}} = \frac{1}{f'(x)} = \frac{1}{f'(g(y))}.$$

Example 1 (of Section **1**).

$$f(x) = x^2+1 \ (x \geqslant 0), \ g(y) = \sqrt{(y-1)}, \ (y \geqslant 1).$$

Here
$$y = x^2+1; \ \frac{dy}{dx} = 2x$$

and so
$$\frac{dx}{dy} = \frac{1}{2x} (x \neq 0) = \frac{1}{2\sqrt{(y-1)}} (y > 1).$$

Hence
$$\frac{d}{dy}\{g(y)\} = \frac{1}{2\sqrt{(y-1)}} (y > 1).$$

Differentiating $g(y)$ directly we have:

$$\frac{d}{dy}\{g(y)\} = \frac{d}{dy}(\sqrt{(y-1)}) = \frac{1}{2\sqrt{(y-1)}} (y > 1).$$

Example 2 (of Section **1**). $f(x) = x^3-3x+1$, $x \geqslant 1$. In this case we cannot easily obtain a formula for $g = f^{-1}$ and so for $\frac{d}{dy}(g(y))$. However we can evaluate this derivative at particular points by using equation (2.1). For example, let us evaluate $g'(-\frac{1}{8})$, i.e. $g'(y)$ at $y = -\frac{1}{8}$.

$$y = x^3-3x+1 \quad \text{gives} \quad \frac{dy}{dx} = 3(x^2-1)$$

and so
$$\frac{dx}{dy} = \frac{1}{3(x^2-1)}, \quad \text{i.e.} \quad g'(y) = \frac{1}{3(x^2-1)}.$$

Hence
$$g'(-\tfrac{1}{8}) = \frac{1}{3(x^2-1)},$$

where
$$x^3-3x+1 = -\tfrac{1}{8} \quad \text{and} \quad x \geqslant 1.$$

In discussing this example in Section **1** we saw that the value of x for which $x^3-3x+1 = -\frac{1}{8}$ and $x \geqslant 1$ is $x = \frac{3}{2}$. Thus

$$g'(-\tfrac{1}{8}) = \frac{1}{3(\frac{9}{4}-1)} = \tfrac{4}{15}.$$

Exercise. For this example show that

$$g'\left(\frac{73}{8}\right) = \frac{4}{63}.$$

3. The inverse trigonometric functions

These important real functions merit special consideration on their own. Following Theorem **4.1** we take restrictions of the trigonometric functions sine, cosine and tangent which are either strictly increasing or strictly decreasing.

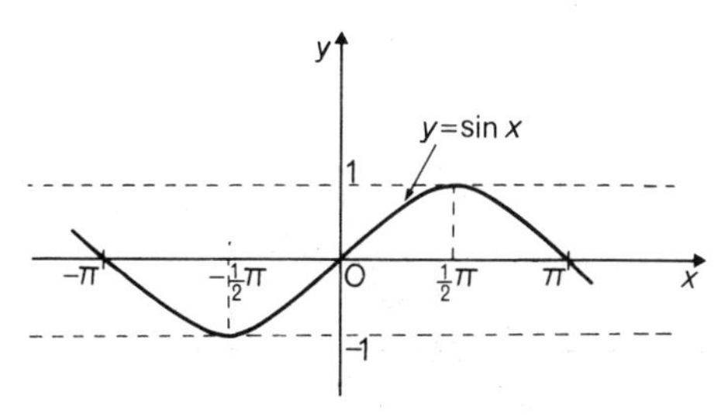

Inverse sine

We choose the simplest possible restriction of the sine function which provides a bijection (whose codomain is the image of the sine function), namely

$$\sin : [-\tfrac{1}{2}\pi, \tfrac{1}{2}\pi] \to [-1, 1].$$

This restriction is a bijection since

$$\frac{d}{dx}(\sin x) = \cos x > 0 \quad \text{on} \quad (-\tfrac{1}{2}\pi, \tfrac{1}{2}\pi).$$

Its inverse is a mapping: $[-1, 1] \to [-\frac{1}{2}\pi, \frac{1}{2}\pi]$ and is denoted by $\sin^{-1}$ or by arcsin and called the **inverse sine function**.

Since $\sin 0 = 0$, $\sin \frac{1}{6}\pi = \frac{1}{2}$, $\sin(-\frac{1}{3}\pi) = -\frac{1}{2}\sqrt{3}$, $\sin \frac{1}{2}\pi = 1$, we have $\sin^{-1} 0 = 0$, $\sin^{-1} \frac{1}{2} = \frac{1}{6}\pi$, $\sin^{-1}(-\frac{1}{2}\sqrt{3}) = -\frac{1}{3}\pi$, $\sin^{-1} 1 = \frac{1}{2}\pi$, etc.

Note that $\sin^{-1}(\sin \pi) = \sin^{-1}(0) = 0$, $\sin^{-1}(\sin \frac{5}{2}\pi) = \sin^{-1} 1 = \frac{1}{2}\pi$, etc.

If $x \in [-\frac{1}{2}\pi, \frac{1}{2}\pi]$ and $y = \sin x$, then $x = \sin^{-1} y \; (-1 \leqslant y \leqslant 1)$.

On $(-1, 1)$, $\dfrac{d}{dy}(\sin^{-1} y)$ exists (by (2.1)) and

$$\frac{d}{dy}(\sin^{-1} y) = \frac{1}{\dfrac{d}{dx}(\sin x)} = \frac{1}{\cos x} = \frac{1}{\sqrt{(1-\sin^2 x)}} = \frac{1}{\sqrt{(1-y^2)}},$$

since $\cos x > 0$.

$$\left[\text{In simpler notation, } y = \sin x \Rightarrow \frac{dy}{dx} = \cos x \Rightarrow \frac{dx}{dy} = \frac{1}{\cos x}, \text{ etc.}\right]$$

Summing up, using x-notation, we have:

$$\sin^{-1} \textit{ is a mapping}: [-1, 1] \to [-\tfrac{1}{2}\pi, \tfrac{1}{2}\pi];$$

it is differentiable on $(-1, 1)$ *and*

$$\frac{d}{dx}(\sin^{-1} x) = \frac{1}{\sqrt{(1-x^2)}}.$$

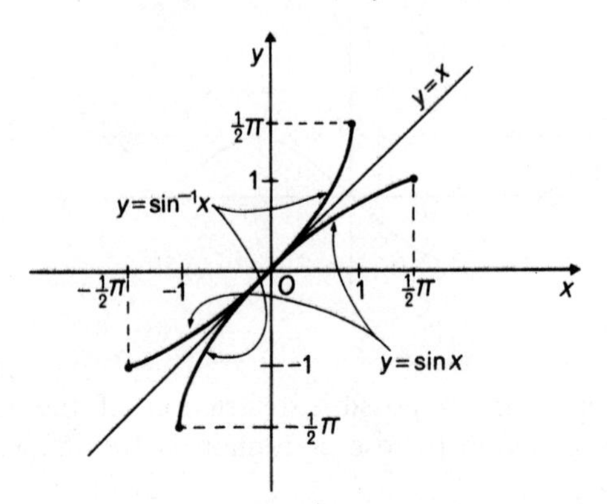

The graph $y = \sin^{-1} x$ is the reflection in the line $y = x$ of the restriction of $y = \sin x$ to $[-\frac{1}{2}\pi, \frac{1}{2}\pi]$. The gradient on

$$y = \sin^{-1} x \to \infty \quad \text{as} \quad x \to 1 \quad \text{and as} \quad x \to -1.$$

Note that $\sin^{-1}$ is an *odd* function, so that $\sin^{-1}(-x) = -\sin^{-1} x$.

Example 1. Differentiate (i) $\sin^{-1}(\sqrt{(1-x)})$, (ii) $(\sin^{-1} x)^2$.

(i) $\dfrac{d}{dx}\sin^{-1}(\sqrt{(1-x)}) = \dfrac{1}{\sqrt{(1-(1-x))}}\cdot\dfrac{d}{dx}(\sqrt{(1-x)}) = -\dfrac{1}{2\sqrt{(x-x^2)}}.$

(ii) $\dfrac{d}{dx}(\sin^{-1} x)^2 = \dfrac{2}{\sqrt{(1-x^2)}}\sin^{-1} x.$

Example 2. Evaluate

$$\sin^{-1}\frac{1}{\sqrt{5}} - \sin^{-1}\left(-\frac{1}{\sqrt{10}}\right).$$

If $\theta = \sin^{-1}\dfrac{1}{\sqrt{5}}$ and $\phi = \sin^{-1}\dfrac{1}{\sqrt{10}}$, then $\sin\theta = \dfrac{1}{\sqrt{5}}$, $\sin\phi = \dfrac{1}{\sqrt{10}}$,

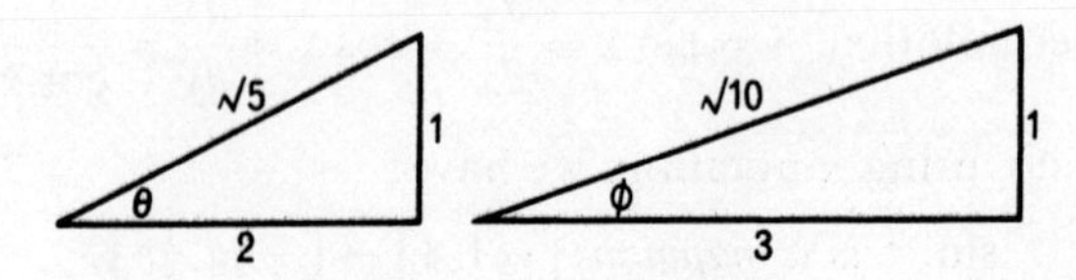

and we require $\theta+\phi$. Now

$$\sin(\theta+\phi) = \sin\theta\cos\phi+\cos\theta\sin\phi$$
$$= \frac{1}{\sqrt{5}}\cdot\frac{3}{\sqrt{10}}+\frac{2}{\sqrt{5}}\cdot\frac{1}{\sqrt{10}}$$
$$= \left(\frac{3}{5}+\frac{2}{5}\right)\frac{1}{\sqrt{2}} = \frac{1}{\sqrt{2}},$$

and so $$\tfrac{1}{4}\pi = \theta+\phi = \sin^{-1}\frac{1}{\sqrt{5}}-\sin^{-1}\left(-\frac{1}{\sqrt{10}}\right).$$

Inverse cosine

Here we choose the restriction $\cos:[0,\pi]\to[-1,1]$.

$$\frac{d}{dx}(\cos x) = -\sin x < 0 \text{ on } (0,\pi),$$

so that cos on $[0,\pi]$ is strictly decreasing and is a bijection. Its inverse is a mapping: $[-1,1]\to[0,\pi]$ and is denoted by $\cos^{-1}$ or arccos and called the **inverse cosine function**.

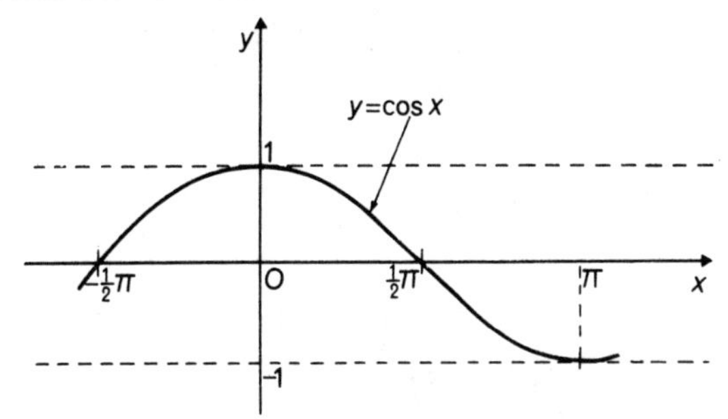

Since $\cos 0 = 1$, $\cos\frac{1}{6}\pi = \frac{1}{2}\sqrt{3}$, $\cos\frac{1}{2}\pi = 0$, $\cos\frac{2}{3}\pi = -\frac{1}{2}$, $\cos\pi = -1$, we have: $\cos^{-1}1 = 0$, $\cos^{-1}(\frac{1}{2}\sqrt{3}) = \frac{1}{6}\pi$, $\cos^{-1}0 = \frac{1}{2}\pi$, $\cos^{-1}(-\frac{1}{2}) = \frac{2}{3}\pi$, $\cos^{-1}(-1) = \pi$, etc.

Note that $\cos^{-1}(\cos(-\frac{1}{4}\pi)) = \cos^{-1}(\frac{1}{\sqrt{2}}) = \frac{1}{4}\pi$, $\cos^{-1}(\cos 2\pi) = \cos^{-1}1 = 0$, etc.

If $x\in[0,\pi]$ and $y = \cos x$, then $x = \cos^{-1}y$ $(-1\leqslant y\leqslant 1)$.

On $(-1,1)$, $\dfrac{d}{dy}(\cos^{-1}y)$ exists (by 2.1) and

$$\frac{d}{dy}(\cos^{-1}y) = \frac{1}{\dfrac{d}{dx}(\cos x)} = -\frac{1}{\sin x} = -\frac{1}{\sqrt{(1-\cos^2 x)}} = -\frac{1}{\sqrt{(1-y^2)}},$$

since $\sin x > 0$.

$$\left[\text{In simpler notation, } y = \cos x \Rightarrow \frac{dy}{dx} = -\sin x \Rightarrow \frac{dx}{dy} = -\frac{1}{\sin x}, \text{ etc.}\right]$$

Summing up, using x-notation, we have:

$\cos^{-1}$ *is a mapping*: $[-1, 1] \to [0, \pi]$;

it is differentiable on $(-1, 1)$ *and*

$$\frac{d}{dx}(\cos^{-1} x) = -\frac{1}{\sqrt{(1-x^2)}}.$$

The graph $y = \cos^{-1} x$ is the reflection in the line $y = x$ of the restriction to $[0, \pi]$ of $y = \cos x$.

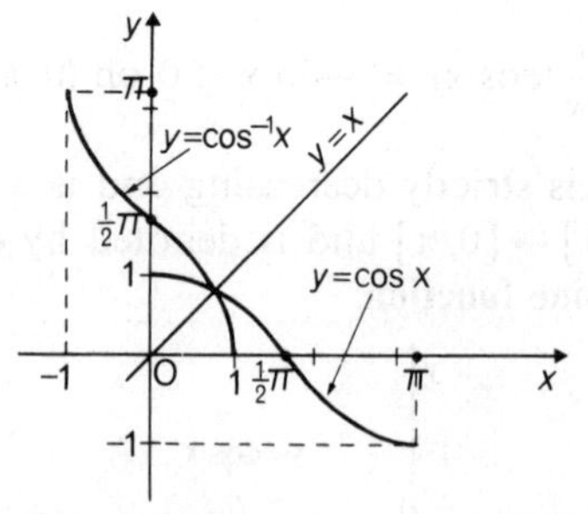

Example 3. Differentiate (i) $\cos^{-1}\dfrac{1}{x}$, (ii) $\cos^{-1}\left(\dfrac{x}{a}\right)$ (a constant).

(i) $$\frac{d}{dx}\cos^{-1}\frac{1}{x} = -\frac{1}{\sqrt{\left(1-\frac{1}{x^2}\right)}}\cdot\left(-\frac{1}{x^2}\right) = \frac{\sqrt{(x^2)}}{x^2\sqrt{(x^2-1)}} = \frac{1}{|x|\sqrt{(x^2-1)}}$$

$$= \frac{1}{x\sqrt{(x^2-1)}} \text{ if } x > 1 \text{ and } -\frac{1}{x\sqrt{(x^2-1)}} \text{ if } x < -1.$$

(ii) $$\frac{d}{dx}\cos^{-1}\left(\frac{x}{a}\right) = -\frac{1}{\sqrt{\left(1-\frac{x^2}{a^2}\right)}}\cdot\frac{1}{a} = -\frac{\sqrt{(a^2)}}{a\sqrt{(a^2-x^2)}} = -\frac{|a|}{a\sqrt{(a^2-x^2)}}$$

$$= -\frac{1}{\sqrt{(a^2-x^2)}} \text{ if } a > 0 \text{ and } \frac{1}{\sqrt{(a^2-x^2)}} \text{ if } a < 0.$$

Exercise. Show that

$$\frac{d}{dx}\sin^{-1}\left(\frac{x}{a}\right) = \frac{1}{\sqrt{(a^2-x^2)}} \text{ if } a > 0 \text{ and } -\frac{1}{\sqrt{(a^2-x^2)}} \text{ if } a < 0.$$

Example 4. Show that $\forall x \in [-1, 1]$, $\cos^{-1} x + \cos^{-1}(-x) = \pi$.

If $\quad f(x) = \cos^{-1} x + \cos^{-1}(-x)$, then, on $(-1, 1)$,

$$f'(x) = -\frac{1}{\sqrt{(1-x^2)}} - \frac{1}{\sqrt{(1-x^2)}} \cdot (-1) = 0.$$

Thus $f(x)$ is constant on $[-1, 1]$, $= f(0) = \pi$, for example; this proves the result.

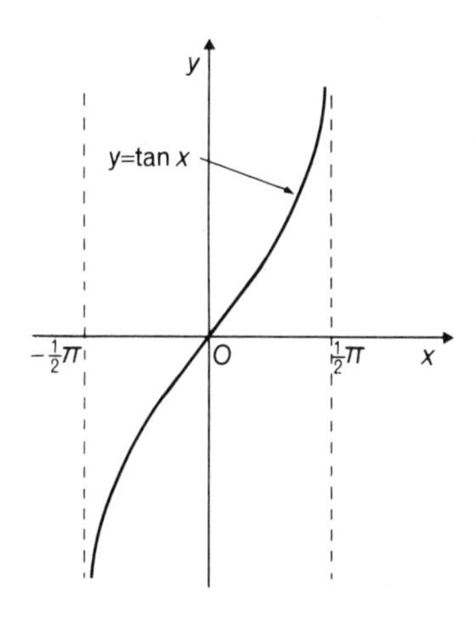

Inverse tangent

In this case we use the restriction

$$\tan : (-\tfrac{1}{2}\pi, \tfrac{1}{2}\pi) \to \mathbf{R}$$

to obtain a bijection.

$$\frac{d}{dx}(\tan x) = \sec^2 x > 0 \;\; \forall x \in (-\tfrac{1}{2}\pi, \tfrac{1}{2}\pi),$$

so that the restriction is a bijection. Its inverse is a mapping: $\mathbf{R} \to (-\frac{1}{2}\pi, \frac{1}{2}\pi)$ and is denoted by $\tan^{-1}$ or by arctan and called the **inverse tangent function.**

Since $\tan 0 = 0$, $\tan \frac{1}{4}\pi = 1$, $\tan(-\frac{1}{6}\pi) = -\frac{1}{\sqrt{3}}$, $\tan(-\frac{1}{3}\pi) = -\sqrt{3}$, we have: $\tan^{-1} 0 = 0$, $\tan^{-1} 1 = \frac{1}{4}\pi$, $\tan^{-1}(-\frac{1}{\sqrt{3}}) = -\frac{1}{6}\pi$, $\tan^{-1}(-\sqrt{3}) = -\frac{1}{3}\pi$, etc.

Note that $\tan^{-1}(\tan \pi) = \tan^{-1} 0 = 0$, $\tan^{-1}(\tan \frac{3}{4}\pi) = \tan^{-1}(-1) = -\frac{1}{4}\pi$, etc.

If $x \in (-\frac{1}{2}\pi, \frac{1}{2}\pi)$ and $y = \tan x$, then $x = \tan^{-1} y$ $(y \in \mathbf{R})$.

$$\frac{d}{dy}(\tan^{-1} y) = \frac{1}{\dfrac{d}{dx}(\tan x)} = \frac{1}{\sec^2 x} = \frac{1}{1+\tan^2 x} = \frac{1}{1+y^2}.$$

$$\left[\text{In simpler notation, } y = \tan x \Rightarrow \frac{dy}{dx} = \sec^2 x \Rightarrow \frac{dx}{dy} = \frac{1}{\sec^2 x}, \text{ etc.}\right]$$

Summing up, using x-notation, we have:

$\tan^{-1}$ *is a mapping*: $\mathbf{R} \to (-\frac{1}{2}\pi, \frac{1}{2}\pi)$;

it is differentiable on $\mathbf{R}$ *and*

$$\frac{d}{dx}(\tan^{-1} x) = \frac{1}{1+x^2}.$$

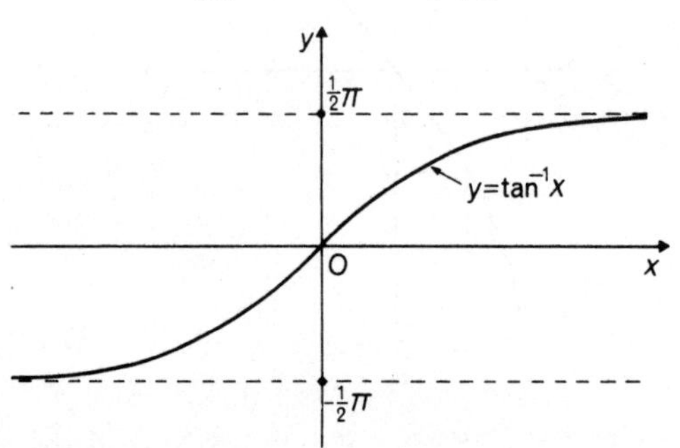

The graph $y = \tan^{-1} x$ is as shown, the reflection in $y = x$ of the restriction to $(-\frac{1}{2}\pi, \frac{1}{2}\pi)$ of $y = \tan x$.

The function $\tan^{-1}$ is an *odd* function, since $\tan^{-1}(-x) = -\tan^{-1} x$.

Note that $\tan^{-1} x \to \frac{1}{2}\pi$ as $x \to \infty$ and $\to -\frac{1}{2}\pi$ as $x \to -\infty$.

Example 5. Differentiate (i) $\tan^{-1}\left(\dfrac{x}{a}\right)$, a constant, (ii) $\tan^{-1}\sqrt{(x-1)}$.

(i) $$\frac{d}{dx}\tan^{-1}\frac{x}{a} = \frac{1}{1+\dfrac{x^2}{a^2}}\cdot\frac{1}{a} = \frac{a}{a^2+x^2};$$

(ii) $$\frac{d}{dx}\tan^{-1}\sqrt{(x-1)} = \frac{1}{1+(x-1)}\cdot\frac{1}{2\sqrt{(x-1)}} = \frac{1}{2x\sqrt{(x-1)}}.$$

Example 6. Evaluate $\tan^{-1} a + \tan^{-1} b, |a| < 1, |b| < 1$.

If $\theta = \tan^{-1} a$ and $\phi = \tan^{-1} b$, then $\tan\theta = a$ and $\tan\phi = b$. Thus

$$\tan(\theta+\phi) = \frac{\tan\theta+\tan\phi}{1-\tan\theta\tan\phi} = \frac{a+b}{1-ab},$$

and so $$\tan^{-1} a+\tan^{-1} b = \theta+\phi = \tan^{-1}\left(\frac{a+b}{1-ab}\right),$$

since $|a| < 1$, $|b| < 1$ imply that $-\frac{1}{2}\pi < \theta+\phi < \frac{1}{2}\pi$.

EXERCISE 4

1. Prove, by using $f'(x)$, that each of the following functions has an inverse, and find a formula for the inverse; in each case the codomain of the given function is the image of the given domain.

   (i) $f(x) = 2x+1$ on $\mathbf{R}$, (ii) $f(x) = x^2-1$ on $\mathbf{R}^+$,
   (iii) $f(x) = 3-2x-x^2$ on $[-1, \infty)$, (iv) $f(x) = x^2-4x+3$ on $(-\infty, 2]$,
   (v) $f(x) = \dfrac{2}{x^2+1}$ on $\mathbf{R}^+$, (vi) $f(x) = \dfrac{2x}{x^2+1}$ on $[-1, 1]$,
   (vii) $f(x) = \dfrac{x}{x^2-x+1}$ on $[-1, 1]$, (viii) $f(x) = \dfrac{x^2+3}{x+1}$ on $(-1, 1]$.

2. In this question g will denote the inverses obtained for (i) to (viii) in question **1**. Evaluate the following numbers [(i) $g'(5)$ means: evaluate the derivative at $y = 5$ of the inverse g arising in (i) of question **1**.]:

   (i) $g'(5)$, (ii) $g'(-\frac{1}{2})$, (iii) $g'(0)$, (iv) $g'(15)$,
   (v) $g'(\frac{1}{5})$, (vi) $g'(-\frac{4}{5})$, (vii) $g'(\frac{3}{7})$, (viii) $g'(\frac{49}{12})$.

3. Show that the restriction of the real function f defined by $f(x) = x^3-12x+5$ to the set $S = \{x \in \mathbf{R} : x \geqslant 2\}$ is a bijection from S to $f(S)$ and describe the inverse of this bijection. If g denotes this inverse, evaluate $g'(-4)$.

4. Find the following numbers:

   (i) $\sin^{-1}(\sin\frac{5}{4}\pi)$, (ii) $\sin^{-1}(\sin 2\pi)$, (iii) $\cos^{-1}(\cos(-\frac{1}{2}\pi))$,
   (iv) $\cos^{-1}(\cos 3\pi)$, (v) $\tan^{-1}(\tan\frac{2}{3}\pi)$, (vi) $\tan^{-1}(\tan\frac{5}{4}\pi)$,
   (vii) $\tan^{-1}\frac{1}{2}+\tan^{-1}\frac{1}{3}$, (viii) $\sin^{-1}(2\sqrt{\frac{3}{13}})-\sin^{-1}(\frac{1}{2}\sqrt{\frac{3}{13}})$.

5. Solve the equations (i) $\sin^{-1} x = \cos^{-1} x$, (ii) $\cos^{-1} x = \tan^{-1} x$.

6. Show that, $\forall x \in [-1, 1]$, $\sin^{-1} x+\cos^{-1} x = \frac{1}{2}\pi$.

7. Show that $\tan^{-1} x+\tan^{-1}\dfrac{1}{x} = \begin{cases} \frac{1}{2}\pi, & \forall x > 0, \\ -\frac{1}{2}\pi, & \forall x < 0. \end{cases}$

8. Find the equations of the following tangents:

   (i) tangent at point $x = \dfrac{1}{\sqrt{2}}$ on $y = \sin^{-1} x$;

   (ii) tangent at point $x = -\frac{3}{2}$ on $y = \cos^{-1}(x+1)$;

   (iii) tangent at point $x = 1$ on $y = \tan^{-1}\dfrac{1}{x}$.

9. Differentiate with respect to x:

(i) $\sin^{-1}(1-x)$, (ii) $\sin^{-1}\left(\dfrac{x-1}{x+1}\right)$, (iii) $\sin^{-1}\sqrt{(1-x^2)}$,

(iv) $x\sin^{-1}x^2$, (v) $\dfrac{1}{\sin^{-1}x}$, (vi) $\dfrac{\sin^{-1}2x}{\sin x}$,

(vii) $\cos^{-1}(3x+5)$, (viii) $\cos^{-1}\dfrac{1}{\sqrt{x}}$, (ix) $\cos^{-1}\sqrt{\left(\dfrac{1-x}{1+x}\right)}$,

(x) $\tan^{-1}\dfrac{1}{x}$, (xi) $\tan^{-1}(1-2x)$, (xii) $\tan^{-1}\sqrt{(1-x)}$,

(xiii) $\tan^{-1}(3\sin 2x)$, (xiv) $\tan^{-1}\dfrac{x}{\sqrt{(1-x^2)}}$, (xv) $\tan^{-1}\left(\dfrac{3x-x^3}{1-3x^2}\right)$.

10. Show that

$$V = \tan^{-1}\frac{x}{y}$$

is *harmonic*, i.e. satisfies the partial differential equation

$$\frac{\partial^2 V}{\partial x^2}+\frac{\partial^2 V}{\partial y^2}=0.$$

Integration, the logarithmic and exponential functions

1. The area problem and the definition of $\int_a^b f(x)dx$

Given a real function f defined on a subset of **R** containing the closed interval $[a, b]$ and such that $f(x) \geqslant 0 \ \forall x \in [a, b]$, an obvious problem is to define clearly what we mean by the area under the graph $y = f(x)$ as shown, and to determine the functions for which such a definition is possible. The method used goes back essentially to the Greeks.

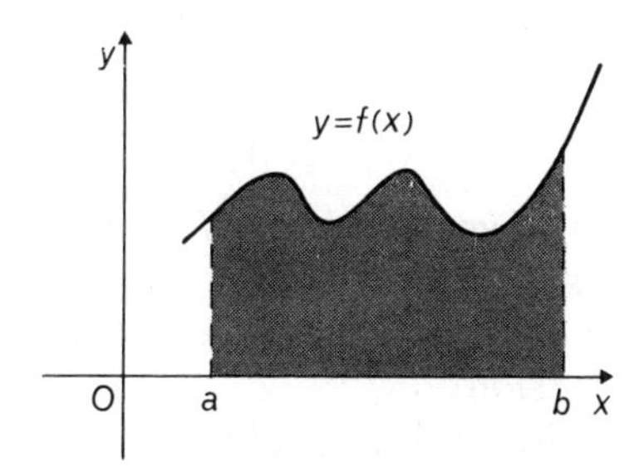

We start by supposing that f *is continuous on* $[a, b]$.

We divide up $[a, b]$ into n subintervals $[x_i, x_{i+1}]$ $(i = 0, \cdots, n-1)$ by $n+1$ points, $a = x_0 < x_1 < x_2 < \cdots < x_{n-1} < x_n = b$. The set of points

$c_0 \quad c_1 \quad c_{n-1}$

$x_0 = a \quad x_1 \quad x_2 \quad x_{n-1} \quad b = x_n \quad x$ (1.1)

$\{x_0 = a, x_1, \cdots, x_n = b\}$ is called a **partition** of $[a, b]$ or a **dissection** D of $[a, b]$;

$$[a, b] = \bigcup_{i=0}^{n-1} [x_i, x_{i+1}].$$

The number
$$\max_{0 \leqslant i \leqslant n-1} (x_{i+1} - x_i),$$

i.e. the largest length of a subinterval, will be denoted by $\| D \|$ and called the **norm of the dissection** D. By adding enough additional points to a dissection we can produce a new dissection with as small a norm as we please.

For each $i = 0, 1, \cdots, n-1$ we take a point c_i in $[x_i, x_{i+1}]$ as shown in (1.1) and form the sum

$$f(c_0)(x_1 - x_0) + f(c_1)(x_2 - x_1) + \cdots + f(c_{n-1})(x_n - x_{n-1}),$$

i.e.
$$\sum_{i=0}^{n-1} f(c_i)(x_{i+1} - x_i).$$

Such a sum is called a **Riemann sum for** f **over** $[a, b]$ (after the famous mathematician Riemann). Geometrically the sum represents, as shown in the diagram, a sum of areas of rectangles which is an approximation to the area under discussion.

Consider each subinterval $[x_i, x_{i+1}]$ $(i = 0, \cdots, n-1)$. Since f is continuous f has a maximum value and a minimum value on this subinterval, so that $\exists$ points s_i and t_i in $[x_i, x_{i+1}]$ such that

$$f(s_i) \leqslant f(x) \leqslant f(t_i), \ \forall x \in [x_i, x_{i+1}] \ (i = 0, \cdots, n-1).$$

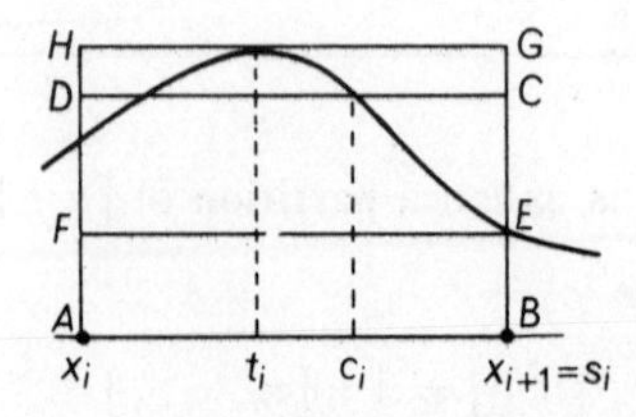

For the particular subinterval shown enlarged, we have: $s_i = x_{i+1}$ and t_i is as indicated. For any choice of c_i in $[x_i, x_{i+1}]$ the area $f(c_i)(x_{i+1} - x_i)$

of rectangle $ABCD$ lies between the area $f(s_i)(x_{i+1}-x_i)$ of rectangle $ABEF$ and the area $f(t_i)(x_{i+1}-x_i)$ of rectangle $ABGH$. Thus,

$$f(s_i)(x_{i+1}-x_i) \leqslant f(c_i)(x_{i+1}-x_i) \leqslant f(t_i)(x_{i+1}-x_i) \ (i = 0, \cdots, n-1),$$

and so $$\sum_{i=0}^{n-1} f(s_i)(x_{i+1}-x_i) \leqslant \sum_{i=0}^{n-1} f(c_i)(x_{i+1}-x_i) \leqslant \sum_{i=0}^{n-1} f(t_i)(x_{i+1}-x_i).$$

Consequently, with a given dissection D of $[a, b]$, every Riemann sum for a continuous function f lies between two particular Riemann sums,

namely $$\sum_{i=0}^{n-1} f(s_i)(x_{i+1}-x_i),$$

called the **lower Riemann sum**, and

$$\sum_{i=0}^{n-1} f(t_i)(x_{i+1}-x_i),$$

called the **upper Riemann sum**.

By taking dissections of $[a, b]$ of smaller and smaller norms we obtain Riemann sums which get closer and closer to the intuitive idea of the area under discussion; for example, by adding additional points to a given

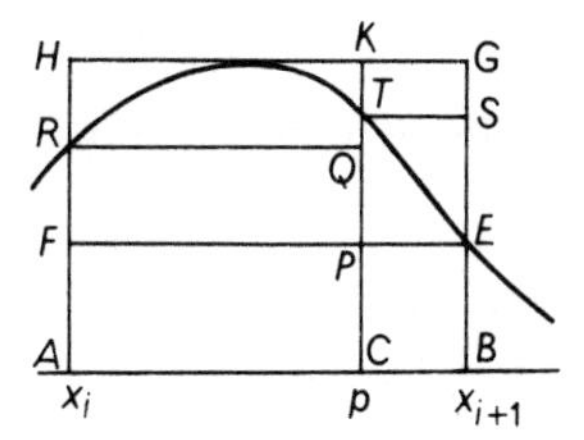

dissection, the new lower and upper Riemann sums are closer together. This is illustrated in the diagram by adding one point p to the subinterval $[x_i, x_{i+1}]$, so producing two subintervals $[x_i, p]$ and $[p, x_{i+1}]$ in the new dissection. The contribution to the old lower Riemann sum was the area of rectangle $ABEF$ which is less than area $ACQR$ + area $CBEP$, the contribution to the new lower Riemann sum; also area $ABGH$, the contribution to the old upper Riemann sum, is greater than area $ACKH$ + area $CBST$, the contribution to the new upper Riemann sum.

Analytically this suggests the following result:

$\exists$ a fixed real number I with the following property: Given any real number $\varepsilon > 0$ we can find $\delta > 0$ such that

$$\left| \sum_{i=0}^{n-1} f(c_i)(x_{i+1}-x_i) - I \right| < \varepsilon \ \textit{whenever} \ \| D \| < \delta,$$

and this is true for all choices of c_i $(i = 0, \cdots, n-1)$ *for a given dissection with* $\| D \| < \delta$.

We often express this statement in the following notation:

$$\lim_{\|D\| \to 0} \sum_{x=a}^{b} f(x)\Delta x = I,$$

where Δx denotes the length $x_{i+1} - x_i$ of a typical subinterval of a dissection, and where

$$\sum_{x=a}^{b} f(x)\Delta x$$

denotes the Riemann sum

$$\sum_{i=0}^{n-1} f(c_i)(x_{i+1} - x_i).$$

It can be proved that, if f is *continuous* on $[a, b]$, as we have supposed, then the number I exists; *we shall assume this result.* The measure of the area bounded by $y = f(x)$, the x-axis and the lines $x = a$ and $x = b$ is defined to be this number I ($f(x) \geqslant 0$ on $[a, b]$). As a further simplification of notation, we denote

$$\lim_{\|D\| \to 0} \sum_{x=a}^{b} f(x)\Delta x \quad \text{by} \quad \int_a^b f(x)dx,$$

and call $I = \displaystyle\int_a^b f(x)dx$ the **Riemann integral over** $[a, b]$ of the *continuous* function f.

So far, we have considered the case $f(x) \geqslant 0$ on $[a, b]$. *If f is continuous on* $[a, b]$ *and* $f(x) \leqslant 0$ $\forall x \in [a, b]$, then the Riemann sum

$$\sum_{i=0}^{n-1} f(c_i)(x_{i+1} - x_i) \text{ is } \leqslant 0, \qquad \text{and} \qquad \int_a^b f(x)dx \leqslant 0.$$

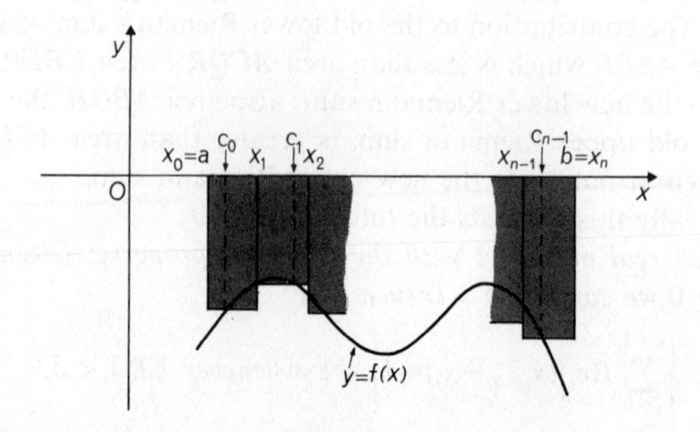

In this case the absolute value of the area between the curve $y = f(x)$, the x-axis and the lines $x = a$ and $x = b$ is

$$\left|\int_a^b f(x)dx\right| = -\int_a^b f(x)dx.$$

Note. If f is continuous on $[a, b]$ we can, by using Riemann sums, form

$$\int_a^b f(x)dx$$

even when $f(x)$ takes positive values *and* negative values on $[a, b]$; in the diagram,

$$\int_a^b f(x)dx = \int_a^c f(x)dx + \int_c^d f(x)dx + \int_d^b f(x)dx$$

$$= \text{area of region } A - \text{area of region } B + \text{area of region } C.$$

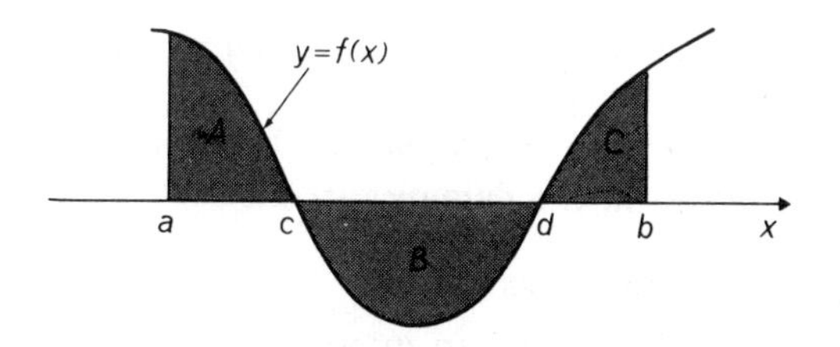

Some properties of the Riemann integral (which we use constantly and which can be proved from the definition).

(1) *If f and g are continuous on $[a, b]$, then*

$$\int_a^b \{f(x)+g(x)\}dx = \int_a^b f(x)dx + \int_a^b g(x)dx.$$

(2) *If f is continuous on $[a, b]$ and $k \in \mathbf{R}$, then*

$$\int_a^b kf(x)dx = k\int_a^b f(x)dx.$$

(3) *If f is continuous on $[a, b]$ and $a < c < b$, then*

$$\int_a^c f(x)dx + \int_c^b f(x)dx = \int_a^b f(x)dx.$$

(4)
$$\int_a^a f(x)dx = 0.$$

(5) *If* $a < b$, $\int_b^a f(x)dx$ *is defined to be* $-\int_a^b f(x)dx$.

(6) (i) $\int_a^b 0dx = 0$; (ii) $\int_a^b 1dx = b-a$; (iii) $\int_a^b kdx = k(b-a)$ $(k \in \mathbf{R})$.

(7) *If* $m \leqslant f(x) \leqslant M$ $\forall x \in [a, b]$, *then*

$$m(b-a) \leqslant \int_a^b f(x)dx \leqslant M(b-a).$$

(8) *If* f *and* g *are continuous on* $[a, b]$ *and* $f(x) \leqslant g(x)$ $\forall x \in [a, b]$, *then*

$$\int_a^b f(x)dx \leqslant \int_a^b g(x)dx.$$

(9) $$\left|\int_a^b f(x)dx\right| \leqslant \int_a^b |f(x)|\,dx, \quad (a \leqslant b).$$

(10) $$\int_a^b f(x)dx = \int_a^b f(t)dt = \int_a^b f(u)du = \cdots,$$

i.e. *the notation used for the variable on* $[a, b]$ *does not affect the value of the integral; we often call it a* **dummy variable**.

Integral of a piecewise continuous function

Let f be a function defined on an interval $[a, b]$, $a < b$. We say that f is **piecewise continuous** on $[a, b]$ if $\exists$ a partition

$$\{a = a_0 < a_1 < \cdots < a_n = b\} \text{ of } [a, b]$$

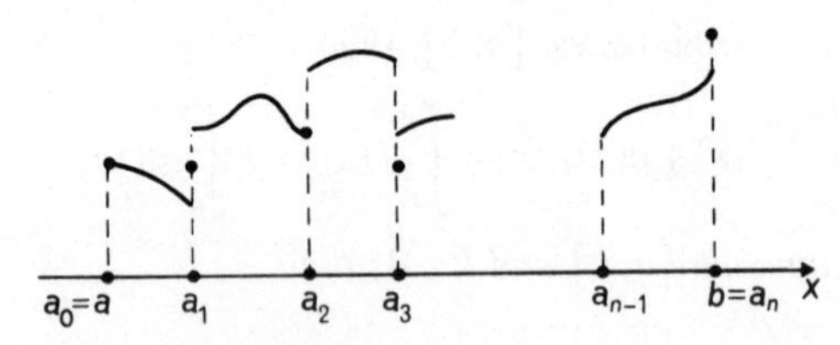

such that on each subinterval $[a_i, a_{i+1}]$ $(i = 0, \cdots, n-1)$ there is a continuous function f_i such that

$$f(x) = f_i(x) \quad \forall x \in (a_i, a_{i+1}).$$

We define $\int_a^b f(x)dx$ by:

$$\int_a^b f(x)dx = \int_{a_0=a}^{a_1} f_0(x)dx + \int_{a_1}^{a_2} f_1(x)dx + \cdots + \int_{a_{n-1}}^{a_n=b} f_{n-1}(x)dx.$$

This definition is possible since each term on the right-hand side exists. For example, if

$$f(x) = \begin{cases} x, & 0 \leqslant x < 1, \\ \frac{3}{2}, & x = 1, \\ 2, & 1 < x \leqslant 2, \end{cases}$$

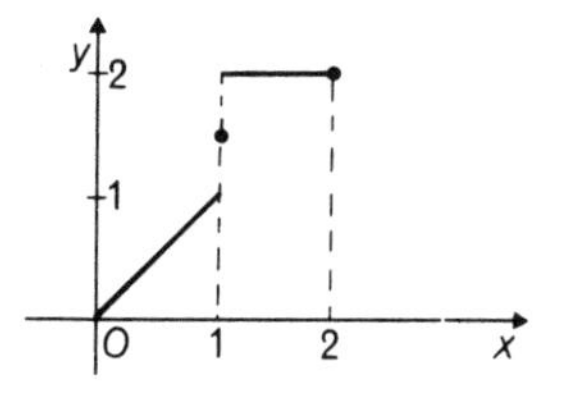

then
$$\int_0^2 f(x)dx = \int_0^1 xdx + \int_1^2 2dx.$$

Note. If $g(x) = \begin{cases} x, & 0 \leqslant x \leqslant 1 \\ 2, & 1 < x \leqslant 2, \end{cases}$ then $\int_0^2 g(x)dx = \int_0^2 f(x)dx$;

f and g differ at $x = 1$ only.

Example 1. *Evaluate* $\int_0^1 x^2dx$.

The number $\int_0^1 x^2dx$ exists since the function involved is continuous. We find this number by taking the very simple dissection

$$D = \left\{0, \frac{1}{n}, \frac{2}{n}, \cdots, \frac{n-1}{n}, \frac{n}{n} = 1\right\}$$

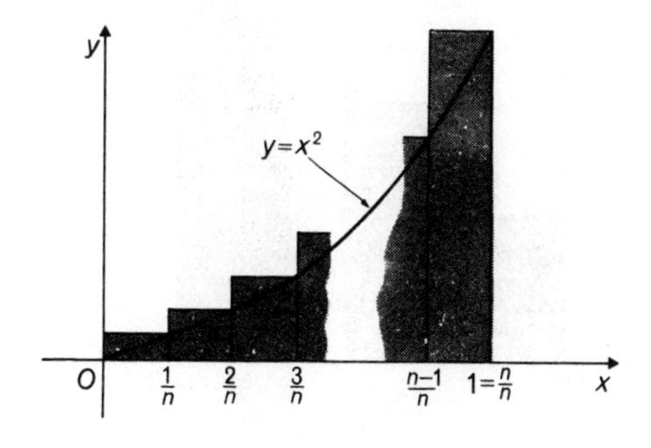

of [0, 1] into n equal parts, so that

$$\| D \| = \frac{1}{n},$$

and in $\left[\frac{i}{n}, \frac{i+1}{n}\right]$ choosing $c_i = \frac{i+1}{n}$ $(i = 0, \cdots, n-1)$.

The corresponding Riemann sum is

$$\sum_{i=0}^{n-1} \left(\frac{i+1}{n}\right)^2 \cdot \frac{1}{n} = \frac{1}{n^3}(1^2 + 2^2 + \cdots + n^2)$$

$$= \frac{1}{n^3} \cdot \frac{n}{6}(n+1)(2n+1)$$

$$= \frac{1}{3}\left(1 + \frac{1}{n}\right)\left(1 + \frac{1}{2n}\right) \to \frac{1}{3} \text{ as } \| D \| \to 0, \text{ i.e. as } n \to \infty.$$

Hence $\int_0^1 x^2 dx = \frac{1}{3}$.

Note. In the earlier notation,

$$s_i = \frac{i}{n} \quad \text{and} \quad t_i = \frac{i+1}{n} \quad \text{for each} \quad i = 0, \cdots, n-1;$$

since the function is strictly increasing on the interval.

Exercise. Show that $\int_0^1 x^3 \, dx = \frac{1}{4} \left[\text{using } \sum_{r=1}^{n} r^3 = \frac{1}{4} n^2(n+1)^2 \right]$.

Example 2. Try to evaluate $\int_0^1 \sqrt{(x)}dx$ *by the same method as that used in Example* 1.

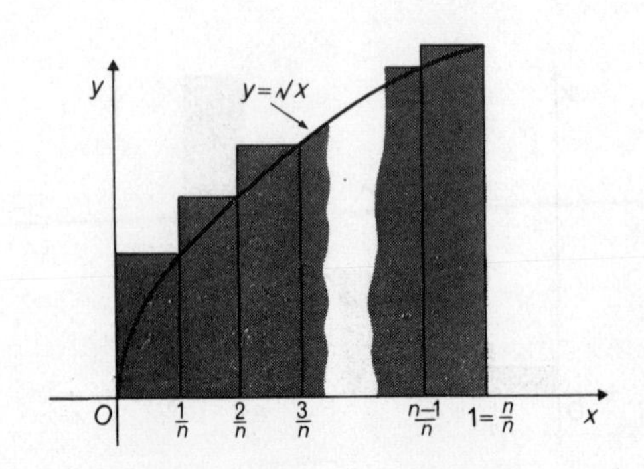

The corresponding Riemann sum is

$$\sum_{i=0}^{n-1} \sqrt{\left(\frac{i+1}{n}\right)} \cdot \frac{1}{n} = \frac{1}{n^{3/2}}(1+\sqrt{2}+\cdots+\sqrt{n}),$$

and
$$\int_0^1 \sqrt{(x)}dx = \lim_{n\to\infty} \left\{\frac{1+\sqrt{2}+\cdots+\sqrt{n}}{n^{3/2}}\right\}.$$

Unfortunately we cannot in this case so easily find a simple expression for the sum involved, and we are forced to look for another method of evaluating $\int_0^1 \sqrt{(x)}dx$, and in fact of evaluating almost all integrals that can be expressed in terms of elementary functions.

In fact almost all the tools that we need are now available. We obtain a suitable method by considering the function F defined by

$$F(x) = \int_c^x f(t)dt, \ \forall x \in [a, b], \tag{1.2}$$

where c is any chosen point in $[a, b]$ and f is *continuous* on $[a, b]$. F has been obtained from f by the "integration process"; we now show that from F we can recover f by differentiation.

Theorem 5.1

If F is defined by (1.2), *then $F'(x)$ exists and*

$$F'(x) = f(x).$$

Proof. *Case* (i), *$x \neq a$ and $x \neq b$:*

Take $x+h \in [a, b]$, $h \neq 0$ and consider

$$\frac{1}{h}\{F(x+h)-F(x)\}.$$

Now
$$F(x+h)-F(x) = \int_c^{x+h} f(t)dt - \int_c^x f(t)dt$$
$$= \int_c^{x+h} f(t)dt + \int_x^c f(t)dt = \int_x^{x+h} f(t)dt.$$

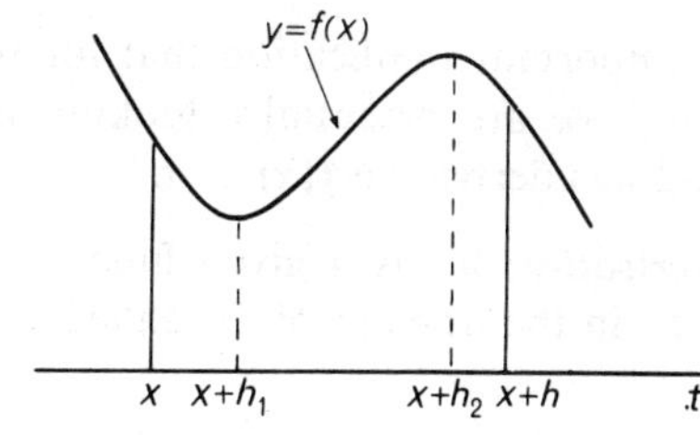

Suppose first that $h > 0$: Since f is continuous on $[x, x+h]$,

$$\exists x+h_1 \in [x, x+h] \quad \text{and} \quad x+h_2 \in [x, x+h]$$

such that $\qquad f(x+h_1) \leqslant f(t) \leqslant f(x+h_2), \ \forall t \in [x, x+h].$

Hence, by property (7) of the Riemann integral,

$$hf(x+h_1) \leqslant \int_x^{x+h} f(t)dt \leqslant hf(x+h_2),$$

and so $$f(x+h_1) \leqslant \frac{F(x+h)-F(x)}{h} \leqslant f(x+h_2),$$

where $0 \leqslant h_1 \leqslant h$, $0 \leqslant h_2 \leqslant h$ and $h > 0$.

Since f is continuous at x, $f(x+h_1) \to f(x)$ and $f(x+h_2) \to f(x)$ as $h \to 0$. Thus

$$\lim_{\substack{h \to 0 \\ (h>0)}} \frac{F(x+h)-F(x)}{h} \text{ exists, and } = f(x),$$

and so $F(x)$ *has right derivative* $f(x)$ *at* x.

Similarly, by examining the case $h < 0$, we can show that $F(x)$ has *left derivative* $f(x)$ *at* x.

Hence $F'(x)$ exists at x and $F'(x) = f(x)$, i.e.

$$\frac{d}{dx}\left\{\int_c^x f(t)dt\right\} = f(x).$$

Case (ii), $x = a$: If f is continuous at a, F has right derivative $f(a)$ at $x = a$.

Case (iii), $x = b$: If f is continuous at b, F has left derivative $f(b)$ at $x = b$.

The details for cases (ii) and (iii) are similar to those for case (i).

2. Antiderivatives

Theorem **5.1** has the important implication that for the integration of a continuous function f we are essentially looking for a function which is differentiable and has derivative $f(x)$ at x.

Definition of an antiderivative: If f is a given function, any function G such that $G'(x) = f(x)$ $\forall x$ in the domain of f is called an **antiderivative** of f.

From Theorem **5.1** it follows that, if f is continuous, then the function F defined by

$$F(x) = \int_c^x f(t)dt$$

is an antiderivative of f; in other words integration and differentiation are "in a certain sense" inverse operations. The phrase "in a certain sense" is used because, as the following theorem shows, an antiderivative is not quite unique.

Theorem 5.2

If G_1, G_2 are both antiderivatives of the continuous function f defined on an interval I, then

$$G_1(x) = G_2(x) + C, \ \forall x \in I,$$

where C is a constant.

Proof. Let $G = G_1 - G_2$, so that $G(x) = G_1(x) - G_2(x)$. Then

$$G'(x) = G_1'(x) - G_2'(x) = f(x) - f(x) = 0 \ \ \forall x \in I.$$

Consequently, from part (i) of Theorem **2.2**, G is a constant function, $G(x) = C$, say, on I, and the result follows.

Notation. If G is an antiderivative of f we often write

$$\int f(x)dx = G(x) + C,$$

and call $G(x)+C$ the **general indefinite integral** of f with respect to x; C is called the **constant of integration** and $f(x)$ is called the **integrand** of the integral $\int f(x)dx$. The notation $\int f(x)dx$ is a bad one since anti-differentiation is involved and not summation, but it is universally accepted.

Note. (i) $\displaystyle\int \{f(x)+g(x)\}dx = \int f(x)dx + \int g(x)dx,$

in the sense that, if F and G are antiderivatives of f and g, then $F+G$ is an antiderivative of $f+g$.

(ii) $\displaystyle\int kf(x)dx = k\int f(x)dx$ for any $k \in \mathbf{R}$.

$\int_a^b f(x)dx$ is often called a **definite integral**; a and b are called, respectively, the **lower** and **upper limits** of **integration**. The next result shows that antidifferentiation has in fact provided a method for determining

$$\int_a^b f(x)dx.$$

Theorem 5.3 (*The Fundamental Theorem of Calculus*).

If G is an antiderivative of f on $[a, b]$, where f is continuous on $[a, b]$, then

$$\int_a^b f(x)dx = G(b) - G(a).$$

Proof. The function F defined by

$$F(x) = \int_a^x f(t)dt$$

is an antiderivative of f on $[a, b]$. Hence, by Theorem **5.2**,

$$\forall x \in [a, b], \int_a^x f(t)dt = G(x) + C, \ C \text{ a constant;}$$

$$x = a \text{ gives:} \quad 0 = G(a) + C,$$

$$x = b \text{ gives:} \int_a^b f(t)dt = G(b) + C,$$

and so, $$\int_a^b f(t)dt = G(b) - G(a), \text{ as required.}$$

Notation. $G(b) - G(a)$ is usually denoted by $[G(x)]_a^b$ or by $G(x)|_a^b$.

Example 1. *Evaluate* $\int_0^1 \sqrt{(x)}dx$ (see Example 2 of Section **1**). An antiderivative of $\sqrt{x}$ is $\frac{2}{3}x^{3/2}$ since

$$\frac{d}{dx}(\tfrac{2}{3}x^{3/2}) = \sqrt{x}.$$

Thus $$\int_0^1 \sqrt{(x)}dx = [\tfrac{2}{3}x^{3/2}]_0^1 = \tfrac{2}{3}(1-0) = \tfrac{2}{3}.$$

From the attempt at evaluating this integral in Section **1** it follows

that
$$\lim_{n\to\infty}\left\{\frac{1+\sqrt{2}+\cdots+\sqrt{n}}{n^{3/2}}\right\}=\frac{2}{3}.$$

By examining the standard derivatives already obtained we can now draw up a useful *table of some antiderivatives*:

$F'(x)=f(x)$	$\int f(x)dx = F(x)+C$
(1) If $n\neq -1$, $\dfrac{d}{dx}\left(\dfrac{x^{n+1}}{n+1}\right)=x^n$	If $n\neq -1$, $\int x^n dx=\dfrac{x^{n+1}}{n+1}+C$
(2) If $n\neq -1$, $a\neq 0$ $\dfrac{d}{dx}\dfrac{(ax+b)^{n+1}}{(n+1)a}=(ax+b)^n$	If $n\neq -1$, $a\neq 0$ $\int(ax+b)^n dx=\dfrac{(ax+b)^{n+1}}{(n+1)a}+C$
(3) $\dfrac{d}{dx}(\sin x)=\cos x$	$\int\cos x\,dx=\sin x+C$
(4) $\dfrac{d}{dx}(-\cos x)=\sin x$	$\int\sin x\,dx=-\cos x+C$
(5) $\dfrac{d}{dx}(\tan x)=\sec^2 x$	$\int\dfrac{dx}{\cos^2 x}=\int\sec^2 x\,dx=\tan x+C$
(6) $\dfrac{d}{dx}(-\cot x)=\operatorname{cosec}^2 x$	$\int\dfrac{dx}{\sin^2 x}=\int\operatorname{cosec}^2 x\,dx=-\cot x+C$
(7) $\dfrac{d}{dx}(\sec x)=\sec x\tan x$	$\int\dfrac{\sin x}{\cos^2 x}dx=\int\sec x\tan x\,dx=\sec x+C$
(8) $\dfrac{d}{dx}(-\operatorname{cosec} x)=\operatorname{cosec} x\cot x$	$\int\dfrac{\cos x}{\sin^2 x}dx=\int\operatorname{cosec} x\cot x\,dx$ $=-\operatorname{cosec} x+C$
(9) If $a\neq 0$, $\dfrac{d}{dx}\left\{\sin^{-1}\dfrac{x}{\lvert a\rvert}\right\}=\dfrac{1}{\sqrt{(a^2-x^2)}}$ and $\dfrac{d}{dx}\left\{-\cos^{-1}\dfrac{x}{\lvert a\rvert}\right\}=\dfrac{1}{\sqrt{(a^2-x^2)}}$	If $a\neq 0$, $\int\dfrac{dx}{\sqrt{(a^2-x^2)}}=\sin^{-1}\dfrac{x}{\lvert a\rvert}+C$ $=-\cos^{-1}\dfrac{x}{\lvert a\rvert}+C$ [For (9) we take $a>0$ if possible.]
(10) If $a\neq 0$, $\dfrac{d}{dx}\left\{\dfrac{1}{a}\tan^{-1}\dfrac{x}{a}\right\}=\dfrac{1}{a^2+x^2}$	If $a\neq 0$, $\int\dfrac{dx}{a^2+x^2}=\dfrac{1}{a}\tan^{-1}\dfrac{x}{a}+C$

3. Improper integrals

Before tackling some problems we introduce some slight extensions of the conditions under which $\int_a^b f(x)dx$ was defined. In the first place we took f to be continuous on the finite closed interval $[a, b]$. We now show that we can often give a meaning to $\int_a^b f(x)dx$ when either f ceases to be continuous at a (or at b) or when the interval of integration is infinite.

I. *Trouble at* $x = a$: Let f be continuous on $a < x \leqslant b$ $(a < b)$; then f is continuous on each interval of the form $[a+h, b]$, where $h > 0$ and $a+h < b$. Thus

$$\int_{a+h}^{b} f(x)dx \text{ exists, for all such } h.$$

If F is an antiderivative of f on $(a, b]$, then

$$\int_{a+h}^{b} f(x)dx = F(b) - F(a+h).$$

If $\lim\limits_{\substack{h\to 0\\(h>0)}} F(a+h)$ exists, we say that the **improper integral** $\int_a^b f(x)dx$ exists or converges and define it by:

$$\int_a^b f(x)dx = F(b) - \lim_{\substack{h\to 0\\(h>0)}} F(a+h);$$

usually contracted to $\Big[F(x)\Big]_a^b$.

Example 1. Consider (i) $\int_0^4 \frac{dx}{\sqrt{x}}$, (ii) $\int_0^4 \frac{dx}{x^{3/2}}$.

In each case the integrand is not defined at $x = 0$ but is continuous on $[h, 4]$ for each h satisfying $0 < h < 4$.

(i) $\int_h^4 \frac{dx}{\sqrt{x}} = \Big[2\sqrt{x}\Big]_h^4 = 4 - 2\sqrt{h} \to 4$ as $h \to 0$ $(h > 0)$.

Thus $\int_0^4 \frac{dx}{\sqrt{x}}$ exists, and $= 4$.

[We often write: $\int_0^4 \frac{dx}{\sqrt{x}} = \Big[2\sqrt{x}\Big]_0^4 = 4$, meaning that $\sqrt{x} \to 0$ as $x \to 0$ $(x > 0)$.]

(ii) $\displaystyle\int_h^4 \frac{dx}{x^{3/2}} = \left[-\frac{2}{\sqrt{x}}\right]_h^4 = -1 + \frac{2}{\sqrt{h}} \nrightarrow$ a limit as $h \to 0$ $(h > 0)$.

Consequently $\displaystyle\int_0^4 \frac{dx}{x^{3/2}}$ does not converge.

II. *Trouble at* $x = b$: Following the pattern in **I**, if f is continuous on $[a, b)$, $a < b$, we say that

$$\int_a^b f(x)dx$$

exists (or is convergent) and has the value

$$\lim_{\substack{h \to 0 \\ (h > 0)}} \int_a^{b-h} f(x)dx,$$

if this limit exists.

Example 2. Consider (i) $\displaystyle\int_0^1 \frac{dx}{(1-x)^{5/4}}$, (ii) $\displaystyle\int_0^1 \frac{dx}{\sqrt{(1-x^2)}}$.

$$\text{(i)} \int_0^{1-h} \frac{dx}{(1-x)^{5/4}} = \left[\frac{4}{(1-x)^{1/4}}\right]_0^{1-h}$$

$$= \frac{4}{h^{1/4}} - 4 \nrightarrow \text{a limit as } h \to 0 \ (h > 0); \text{ thus}$$

$\displaystyle\int_0^1 \frac{dx}{(1-x)^{5/4}}$ does not exist.

$$\text{(ii)} \int_0^{1-h} \frac{dx}{\sqrt{(1-x^2)}} = \left[\sin^{-1} x\right]_0^{1-h} = \sin^{-1}(1-h) - \sin^{-1} 0$$

$$= \sin^{-1}(1-h) \to \sin^{-1} 1 \text{ as } h \to 0 \ (h > 0).$$

Hence $\displaystyle\int_0^1 \frac{dx}{\sqrt{(1-x^2)}}$ exists and $= \frac{1}{2}\pi$.

[In practice this work is written as:

$$\int_0^1 \frac{dx}{\sqrt{(1-x^2)}} = \left[\sin^{-1} x\right]_0^1 = \sin^{-1} 1 - \sin^{-1} 0 = \tfrac{1}{2}\pi.]$$

III. *Upper limit* ∞: Let f be continuous on $[a, \infty)$; then

$$\int_a^p f(x)dx \text{ exists for every } p > a.$$

If F is an antiderivative of f, then

$$\int_a^p f(x)dx = F(p) - F(a).$$

We define
$$\int_a^\infty f(x)dx = \lim_{p\to\infty} F(p) - F(a),$$

provided $\lim_{p\to\infty} F(p)$ exists. When it does exist, we say that the **improper integral** $\int_a^\infty f(x)dx$ exists or converges, and write

$$\int_a^\infty f(x)dx = \lim_{p\to\infty}\int_a^p f(x)dx.$$

Example 3. Consider (i) $\displaystyle\int_1^\infty \frac{dx}{x^4}$, (ii) $\displaystyle\int_0^\infty \frac{dx}{1+x^2}$, (iii) $\displaystyle\int_1^\infty \frac{dx}{\sqrt{x}}$.

(i) $\displaystyle\int_1^p \frac{dx}{x^4} = \left[-\frac{1}{3x^3}\right]_1^p = \frac{1}{3} - \frac{1}{3p^3} \to \frac{1}{3}$ as $p\to\infty$; thus

$$\int_1^\infty \frac{dx}{x^4} \text{ exists, and } = \frac{1}{3}.$$

[We often write: $\displaystyle\int_1^\infty \frac{dx}{x^4} = \left[-\frac{1}{3x^3}\right]_1^\infty = \frac{1}{3}$,

noting that $\dfrac{1}{x^3}\to 0$ as $x\to\infty$.]

(ii) Here

$$\int_0^p \frac{dx}{1+x^2} = \left[\tan^{-1}x\right]_0^p = \tan^{-1}p - \tan^{-1}0 = \tan^{-1}p$$

$$\to \tfrac{1}{2}\pi \text{ as } p\to\infty,$$

so that
$$\int_0^\infty \frac{dx}{1+x^2} \text{ exists, and } = \tfrac{1}{2}\pi.$$

[Again we usually simplify this to:

$\displaystyle\int_0^\infty \frac{dx}{1+x^2} = \left[\tan^{-1}x\right]_0^\infty = \tfrac{1}{2}\pi$ (since $\tan^{-1}x\to\tfrac{1}{2}\pi$ as $x\to\infty$).]

(iii) $\displaystyle\int_1^p \frac{dx}{\sqrt{x}} = \left[2\sqrt{x}\right]_1^p = 2\sqrt{p}-2 \not\to$ a limit as $p\to\infty$, and so $\int_1^{\infty} \frac{dx}{\sqrt{x}}$ is not convergent.

IV. *Lower limit* $-\infty$: Here $\int_{-\infty}^{b} f(x)dx$ is said to exist or be convergent if $\lim_{q\to\infty} \int_{-q}^{b} f(x)dx$ exists and we define:

$$\int_{-\infty}^{b} f(x)dx = \lim_{q\to\infty} \int_{-q}^{b} f(x)dx.$$

Note. More than one of the troubles listed in **I** to **IV** may occur in the same integral; e.g.

$$\int_{-\infty}^{\infty} f(x)dx \text{ exists and is defined to be } \lim_{\substack{p\to\infty\\ q\to\infty}} \int_{-q}^{p} f(x)dx,$$

where $p \to \infty$ and $q \to \infty$ independently, provided this limit exists.

Example 4. Consider $\int_{-\infty}^{\infty} \frac{dx}{1+x^2}$.

$$\int_{-q}^{p} \frac{dx}{1+x^2} = \Big[\tan^{-1} x\Big]_{-q}^{p} = \tan^{-1} p - \tan^{-1}(-q) = \tan^{-1} p + \tan^{-1} q$$

$$\to \tfrac{1}{2}\pi + \tfrac{1}{2}\pi \text{ as } p, q \to \infty,$$

and so $\int_{-\infty}^{\infty} \frac{dx}{1+x^2}$ exists, and $= \pi$.

4. Some worked examples

1. A function f is defined on the interval $[0, 4]$ by

$$f(x) = \begin{cases} 3x+1, & 0 \leqslant x \leqslant 1, \\ 2/x^2, & 1 < x \leqslant 4. \end{cases}$$

Sketch the graph of f and evaluate $\int_0^4 f(x)dx$.

$$\begin{aligned} \int_0^4 f(x)dx &= \int_0^1 (3x+1)dx + \int_1^4 \frac{2}{x^2}dx \\ &= \left[\frac{3}{2}x^2 + x\right]_0^1 + 2\left[-\frac{1}{x}\right]_1^4 \\ &= \frac{5}{2} + 2\left(1 - \frac{1}{4}\right) = 4. \end{aligned}$$

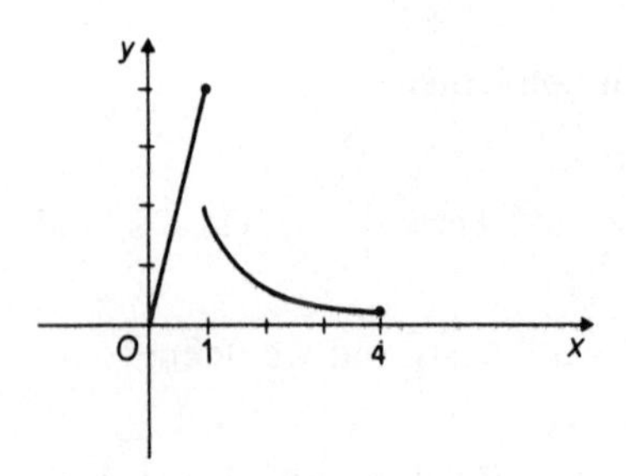

2. Evaluate

$$\lim_{n\to\infty} n\left\{\frac{1}{n^2+1^2}+\frac{1}{n^2+2^2}+\cdots+\frac{1}{n^2+n^2}\right\},$$

by interpreting this as a definite integral.

$$\lim_{n\to\infty} n\left\{\frac{1}{n^2+1^2}+\frac{1}{n^2+2^2}+\cdots+\frac{1}{n^2+n^2}\right\}=\lim_{n\to\infty}\sum_{r=1}^{n}\frac{1}{1+\left(\dfrac{r}{n}\right)^2}\cdot\frac{1}{n}$$

$$=\int_0^1\frac{dx}{1+x^2}=\Big[\tan^{-1}x\Big]_0^1=\frac{1}{4}\pi.$$

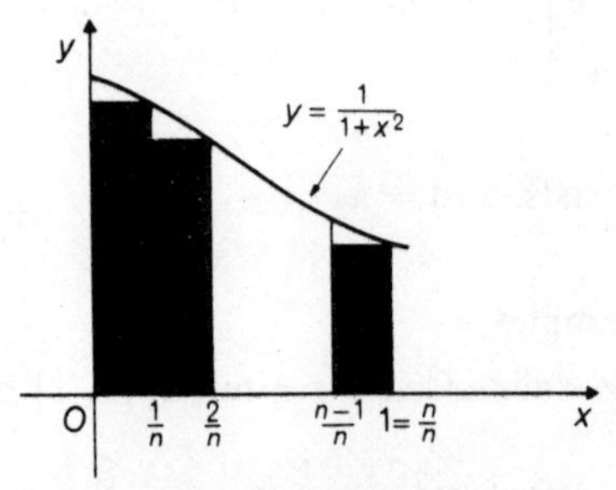

3. Integrate (i.e. find the general indefinite integrals):

(i) $\dfrac{1}{9+4x^2}$, (ii) $\dfrac{1}{(1-3x)^2}$, (iii) $\dfrac{1}{\sqrt{(1-4x^2)}}$, (iv) $\dfrac{1}{5-2x+x^2}$.

(i) $$\int\frac{dx}{9+4x^2}=\frac{1}{4}\int\frac{dx}{\frac{9}{4}+x^2}=\frac{1}{4}\cdot\frac{1}{3/2}\tan^{-1}\frac{x}{3/2}+C$$

$$=\frac{1}{6}\tan^{-1}\frac{2}{3}x+C;$$

(ii) $$\int\frac{dx}{(1-3x)^2}=\frac{1}{(-1)}\cdot\frac{1}{(-3)}(1-3x)^{-1}+C=\frac{1}{3(1-3x)}+C;$$

(iii) $$\int \frac{dx}{\sqrt{(1-4x^2)}} = \frac{1}{2}\int \frac{dx}{\sqrt{((\frac{1}{2})^2 - x^2)}} = \frac{1}{2}\sin^{-1} 2x + C;$$

(iv) $$\int \frac{dx}{5-2x+x^2} = \int \frac{dx}{4+(x-1)^2} = \frac{1}{2}\tan^{-1}\frac{x-1}{2} + C.$$

4. Evaluate (i) $\displaystyle\int_{-1}^{\sqrt{3}} \frac{dx}{1+x^2}$, (ii) $\displaystyle\int_{\frac{1}{4}\sqrt{3}}^{3/4} \frac{dx}{\sqrt{(9-4x^2)}}$.

(i) $$\int_{-1}^{\sqrt{3}} \frac{dx}{1+x^2} = \Big[\tan^{-1} x\Big]_{-1}^{\sqrt{3}} = \tan^{-1}\sqrt{3} - \tan^{-1}(-1)$$

$$= \frac{1}{3}\pi - \left(-\frac{1}{4}\pi\right) = \frac{7}{12}\pi;$$

(ii) $$\int_{\frac{1}{4}\sqrt{3}}^{3/4} \frac{dx}{\sqrt{(9-4x^2)}} = \frac{1}{2}\int_{\frac{1}{4}\sqrt{3}}^{3/4} \frac{dx}{\sqrt{((\frac{3}{2})^2 - x^2)}} = \frac{1}{2}\left[\sin^{-1}\left(\frac{2}{3}x\right)\right]_{\frac{1}{4}\sqrt{3}}^{3/4}$$

$$= \frac{1}{2}\left[\sin^{-1}\frac{1}{2} - \sin^{-1}\frac{1}{2\sqrt{3}}\right] = \frac{1}{12}\pi - \frac{1}{2}\sin^{-1}\frac{1}{2\sqrt{3}}.$$

5. Discuss the convergence of the integrals

(i) $\displaystyle\int_{-a}^{a} \frac{dx}{\sqrt{(a^2-x^2)}}$ $(a > 0)$, (ii) $\displaystyle\int_{0}^{\infty} \frac{x^2}{x^2+1}\,dx$.

(i) Using simplified notation,

$$\int_{-a}^{a} \frac{dx}{\sqrt{(a^2-x^2)}} = \left[\sin^{-1}\frac{x}{a}\right]_{-a}^{a} \ (a > 0) = \sin^{-1} 1 - \sin^{-1}(-1) = \pi,$$

and the integral exists.

(ii) $$\int_0^p \frac{x^2}{x^2+1}\,dx = \int_0^p \left(1 - \frac{1}{x^2+1}\right)dx = \Big[x - \tan^{-1} x\Big]_0^p$$

$$= p - \tan^{-1} p \nrightarrow \text{a limit as } p \to \infty,$$

and so the integral is not convergent.

6. Find the area of the finite region bounded by the x-axis and the parabola $y = 5-4x-x^2$.

$$y = 9-(x+2)^2 \leqslant 9 \text{ and } = 9 \Leftrightarrow x = -2;$$

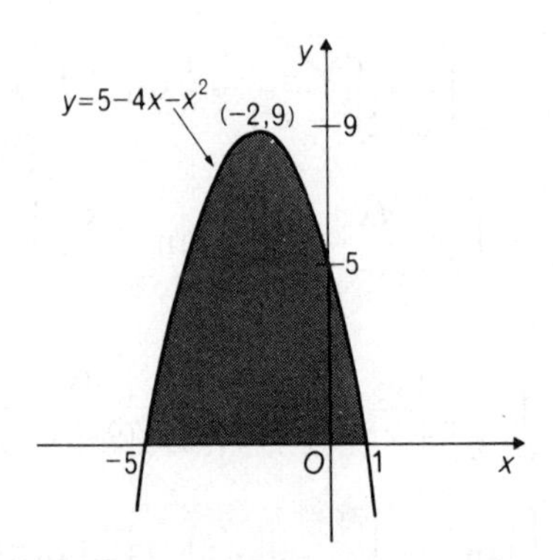

also the parabola meets the x-axis where $x = -5, 1$. The required area is

$$\int_{-5}^{1} (5-4x-x^2)dx = \left[5x-2x^2-\frac{1}{3}x^3\right]_{-5}^{1}$$
$$= \left(5-2-\frac{1}{3}\right)-\left(-25-50+\frac{125}{3}\right) = 36.$$

7. [*Use of symmetry for definite integrals and areas.*]

(i) Evaluate $\int_0^{\frac{1}{2}\pi} \sin x\, dx$ and $\int_0^{\pi} \sin x\, dx$ and explain graphically why $\int_0^{\pi} \sin x\, dx = 2\int_0^{\frac{1}{2}\pi} \sin x\, dx$. $\left[\text{Check that } \int_0^{\frac{1}{2}\pi} \sin x\, dx = 1.\right]$

(ii) Show that $\int_0^{\pi} \cos x\, dx = 0$ and explain this result graphically.

(iii) If f is an *even* continuous function, then, by symmetry,

$$\int_{-a}^{a} f(x)dx = 2\int_0^{a} f(x)dx \quad (a > 0);$$

e.g.
$$\int_{-1}^{1} x^4\, dx = 2\int_0^{1} x^4\, dx.$$

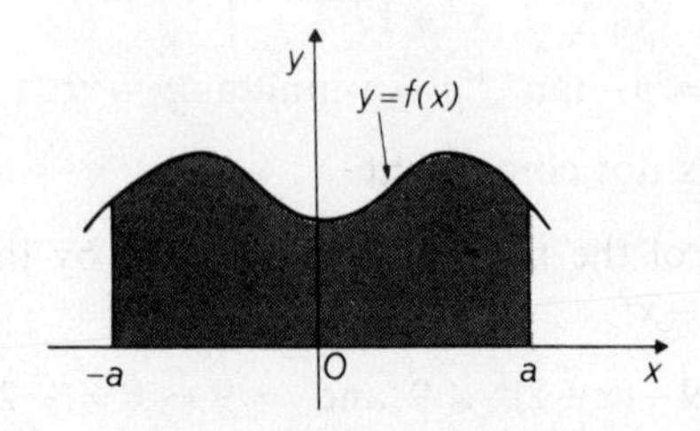

(iv) If the *odd* continuous function f is defined on the interval $[-a, a]$ $(a > 0)$, then, by the half-turn symmetry about the origin O,

$$\int_{-a}^{a} f(x)dx = 0;$$

e.g.

$$\int_{-1}^{1} x^3\, dx = 0.$$

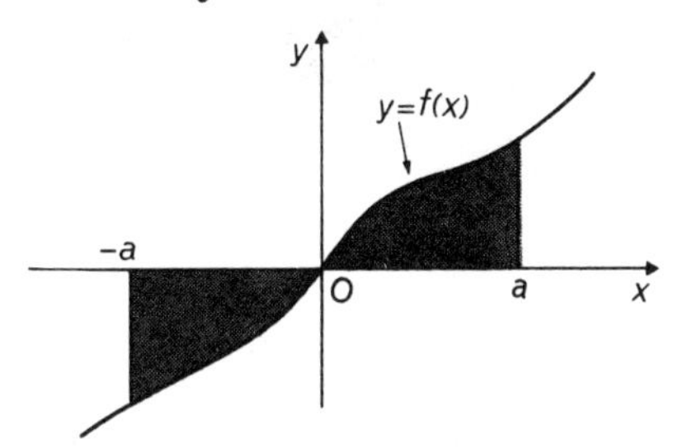

8. By interpreting $\int_0^1 \sqrt{(1-x^2)}dx$ as the measure of the area of a region, evaluate the integral.

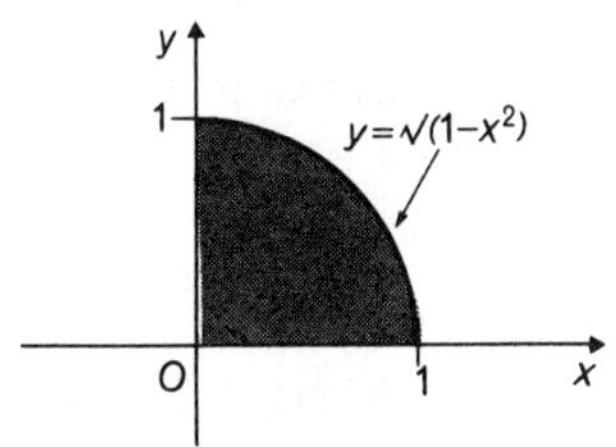

The integral is the area of the quarter-circular region shown, and so equals $\frac{1}{4}\pi$.

9. Evaluate $\dfrac{d}{dx}\displaystyle\int_{g(x)}^{h(x)} f(t)dt$, where f is continuous and g and h are differentiable.

If F is an antiderivative of f, so that $F'(t) = f(t)$, then

$$\begin{aligned}\frac{d}{dx}\int_{g(x)}^{h(x)} f(t)dt &= \frac{d}{dx}\{[F(t)]_{g(x)}^{h(x)}\} = \frac{d}{dx}\{F(h(x)) - F(g(x))\} \\ &= F'(h(x)).h'(x) - F'(g(x)).g'(x) \\ &= f(h(x)).h'(x) - f(g(x)).g'(x).\end{aligned}$$

For example,
$$\frac{d}{dx}\int_x^{x^2} \frac{dt}{1+t^2} = \frac{2x}{1+x^4} - \frac{1}{1+x^2}.$$

5. The logarithmic and exponential functions

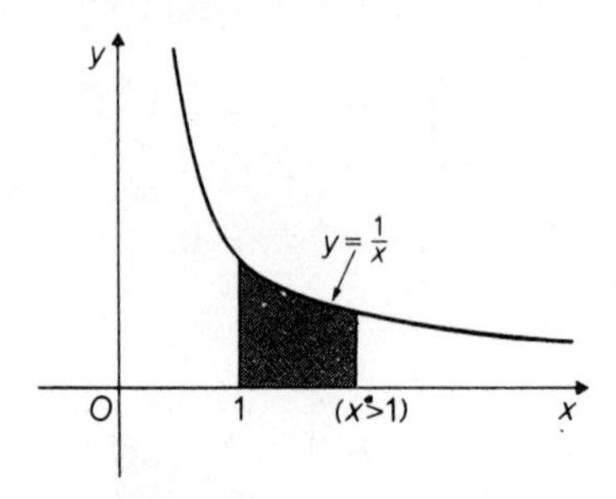

Let f be the function defined for $x > 0$ by

$$f(x) = \frac{1}{x}.$$

For given $x > 0$, f is continuous on the closed interval determined by x and 1. Thus

$$F(x) = \int_1^x \frac{dt}{t}$$

exists for each $x > 0$ and so defines a function F of x on $x > 0$. Also F is differentiable on $x > 0$ and

$$F'(x) = \frac{1}{x}; \quad \text{since} \quad \frac{1}{x} > 0 \text{ for } x > 0,$$

F is strictly increasing on $x > 0$. The function F is continuous on $x > 0$ since it is differentiable there. Since

$$F''(x) = -\frac{1}{x^2} < 0 \ \forall x > 0,$$

the graph $y = F(x)$ is concave down on $x > 0$.

We denote F by $\log_e$ (a meaning for e is given later in Section **6** of this chapter) or simply by log or by ln (especially when dealing with numerical work) and call it the **logarithmic function**. Thus

$$\log_e x (= \log x = \ln x) = \int_1^x \frac{dt}{t} \ (x > 0), \text{ and } \frac{d}{dx}(\log_e x) = \frac{1}{x}.$$

Clearly, for $x > 1$, $\log_e x > 0$, and represents the area shown;

$$\log_e 1 = \int_1^1 \frac{dt}{t} = 0; \quad \text{for} \quad 0 < x < 1, \quad \log_e x = \int_1^x \frac{dt}{t} = -\int_x^1 \frac{dt}{t} < 0.$$

Basic properties of $\log_e$ (to simplify notation we shall mainly use log for $\log_e$).

I. *If* $a > 0$ *and* $b > 0$, *then*

$$\log(ab) = \log a + \log b. \tag{5.1}$$

Proof. Define a function H on $x > 0$ by

$$H(x) = \log(ax) - \log a - \log x$$

Then
$$H'(x) = \frac{a}{ax} - \frac{1}{x} = 0$$

for $x > 0$, and so $H(x)$ is constant on $x > 0$; thus $H(x) = H(1) = 0$, for $x > 0$. Consequently $H(b) = 0$, so that

$$\log(ab) = \log a + \log b.$$

II. *If* $b > 0$, *then*

$$\log\left(\frac{1}{b}\right) = -\log b. \tag{5.2}$$

Proof. From (5.1), if $b > 0$, then

$$\log\left(b \cdot \frac{1}{b}\right) = \log b + \log\left(\frac{1}{b}\right),$$

and so
$$0 = \log 1 = \log b + \log\left(\frac{1}{b}\right);$$

from this (5.2) follows.

III. *If* $a > 0$ *and* $b > 0$, then

$$\log\left(\frac{a}{b}\right) = \log a - \log b. \tag{5.3}$$

Proof. $\log\left(\frac{a}{b}\right) = \log\left(a \cdot \frac{1}{b}\right) = \log a + \log\left(\frac{1}{b}\right) = \log a - \log b,$

using the results (5.1) and (5.2).

IV. *If* $a > 0$ *and* $\frac{p}{q} \in \mathbf{Q}$, *then*

$$\log(a^{p/q}) = \frac{p}{q}\log a. \tag{5.4}$$

Proof. The result (5.4) can be established by the following four steps:

(i) Show, by induction, that $\forall n \in \mathbf{N}$, $\log(a^n) = n \log a$. [The details are left to the reader; note that $a^{n+1} = a^n . a$.]

(ii) Show that, $\forall n \in \mathbf{N}$, $\log(a^{-n}) = (-n)\log a$.

$$\left[\log(a^{-n}) = \log\left(\frac{1}{a^n}\right) = -\log(a^n) = -(n \log a) = (-n)\log a.\right]$$

(iii) Show that, if $q \in \mathbf{N}$, then

$$\log(a^{1/q}) = \frac{1}{q}\log a.$$

$$\left[\log(a^{1/q})^q = q \log a^{1/q} \Rightarrow \log a = q \log a^{1/q} \Rightarrow \log a^{1/q} = \frac{1}{q}\log a.\right]$$

(iv) *Final step*: Take $\frac{p}{q} \in \mathbf{Q}$, $q \in \mathbf{N}$; then

$$\log(a^{p/q}) = \log((a^{1/q})^p) = p \log(a^{1/q}) = \frac{p}{q}\log a.$$

V. *The image of* log *is* **R**. We show that

$$\log x \to \infty \text{ as } x \to \infty \quad \text{and} \quad \log x \to -\infty \text{ as } x \to 0 \ (x > 0).$$

The required result will then follow by the intermediate-value theorem which ensures that a continuous function takes every value between any two of its values.

We first note that log is strictly increasing on $x > 0$. Also, since $\log 1 = 0$, it follows that

$$\log 2 = \int_1^2 \frac{dt}{t} > 0.$$

If M is any positive real number, we can choose a positive integer n such that

$$n > \frac{M}{\log 2} > 0,$$

i.e. such that $\log(2^n) > M$. Since M can be chosen arbitrarily, it follows that $\log x$ is unbounded as $x \to \infty$, i.e. $\log x \to \infty$ as $x \to \infty$.

Similarly, we can choose a positive integer k such that

$$-k < -\frac{M}{\log 2} < 0,$$

i.e. such that $$\log\left(\frac{1}{2^k}\right) < -M.$$

Since M can be chosen arbitrarily, it follows that $\log x \to -\infty$ as $x \to 0$ $(x > 0)$.

VI. *The graph of* $\log : \mathbf{R}^+ - \{0\} \to \mathbf{R}$. Combining the facts now obtained for log we see that its graph is of the following shape:

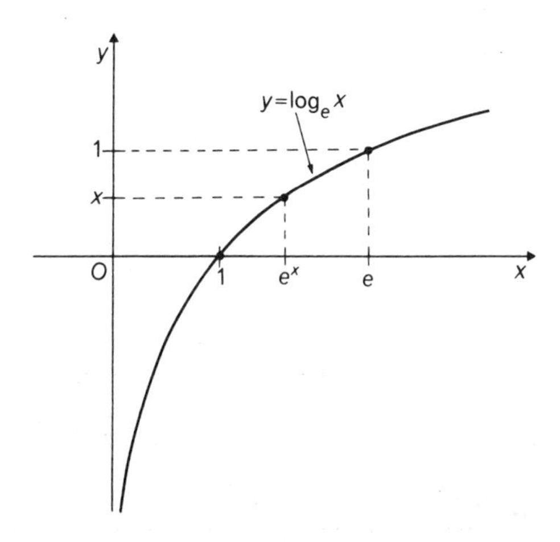

For actual coordinates of points we require later information.

The exponential function exp

Since $\log : \mathbf{R}^+ - \{0\} \to \mathbf{R}$ is strictly increasing on its domain

$$\mathbf{R}^+ - \{0\} = \{x \in \mathbf{R} : x > 0\},$$

it is a bijection and so has an inverse mapping: $\mathbf{R} \to \mathbf{R}^+ - \{0\}$. This inverse mapping is denoted by exp and called the **exponential function** to base e, its value at $x \in \mathbf{R}$ being denoted by $\exp x$ or e^x. Thus

$$y = \log_e x \Leftrightarrow x = \exp y = e^y; \tag{5.5}$$

also, since $\log_e$ and exp are inverse functions,

$$\forall x \in \mathbf{R},\ \log_e(\exp x) = x, \quad \text{i.e. } \log_e(e^x) = x, \tag{5.6}$$

and $$\forall x \in \mathbf{R}^+ - \{0\},\ \exp(\log_e x) = x, \quad \text{i.e. } e^{\log_e x} = x. \tag{5.7}$$

The statement (5.6) shows that e^x is the real number (>0) mapped by $\log_e$ to x (see the graph of $\log_e$); in particular, e is the unique positive real number mapped by $\log_e$ to 1, and this gives a meaning to the number

e introduced earlier. The statement (5.5), i.e. $y = \log_e x \Leftrightarrow x = e^y$, agrees with the usual elementary notion of a logarithm to a given **base**; e.g. for logarithms to base 10, $y = \log_{10} x \Leftrightarrow x = 10^y$.

The graph $y = e^x$ of the exponential function is the reflection of $y = \log_e x$ in the line $y = x$.

$$\frac{d}{dy}(e^y) = \frac{1}{\dfrac{d}{dx}(\log_e x)}, \text{ where } y = \log_e x \text{ and } x = e^y,$$

$$= \frac{1}{1/x}$$

$$= x = e^y.$$

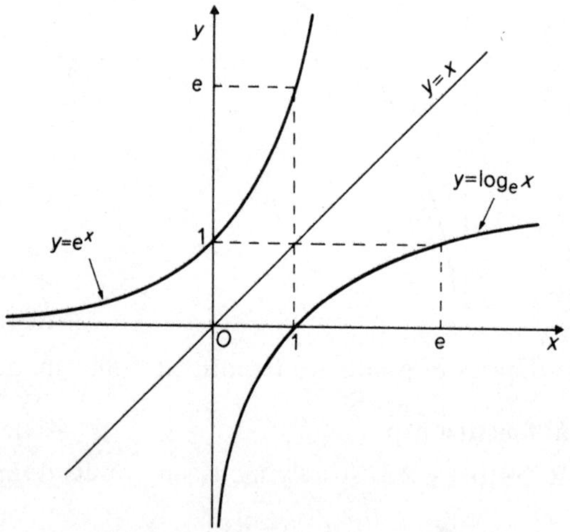

Thus, $$\forall x \in \mathbf{R}, \ \frac{d}{dx}(e^x) = e^x,$$

and, by antidifferentiation,

$$\int e^x \, dx = e^x + C.$$

exp is strictly increasing and differentiable (and so continuous) on $\mathbf{R}$;

$$e^0 = 1, \quad e^x > 1 \ \forall x > 0, \quad 0 < e^x < 1 \ \forall x < 0.$$

Basic properties of exp

These correspond to and can be deduced from the corresponding properties of $\log_e$.

I. $\forall x, y \in \mathbf{R}, e^{x+y} = e^x . e^y$.

Proof. $\log(e^{x+y}) = x + y = \log(e^x) + \log(e^y) = \log(e^x . e^y)$, and so

$$e^{x+y} = e^x . e^y, \text{ since log is injective.}$$

II. $\forall y \in \mathbf{R}, \dfrac{1}{e^y} = e^{-y}$.

III. $\forall x, y \in \mathbf{R}, \dfrac{e^x}{e^y} = e^{x-y}$

IV. $\forall x \in \mathbf{R}, \dfrac{p}{q} \in \mathbf{Q}, (e^x)^{p/q} = e^{(p/q)x}$

V. $e^x \to \infty$ as $x \to \infty$; $e^x \to 0$ as $x \to -\infty$.

The proofs of **II** to **V** are left to the reader.

Some limits involving log **and** exp

$$\text{(i) } \lim_{x\to\infty} x\,e^{-x} = 0, \quad \text{(ii) } \lim_{x\to\infty} \frac{\log x}{x} = 0, \quad \text{(iii) } \lim_{x\to 0} x \log x = 0.$$

Proof of (i). Since $\dfrac{d}{dx}(x\,e^{-x}) = e^{-x} - x\,e^{-x} = -(x-1)e^{-x} < 0$ for $x > 1$,

it follows that $x\,e^{-x}$ is strictly decreasing for $x > 1$.

Since $e > 1$, we can write $e = 1 + h$ where $h > 0$.

If n is a large positive integer,

$$\frac{n}{e^n} = \frac{n}{(1+h)^n} = \frac{n}{1 + nh + \frac{1}{2}n(n-1)h^2 + b}, \quad \text{where } b \geqslant 0,$$

$$= \frac{1}{\dfrac{1}{n} + h + n\left(\frac{1}{2} - \dfrac{1}{2n}\right)h^2 + \dfrac{b}{n}}$$

$$< \frac{1}{\frac{1}{4}nh^2} \quad (n \geqslant 2)$$

$$\to 0 \text{ as } n \to \infty.$$

Thus $\qquad x\,e^{-x} \to 0$ as $x \to \infty$.

Proof of (ii). $\displaystyle \lim_{x\to\infty} \frac{\log x}{x} = \lim_{y\to\infty} \frac{y}{e^y} \; (x = e^y) = 0.$

Proof of (iii). $\displaystyle \lim_{x\to 0} x \log x = \lim_{y\to\infty} (-y\,e^{-y}) \; (x = e^{-y}) = 0.$

In fact, if k is any fixed positive integer,

$$\lim_{x\to\infty} x^k e^{-x} = 0, \quad \lim_{x\to\infty} \frac{\log x}{x^k} = 0, \quad \text{and} \quad \lim_{x\to 0} x^k \log x = 0.$$

Before listing some worked examples we add to the table of standard derivatives and antiderivatives inserted at the end of Section **2**.

$F'(x) = f(x)$	$\int f(x)dx = F(x)+C$
(11) If $a \in \mathbf{R}$, $\frac{d}{dx}(e^{ax}) = a\,e^{ax}$	If $a \neq 0$, $\int e^{ax}\,dx = \frac{1}{a}\,e^{ax}+C$
(12) If $x > 0$, $\frac{d}{dx}(\log x) = \frac{1}{x}$ If $x < 0$, $\frac{d}{dx}(\log(-x)) = \frac{(-1)}{(-x)} = \frac{1}{x}$	$\int \frac{1}{x}\,dx = \log\lvert x\rvert + C$
(13) If $ax+b > 0$, $\frac{d}{dx}\log(ax+b) = \frac{a}{ax+b}$ If $ax+b < 0$, $\frac{d}{dx}\log(-ax-b) = \frac{a}{ax+b}$	$\int \frac{dx}{ax+b}$ $= \frac{1}{a}\log\lvert ax+b\rvert + C,\ a \neq 0$
(14) If $x+\sqrt{(x^2+k)} > 0$, $\frac{d}{dx}\log\{x+\sqrt{(x^2+k)}\} = \dfrac{1+\dfrac{x}{\sqrt{(x^2+k)}}}{x+\sqrt{(x^2+k)}} = \frac{1}{\sqrt{(x^2+k)}}$ If $x+\sqrt{(x^2+k)} < 0$, $\frac{d}{dx}\log\{-x-\sqrt{(x^2+k)}\} = \dfrac{-1-\dfrac{x}{\sqrt{(x^2+k)}}}{-x-\sqrt{(x^2+k)}} = \frac{1}{\sqrt{(x^2+k)}}$	$\int \frac{dx}{\sqrt{(x^2+k)}}$ $= \log\lvert x+\sqrt{(x^2+k)}\rvert + C$ [$\lvert\cdots\rvert$ is not required when $k > 0$.]

Example 1. Show that, $\forall x \geqslant 1$, $\log x < x$.
If $f(x) = x - \log x$, then

$$f'(x) = 1 - \frac{1}{x} = \frac{x-1}{x} > 0 \text{ for } x > 1.$$

Thus f is strictly increasing on $[1, \infty)$, so that $f(x) \geqslant f(1)$ for $x \geqslant 1$. Since $f(1) = 1$, it follows that $x - \log x \geqslant 1 > 0$ for $x \geqslant 1$.

Example 2. Find the critical points and the x-coordinates of the points of inflexion on the curve $y = x^2 e^{-x}$, and sketch the curve.

$$\frac{dy}{dx} = (2x - x^2)e^{-x} \quad \text{and} \quad \frac{d^2y}{dx^2} = (2-4x+x^2)e^{-x}.$$

The critical points are $(0, 0)$ and $\left(2, \frac{4}{e^2}\left(\doteqdot \frac{4}{7}\right)\right)$.

For $x = 0$,
$$\frac{d^2y}{dx^2} = 2 > 0$$

and so $(0, 0)$ is a local minimum point; for $x = 2$,
$$\frac{d^2y}{dx^2} \text{ is } -\text{ve} \quad \text{and so} \quad \left(2, \frac{4}{e^2}\right)$$

is a local maximum point.

$\frac{d^2y}{dx^2} = 0 \Leftrightarrow x^2 - 4x + 2 = 0 \Leftrightarrow x = 2 - \sqrt{2}$ (α, say) or $x = 2 + \sqrt{2}$ (β, say).

Then
$$\frac{d^2y}{dx^2} = (x-\alpha)(x-\beta)e^{-x}, \ \alpha < \beta;$$

clearly $\frac{d^2y}{dx^2}$ is > 0 for $x < \alpha$, < 0 for $\alpha < x < \beta$ and > 0 for $x > \beta$. Consequently concavity changes direction at $x = \alpha$ and at $x = \beta$, and these are the x-coordinates of the points of inflexion on the curve.

Since $x^2 e^{-x} \to \infty$ as $x \to -\infty$ and $x^2 e^{-x} \to 0$ as $x \to \infty$, it follows that the curve is as shown.

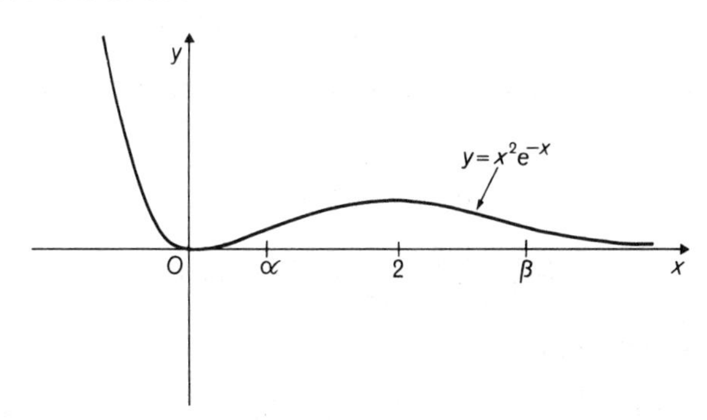

Example 3. A radioactive material disintegrates at a rate proportional to the amount present. At the end of 60 seconds 20% of the original amount has disintegrated. When will half the original amount have disintegrated?

If $f(t)$ denotes the amount (in a given unit of measure) of the material present at time t seconds, then

$$\frac{d}{dt}(f(t)) = -kf(t), \tag{5.8}$$

where k is a positive constant, is the mathematical model for the physical statement about the disintegration of the material. [Note that the coefficient of $f(t)$ on the right-hand side of (5.8), $-k$, is negative, since the rate of change of $f(t)$ with respect to t is negative.]

From (5.8),
$$\frac{1}{f(t)}\frac{d}{dt}(f(t)) = -k,$$

and so
$$\frac{d}{dt}(\log f(t)) = -k.$$

On integrating both sides with respect to t, we have

$$\log f(t) = -kt+C, \text{ with } C \text{ a constant.}$$

If $f(0)$ denotes the amount present initially, i.e. at $t = 0$, then

$$\log f(0) = 0+C = C.$$

Consequently,
$$\log f(t)-\log f(0) = -kt,$$

$$\log\frac{f(t)}{f(0)} = -kt,$$

and so
$$f(t) = f(0) . e^{-kt}. \tag{5.9}$$

Since $f(60) = \frac{4}{5}f(0)$, equation (5.9) gives

$$\tfrac{4}{5} = e^{-60k}, \quad \text{so that} \quad e^{-k} = (\tfrac{4}{5})^{1/60}. \tag{5.10}$$

If $f(t) = \frac{1}{2}f(0)$ when $t = T$, then T is given, from (5.9) and (5.10), by:

$$\tfrac{1}{2} = e^{-kT} = (\tfrac{4}{5})^{T/60},$$

and so by:
$$\log\tfrac{1}{2} = \frac{T}{60}\log\tfrac{4}{5},$$

i.e. by
$$T = 60\frac{\log 2}{\log 5-\log 4} \doteqdot 186{\cdot}4 \text{ seconds.}$$

Example 4. Integrate

$$\text{(i)}\ \frac{1}{2x+3}, \quad \text{(ii)}\ \frac{1}{-2x-3}, \quad \text{(iii)}\ \frac{1}{\sqrt{(4x^2-1)}}.$$

(i) $\displaystyle\int\frac{dx}{2x+3} = \tfrac{1}{2}.\log|2x+3|+C;$

[*Note.* $\displaystyle\int\frac{dx}{2x+3} = \tfrac{1}{2}\int\frac{dx}{x+\frac{3}{2}} = \tfrac{1}{2}\log|x+\tfrac{3}{2}|+C$; the antiderivatives $\tfrac{1}{2}\log|2x+3|$ and $\tfrac{1}{2}\log|x+\tfrac{3}{2}|$ differ by the constant $\tfrac{1}{2}\log 2.$]

(ii) $\displaystyle\int \frac{dx}{-2x-3} = -\int \frac{dx}{2x+3} = -\tfrac{1}{2}\log|2x+3|+C;$

(iii) $\displaystyle\int \frac{dx}{\sqrt{(4x^2-1)}} = \tfrac{1}{2}\int \frac{dx}{\sqrt{(x^2-\frac{1}{4})}} = \tfrac{1}{2}\log|x+\sqrt{(x^2-\tfrac{1}{4})}|+C.$

Example 5. Evaluate

$$\text{(i)} \int_{-3}^{-2} \frac{dx}{3x+4}, \quad \text{(ii)} \int_0^1 \frac{x}{x+1}\,dx, \quad \text{(iii)} \int_{-1}^{1} \frac{dx}{\sqrt{(x^2+2x+2)}}.$$

(i) $\displaystyle\int_{-3}^{-2} \frac{dx}{3x+4} = [\tfrac{1}{3}\log|3x+4|]_{-3}^{-2} = \tfrac{1}{3}(\log 2-\log 5) = \tfrac{1}{3}\log(\tfrac{2}{5});$

(ii) $\displaystyle\int_0^1 \frac{x}{x+1}\,dx = \int_0^1 \left(1-\frac{1}{x+1}\right)dx = [x-\log|x+1|]_0^1 = 1-\log 2;$

(iii) $\displaystyle\int_{-1}^{1} \frac{dx}{\sqrt{(x^2+2x+2)}} = \int_{-1}^{1} \frac{dx}{\sqrt{\{(x+1)^2+1\}}}$

$$= [\log|(x+1)+\sqrt{\{(x+1)^2+1\}}|]_{-1}^{1},$$

(check by differentiation), $= \log(2+\sqrt{5}).$

Note. **Logarithmic differentiation** (suggested by Example 3). If

$$y = f_1(x).f_2(x), \quad \text{where} \quad f_1(x) > 0 \text{ and } f_2(x) > 0, \tag{5.11}$$

then $\qquad \log y = \log(f_1(x).f_2(x)) = \log f_1(x)+\log f_2(x),$

and, differentiating with respect to x,

$$\frac{1}{y}\frac{dy}{dx} = \frac{1}{f_1(x)}\frac{df_1(x)}{dx}+\frac{1}{f_2(x)}\frac{df_2(x)}{dx}. \tag{5.12}$$

In terms of differentials we obtain

$$\frac{dy}{y} = \frac{df_1}{f_1(x)}+\frac{df_2}{f_2(x)}. \tag{5.13}$$

The equations (5.12) and (5.13) are said to have been obtained from (5.11) by **logarithmic differentiation**. The process is very useful when percentage errors have to be obtained. Suppose that Δf_1, Δf_2, Δy, where y, f_1, f_2 are connected by (5.11), are errors in $f_1(x)$, $f_2(x)$ and y due to a small error $\Delta x (= dx)$ in x. If the percentage errors in $f_1(x)$ and $f_2(x)$ are at most 1% and 2%, respectively, what can be said about the error in y?

At the end of Section **2** of Chapter 1 we saw that, for small Δx,

$\Delta f_1 \doteqdot df_1$, $\Delta f_2 \doteqdot df_2$ and $\Delta y \doteqdot dy$. The percentage errors in $f_1(x)$, $f_2(x)$, y are

$$\frac{\Delta f_1}{f_1} \times 100, \ \frac{\Delta f_2}{f_2} \times 100, \ \frac{\Delta y}{y} \times 100;$$

so, by (5.13), the percentage error in y is $\doteqdot$ percentage error in $f_1(x)$ + percentage error in $f_2(x)$, and so 3% (approximately) at most.

6. The general exponential function to base a **(**a^x, $a > 0$**)**

Let $a > 0$ be given; for $x \in \mathbf{R}$ we define a^x by:

$$a^x = \exp(x \log_e a) = e^{x \log_e a}, \text{ so that } \log_e a^x = x \log_e a. \qquad (6.1)$$

For example,

$$a^{\sqrt{2}} = e^{\sqrt{2} \log a} \ (a > 0) \text{ (we usually omit } e \text{ from } \log_e); \ 3^\pi = e^{\pi \log 3};$$

$$(\sqrt{3})^{\sqrt{2}} = e^{\sqrt{2} \log(\sqrt{3})} = e^{\frac{1}{2}\sqrt{2} \log 3}; \ (e^{\sqrt{2}})^\pi = e^{\pi \log e^{\sqrt{2}}} = e^{\pi\sqrt{2}}.$$

Some properties of a^x:

I. $a^{x+y} = a^x . a^y$.

$[a^{x+y} = e^{(x+y)\log a} = e^{x \log a + y \log a} = e^{x \log a} . e^{y \log a} = a^x . a^y.]$

II. $a^{x-y} = a^x/a^y$. [Proof is similar.]

III. $(a^x)^y = a^{xy}$

$[(a^x)^y = e^{y \log a^x} = e^{yx \log a} = e^{xy \log a} = a^{xy}$; in particular $(e^x)^y = e^{xy}$.]

IV. *If* x *is a positive integer,* n *say, then* a^n, *as defined by* (6.1) *is simply* $a . a . \cdots . a$ *(*n *of these).*

$[a^n = e^{n \log a} = e^{\log a} . e^{(n-1)\log a} = a . e^{(n-1)\log a}$, and the result is now easily obtained by induction.]

Also, $a^{1/n}$ *is simply* $\sqrt[n]{a}$. [Consider $(a^{1/n})^n$.]

V. $\dfrac{d}{dx}(a^x) = \dfrac{d}{dx}(e^{x \log a}) = e^{x \log a} \dfrac{d}{dx}(x \log a) = a^x \log a;$

$$\int a^x \, dx = \frac{1}{\log a} a^x + C.$$

Note. $\dfrac{d}{dx}(a^x) = a^x \Leftrightarrow \log a = 1 \Leftrightarrow a = e$. Thus $\log_e$ and exp have the simplest derivatives of all the logarithmic and exponential functions given by different bases.

Example 1. Differentiate

$$\text{(i) } x^x, \quad \text{(ii) } 2^{\sin x}, \quad \text{(iii) } (\log x)^x.$$

(i) $\dfrac{d}{dx}(x^x) = \dfrac{d}{dx} e^{x \log x} = e^{x \log x}.(\log x + 1) = (1 + \log x)x^x;$

(ii) $\dfrac{d}{dx}(2^{\sin x}) = \dfrac{d}{dx}(e^{\sin x . \log 2})$

$= e^{\sin x . \log 2}.(\cos x . \log 2) = \log 2 . \cos x . 2^{\sin x};$

(iii) $\dfrac{d}{dx}(\log x)^x = \dfrac{d}{dx} e^{x \log(\log x)} = e^{x \log(\log x)}.\left(\dfrac{1}{\log x} + \log(\log x)\right)$

$= \left(\dfrac{1}{\log x} + \log(\log x)\right)(\log x)^x.$

Example 2. Evaluate

$$\text{(i) } \lim_{x \to \infty} x^{\frac{1}{x}}, \quad \text{(ii) } \lim_{h \to 0} \frac{2^h - 1}{h}.$$

$$\text{(i) } \lim_{x \to \infty} x^{\frac{1}{x}} = \lim_{x \to \infty} e^{\frac{1}{x}\log x} = e^{\lim_{x \to \infty} \frac{1}{x} \log x} = e^0 = 1.$$

[This uses the continuity of exp at $x = 0$.]

$$\text{(ii) } \lim_{h \to 0} \frac{2^h - 1}{h} = \lim_{h \to 0} \frac{2^h - 2^0}{h} = \text{derivative of } 2^x \text{ at } x = 0$$

$$= [2^x \log 2]_{x=0} = \log 2.$$

e as a limit

We are now in a position to prove that

$$e = \lim_{h \to 0} (1 + h)^{1/h}. \tag{6.2}$$

Since $\log'(1) = 1$, it follows that

$$\lim_{h \to 0} \frac{1}{h}\{\log(1 + h) - \log 1\} = 1, \quad \text{so that} \quad \lim_{h \to 0} \left\{\frac{1}{h} \log(1 + h)\right\} = 1.$$

Now $$(1 + h)^{\frac{1}{h}} = e^{\frac{1}{h} \log(1 + h)},$$

so that $$\lim_{h \to 0} (1 + h)^{1/h} = e^{\lim_{h \to 0} \frac{1}{h} \log(1 + h)} = e^1 = e,$$

using the continuity of exp at $x = 1$, and this proves (6.2).

In particular, if we let $h = \frac{1}{n}$, where n is a positive integer, we have:

$$\lim_{n\to\infty}\left(1+\frac{1}{n}\right)^n = e.$$

We can show that $e = 2{\cdot}7182818\cdots \doteqdot 2{\cdot}72.$

7. The general power function (x^c for given $c \in \mathbf{R}$)

For given $c \in \mathbf{R}$ the power x^c is defined for $x > 0$ by:

$$x^c = e^{c\log x},\ x > 0. \tag{7.1}$$

For $c = \frac{p}{q}$, where $p \in \mathbf{Z}$ and $q \in \mathbf{N}$, the definition (7.1) agrees with $\left(x^{\frac{1}{q}}\right)^p$; for,

$$x^{\frac{p}{q}} = e^{\frac{p}{q}\log x} = \left(e^{\frac{1}{q}\log x}\right)^p = \left(x^{\frac{1}{q}}\right)^p.$$

$$\frac{d}{dx}(x^c) = \frac{d}{dx}(e^{c\log x}) = e^{c\log x}.\frac{c}{x} = \frac{c}{x}\cdot x^c = cx^{c-1}.$$

For example, $\frac{d}{dx}(x^\pi) = \pi x^{\pi-1}$; $\int x^\pi\,dx = \frac{1}{\pi+1}x^{\pi+1}+C.$

8. The hyperbolic functions

These are the functions cosh, sinh, tanh, sech, cosech, coth defined as follows:

$\cosh x = \frac{1}{2}(e^x+e^{-x}),\ \forall x \in \mathbf{R};$ $\quad$ $\operatorname{sech} x = \frac{1}{\cosh x},\ \forall x \in \mathbf{R},$

$\sinh x = \frac{1}{2}(e^x-e^{-x}),\ \forall x \in \mathbf{R};$ $\quad$ $\operatorname{cosech} x = \frac{1}{\sinh x},\ \forall x \in \mathbf{R}-\{0\};$

$\tanh x = \frac{\sinh x}{\cosh x} = \frac{e^x-e^{-x}}{e^x+e^{-x}},\ \forall x \in \mathbf{R};$ $\quad$ $\coth x = \frac{1}{\tanh x},\ \forall x \in \mathbf{R}-\{0\}.$

Now,

$$\frac{d}{dx}(\cosh x) = \tfrac{1}{2}(e^x-e^{-x}) = \sinh x; \quad \int \sinh x\,dx = \cosh x + C;$$

$$\frac{d}{dx}(\sinh x) = \tfrac{1}{2}(e^x+e^{-x}) = \cosh x; \quad \int \cosh x\,dx = \sinh x + C;$$

$$\frac{d}{dx}(\tanh x) = \frac{\cosh^2 x-\sinh^2 x}{\cosh^2 x} = \frac{1}{\cosh^2 x} = \operatorname{sech}^2 x,$$

noting that

$$\cosh^2 x - \sinh^2 x = \tfrac{1}{4}(e^{2x} + 2 + e^{-2x} - e^{2x} + 2 - e^{-2x}) = 1;$$

$$\int \operatorname{sech}^2 x\, dx = \tanh x + C.$$

Similarly, the derivatives of the other three hyperbolic functions can be obtained.

The functions are in some ways similar to the trigonometric functions (especially when we introduce complex numbers) and have many corresponding properties. For example,

$$\cosh(x+y) = \cosh x \cosh y + \sinh x \sinh y,$$

$$\sinh(x+y) = \sinh x \cosh y + \cosh x \sinh y,$$

$$\cosh 2x = \cosh^2 x + \sinh^2 x = 2\cosh^2 x - 1 = 2\sinh^2 x + 1,$$

$$\sinh 2x = 2 \sinh x \cosh x, \quad \operatorname{sech}^2 x = 1 - \tanh^2 x.$$

These are all easily proved from the definitions; e.g.

$$\begin{aligned}\cosh(x+y) &= \tfrac{1}{2}(e^{x+y} + e^{-x-y}) \\ &= \tfrac{1}{2}(e^x + e^{-x}) \cdot \tfrac{1}{2}(e^y + e^{-y}) + \tfrac{1}{2}(e^x - e^{-x}) \cdot \tfrac{1}{2}(e^y - e^{-y}) \\ &= \cosh x \cosh y + \sinh x \sinh y.\end{aligned}$$

The graphs of the functions are as follows:

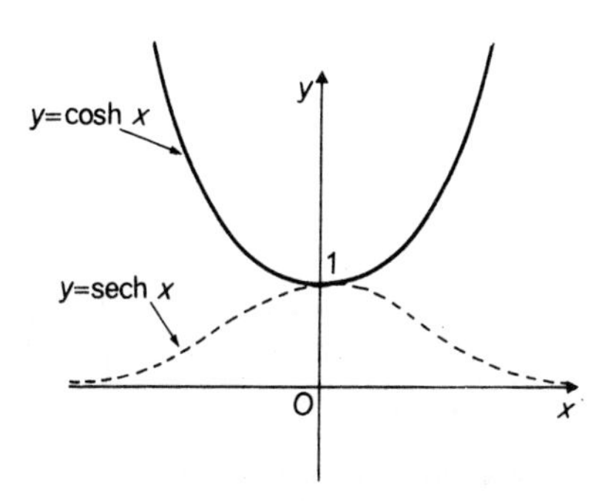

$\cosh 0 = 1$; $\cosh x \sim \tfrac{1}{2}e^x$ as $x \to \infty$,
$\sim \tfrac{1}{2}e^{-x}$ as $x \to -\infty$;

cosh is an *even* function (so is sech);
$\cosh x \geqslant 1, \ \forall x \in \mathbf{R}$.

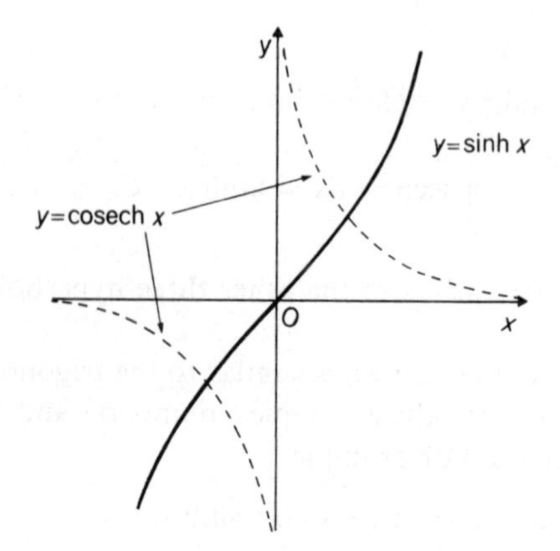

$\sinh 0 = 0$: $\sinh x \sim \frac{1}{2}e^x$ as $x \to \infty$
$\sim -\frac{1}{2}e^{-x}$ as $x \to -\infty$;
sinh is an *odd* function (so is cosech).

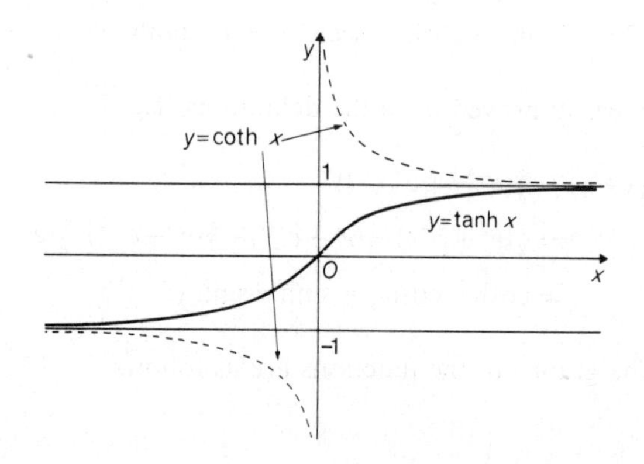

$\tanh 0 = 0$; $\tanh x \to 1$ as $x \to \infty$ and $\to -1$ as $x \to -\infty$;
tanh is an *odd* function (so is coth); $|\tanh x| < 1$, $\forall x \in \mathbf{R}$.

It is clear from the graphs that

$\cosh : \mathbf{R}^+ \to [1, \infty)$ has an inverse $\cosh^{-1} : [1, \infty) \to \mathbf{R}^+$,
$\sinh : \mathbf{R} \to \mathbf{R}$ has an inverse $\sinh^{-1} : \mathbf{R} \to \mathbf{R}$,
$\tanh : \mathbf{R} \to (-1, 1)$ has an inverse $\tanh^{-1} : (-1, 1) \to \mathbf{R}$.

These three **inverse hyperbolic functions** are given by the following formulae:

(i) $\forall x \geqslant 1$, $\cosh^{-1} x = \log\{x + \sqrt{(x^2 - 1)}\}$,
(ii) $\forall x \in \mathbf{R}$, $\sinh^{-1} x = \log\{x + \sqrt{(x^2 + 1)}\}$,

(iii) $\forall x \in (-1, 1)$, $\tanh^{-1} x = \frac{1}{2} \log\left(\dfrac{1+x}{1-x}\right)$.

Proof of (i). If $y = \cosh x$, $x \geqslant 0$, then $x = \cosh^{-1} y$, and, for $y > 1$,

$$\frac{d}{dy} \cosh^{-1} y = \frac{dx}{dy} = \frac{1}{\dfrac{dy}{dx}} = \frac{1}{\sinh x} = \frac{1}{\sqrt{(\cosh^2 x - 1)}} = \frac{1}{\sqrt{(y^2-1)}}.$$

Thus $\quad \cosh^{-1} y = \log\{y + \sqrt{(y^2-1)}\} + C$ (noting that $y \geqslant 1$);

$y = 1$ gives $C = 0$, and the result (i) follows (changing to x notation).

Exercise. Prove (ii) and (iii).

$$\left[\text{For (iii), note that } \frac{1}{1-y^2} = \frac{1}{2}\left(\frac{1}{1+y} + \frac{1}{1-y}\right).\right]$$

Note. We have now introduced all the elementary functions of calculus; we can differentiate any compositions of these, but at present we can find antiderivatives only of functions very like the standard functions. In Chapter 6 we extend the classes of functions for which antiderivatives can be found.

EXERCISE 5

1. Differentiate:

(i) $e^{\cos x}$, (ii) $x\, e^{x-x^2}$, (iii) $x^2 e^{\sin^2 x}$,
(iv) $\log(\sin x)$, (v) $\log(\cos x)$, (vi) $\log(\sec x + \tan x)$,
(vii) $\log(\operatorname{cosec} x + \cot x)$, (viii) $\log(1 - 2\cos 2x)$, (ix) $\log(\tan^{-1} \sqrt{x})$,
(x) $\sin^{-1}(e^{-3x})$, (xi) $\cos^{-1}(\log 2x)$, (xii) $(\sin x)^x$,
(xiii) x^{x^2}, (xiv) $x^2 . 2^x$, (xv) $x\pi^{x^2}$,
(xvi) $(\log x)^{\log x}$, (xvii) $(\sqrt{2})^x . x^{\sqrt{2}}$, (xviii) $\sinh 2x \cosh^2 x$.

2. Find the nth derivative of each of

(i) $\log x$, (ii) $\log \dfrac{x-1}{x+1}$, (iii) $x\,e^x$, (iv) $e^x \cos x$.

3. Integrate [Note that an antiderivative can always be checked by differentiation.]:

(i) $4x^3 - 6x^2 + 5$ (ii) $\dfrac{x^4+1}{x^2}$, (iii) $\dfrac{1}{(2x-1)^4}$,

(iv) $\dfrac{1}{(3-2x)^3}$, (v) $\sin 2x$, (vi) $\cos(1-3x)$,

(vii) $\sec^2(2x+1)$, (viii) $\cot x$, (ix) $\tan x$.

(x) $\sec x$, (xi) $\operatorname{cosec} x$, (xii) $\dfrac{(x+1)^2}{x}$,

[For (viii), (ix), (x), (xi) see (iv), (v), (vi), (vii), respectively, of **1**.]

(xiii) $\dfrac{x}{(x+1)^2}$, (xiv) $\dfrac{1}{2x^2+3}$, (xv) $\dfrac{1}{x^2-4x+5}$,

(xvi) $\dfrac{1}{\sqrt{(1-9x^2)}}$, (xvii) $\dfrac{1}{\sqrt{(3+2x-x^2)}}$, (xviii) $\dfrac{x+5}{x+2}$,

(xix) $\dfrac{x}{3x+1}$, (xx) $\dfrac{1}{\sqrt{(1+4x^2)}}$, (xxi) $\dfrac{1}{\sqrt{(x^2+4x+3)}}$,

(xxii) 3^x, (xxiii) $\cosh 2x$, (xxiv) $\sinh^2 2x$.

4. Evaluate:

(i) $\displaystyle\int_{-1}^{2} (5x^4+3x^2-4x)dx$, (ii) $\displaystyle\int_{1}^{2} \frac{x^3+1}{x^2}\,dx$, (iii) $\displaystyle\int_{1}^{3} \frac{(x-1)^2}{x^4}\,dx$,

(iv) $\displaystyle\int_{0}^{1} \frac{dx}{(3x+1)^2}$, (v) $\displaystyle\int_{0}^{\frac{1}{4}\pi} \cos 2x\,dx$, (vi) $\displaystyle\int_{\frac{1}{12}\pi}^{\frac{1}{6}\pi} \sin 3x\,dx$,

(vii) $\displaystyle\int_{0}^{\frac{1}{8}\pi} \sec^2 2x\,dx$, (viii) $\displaystyle\int_{0}^{\frac{1}{4}\pi} \sec x\,dx$, (ix) $\displaystyle\int_{0}^{\frac{1}{4}\pi} \tan x\,dx$,

(x) $\displaystyle\int_{\frac{1}{2}}^{\frac{1}{2}\sqrt{3}} \frac{dx}{4x^2+1}$, (xi) $\displaystyle\int_{2}^{3} \frac{dx}{x^2-4x+5}$, (xii) $\displaystyle\int_{1}^{2} \frac{dx}{\sqrt{(4-x^2)}}$,

(xiii) $\displaystyle\int_{2}^{5} \frac{dx}{\sqrt{(5+4x-x^2)}}$, (xiv) $\displaystyle\int_{2}^{3} \frac{x}{x-1}\,dx$, (xv) $\displaystyle\int_{0}^{1} \frac{x}{1+2x}\,dx$,

(xvi) $\displaystyle\int_{0}^{2} \frac{dx}{\sqrt{(9+x^2)}}$, (xvii) $\displaystyle\int_{0}^{\frac{1}{4}} \frac{dx}{\sqrt{(1+9x^2)}}$, (xviii) $\displaystyle\int_{-1}^{0} \frac{dx}{\sqrt{(x^2+2x+2)}}$,

(xix) $\displaystyle\int_{0}^{1} 2^x\,dx$, (xx) $\displaystyle\int_{0}^{\log 2} \sinh 2x\,dx$, (xxi) $\displaystyle\int_{0}^{\log 3} \cosh^2 2x\,dx$.

5. (i) Evaluate $\displaystyle\int_{0}^{3} f(x)dx$, where
$$f(x) = \begin{cases} x+2, & 0 \leqslant x < 1, \\ 2, & x = 1, \\ \dfrac{1}{x}, & 1 < x \leqslant 3. \end{cases}$$

(ii) Evaluate $\displaystyle\int_{-1}^{2} f(x)dx$, where
$$f(x) = \begin{cases} \dfrac{1}{x^2+1}, & -1 \leqslant x \leqslant 1, \\ \dfrac{1}{x+1}, & 1 < x \leqslant 2. \end{cases}$$

6. By interpreting each as a definite integral, evaluate each of the following limits:

(i) $\lim_{n\to\infty} \frac{1}{n^{3/2}}(1+\sqrt{2}+\cdots+\sqrt{(n-1)})$ (ii) $\lim_{n\to\infty} \frac{1}{n^{5/2}} \sum_{r=1}^{n} r^{3/2}$,

(iii) $\lim_{n\to\infty} \sum_{r=1}^{n} \frac{1}{n+r}$, (iv) $\lim_{n\to\infty} \sum_{r=0}^{n-1} \frac{1}{\sqrt{(n^2-r^2)}}$.

7. Find the area of each of the following regions:
(i) the finite region bounded by the x-axis and the parabola $y = x^2-2x-3$;
(ii) the finite region bounded by the line $x = 4$ and the parabola $y^2 = x$;
(iii) the region between the x-axis and the curve $y = \frac{1}{x^2+1}$;
(iv) the three finite regions between the x-axis and the curve

$$y = x(x+1)(x-1)(x-2).$$

8. Evaluate $\int_0^{\sqrt{2}} \sqrt{(2-x^2)}dx$ by interpreting it as the area of a region in the plane.

9. Find the critical point and point of inflexion on the curve

$$y = \frac{1}{x}\log x,\ x > 0,$$

and sketch the curve.

10. Find the critical point and the point of inflexion on the curve $y = x\,e^{-x}$, and sketch the curve.

11. Find the critical points and the points of inflexion on the curve $y = x\,e^{-x^2}$, and sketch the curve.

12. Sketch the curve $y = x^x$, $x > 0$, by showing that it has a critical point and that $x^x \to 1$ as $x \to 0$ ($x > 0$).

13. Discuss the convergence of the following integrals:

(i) $\int_0^1 \frac{dx}{x}$, (ii) $\int_{-1}^{2} \frac{dx}{\sqrt{(x+1)}}$, (iii) $\int_1^2 \frac{dx}{\sqrt{(x^2-1)}}$,

(iv) $\int_{-3}^{-2} \frac{dx}{(x+2)^2}$, (v) $\int_{3/2}^{\infty} \frac{dx}{9+4x^2}$, (vi) $\int_1^{\infty} e^x\,dx$,

(vii) $\int_1^{\infty} e^{-x}\,dx$, (viii) $\int_2^{\infty} x^{-4/3}\,dx$, (ix) $\int_0^{\frac{1}{2}\pi} \frac{dx}{\cos x}$.

14. Evaluate:

(i) $\lim_{x\to 0} x^{x^2}$, (ii) $\lim_{x\to\infty} x^{1/x^2}$,

(iii) $\lim_{h\to 0} \frac{3^h-1}{h}$, (iv) $\lim_{h\to 0} \frac{(1+h)^{1+h}-1}{h}$.

15. Differentiate with respect to x:

(i) $\displaystyle\int_0^x \frac{dt}{4+t^4}$, (ii) $\displaystyle\int_{x^2}^x \frac{dt}{\sqrt{(1-t^3)}}$, (iii) $\displaystyle\int_x^{2x} 2^{t^2}\,dt$.

16. Use logarithmic differentiation to evaluate

$$\frac{1}{y}\frac{dy}{dx}, \quad \text{where} \quad y = x^3 e^{-x^2} \sin^2 x.$$

17. Show that $\operatorname{sech} : \mathbf{R}^+ \to (0, 1]$ is a bijection and *verify* that $\operatorname{sech}^{-1} : (0, 1] \to \mathbf{R}^+$ is given by the formula

$$\operatorname{sech}^{-1} y = \log\left\{\frac{1+\sqrt{(1-y^2)}}{y}\right\}, \quad 0 < y \leqslant 1.$$

18. Show that $x = a \cosh t$, $y = b \sinh t$ $(t \in \mathbf{R})$ are parametric equations for the right-hand branch of the hyperbola $x^2/a^2 - y^2/b^2 = 1$ $(a > 0, b > 0)$. Find the equation of the tangent at the point with parameter t_1 on the hyperbola.

Give parametric equations of the same form for the left-hand branch of the hyperbola.

19. A particle moves on the x-axis so that its distance $x(t)$ at time t seconds from the origin O satisfies the equation

$$\frac{dx}{dt} = -kx,$$

where k is a constant. If the particle starts initially with velocity -10 units/second at the point $x = 5$, find the time at which the speed is half its initial value. Describe what happens to the particle as $t \to \infty$.

20. The temperature difference $T(t)$ at time t seconds between a body of gas and the surrounding air decreases at a rate proportional to its value at time t seconds. If the initial temperature difference is 100° and $T(60) = 50^\circ$, find (i) the time at which the temperature difference is 40° and (ii) the temperature difference when $t = 120$.

Methods of integration

1. The two main methods for finding antiderivatives

In dealing with differentiation it was clear that progress without the chain rule and the product rule would have been very limited. With antidifferentiation we made some progress in Chapter 5, but as yet we lack tools which would enable us to make the subject more comprehensive. There are two basic such tools (1) the **method of change of variable** which is based on the chain rule for differentiation, and (2) the **method of integration by parts**, based on the product rule for differentiation. We establish both of these in this section and illustrate their uses and some other techniques in the remainder of the chapter.

I. Method of change of variable

The aim is to reduce an integral to a standard integral or a sum of standard integrals by suitable changes of variable. The method for indefinite integrals is based on the following result.

Theorem 6.1

Let the real function f be continuous and the real function g be differentiable and its derived function g' be continuous; if F is an antiderivative of f, then $F(g(x))$ is an antiderivative of

$$f(g(x))\frac{dg}{dx}, \text{ i.e.}$$

$$F(g(x)) = \int f(g(x))\frac{dg}{dx}\,dx. \tag{1.1}$$

Proof. $\dfrac{d}{dx}\{F(g(x))\} = F'(g(x))\cdot\dfrac{dg}{dx}$, by the chain rule,

$$= f(g(x))\cdot\frac{dg}{dx}, \quad \text{by the definition of } F,$$

and so, by the definition of an antiderivative,

$$\int f(g(x)) \cdot \frac{dg}{dx}\, dx = F(g(x)).$$

Notation. We usually write $u = g(x)$, and

$$\int f(g(x)) \cdot \frac{dg}{dx}\, dx = F(u) = \int f(u)\, du;$$

we say that the complicated integral

$$\int f(g(x)) \cdot \frac{dg}{dx}\, dx \text{ becomes } \int f(u)\, du$$

by the **change of variable** $u = g(x)$.

Example 1. Find $\int (x^2+1)^{5/2} x\, dx$.

With the notation of Theorem **6.1** in mind, we take $g(x) = x^2+1$,

so that
$$\frac{dg}{dx} = 2x;$$

with $\quad u = g(x) = x^2+1, \; du = 2x\, dx$ (in differential notation)

and the integral $= \int u^{5/2} \cdot \tfrac{1}{2} du = \tfrac{1}{2} \int u^{5/2}\, du = \tfrac{1}{2}(\tfrac{2}{7} u^{7/2}) + C,$

since $\tfrac{2}{7}u^{7/2}$ is an antiderivative of $u^{5/2}$. Hence

$$\int (x^2+1)^{5/2} x\, dx = \tfrac{1}{7}(x^2+1)^{7/2} + C.$$

Example 2. Find
$$\int \frac{x^3}{1+x^8}\, dx.$$

If $u = x^4$, then $du = 4x^3\, dx$, and the integral

$$= \int \frac{1}{1+u^2} \tfrac{1}{4}\, du = \tfrac{1}{4} \tan^{-1} u + C = \tfrac{1}{4} \tan^{-1} x^4 + C.$$

Note. With practice, in many cases the integration can be performed without actually making the change of variable.

Theorem 6.2

[**Change of variable for a definite integral.**] *Let g be differentiable on the interval $[a, b]$ and let its derived function be continuous. Let f be a* *continuous function ⁻ned on an interval containing the values of g. Then*

$$\int \frac{dg}{dx}\,dx = \int_{g(a)}^{g(b)} f(u)du. \qquad (1.2)$$

Proof. If F is an antiderivative of f, then, by Theorem **6.1**,

$$F(g(x)) = \int f(g(x))\frac{dg}{dx}\,dx.$$

Hence, by the fundamental theorem of calculus,

$$\int_a^b f(g(x))\frac{dg}{dx}\,dx = F(g(b)) - F(g(a)) = \int_{g(a)}^{g(b)} f(u)du.$$

Note. In applying (1.2) we formally make the change of variable $u = g(x)$ on the left-hand side, putting

$$du = \frac{dg}{dx}\,dx$$

and drawing up a table of values for the limits:

x	a	b
u	$g(a)$	$g(b)$

Example 3. Evaluate

$$\int_0^{\frac{1}{2}\pi} \frac{\sin x}{\sqrt{(1+\cos^2 x)}}\,dx.$$

Put $u = \cos x$; then $du = -\sin x\,dx$ and the table of limits is

x	0	$\frac{1}{2}\pi$
u	1	0

The integral is

$$\int_1^0 \frac{-du}{\sqrt{(1+u^2)}} = \int_0^1 \frac{du}{\sqrt{(1+u^2)}} = [\log\{u+\sqrt{(1+u^2)}\}]_0^1 = \log(1+\sqrt{2}).$$

[Note that $u+\sqrt{(1+u^2)} > 0\ \forall u \in \mathbf{R}$.]

Example 4. Evaluate

$$\int_1^e \frac{1}{\sqrt{\{4-(\log x)^2\}}}\frac{dx}{x}.$$

Put $u = \log x$; then $du = \dfrac{1}{x}dx$ and the table of limits is

x	1	e
u	0	1

The integral is

$$\int_0^1 \frac{du}{\sqrt{(4-u^2)}} = [\sin^{-1}\tfrac{1}{2}u]_0^1 = \tfrac{1}{6}\pi.$$

II. Method of integration by parts

This is based on the following result:

Theorem 6.3. *If the derivatives f', g' of the functions f and g are continuous, then*

$$\int f(x)g'(x)dx = f(x)g(x) - \int g(x)f'(x)dx. \tag{1.3}$$

Proof. By the product rule for differentiation,

$$\frac{d}{dx}\{f(x)g(x)\} = f(x)g'(x)+g(x)f'(x).$$

Consequently,
$$f(x)g(x) = \int \{f(x)g'(x)+g(x)f'(x)\}dx$$
$$= \int f(x)g'(x)dx + \int g(x)f'(x)dx,$$

and so
$$\int f(x)g'(x)dx = f(x)g(x) - \int g(x)f'(x)dx.$$

Notes **1.** Equation (1.3) is called the **rule for integration by parts**; it is useful if

$$\int g(x)f'(x)dx \quad \text{is easier to find than} \quad \int f(x)g'(x)dx.$$

2.
$$\int_a^b f(x)g'(x)dx = [f(x)g(x)]_a^b - \int_a^b g(x)f'(x)dx.$$

3. Writing $u(x) = f(x)$ and $v(x) = g'(x)$, equation (1.3) becomes

$$\int u(x)v(x)dx = u(x)v_1(x) - \int v_1(x)u'(x)dx, \tag{1.4}$$

where
$$v_1(x) = \int v(x)dx.$$

4. The extended rule for integration by parts.

$$\int u(x)v(x)dx = u(x)v_1(x) - u'(x)v_2(x) + u''(x)v_3(x) - u'''(x)v_4(x) + \cdots, \tag{1.5}$$

where $v_1(x) = \int v(x)dx$, $v_2(x) = \int v_1(x)dx$, $v_3(x) = \int v_2(x)dx$, etc.

Proof. $\int u(x)v(x)dx = u(x)v_1(x) - \int u'(x)v_1(x)dx$, by (1.4),

$$= u(x)v_1(x) - \left\{u'(x)v_2(x) - \int u''(x)v_2(x)dx\right\}$$

$$= u(x)v_1(x) - u'(x)v_2(x) + \left\{u''(x)v_3(x) - \int u'''(x)v_3(x)dx\right\}$$

$$= u(x)v_1(x) - u'(x)v_2(x) + u''(x)v_3(x) - \left\{u'''(x)v_4(x) - \int u^{iv}(x)v_4(x)dx\right\},$$

and so on.

Rule (1.5) is useful when $u(x)$ is a polynomial, since $u^{(n)}(x) = 0$ when n is greater than the degree of $u(x)$.

Example 5. Find
$$\int x \cosh x \, dx.$$

Using (1.4) with $u(x) = x$ and $v(x) = \cosh x$,

$$\int x \cosh x \, dx = x \sinh x - \int 1 . \sinh x \, dx, \text{ since } \frac{d}{dx}(\sinh x) = \cosh x,$$

$$= x \sinh x - \cosh x + C.$$

Example 6. (*Illustrating a use of* (1.5)). Evaluate

$$\int_0^\infty x^3 e^{-2x} dx.$$

Using (1.5),

$$\int_0^\infty x^3 e^{-2x} dx$$

$$= [x^3(-\tfrac{1}{2}e^{-2x}) - 3x^2(\tfrac{1}{4}e^{-2x}) + 6x(-\tfrac{1}{8}e^{-2x}) - 6(\tfrac{1}{16}e^{-2x}) + 0]_0^\infty$$

$= \frac{6}{16} = \frac{3}{8}$ (noting that $x^k e^{-2x} \to 0$ as $x \to \infty$, for any $k \in \mathbf{Z}$).

Example 7. (*Illustrating use of* (1.4) *with* $v(x) = 1$.)

Find

(i) $\int \log x \, dx$, (ii) $\int \tan^{-1} x \, dx$, (iii) $\int \sin^{-1} x \, dx$,

(iv) $\int \sqrt{(a^2 - x^2)}dx$, $(a > 0)$, (v) $\int \sqrt{(x^2 + k)}dx$.

(i) $\int \log x\,dx = \int 1\,.\log x\,dx$

$$= x\log x - \int x\,.\frac{1}{x}\,dx \text{ (using (1.4) with } v(x)=1,\ u(x)=\log x),$$

$$= x\log x - x + C.$$

(ii) $\int \tan^{-1} x\,dx = \int 1\,.\tan^{-1} x\,dx$

$$= x\tan^{-1} x - \int \frac{x}{1+x^2}\,dx$$

$$= x\tan^{-1} x - \tfrac{1}{2}\log(1+x^2) + C$$

(putting $u = 1+x^2$ in the integral on the right-hand side).

(iii) $\int \sin^{-1} x\,dx = \int 1\,.\sin^{-1} x\,dx$

$$= x\sin^{-1} x - \int \frac{x}{\sqrt{(1-x^2)}}\,dx$$

$$= x\sin^{-1} x + \sqrt{(1-x^2)} + C,$$

(putting $u = 1-x^2$ in the integral on the right-hand side).

(iv) If $I = \int \sqrt{(a^2-x^2)}dx\ (a>0)$, then

$$I = \int 1\,.\sqrt{(a^2-x^2)}dx = x\sqrt{(a^2-x^2)} - \int x\,.\frac{(-x)}{\sqrt{(a^2-x^2)}}\,dx$$

$$= x\sqrt{(a^2-x^2)} - \int \frac{(a^2-x^2)-a^2}{\sqrt{(a^2-x^2)}}\,dx$$

$$= x\sqrt{(a^2-x^2)} - \int \sqrt{(a^2-x^2)}dx + a^2\int \frac{dx}{\sqrt{(a^2-x^2)}}.$$

Thus $$2I = x\sqrt{(a^2-x^2)} + a^2\sin^{-1}\frac{x}{a} + 2C,$$

and so $$\int \sqrt{(a^2-x^2)}dx = \tfrac{1}{2}x\sqrt{(a^2-x^2)} + \tfrac{1}{2}a^2\sin^{-1}\frac{x}{a} + C\ (a>0).$$

(v) Show, using a similar method, that

$$\int \sqrt{(x^2+k)}dx = \tfrac{1}{2}x\sqrt{(x^2+k)} + \tfrac{1}{2}k\log|x+\sqrt{(x^2+k)}| + C.$$

[*Note.* If $k>0$, the modulus sign $|\ \ |$ is not required.]

Example 8. (*Illustrating a double use of* (1.4) (or (1.3)).) Find

$$\text{(i) } I = \int e^{ax} \cos bx\, dx, \qquad \text{(ii) } J = \int e^{ax} \sin bx\, dx \; (a, b \in \mathbf{R}).$$

(i)
$$I = \frac{e^{ax}}{a} \cos bx + \frac{b}{a} \int e^{ax} \sin bx\, dx = \frac{e^{ax}}{a} \cos bx + \frac{b}{a} J \tag{1.6}$$

$$= \frac{e^{ax}}{a} \cos bx + \frac{b}{a} \left\{ \frac{e^{ax}}{a} \sin bx - \frac{b}{a} \int e^{ax} \cos bx\, dx \right\},$$

and so
$$\left(1 + \frac{b^2}{a^2}\right) I = \frac{e^{ax}}{a} \cos bx + \frac{b}{a^2} e^{ax} \sin bx + C_1,$$

which gives
$$I = \frac{e^{ax}}{a^2 + b^2} (a \cos bx + b \sin bx) + C, \; a^2 + b^2 \neq 0. \tag{1.7}$$

(ii) Similarly, we can show that

$$J = \frac{e^{ax}}{a^2 + b^2} (a \sin bx - b \cos bx) + C, \; a^2 + b^2 \neq 0; \tag{1.8}$$

or, we can obtain (1.7) and (1.8) by solving equation (1.6) with the corresponding equation expressing J in terms of I, namely

$$J = \frac{e^{ax}}{a} \sin bx - \frac{b}{a} I.$$

Note. Using complex numbers, we can find I and J as follows:

$$\begin{aligned} I + iJ &= \int e^{ax} (\cos bx + i \sin bx) dx \\ &= \int e^{(a+ib)x}\, dx \\ &= \frac{1}{a+ib} e^{(a+ib)x} + \text{a complex constant } (a + ib \neq 0) \\ &= \frac{a - ib}{a^2 + b^2} e^{ax} (\cos bx + i \sin bx) + \text{a complex constant } (a^2 + b^2 \neq 0). \end{aligned}$$

Equating real and imaginary parts now gives the results.

Exercise. Show that

$$\int x \sin^2 x\, dx = \tfrac{1}{4}x^2 - \tfrac{1}{4}x \sin 2x - \tfrac{1}{8} \cos 2x + C.$$

[Use $v(x) = \sin^2 x = \frac{1}{2}(1 - \cos 2x)$.]

2. Trigonometric integrals, some suitable changes of variable

In Chapter 5 we listed some standard integrals involving trigonometric functions and in Exercise **5** [3 (viii), (ix), (x), (xi)] the following anti-derivatives were set:

$$\text{(a)} \int \cot x\,dx, \quad \text{(b)} \int \tan x\,dx, \quad \text{(c)} \int \sec x\,dx, \quad \text{(d)} \int \operatorname{cosec} x\,dx.$$

We now examine these in more detail.

$$\text{(a)} \int \cot x\,dx = \int \frac{\cos x}{\sin x}\,dx = \int \frac{d(\sin x)}{\sin x} = \log|\sin x| + C.$$

[Note the simplified formal use of the change of variable $u = \sin x$.]

$$\text{(b)} \int \tan x\,dx = \int \frac{\sin x}{\cos x}\,dx = -\int \frac{d(\cos x)}{\cos x} = -\log|\cos x| + C.$$

(c) If $\sec x + \tan x > 0$, $\dfrac{d}{dx}\{\log(\sec x + \tan x)\} = \dfrac{\sec x \tan x + \sec^2 x}{\sec x + \tan x}$

$$= \sec x;$$

if $\sec x + \tan x < 0$, $\dfrac{d}{dx}\{\log(-\sec x - \tan x)\} = \dfrac{-\sec x \tan x - \sec^2 x}{-\sec x - \tan x}$

$$= \sec x.$$

Thus
$$\int \frac{dx}{\cos x} = \int \sec x\,dx = \log|\sec x + \tan x| + C.$$

(d) Show similarly that

$$\int \frac{dx}{\sin x} = \int \operatorname{cosec} x\,dx = -\log|\operatorname{cosec} x + \cot x| + C.$$

We now consider in turn several types of trigonometric integrals.

I. $\displaystyle\int \sin mx \sin nx\,dx, \int \sin mx \cos nx\,dx, \int \cos mx \cos nx\,dx$

The method is to express the products linearly in terms of sines or cosines of multiples of x.

Example 1. Find

$$\text{(i)} \int \sin 2x \sin 3x\,dx, \qquad \text{(ii)} \int \cos x \cos^2 3x\,dx.$$

(i) $\int \sin 2x \sin 3x \, dx = \frac{1}{2}\int (\cos x - \cos 5x)dx = \frac{1}{2}(\sin x - \frac{1}{5}\sin 5x) + C.$

(ii) $$\begin{aligned}\int \cos x \cos^2 3x \, dx &= \tfrac{1}{2}\int \cos x(1+\cos 6x)dx \\ &= \tfrac{1}{2}\sin x + \tfrac{1}{2}\int \cos x \cos 6x \, dx \\ &= \tfrac{1}{2}\sin x + \tfrac{1}{4}\int (\cos 7x + \cos 5x)dx \\ &= \tfrac{1}{2}\sin x + \tfrac{1}{28}\sin 7x + \tfrac{1}{20}\sin 5x + C.\end{aligned}$$

II. $\int \cos^m x \sin^n x \, dx \ (m, n \in \mathbf{N})$

A method is: if n is *odd*, put $u = \cos x$; if m is *odd*, put $u = \sin x$; if m, n are both *even*, express $\cos^m x \sin^n x$ in terms of sines or cosines of multiples of x.

Example 2. Find

(i) $\int \cos^4 x \sin x \, dx$, (ii) $\int \sin^3 x \cos^5 x \, dx$, (iii) $\int \sin^2 x \cos^2 x \, dx$.

(i) $\int \cos^4 x \sin x \, dx = -\int \cos^4 x \, d(\cos x) = -\frac{1}{5}\cos^5 x + C;$

(ii) $$\begin{aligned}\int \sin^3 x \cos^5 x \, dx &= \int \sin^3 x(1-\sin^2 x)^2 \cos x \, dx \\ &= \int u^3(1-u^2)^2 du \quad (u = \sin x) \\ &= \int (u^3 - 2u^5 + u^7)du \\ &= \tfrac{1}{4}u^4 - \tfrac{1}{3}u^6 + \tfrac{1}{8}u^8 + C \\ &= \tfrac{1}{4}\sin^4 x - \tfrac{1}{3}\sin^6 x + \tfrac{1}{8}\sin^8 x + C;\end{aligned}$$

(iii) $$\begin{aligned}\int \sin^2 x \cos^2 x \, dx = \tfrac{1}{4}\int \sin^2 2x \, dx &= \tfrac{1}{8}\int (1-\cos 4x)dx \\ &= \tfrac{1}{8}x - \tfrac{1}{32}\sin 4x + C.\end{aligned}$$

III. Reduction formulae for $\int \sin^n x \, dx$ **and** $\int \cos^n x \, dx$ $(n \in \mathbf{N})$

If

$$I_n = \int \sin^n x \, dx, \ (n = 1, 2, 3, \cdots), \text{ then}$$

$$\begin{aligned} I_n &= \int \sin^{n-1} x \,.\, \sin x \, dx \\ &= -\sin^{n-1} x \cos x + (n-1) \int \sin^{n-2} x \,.\, \cos^2 x \, dx \ (n \geqslant 2) \\ &= -\sin^{n-1} x \cos x + (n-1) \int \sin^{n-2} x (1 - \sin^2 x) dx \\ &= -\sin^{n-1} x \cos x + (n-1) I_{n-2} - (n-1) I_n, \end{aligned}$$

and so $$I_n = -\frac{1}{n} \sin^{n-1} x \cos x + \frac{n-1}{n} I_{n-2} \ (n \geqslant 2). \tag{2.1}$$

Equation (2.1) is called a **reduction formula** for I_n; it relates the integral to a similar integral with a *smaller suffix*.

Similarly, if

$$J_n = \int \cos^n x \, dx,$$

we can show that

$$J_n = \frac{1}{n} \cos^{n-1} x \sin x + \frac{n-1}{n} J_{n-2} \ (n \geqslant 2).$$

Formulae for $I_n = \int_0^{\frac{1}{2}\pi} \sin^n x \, dx$ **and** $J_n = \int_0^{\frac{1}{2}\pi} \cos^n x \, dx \ (n \in \mathbf{Z}^+)$.

We first note that $I_0 = J_0 = \frac{1}{2}\pi$ and $I_1 = J_1 = 1$. Also,

$$J_n = -\int_{\frac{1}{2}\pi}^{0} \cos^n (\tfrac{1}{2}\pi - t) dt \ (x = \tfrac{1}{2}\pi - t) = \int_0^{\frac{1}{2}\pi} \sin^n t \, dt = \int_0^{\frac{1}{2}\pi} \sin^n x \, dx = I_n.$$

We show that

$$I_n (= J_n) = \frac{(n-1)(n-3)(n-5)\cdots}{n(n-2)(n-4)\cdots} \times \alpha, \tag{2.2}$$

where $\alpha = \frac{1}{2}\pi$ when n is *even* and $\alpha = 1$ when n is *odd*.

Proof of (2.2) From (2.1),

$$I_n = \left[-\frac{1}{n} \sin^{n-1} x \cos x \right]_0^{\frac{1}{2}\pi} + \frac{n-1}{n} I_{n-2} \ (n \geqslant 2),$$

so that
$$I_n = \frac{n-1}{n} I_{n-2} \; (n \geqslant 2)$$
$$= \frac{n-1}{n} \cdot \frac{n-3}{n-2} I_{n-4} \; (n \geqslant 4)$$
$$= \frac{n-1}{n} \cdot \frac{n-3}{n-2} \cdot \frac{n-5}{n-4} I_{n-6} \; (n \geqslant 6), \text{ etc.}$$

If n is *even*,
$$I_n = \frac{n-1}{n} \cdot \frac{n-3}{n-2} \cdot \frac{n-5}{n-4} \cdots \tfrac{1}{2} \times I_0 = \frac{(n-1)(n-3)(n-5)\cdots}{n(n-2)(n-4)\cdots} \times \tfrac{1}{2}\pi;$$

if n is *odd*,
$$I_n = \frac{n-1}{n} \cdot \frac{n-3}{n-2} \cdot \frac{n-5}{n-4} \cdots \tfrac{2}{3} \times I_1 = \frac{(n-1)(n-3)(n-5)\cdots}{n(n-2)(n-4)\cdots} \times 1.$$

Example 3. Evaluate
$$\text{(i)} \int_0^\pi \sin^6 \theta \, d\theta, \quad \text{(ii)} \int_0^\pi \cos^6 \theta \, d\theta, \quad \text{(iii)} \int_0^\pi \cos^5 \theta \, d\theta.$$

(i) By symmetry, $\displaystyle\int_0^\pi \sin^6 \theta \, d\theta = 2\int_0^{\frac{1}{2}\pi} \sin^6 \theta \, d\theta = 2 . \frac{5.3.1}{6.4.2} \cdot \frac{\pi}{2} = \tfrac{5}{16}\pi;$

(ii) clearly $\displaystyle\int_0^\pi \cos^6 \theta \, d\theta = 2\int_0^{\frac{1}{2}\pi} \cos^6 \theta \, d\theta = \int_0^\pi \sin^6 \theta \, d\theta = \tfrac{5}{16}\pi;$

(iii) again by symmetry,
$$\int_0^\pi \cos^5 \theta \, d\theta = 0.$$

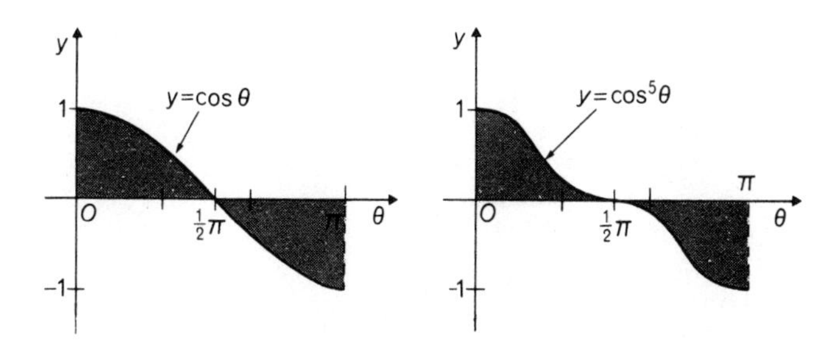

[In dealing with such examples a graph is often helpful.]

Extension of (2.2). *If m and $n \in \mathbf{Z}^+$ (m and n not both zero), then*

$$\int_0^{\frac{1}{2}\pi} \sin^n x \cos^m x \, dx = \frac{(n-1)(n-3)\cdots.(m-1)(m-3)\cdots}{(m+n)(m+n-2)\cdots} \times \alpha, \quad (2.3)$$

where $\alpha = 1$ unless m and n are both even, in which case $\alpha = \frac{1}{2}\pi$.

Proof of (2.3). If $\quad I_{n,m} = \int_0^{\frac{1}{2}\pi} \sin^n x \cos^m x \, dx$, then

$$\begin{aligned} I_{n,m} &= \int_0^{\frac{1}{2}\pi} \sin^{n-1} x (\sin x \cos^m x) dx \\ &= \left[-\sin^{n-1} x . \frac{\cos^{m+1} x}{m+1} \right]_0^{\frac{1}{2}\pi} + \frac{n-1}{m+1} \int_0^{\frac{1}{2}\pi} \sin^{n-2} x \cos^m x (1 - \sin^2 x) dx \\ &= \frac{n-1}{m+1} I_{n-2,m} - \frac{n-1}{m+1} I_{n,m} \; (n \geqslant 2), \end{aligned}$$

and so

$$\begin{aligned} I_{n,m} &= \frac{n-1}{m+n} I_{n-2,m} \; (n \geqslant 2) \\ &= \frac{n-1}{m+n} \cdot \frac{n-3}{m+n-2} I_{n-4,m} \; (n \geqslant 4), \text{ etc.} \end{aligned}$$

If n is *odd*,

$$\begin{aligned} I_{n,m} &= \frac{n-1}{m+n} \cdot \frac{n-3}{m+n-2} \cdots \frac{2}{m+3} I_{1,m} \\ &= \frac{n-1}{m+n} \cdot \frac{n-3}{m+n-2} \cdots \frac{2}{m+3} \left[-\frac{\cos^{m+1} x}{m+1} \right]_0^{\frac{1}{2}\pi} \\ &= \frac{(n-1)(n-3)\cdots 2}{(m+n)(m+n-2)\cdots(m+3)(m+1)} \times \frac{(m-1)(m-3)\cdots}{(m-1)(m-3)\cdots} \times 1. \end{aligned} \quad (2.4)$$

If n is *even*,

$$\begin{aligned} I_{n,m} &= \frac{n-1}{m+n} \cdot \frac{n-3}{m+n-2} \cdots \frac{1}{m+2} I_{0,m} \\ &= \frac{(n-1)(n-3)\cdots(m-1)(m-3)\cdots}{(m+n)(m+n-2)\cdots} \times \alpha, \end{aligned} \quad (2.5)$$

using (2.2), where α is 1 when m is *odd* and α is $\frac{1}{2}\pi$ when m is *even*.

The result (2.3) now follows from (2.4) and (2.5).

Example 4. Evaluate

$$\text{(i)} \int_0^{2\pi} \cos^4 x \sin^8 x \, dx, \qquad \text{(ii)} \int_0^{\pi} \sin^3 x \cos^5 x \, dx.$$

$$\text{(i)} \int_0^{2\pi} \cos^4 x \sin^8 x \, dx = 4 \int_0^{\frac{1}{2}\pi} \cos^4 x \sin^8 x \, dx$$

$$= 4 \,.\, \frac{3.1.7.5.3.1}{12.10.8.6.4.2} \cdot \frac{\pi}{2} = \frac{7}{512}\pi.$$

$$\text{(ii)} \int_0^{\pi} \sin^3 x \cos^5 x \, dx = 0 \quad \text{(from graphical considerations).}$$

IV. Reduction formulae for $\int \tan^n x \, dx$, $\int \sec^n x \, dx$, $\int \tan^n x \sec^m x \, dx$, $n, m \in \mathbf{Z}^+$

If
$$I_n = \int \tan^n x \, dx, \text{ then}$$

$$I_n = \int \tan^{n-2} x \tan^2 x \, dx = \int \tan^{n-2} x \, (\sec^2 x - 1) dx$$

$$= \int \tan^{n-2} x \sec^2 x \, dx - I_{n-2},$$

and so
$$I_n = \frac{1}{n-1} \tan^{n-1} x - I_{n-2} \;\; (n \geqslant 2). \tag{2.6}$$

If
$$J_n = \int \sec^n x \, dx, \text{ then}$$

$$J_n = \int \sec^{n-2} x \sec^2 x \, dx = \sec^{n-2} x \tan x - (n-2) \int \sec^{n-3} x \sec x \tan^2 x \, dx$$

$$= \sec^{n-2} x \tan x - (n-2) \int \sec^{n-2} x \, (\sec^2 x - 1) dx,$$

and so
$$J_n = \frac{1}{n-1} \sec^{n-2} x \tan x + \frac{n-2}{n-1} J_{n-2} \;\; (n \geqslant 2). \tag{2.7}$$

Example 5. $\left(\text{Illustrating} \int \tan^n x \sec^m x \, dx\right)$ Find

$$\text{(i)} \int \frac{\sin^2 x}{\cos^6 x} dx = \int \tan^2 x \sec^4 x \, dx. \quad \text{(ii)} \int \frac{\sin^5 x}{\cos^8 x} dx = \int \sec^3 x \tan^5 x \, dx.$$

(i) $$\int \tan^2 x \sec^4 x \, dx = \int \tan^2 x (1+\tan^2 x) \sec^2 x \, dx$$
$$= \int (u^2+u^4) du \quad (u = \tan x)$$
$$= \tfrac{1}{3}u^3 + \tfrac{1}{5}u^5 + C = \tfrac{1}{3}\tan^3 x + \tfrac{1}{5}\tan^5 x + C.$$

(ii) $$\int \sec^3 x \tan^5 x \, dx = \int \sec^2 x (\sec^2 x - 1)^2 \sec x \tan x \, dx$$
$$= \int (t^6 - 2t^4 + t^2) dt \quad (t = \sec x)$$
$$= \tfrac{1}{7}\sec^7 x - \tfrac{2}{5}\sec^5 x + \tfrac{1}{3}\sec^3 x + C. \tag{2.8}$$

Note. This integral can also be evaluated by using the change of variable $u = \cos x$; for,

$$\int \frac{\sin^5 x}{\cos^8 x} dx = -\int \frac{(1-u^2)^2}{u^8} du = \int \left(-\frac{1}{u^8} + \frac{2}{u^6} - \frac{1}{u^4}\right) du,$$

and this also leads to the result (2.8).

V. Reduction formulae for $\int \cot^n x \, dx$, $\int \operatorname{cosec}^m x \, dx$, $\int \cot^n x \operatorname{cosec}^m x \, dx$

These integrals can be obtained by methods similar to those used in **IV**, but with the identity $\operatorname{cosec}^2 x = 1 + \cot^2 x$ replacing the identity $\sec^2 x = 1 + \tan^2 x$.

VI. *The integral* $\int \frac{dx}{a\cos x + b \sin x + c}$, $a, b, c \in \mathbf{R}$ (a, b not both zero)

We use the substitution, i.e. change of variable, $u = \tan \tfrac{1}{2}x$. Then

$$du = \tfrac{1}{2}\sec^2 \tfrac{1}{2}x \, dx = \tfrac{1}{2}(1+u^2) dx, \quad \text{so that} \quad dx = \frac{2}{1+u^2} du,$$

and $$\sin x = 2 \sin \tfrac{1}{2}x \cos \tfrac{1}{2}x = \frac{2 \sin \frac{1}{2}x \cos \frac{1}{2}x}{\cos^2 \frac{1}{2}x + \sin^2 \frac{1}{2}x} = \frac{2u}{1+u^2},$$

$$\cos x = \cos^2 \tfrac{1}{2}x - \sin^2 \tfrac{1}{2}x = \frac{\cos^2 \frac{1}{2}x - \sin^2 \frac{1}{2}x}{\cos^2 \frac{1}{2}x + \sin^2 \frac{1}{2}x} = \frac{1-u^2}{1+u^2}.$$

$$\int \frac{dx}{a \cos x + b \sin x + c} = 2 \int \frac{du}{a(1-u^2) + 2bu + c(1+u^2)},$$

and we have reduced the problem to that of dealing with rational functions which we shall consider in detail in Section **4**.

Example 6. Evaluate

$$\text{(i)} \int_0^{\pi} \frac{dx}{5+4\cos x}, \quad \text{(ii)} \int_{\alpha}^{\frac{1}{4}\pi} \frac{dx}{\cos^2 x + 16\sin^2 x}, \ \alpha = \tan^{-1}\tfrac{1}{2}.$$

$$\text{(i)} \int_0^{\pi} \frac{dx}{5+4\cos x} = \int_0^{\infty} \frac{2\,du}{5(1+u^2)+4(1-u^2)}, \ u = \tan\tfrac{1}{2}x, \ \begin{array}{c|c|c} x & 0 & \pi \\ \hline u & 0 & \infty \end{array}.$$

$$= 2\int_0^{\infty} \frac{du}{9+u^2} = \tfrac{2}{3}[\tan^{-1}\tfrac{1}{3}u]_0^{\infty} = \tfrac{1}{3}\pi.$$

(ii) We first note that

$$\int \frac{dx}{a\cos^2 x + 2b\cos x \sin x + c\sin^2 x}$$

can be expressed in the form

$$\int \frac{dx}{\alpha\cos 2x + \beta\sin 2x + \gamma},$$

by using $\cos^2 x = \frac{1}{2}(1+\cos 2x)$, $\sin^2 x = \frac{1}{2}(1-\cos 2x)$, $\sin x \cos x = \frac{1}{2}\sin 2x$. It follows, from the work in **VI**, that the substitution $u = \tan x$ reduces the integral to that of a rational function.

$$\int_{\alpha}^{\frac{1}{4}\pi} \frac{dx}{\cos^2 x + 16\sin^2 x} = \int_{\alpha}^{\frac{1}{4}\pi} \frac{\sec^2 x\,dx}{1+16\tan^2 x}$$

$$= \tfrac{1}{16}\int_{\frac{1}{2}}^{1} \frac{du}{\frac{1}{16}+u^2} = \tfrac{1}{4}[\tan^{-1} 4u]_{\frac{1}{2}}^{1}$$

$$= \tfrac{1}{4}(\tan^{-1} 4 - \tan^{-1} 2) = \tfrac{1}{4}\tan^{-1}\tfrac{2}{9}.$$

3. Integrals involving irrational functions

We have already met some standard integrals of this type, e.g.

$$\int (ax+b)^{\frac{p}{q}}\,dx = \frac{1}{\left(\frac{p}{q}+1\right)a}(ax+b)^{\frac{p}{q}+1} + C \left(\frac{p}{q} \in \mathbf{Q}-\mathbf{Z}, \ a \neq 0\right),$$

$$\int \frac{dx}{\sqrt{(a^2-x^2)}} = \sin^{-1}\frac{x}{a} + C \ (a>0), \quad \int \frac{dx}{\sqrt{(x^2+k)}} = \log|x+\sqrt{(x^2+k)}| + C.$$

We now consider in turn several types of integrals involving irrational functions.

I. $\int (a^2+x^2)^n\,dx, \ n \in \mathbf{Q}, \ a > 0$

It is often useful to use the substitution

$$\theta = \tan^{-1}\frac{x}{a};$$

then $\qquad x = a\tan\theta,\ dx = a\sec^2\theta\,d\theta,\ a^2+x^2 = a^2\sec^2\theta,$

and $\qquad -\tfrac{1}{2}\pi < \theta < \tfrac{1}{2}\pi.$

Example 1. Evaluate

$$\int_0^1 \frac{dx}{(1+x^2)^{3/2}}.$$

Put $\theta = \tan^{-1}x$; then $x = \tan\theta$, $1+x^2 = \sec^2\theta$, $dx = \sec^2\theta\,d\theta$ and the table of limits is

x	0	1
θ	0	$\frac{1}{4}\pi$

$$\int_0^1 \frac{dx}{(1+x^2)^{3/2}} = \int_0^{\frac{1}{4}\pi} \frac{\sec^2\theta\,d\theta}{\sec^3\theta} = \int_0^{\frac{1}{4}\pi} \cos\theta\,d\theta = [\sin\theta]_0^{\frac{1}{4}\pi} = \frac{1}{\sqrt{2}}.$$

The method can also be useful when n is an integer.

Example 2. Evaluate

$$\int_0^{a\sqrt{3}} \frac{dx}{(a^2+x^2)^2} \quad (a > 0).$$

Put $\qquad \theta = \tan^{-1}\dfrac{x}{a};$

then $x = a\tan\theta$, $a^2+x^2 = a^2\sec^2\theta$, $dx = a\sec^2\theta\,d\theta$ and the table of limits is:

x	0	$a\sqrt{3}$
θ	0	$\frac{1}{3}\pi$

$$\int_0^{a\sqrt{3}} \frac{dx}{(a^2+x^2)^2} = \int_0^{\frac{1}{3}\pi} \frac{a\sec^2\theta\,d\theta}{a^4\sec^4\theta} = \frac{1}{a^3}\int_0^{\frac{1}{3}\pi} \cos^2\theta\,d\theta$$

$$= \frac{1}{2a^3}\int_0^{\frac{1}{3}\pi} (1+\cos 2\theta)d\theta = \frac{1}{2a^3}\left[\theta + \frac{\sin 2\theta}{2}\right]_0^{\frac{1}{3}\pi}$$

$$= \frac{1}{a^3}\left(\tfrac{1}{6}\pi + \tfrac{1}{8}\sqrt{3}\right).$$

II. $\int (a^2 - x^2)^n dx$, $n \in \mathbf{Q}$, $a > 0$

It is often useful to use the substitution

$$\theta = \sin^{-1}\frac{x}{a};$$

then $$x = a \sin\theta,\ dx = a\cos\theta\, d\theta,\ a^2 - x^2 = a^2\cos^2\theta$$

and $$-\tfrac{1}{2}\pi \leqslant \theta \leqslant \tfrac{1}{2}\pi.$$

[Note that $\cos\theta > 0$ on $(-\tfrac{1}{2}\pi, \tfrac{1}{2}\pi)$.]

Example 3. Find $\displaystyle\int \frac{dx}{(a^2-x^2)^{3/2}}$, $a > 0$.

Put $$\theta = \sin^{-1}\frac{x}{a};$$

then $$x = a\sin\theta,\ a^2 - x^2 = a^2\cos^2\theta,\ dx = a\cos\theta\, d\theta.$$

$$\int \frac{dx}{(a^2-x^2)^{3/2}} = \int \frac{a\cos\theta\, d\theta}{a^3\cos^3\theta} = \frac{1}{a^2}\int \sec^2\theta\, d\theta$$

$$= \frac{1}{a^2}\tan\theta + C = \frac{x}{a^2\sqrt{(a^2-x^2)}} + C.$$

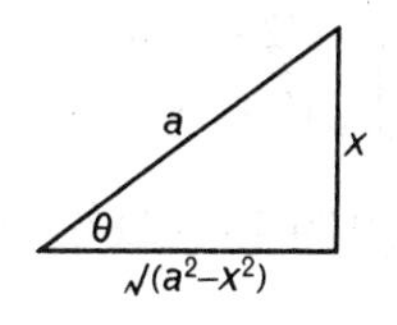

[Note that $\tan\theta$ and $\sin\theta$ have the same sign, namely that of x.]

III. Integrals of form

$$\int \frac{px+q}{\sqrt{(ax^2+bx+c)}}dx,\ \int (px+q)\sqrt{(ax^2+bx+c)}dx, \text{ etc., } a \neq 0$$

We note that

$$\frac{d}{dx}(ax^2+bx+c) = 2ax + b,$$

and express $px+q$ as

$$\frac{p}{2a}(2ax+b)+\left(q-\frac{pb}{2a}\right). \quad \text{Then}$$

$$\int\frac{px+q}{\sqrt{(ax^2+bx+c)}}dx = \frac{p}{2a}\int\frac{(2ax+b)dx}{\sqrt{(ax^2+bx+c)}}+\left(q-\frac{pb}{2a}\right)$$
$$\times\int\frac{dx}{\sqrt{\left\{a\left(x+\frac{b}{2a}\right)^2+\left(c-\frac{b^2}{4a}\right)\right\}}}$$
$$=\frac{p}{a}\sqrt{(ax^2+bx+c)}+\left(q-\frac{pb}{2a}\right)$$
$$\times\int\frac{du}{\sqrt{(au^2+g)}}\left(u = x+\frac{b}{2a},\ g = c-\frac{b^2}{4a}\right),$$

and $\int\frac{du}{\sqrt{(au^2+g)}}$ is now effectively a standard integral.

Example 4. Find $\int\frac{x+2}{\sqrt{(1+2x-2x^2)}}dx.$

$$\frac{d}{dx}(1+2x-2x^2) = 2-4x, \quad \text{and} \quad x+2 = -\tfrac{1}{4}(2-4x)+\tfrac{5}{2}.$$

$$\int\frac{x+2}{\sqrt{(1+2x-2x^2)}}dx = -\tfrac{1}{4}\int\frac{(2-4x)dx}{\sqrt{(1+2x-2x^2)}}+\frac{5}{2\sqrt{2}}\int\frac{dx}{\sqrt{(\frac{1}{2}+x-x^2)}}$$
$$= -\tfrac{1}{2}\sqrt{(1+2x-2x^2)}+\frac{5}{2\sqrt{2}}\int\frac{d(x-\frac{1}{2})}{\sqrt{\{\frac{3}{4}-(x-\frac{1}{2})^2\}}}$$
$$= -\tfrac{1}{2}\sqrt{(1+2x-2x^2)}+\frac{5}{2\sqrt{2}}\sin^{-1}\frac{2x-1}{\sqrt{3}}+C.$$

IV. Irrational integrals reduced to rational integrals by suitable changes of variable

We illustrate some useful methods with examples.

Example 5. Find $\int\frac{x\,dx}{1+\sqrt{(x-1)}}$.

Put $$u = \sqrt{(x-1)};$$
then $$x = u^2+1,\ dx = 2u\,du$$

and

$$\begin{aligned}\int \frac{x\,dx}{1+\sqrt{(x-1)}} &= \int \frac{u^2+1}{u+1}\,2u\,du \\ &= 2\int\left(u^2-u+2-\frac{2}{u+1}\right)du \\ &= \tfrac{2}{3}u^3-u^2+4u-4\log|1+u|+C_1 \\ &= \tfrac{2}{3}(x-1)^{3/2}-x+4\sqrt{(x-1)}-4\log|1+\sqrt{(x-1)}|+C.\end{aligned}$$

$$\begin{array}{r|l} & u^2-u+2 \\ \hline u+1 & u^3+u \\ & \underline{u^3+u^2} \\ & \quad -u^2+u \\ & \quad \underline{-u^2-u} \\ & \qquad\quad 2u \\ & \qquad\quad \underline{2u+2} \\ & \qquad\qquad -2 \end{array}$$

Example 6. Find $\displaystyle\int \frac{(x+1)^{3/2}}{x^2-x-1}\,dx.$

Put $\qquad u=\sqrt{(x+1)};$

then $\qquad x=u^2-1,\ dx=2u\,du$

and $\qquad \displaystyle\int \frac{(x+1)^{3/2}}{x^2-x-1}\,dx=\int \frac{2u^4}{u^4-3u^2+1}\,du,$

and this is a rational integral of a type to be discussed in Section **4**.

Example 7. Evaluate $\displaystyle\int_0^1 \frac{dx}{(2-x)\sqrt{(4-x^2)}}.$

Put $\qquad 2-x=\dfrac{1}{u};$

then $\qquad dx=\dfrac{du}{u^2},\ 4-x^2=\dfrac{4}{u^2}(u-\tfrac{1}{4}),\quad \begin{array}{c|c|c} x & 0 & 1 \\ \hline u & \frac{1}{2} & 1 \end{array}.$

and $\qquad \displaystyle\int_0^1 \frac{dx}{(2-x)\sqrt{(4-x^2)}}=\tfrac{1}{2}\int_{\frac{1}{2}}^{1}\frac{du}{\sqrt{(u-\frac{1}{4})}}=[\sqrt{(u-\tfrac{1}{4})}]_{\frac{1}{2}}^{1}=\tfrac{1}{2}(\sqrt{3}-1).$

[Or, put $\theta=\sin^{-1}\frac{1}{2}x$, i.e. $x=2\sin\theta$.]

Example 8. Find $\int \frac{dx}{\sqrt{(1+e^{-2x})}}$.

$$\int \frac{dx}{\sqrt{(1+e^{-2x})}} = \int \frac{e^x\,dx}{\sqrt{(e^{2x}+1)}} = \int \frac{du}{\sqrt{(u^2+1)}} \quad (u = e^x)$$

$$= \log(u+\sqrt{(u^2+1)})+C = \log(e^x+\sqrt{(e^{2x}+1)})+C.$$

Example 9. Evaluate $\int_0^{\sqrt{3}} \frac{dx}{(1+x^2)\sqrt{(3-x^2)}}$.

Put
$$x = \frac{1}{u};$$

then
$$dx = -\frac{du}{u^2},$$

x	0	$\sqrt{3}$
u	∞	$\frac{1}{\sqrt{3}}$

and
$$\int_0^{\sqrt{3}} \frac{dx}{(1+x^2)\sqrt{(3-x^2)}} = \int_{\frac{1}{\sqrt{3}}}^{\infty} \frac{u\,du}{(1+u^2)\sqrt{(3u^2-1)}}.$$

Now put $v = \sqrt{(3u^2-1)}$; $u^2 = \frac{1}{3}(v^2+1)$, $u\,du = \frac{1}{3}v\,dv$,

u	$1/\sqrt{3}$	∞
v	0	∞

and the integral equals

$$\int_0^{\infty} \frac{dv}{v^2+4} = [\tfrac{1}{2}\tan^{-1}\tfrac{1}{2}v]_0^{\infty} = \tfrac{1}{4}\pi.$$

[Alternatively, put $\theta = \sin^{-1}\frac{x}{\sqrt{3}}$ and then $t = \tan\theta$.]

Example 10. Evaluate $\int_a^b \sqrt{\{(x-a)(b-x)\}}\,dx$, $0 < a < b$.

Put
$$x = a\cos^2\theta + b\sin^2\theta,\ 0 \leqslant \theta \leqslant \tfrac{1}{2}\pi;$$

$dx = 2(b-a)\sin\theta\cos\theta\,d\theta,\ x-a = (b-a)\sin^2\theta,\ b-x = (b-a)\cos^2\theta,$

x	a	b
θ	0	$\frac{1}{2}\pi$

$$\int_a^b \sqrt{\{(x-a)(b-x)\}}\,dx = 2(b-a)^2\int_0^{\frac{1}{2}\pi}\sin^2\theta\cos^2\theta\,d\theta$$

$$= 2(b-a)^2\cdot\frac{1.1}{4.2}\cdot\frac{\pi}{2} = \frac{1}{8}(b-a)^2\pi.$$

4. Integrals of rational functions, partial fractions

We already have as standard integrals: If $a \neq 0$,

$$\int (ax+b)^n dx = \frac{1}{(n+1)a}(ax+b)^{n+1}+C \quad (n \in \mathbf{Z},\ n \neq -1),$$

$$\int \frac{dx}{ax+b} = \frac{1}{a}\log|ax+b|+C,\quad \int\frac{dx}{a^2+x^2} = \frac{1}{a}\tan^{-1}\frac{x}{a}+C.$$

An important class of rational integrals consists of those of the form

$$\int \frac{px+q}{ax^2+bx+c}\,dx, \tag{4.1}$$

where $a > 0$ and ax^2+bx+c does not have real *linear* factors, so that b^2-4ac, the discriminant of the quadratic ax^2+bx+c, is negative.

We first note that

$$\frac{d}{dx}(ax^2+bx+c) = 2ax+b$$

and express $px+q$ in the form

$$\frac{p}{2a}(2ax+b)+\left(q-\frac{pb}{2a}\right).$$

Then

$$\int\frac{px+q}{ax^2+bx+c}\,dx = \frac{p}{2a}\int\frac{2ax+b}{ax^2+bx+c}\,dx+\left(q-\frac{pb}{2a}\right)\int\frac{dx}{ax^2+bx+c}$$

$$= \frac{p}{2a}\log(ax^2+bx+c)+\frac{(2aq-pb)}{2a^2}\int\frac{d\left(x+\dfrac{b}{2a}\right)}{\left(x+\dfrac{b}{2a}\right)^2+\dfrac{4ac-b^2}{4a^2}}$$

$$= \frac{p}{2a}\log(ax^2+bx+c)+\frac{(2aq-pb)}{a\sqrt{(4ac-b^2)}}\tan^{-1}\left(\frac{2ax+b}{\sqrt{(4ac-b^2)}}\right)+C. \tag{4.2}$$

[Note that $ax^2+bx+c>0\ \forall x\in\mathbf{R}$ (since $a>0$ and $b^2-4ac<0$), and that $4ac-b^2>0$; clearly it is better to deal with each example of this type on its own rather than try to apply (4.2).]

Example 1. Find $\displaystyle\int\frac{1-x}{2x^2+4x+5}\,dx.$

Here $a=2$ and $b^2-4ac=-24<0$, and so the integral is of type (4.1).

$$\frac{d}{dx}(2x^2+4x+5)=4x+4 \quad\text{and}\quad 1-x=-\tfrac{1}{4}(4x+4)+2.$$

$$\begin{aligned}\int\frac{1-x}{2x^2+4x+5}\,dx &= -\tfrac{1}{4}\int\frac{4x+4}{2x^2+4x+5}\,dx+\int\frac{dx}{x^2+2x+\frac{5}{2}}\\ &= -\tfrac{1}{4}\log(2x^2+4x+5)+\int\frac{d(x+1)}{(x+1)^2+\frac{3}{2}}\\ &= -\tfrac{1}{4}\log(2x^2+4x+5)+\sqrt{(\tfrac{2}{3})}\tan^{-1}\{(x+1)\sqrt{(\tfrac{2}{3})}\}+C.\end{aligned}$$

Example 2. Evaluate $\displaystyle\int_0^{\pi}\frac{dx}{2+\sin x}.$

Put
$$u=\tan\tfrac{1}{2}x;$$

then
$$dx=\frac{2du}{1+u^2},\quad \sin x=\frac{2u}{1+u^2},$$

x	0	π
u	0	∞

and
$$\begin{aligned}\int_0^{\pi}\frac{dx}{2+\sin x} &= \int_0^{\infty}\frac{du}{u^2+u+1}=\int_0^{\infty}\frac{d(u+\frac{1}{2})}{(u+\frac{1}{2})^2+\frac{3}{4}}\\ &= \left[\frac{2}{\sqrt{3}}\tan^{-1}\frac{2u+1}{\sqrt{3}}\right]_0^{\infty}=\frac{2}{\sqrt{3}}(\tfrac{1}{2}\pi-\tfrac{1}{6}\pi)=\frac{2\pi}{3\sqrt{3}}.\end{aligned}$$

Example 3. Find $\displaystyle\int\frac{dx}{\cosh x}.$

$$\begin{aligned}\int\frac{dx}{\cosh x} &= 2\int\frac{dx}{e^x+e^{-x}}=2\int\frac{e^x\,dx}{e^{2x}+1}\\ &= 2\int\frac{d(e^x)}{1+(e^x)^2}=2\tan^{-1}(e^x)+C.\end{aligned}$$

As an introduction to the basic method for dealing with antiderivatives of rational functions we consider

$$\int \frac{dx}{x^2-a^2} \ (a \neq 0).$$

We first note that

$$\frac{1}{x^2-a^2} = \frac{1}{(x-a)(x+a)} = \frac{\frac{1}{2a}}{x-a} - \frac{\frac{1}{2a}}{x+a}. \tag{4.3}$$

Hence $\displaystyle\int \frac{dx}{x^2-a^2} = \frac{1}{2a}\log|x-a| - \frac{1}{2a}\log|x+a| + C = \frac{1}{2a}\log\left|\frac{x-a}{x+a}\right| + C.$

Equation (4.3) is said to express $\dfrac{1}{x^2-a^2}$ in terms of **partial fractions.** We now describe how every rational function can be expressed in a standard form involving fractions which lead, so far as antidifferentiation is concerned, to integrals of polynomials, integrals of the form

$$\int \frac{dx}{(ax+b)^n} \ (n \in \mathbf{N})$$

and integrals of the form (4.1) or (4.1) with denominator $(ax^2+bx+c)^n$, where $n \in \mathbf{N}$, $n \geqslant 2$.

Partial fractions for rational expressions

$$\frac{f(x)}{g(x)}, \quad \text{where} \quad f(x),\, g(x)$$

are real polynomials with no common factor of degree $\geqslant 1$.

If $\partial f \geqslant \partial g$, where ∂f means the degree of a polynomial $f(x)$, we can divide $f(x)$ by $g(x)$, obtaining, say, $f(x) = g(x)q(x) + r(x)$, where $q(x)$ is the *quotient* and $r(x)$ is the *remainder* and $\partial r < \partial g$. Then

$$\frac{f(x)}{g(x)} = q(x) + \frac{r(x)}{g(x)},$$

and we are now concerned with

$$\frac{r(x)}{g(x)}, \quad \text{where} \quad \partial r < \partial g.$$

In work on complex numbers it is shown that a *real* polynomial $g(x)$ can be factorised as a product of powers of *real linear* factors and (or) *irreducible real quadratic* factors. For example,

$$x^2-a^2=(x-a)(x+a) \quad (a\in\mathbf{R}),$$
$$x^3-a^3=(x-a)(x^2+ax+a^2) \quad (a\in\mathbf{R}-\{0\}),$$
$$x^3+1=(x+1)(x^2-x+1),$$
$$(x^4-1)^2=(x-1)^2(x+1)^2(x^2+1)^2,$$
$$x^4+1=(x^2+1)^2-2x^2=(x^2+\sqrt{2}x+1)(x^2-\sqrt{2}x+1), \text{ etc.}$$

If $g(x)$

$$=(x-\alpha_1)^{m_1}(x-\alpha_2)^{m_2}\cdots(x-\alpha_r)^{m_r}(a_1x^2+b_1x+c_1)^{n_1}\cdots(a_sx^2+b_sx+c_s)^{n_s}$$

is a factorisation of $g(x)$ into real linear and irreducible real quadratic factors, then it can be proved that, provided $\partial r<\partial g$,

$$\frac{r(x)}{g(x)}=\sum_{i=1}^{r}\left\{\frac{A_{i1}}{x-\alpha_i}+\frac{A_{i2}}{(x-\alpha_i)^2}+\cdots+\frac{A_{im_i}}{(x-\alpha_i)^{m_i}}\right\}$$
$$+\sum_{j=1}^{s}\left\{\frac{B_{j1}x+C_{j1}}{a_jx^2+b_jx+c_j}+\frac{B_{j2}x+C_{j2}}{(a_jx^2+b_jx+c_j)^2}+\cdots+\frac{B_{jn_j}x+C_{jn_j}}{(a_jx^2+b_jx+c_j)^{n_j}}\right\}, \quad (4.4)$$

where the coefficients A_{ij}, B_{ij}, C_{ij} are unique real numbers. The right-hand side of (4.4) is said to be an **expression in partial fractions** for $r(x)/g(x)$, where $\partial r<\partial g$. Methods for determining the coefficients in the expression are given in the solutions of the following examples.

Example 4. Find (i) $\displaystyle\int\frac{x}{2x+1}dx$, (ii) $\displaystyle\int\frac{x^2}{x^2+4}dx$, (iii) $\displaystyle\int\frac{x^2}{x^2-4}dx$.

(i) $$\int\frac{x}{2x+1}dx=\int\frac{\frac{1}{2}(2x+1)-\frac{1}{2}}{2x+1}dx=\int\left(\frac{1}{2}-\frac{\frac{1}{2}}{2x+1}\right)dx$$
$$=\tfrac{1}{2}x-\tfrac{1}{4}\log|2x+1|+C;$$

(ii) $$\int\frac{x^2}{x^2+4}dx=\int\left(1-\frac{4}{x^2+4}\right)dx=x-2\tan^{-1}\tfrac{1}{2}x+C;$$

(iii) $$\int\frac{x^2}{x^2-4}dx=\int\left(1+\frac{4}{x^2-4}\right)dx=x+\int\frac{4}{x^2-4}dx.$$

We now find partial fractions for

$$\frac{4}{x^2-4}=\frac{4}{(x-2)(x+2)};$$

by (4.4), $$\frac{4}{x^2-4}=\frac{A}{x-2}+\frac{B}{x+2},$$

where A, B are unique real numbers. We have: $4 = A(x+2)+B(x-2)$; $x = 2$ in this identity gives $4 = 4A$, and so $A = 1$, and $x = -2$ in the identity gives $4 = -4B$, and so $B = -1$. Thus

$$\int \frac{4}{x^2-4}\,dx = \int \left(\frac{1}{x-2} - \frac{1}{x+2}\right) dx = \log\left|\frac{x-2}{x+2}\right| + C,$$

and so
$$\int \frac{x^2}{x^2-4}\,dx = x + \log\left|\frac{x-2}{x+2}\right| + C.$$

Example 5. Find $I = \displaystyle\int \frac{x^3-4x^2-x+2}{x(x^2-1)}\,dx.$

$$\begin{array}{r|l} & 1 \\ \hline x^3 - x & x^3 - 4x^2 - x + 2 \\ & x^3 \qquad\quad - x \\ \hline & \quad -4x^2 \qquad + 2 \end{array}$$

Here ∂ (numerator) = ∂ (denominator), so we divide numerator by denominator and obtain

$$I = \int \left(1 + \frac{2-4x^2}{x(x-1)(x+1)}\right) dx = x + J,$$

where
$$J = \int \frac{2-4x^2}{x(x-1)(x+1)}\,dx.$$

Now
$$\frac{2-4x^2}{x(x-1)(x+1)} = \frac{A}{x} + \frac{B}{x-1} + \frac{C}{x+1},$$

where
$$2-4x^2 = A(x-1)(x+1) + Bx(x+1) + Cx(x-1). \tag{4.5}$$

$x = 0$ in (4.5) gives $A = -2$; $x = 1$ gives $B = -1$; $x = -1$ gives $C = -1$.

Thus
$$\begin{aligned} J &= \int \left(\frac{-2}{x} - \frac{1}{x-1} - \frac{1}{x+1}\right) dx \\ &= -2\log|x| - \log|x-1| - \log|x+1| + C, \end{aligned}$$

and
$$I = x + \log\frac{1}{x^2|x^2-1|} + C.$$

Example 6. Find $I = \displaystyle\int \frac{x^2+4x+2}{(x+1)^2(x^2+x+1)}\,dx.$

Here
$$\frac{x^2+4x+2}{(x+1)^2(x^2+x+1)} = \frac{A}{x+1} + \frac{B}{(x+1)^2} + \frac{Cx+D}{x^2+x+1},$$

where

$$x^2+4x+2 = A(x+1)(x^2+x+1)+B(x^2+x+1)+(Cx+D)(x+1)^2. \quad (4.6)$$

$x = -1$ in (4.6) gives $B = -1$; then, from (4.6),

$$2x^2+5x+3 = A(x+1)(x^2+x+1)+(Cx+D)(x+1)^2,$$

$$(x+1)(2x+3) = A(x+1)(x^2+x+1)+(Cx+D)(x+1)^2,$$

and so

$$2x+3 = A(x^2+x+1)+(Cx+D)(x+1). \quad (4.7)$$

[Note that, by the remainder theorem, the polynomial given by (right-hand side of (4.6))—(left-hand side of (4.6)), with $B = -1$, must have a factor $x+1$.]

Now $x = -1$ in (4.7) gives $A = 1$; then, from (4.7),

$$-x^2+x+2 = (Cx+D)(x+1),$$

$$(x+1)(-x+2) = (Cx+D)(x+1),$$

and so

$$Cx+D = -x+2 \text{ (i.e. } C = -1, D = 2).$$

Hence

$$I = \int\left(\frac{1}{x+1}-\frac{1}{(x+1)^2}+\frac{2-x}{x^2+x+1}\right)dx.$$

Exercise. Check that

$$I = \log|x+1|+\frac{1}{x+1}-\tfrac{1}{2}\log(x^2+x+1)+\frac{5}{\sqrt{3}}\tan^{-1}\frac{2x+1}{\sqrt{3}}+C.$$

Example 7. Find $I = \displaystyle\int\frac{3(x^3-x^2)}{(x^2+1)(x^3+1)}\,dx.$

Here the integrand is

$$\frac{3(x^3-x^2)}{(x+1)(x^2+1)(x^2-x+1)} = \frac{A}{x+1}+\frac{Bx+C}{x^2+1}+\frac{Dx+E}{x^2-x+1},$$

where

$$3x^3-3x^2 = A(x^2+1)(x^2-x+1) +(Bx+C)(x+1)(x^2-x+1)+(Dx+E)(x+1)(x^2+1). \quad (4.8)$$

$x = -1$ in (4.8) gives $A = -1$; then, from (4.8),

$$x^4+2x^3-x^2-x+1 = (Bx+C)(x+1)(x^2-x+1)+(Dx+E)(x+1)(x^2+1),$$

$$(x+1)(x^3+x^2-2x+1) = (Bx+C)(x+1)(x^2-x+1)+(Dx+E)(x+1)(x^2+1),$$

and so

$$x^3+x^2-2x+1 = (Bx+C)(x^2-x+1)+(Dx+E)(x^2+1). \quad (4.9)$$

Equating coefficients of corresponding powers of x in the polynomial identity (4.9) we have:

from the coefficients of x^3, x^2, x and the constant terms, in turn,

$$\begin{aligned}
(1)\quad 1 &= B+D,\\
(2)\quad 1 &= -B+C+E,\\
(3)\quad -2 &= B-C+D,\\
(4)\quad 1 &= C+E.
\end{aligned}$$

(2)−(4) gives $B = 0$; then (1) gives $D = 1$, (3) gives $C = 3$ and (4) gives $E = -2$.

Hence $$I = \int\left(-\frac{1}{x+1}+\frac{3}{x^2+1}+\frac{x-2}{x^2-x+1}\right)dx.$$

Exercise. Check that

$$I = -\log|x+1|+3\tan^{-1}x+\tfrac{1}{2}\log(x^2-x+1)-\sqrt{3}\tan^{-1}\frac{2x-1}{\sqrt{3}}+C.$$

5. A useful special method

Some definite integrals can be evaluated by using the following result.

Theorem 6.4

$$\int_0^a f(x)dx = \int_0^a f(a-x)dx. \tag{5.1}$$

Proof. Put $x = a-t$ in the left-hand side; then $dx = -dt$,

x	0	a
t	a	0

and $$\int_0^a f(x)dx = \int_a^0 f(a-t)(-dt) = \int_0^a f(a-t)dt = \int_0^a f(a-x)dx,$$

noting that t, x are dummy variables for the right-hand side of (5.1).

Example 1. Evaluate $I = \displaystyle\int_0^\pi \frac{x\sin x}{1+\cos^2 x}dx.$

By (5.1), $$I = \int_0^\pi \frac{(\pi-x)\sin(\pi-x)}{1+\cos^2(\pi-x)}dx = \int_0^\pi \frac{(\pi-x)\sin x}{1+\cos^2 x}d.$$

$$= \pi\int_0^\pi \frac{\sin x}{1+\cos^2 x}dx - I,$$

and so $$I = \tfrac{1}{2}\pi \int_0^\pi \frac{-d(\cos x)}{1+\cos^2 x}$$
$$= \tfrac{1}{2}\pi[-\tan^{-1}(\cos x)]_0^\pi = \tfrac{1}{2}\pi[\tfrac{1}{4}\pi + \tfrac{1}{4}\pi] = \tfrac{1}{4}\pi^2.$$

Example 2. Evaluate $I = \int_0^{\frac{1}{2}\pi} \log(\sin x)dx.$

By (5.1), $I = \int_0^{\frac{1}{2}\pi} \log\sin(\tfrac{1}{2}\pi - x)dx = \int_0^{\frac{1}{2}\pi} \log(\cos x)dx.$

Thus
$$I = \tfrac{1}{2}\int_0^{\frac{1}{2}\pi} \{\log(\sin x) + \log(\cos x)\}\,dx$$
$$= \tfrac{1}{2}\int_0^{\frac{1}{2}\pi} \log(\tfrac{1}{2}\sin 2x)dx$$
$$= \tfrac{1}{2}\int_0^{\frac{1}{2}\pi} \log(\sin 2x)dx - \tfrac{1}{2}\log 2 \int_0^{\frac{1}{2}\pi} dx$$
$$= \tfrac{1}{4}\int_0^{\pi} \log(\sin u)du - \tfrac{1}{4}\pi\log 2 \quad (u = 2x)$$
$$= \tfrac{1}{2}\int_0^{\frac{1}{2}\pi} \log(\sin u)du - \tfrac{1}{4}\pi\log 2 \quad (\sin \text{ is symmetrical about } \tfrac{1}{2}\pi)$$
$$= \tfrac{1}{2}I - \tfrac{1}{4}\pi\log 2,$$

and so $$\int_0^{\frac{1}{2}\pi} \log(\sin x)dx = -\tfrac{1}{2}\pi\log 2.$$

6. Numerical integration for definite integrals

Many functions expressible in terms of elementary functions do not have antiderivatives expressible in terms of elementary functions, e.g.

$$\sin x^2,\ e^{x^2},\ \frac{1}{x}\cos x,\ \frac{1}{x}e^x,\ e^x\log x,\ \frac{1}{\sqrt{(x^5+1)}},\ \text{etc.}$$

In many applications approximations to the values of definite integrals have to be obtained by numerical techniques, often with the use of a computer. We describe some of the ideas behind one of these methods of numerical integration, namely:

Simpson's rule

We begin by approximating to the shaded area shown (bounded by the graph of the continuous function f, the x-axis and the ordinates

$x = x_i, x = x_{i+1}$) by the parabola indicated by the broken curve which has axis parallel to the y-axis and passes through the points

$$A(x_i, f(x_i)),\ B\left(\frac{x_i + x_{i+1}}{2}, f\left(\frac{x_i + x_{i+1}}{2}\right)\right),\ C(x_{i+1}, f(x_{i+1})).$$

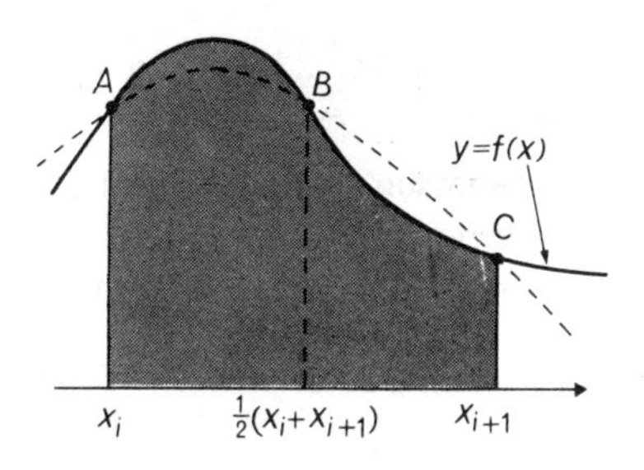

If the parabola has equation $y = \alpha x^2 + \beta x + \gamma$, then the area under the parabola is

$$\int_{x_i}^{x_{i+1}} (\alpha x^2 + \beta x + \gamma)dx$$

$$= \tfrac{1}{3}\alpha(x_{i+1}^3 - x_i^3) + \tfrac{1}{2}\beta(x_{i+1}^2 - x_i^2) + \gamma(x_{i+1} - x_i)$$

$$= \tfrac{1}{6}(x_{i+1} - x_i)[2\alpha(x_{i+1}^2 + x_{i+1}x_i + x_i^2) + 3\beta(x_{i+1} + x_i) + 6\gamma]$$

$$= \tfrac{1}{6}(x_{i+1} - x_i)$$

$$\times [(\alpha x_i^2 + \beta x_i + \gamma) + (\alpha x_{i+1}^2 + \beta x_{i+1} + \gamma) + \alpha(x_i + x_{i+1})^2 + 2\beta(x_i + x_{i+1}) + 4\gamma]$$

$$= \tfrac{1}{6}(x_{i+1} - x_i)\left[f(x_i) + f(x_{i+1}) + 4\left\{\alpha\left(\frac{x_i + x_{i+1}}{2}\right)^2 + \beta\left(\frac{x_i + x_{i+1}}{2}\right) + \gamma\right\}\right]$$

$$= \tfrac{1}{6}(x_{i+1} - x_i)\left[f(x_i) + 4f\left(\frac{x_i + x_{i+1}}{2}\right) + f(x_{i+1})\right]. \tag{6.1}$$

Consider now $$\int_a^b f(x)dx.$$

We divide $[a, b]$ into n equal parts by the dissection

$$a = x_0 < x_1 < x_2 < \cdots < x_n = b,$$

where $$x_{i+1} - x_i = \frac{b-a}{n}.$$

Using the above parabolic approximation for $i = 0, 1, \cdots, n-1$, we have, from (6.1),

$$\int_a^b f(x)dx \doteqdot \sum_{i=0}^{n-1} \frac{(b-a)}{6n}\left[f(x_i)+4f\left(\frac{x_i+x_{i+1}}{2}\right)+f(x_{i+1})\right]$$

$$= \frac{(b-a)}{6n}\left[f(x_0)+f(x_n)+2\{f(x_1)+\cdots+f(x_{n-1})\}\right.$$

$$\left.+4\left\{f\left(\frac{x_0+x_1}{2}\right)+\cdots+f\left(\frac{x_{n-1}+x_n}{2}\right)\right\}\right]. \quad (6.2)$$

The statement (6.2) is **Simpson's rule** for numerical integration.

A discussion on the important question of just how accurate the approximation is can be found in books on numerical methods.

Example. By using Simpson's rule with $n = 5$, obtain an approximation to

$$I = \int_0^1 \frac{dx}{\sqrt{(1+x^4)}}.$$

We first show, for interest, that we can obtain bounds for I by the use of inequalities.

$$\forall x \in [0, 1], \quad 1 \leqslant 1+x^4 \leqslant 1+x^2,\ 1 \leqslant \sqrt{(1+x^4)} \leqslant \sqrt{(1+x^2)},$$

and so
$$\frac{1}{\sqrt{(1+x^2)}} \leqslant \frac{1}{\sqrt{(1+x^4)}} \leqslant 1.$$

Consequently,
$$\int_0^1 \frac{dx}{\sqrt{(1+x^2)}} \leqslant \int_0^1 \frac{dx}{\sqrt{(1+x^4)}} \leqslant \int_0^1 1\,dx.$$

$$[\log(x+\sqrt{(1+x^2)})]_0^1 \leqslant I \leqslant 1,$$

and so $\log(1+\sqrt{2}) \leqslant I \leqslant 1$, giving $0{\cdot}881 < I < 1$.

Now using Simpson's rule with

$$f(x) = \frac{1}{\sqrt{(1+x^4)}},\ a = 0,\ b = 1,\ n = 5, \quad \text{we have} \quad \frac{b-a}{6n} = \frac{1}{30},$$

and
$$I \doteqdot \frac{1}{30}\left[1+\frac{1}{\sqrt{2}}+2\left\{\frac{1}{\sqrt{1{\cdot}0016}}+\frac{1}{\sqrt{1{\cdot}0256}}+\frac{1}{\sqrt{1{\cdot}1296}}+\frac{1}{\sqrt{1{\cdot}4096}}\right\}\right.$$

$$\left.+4\left\{\frac{1}{\sqrt{1{\cdot}0001}}+\frac{1}{\sqrt{1{\cdot}0081}}+\frac{1}{\sqrt{1{\cdot}0625}}+\frac{1}{\sqrt{1{\cdot}2401}}+\frac{1}{\sqrt{1{\cdot}6561}}\right\}\right]$$

$$= \frac{1}{30}[1{\cdot}7071+7{\cdot}5396+18{\cdot}5645] = 0{\cdot}927.$$

EXERCISE 6

1. Integrate with respect to x:

(1) $\dfrac{x^3}{1+x^4}$, (2) $\dfrac{x}{\sqrt{(2+x^2)}}$, (3) $\dfrac{x^4}{(x^5-4)^{3/2}}$,

(4) $\dfrac{x^4}{\sqrt{(x^{10}-4)}}$, (5) $\dfrac{x^2}{\sqrt{(2-x^6)}}$, (6) $\dfrac{x}{4x^4+9}$,

(7) $x^3 e^{-x^4}$, (8) $(2x-1)e^{x^2-x}$, (9) $x \sin x^2$,

(10) $x^3(x^2+a^2)^{51}$ $(a \neq 0)$, (11) $\tanh x$, (12) $\dfrac{1}{x}\log x$,

(13) $\dfrac{1}{2x+1}\log(2x+1)$, (14) $x \sin 2x$, (15) $x^2 \cos x$,

(16) $x^2 e^{-x}$, (17) $e^{-2x}\sin x$, (18) $e^x \cos^2 x$,

(19) $\cos(\log x)$, (20) $\sin(\log x)$, (21) $x^2 \log x$,

(22) $\dfrac{1}{x^2}\sin(\log x)$, (23) $x \tan^{-1} x$, (24) $x \log(x^2+1)$,

(25) $\cos x \log(\sin x)$, (26) $x \sinh x$, (27) $x\,2^x$,

(28) $x e^x \sin x$, (29) $\sin 2x \cos 4x$, (30) $\sin x \sin 3x$,

(31) $\sin^3 x \cos^2 x$, (32) $\sin^4 x \cos^5 x$, (33) $\sin^2 x \cos^4 x$,

(34) $\sin^4 x \cos^4 x$, (35) $\tan^4 x$, (36) $\operatorname{cosec}^4 x$,

(37) $\dfrac{\sin^2 x}{\cos^4 x}$, (38) $\dfrac{1}{1+\sin x}$, (39) $\dfrac{1}{\cos x+2\sin x+5}$,

(40) $\dfrac{1}{\cos^2 x+4\sin^2 x}$, (41) $\dfrac{1}{(1+x^2)^{5/2}}$, (42) $\dfrac{1}{(a^2-x^2)^{5/2}}$ $(a>0)$,

(43) $\dfrac{1+x}{\sqrt{(1+x^2)}}$, (44) $\dfrac{1}{\sqrt{(x^2+2x+3)}}$, (45) $\dfrac{1-2x}{\sqrt{(2+x-2x^2)}}$,

(46) $\dfrac{x}{x+\sqrt{(x-1)}}$, (47) $\dfrac{1}{x\sqrt{(2-x^2)}}$, (48) $\dfrac{1}{\sqrt{(1+e^{2x})}}$,

(49) $\dfrac{1}{(1+x^2)\sqrt{(1-x^2)}}$, (50) $\dfrac{1}{\sqrt{\{(x-a)(b-x)\}}}$ $(0<a<b)$,

(51) $\dfrac{1}{4-x^2}$, (52) $\dfrac{1}{\sinh x}$, (53) $\dfrac{x^2+x}{x^2+1}$,

(54) $\dfrac{x}{x^2+2x+3}$, (55) $\dfrac{x^3+5x}{x^2-4}$, (56) $\dfrac{x^4-x^3+6x-2}{x(x+1)(x-2)}$,

(57) $\dfrac{1}{x^3+1}$, (58) $\dfrac{x^2-x+2}{(x+1)(x^2+1)}$, (59) $\dfrac{2x^4+3x^2-x+1}{x(x^2+1)^2}$,

(60) $\dfrac{x^5+3x^4+x^3+x^2-3x+3}{(x+2)(x^4+x^2+1)}$.

2. Evaluate:

(1) $\displaystyle\int_0^1 \frac{x^2}{1+x^3}\,dx$, (2) $\displaystyle\int_0^1 \frac{x}{\sqrt{(3+x^2)}}\,dx$, (3) $\displaystyle\int_1^{\sqrt[4]{3}} \frac{x}{\sqrt{(4-x^4)}}\,dx$,

(4) $\displaystyle\int_{\sqrt{2}}^{\infty} \frac{x}{x^4+4}\,dx$, (5) $\displaystyle\int_0^{\sqrt{(\pi/2)}} x\cos x^2\,dx$, (6) $\displaystyle\int_1^{e^{\pi/4}} \frac{1}{x}\sin(\log x)\,dx$,

(7) $\displaystyle\int_1^{e} \frac{1}{x^2}\log x\,dx$, (8) $\displaystyle\int_0^{\infty} x^3 e^{-x}\,dx$, (9) $\displaystyle\int_0^{\infty} e^{-x}\sin 2x\,dx$,

(10) $\displaystyle\int_0^1 \tan^{-1} x\,dx$, (11) $\displaystyle\int_{\frac{1}{2}}^1 x\sin^{-1} x\,dx$, (12) $\displaystyle\int_0^{\sqrt{2}} \sqrt{(2-x^2)}\,dx$,

(13) $\displaystyle\int_0^1 \sqrt{(x^2+2)}\,dx$, (14) $\displaystyle\int_0^{1/\log 3} x^2\,3^x\,dx$, (15) $\displaystyle\int_0^{\pi/4} \cos 2x\sin 4x\,dx$,

(16) $\displaystyle\int_0^{\pi/6} \sin 3x\sin^3 x\,dx$, (17) $\displaystyle\int_0^{\frac{1}{2}\pi} \sin^3 x\cos^4 x\,dx$, (18) $\displaystyle\int_0^{\frac{1}{2}\pi} \sin^6 x\cos^4 x\,dx$,

(19) $\displaystyle\int_0^{\pi/4} \sin^2 x\cos^4 x\,dx$, (20) $\displaystyle\int_0^{\pi/4} \tan^3 x\,dx$, (21) $\displaystyle\int_{\pi/4}^{\pi/2} \operatorname{cosec}^3 x\,dx$,

(22) $\displaystyle\int_0^{2\pi/3} \frac{3\,dx}{5+4\cos x}$, (23) $\displaystyle\int_0^{\frac{1}{2}\pi} \frac{dx}{3+\sin x}$, (24) $\displaystyle\int_0^{\pi/4} \frac{\sin x}{\sin x+\cos x}\,dx$ $(t = \tan x)$,

(25) $\displaystyle\int_1^{\sqrt{3}} \frac{dx}{x^2\sqrt{(1+x^2)}}$, (26) $\displaystyle\int_0^1 \frac{x^2\,dx}{(4-x^2)^{3/2}}$, (27) $\displaystyle\int_0^{\frac{1}{2}} \frac{1+x}{\sqrt{(1-x^2)}}\,dx$,

(28) $\displaystyle\int_1^2 \frac{x+1}{\sqrt{(x^2-2x+2)}}\,dx$, (29) $\displaystyle\int_1^3 \frac{dx}{1+\sqrt{(x-1)}}$, (30) $\displaystyle\int_0^1 \sqrt{\{x(1-x)\}}\,dx$,

(31) $\displaystyle\int_{-\infty}^{0} \frac{e^{x/2}\,dx}{\sqrt{(\cosh x)}}$, (32) $\displaystyle\int_0^1 \frac{x^2+2x}{x^2+1}\,dx$, (33) $\displaystyle\int_2^3 \frac{2x^2-2x-2}{x(x^2-1)}\,dx$,

(34) $\displaystyle\int_1^2 \frac{3x}{x^3+1}\,dx$, (35) $\displaystyle\int_0^{\sqrt{2}} \frac{3\,dx}{(x+1)(x^2+2)}$, (36) $\displaystyle\int_1^{\sqrt{3}} \frac{2x^2-x+1}{x^2(x^2+1)}\,dx$.

3. For any $n\in\mathbf{Z}^+$, let $I_n = \displaystyle\int_1^e x(\log x)^n\,dx$.

Prove that, for $n \geqslant 1$, $I_n = \frac{1}{2}e^2-\frac{1}{2}nI_{n-1}$, and hence find the value of I_3.

4. Find

$$\int x\sqrt{(1-x^2)}\,dx.$$

If $I_n = \displaystyle\int_0^1 x^n\sqrt{(1-x^2)}\,dx$, where $n\in\mathbf{Z}^+$, show, by writing the integrand as $\{x\sqrt{(1-x^2)}\}x^{n-1}$, that, for $n \geqslant 2$,

$$I_n = \frac{n-1}{n+2}I_{n-2},$$

and hence evaluate I_5.

5. If
$$I_n = \int_0^{\frac{1}{2}\pi} x \cos^n x \, dx,$$
where $n \in \mathbf{Z}^+$, show by writing the integrand as $(x \cos^{n-1} x) \cos x$ and integrating by parts, that, for $n \geqslant 2$,
$$I_n = -\frac{1}{n^2} + \frac{n-1}{n} I_{n-2},$$
and hence evaluate I_6.

6. By using the result $\int_0^a f(x) dx = \int_0^a f(a-x) dx$, evaluate

(i) $\displaystyle\int_0^{\pi} \frac{x \sin^3 x}{1+\cos^2 x} dx$, (ii) $\displaystyle\int_0^{\frac{1}{2}\pi} \frac{\cos^3 x}{\sin x + \cos x} dx$,

(iii) $\displaystyle\int_0^{\frac{1}{2}\pi} \frac{\sin^2 x \cos x}{\sin x + \cos x} dx$, (iv) $\displaystyle\int_0^{\frac{1}{2}\pi} \frac{x}{\sin x + \cos x} dx$,

(v) $\displaystyle\int_0^{\frac{1}{2}\pi} \frac{(\cos x - \sin x)^3}{(\sin x + \cos x)^5} dx$, (vi) $\displaystyle\int_0^{\pi/4} \log(1+\tan x) dx$.

7. Show that $\sin x \geqslant 2x/\pi$ for $0 \leqslant x \leqslant \frac{1}{2}\pi$, and deduce that
$$\int_0^{\frac{1}{2}\pi} \frac{dx}{\sqrt{(1+\sin^2 x)}} \leqslant \tfrac{1}{2}\pi \int_0^{\frac{1}{2}\pi} \frac{dx}{\sqrt{(x^2 + \frac{1}{4}\pi^2)}}.$$
Hence show that
$$\int_0^{\frac{1}{2}\pi} \frac{dx}{\sqrt{(1+\sin^2 x)}} \leqslant \tfrac{1}{2}\pi \log(1+\sqrt{2}).$$
By using Simpson's rule with $n = 5$, find an approximation to the integral.

8. Show that
$$\forall x \in [0, 1], \quad \tfrac{1}{2} \leqslant \frac{1}{\sqrt{(4-x^2+x^3)}} \leqslant \frac{1}{\sqrt{(4-x^2)}},$$
and deduce that
$$\tfrac{1}{2} < \int_0^1 \frac{dx}{\sqrt{(4-x^2+x^3)}} < \tfrac{1}{6}\pi.$$
By using Simpson's rule with $n = 5$, find an approximation to the integral.

9. Find an approximation to
$$\int_{-1}^{1} \frac{x^2}{x+2} dx$$
by using Simpson's rule with $n = 5$. Evaluate the integral exactly and hence obtain an approximation to log 3.

10. Find an approximation to
$$\int_0^{\frac{1}{2}} \frac{dx}{\sqrt{(1-x^2)}}$$
by using Simpson's rule with $n = 5$. Evaluate the integral exactly and hence obtain an approximation to π.

Some applications of integration and differentiation

1. Length of an arc of a curve

We consider the graph of a function f differentiable on a closed interval $[a, b]$, $a < b$ and suppose that f' is continuous on $[a, b]$. The

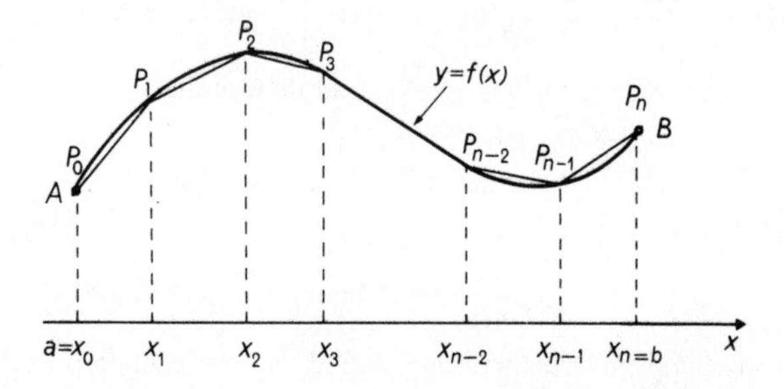

length of arc AB **of curve** $y = f(x)$, where A is the point $(a, f(a))$ and B is the point $(b, f(b))$ can be defined as follows. Take a dissection

$$D = \{a = x_0 < x_1 < x_2 < \cdots < x_n = b\} \text{ of } [a, b]$$

and form
$$\sum_{i=0}^{n-1} |P_i P_{i+1}|,$$

where P_i is the point $(x_i, f(x_i))$, so that the sum is the length of the **approximating polygon** $P_0 P_1 \cdots P_n$ ($P_0 = A$, $P_n = B$). If

$$\lim_{||D|| \to 0} \sum_{i=0}^{n-1} |P_i P_{i+1}|$$

exists, then this number is called the **length of the arc of the curve** $y = f(x)$ **from** A **to** B. We show that, when f' is continuous, the limit does exist and we have:

$$\text{arc length of } y = f(x) \text{ from } A \text{ to } B = \int_a^b \sqrt{\{1 + (f'(x))^2\}}\, dx. \quad (1.1)$$

Proof of (1.1). Since

$$|P_iP_{i+1}| = \sqrt{\{(x_{i+1}-x_i)^2+(f(x_{i+1})-f(x_i))^2\}},$$

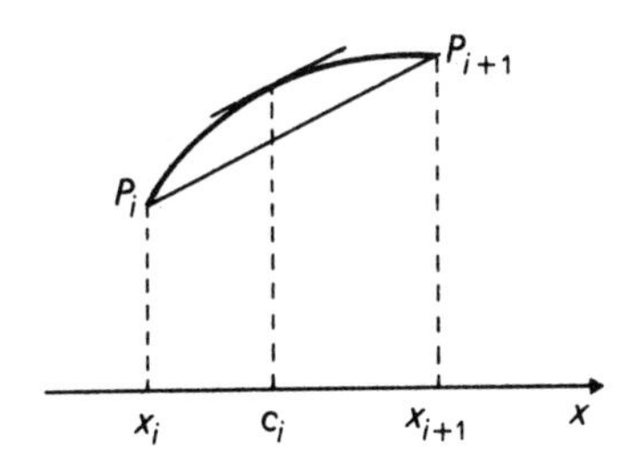

and, by the mean-value theorem,

$$\frac{f(x_{i+1})-f(x_i)}{x_{i+1}-x_i} = f'(c_i), \quad \text{where} \quad x_i < c_i < x_{i+1},$$

we have

$$|P_iP_{i+1}| = \sqrt{\{1+(f'(c_i))^2\}}(x_{i+1}-x_i)(i = 0, \cdots, n-1).$$

Thus $$\lim_{||D||\to 0} \sum_{i=0}^{n-1} |P_iP_{i+1}| = \lim_{||D||\to 0} \sum_{i=0}^{n-1} \sqrt{\{1+(f'(c_i))^2\}}(x_{i+1}-x_i)$$
$$= \int_a^b \sqrt{\{1+(f'(x))^2\}}\,dx,$$

by the definition of the Riemann integral, noting that $\sqrt{\{1+(f'(x))^2\}}$ defines a continuous function on $[a, b]$. The result now follows.

Note. If $s(x)$ denotes the arc length on $y = f(x)$ from $A(a, f(a))$ to $P(x, f(x))$, then

$$s(x) = \int_a^x \sqrt{\{1+(f'(t))^2\}}\,dt;$$

this formula defines a differentiable function on $[a, b]$ and

$$\frac{ds}{dx} = \sqrt{\{1+(f'(x))^2\}} = \sqrt{\left\{1+\left(\frac{dy}{dx}\right)^2\right\}}, \tag{1.2}$$

so that

$$\left(\frac{ds}{dx}\right)^2 = 1+\left(\frac{dy}{dx}\right)^2. \tag{1.3}$$

In finding $s(x)$ and $s(b)$ it is usually simpler to start with (1.3) and (1.2).

Curve in parametric form: $x = x(t)$, $y = y(t)$, $\alpha \leqslant t \leqslant \beta$

Here

$$\frac{ds}{dt} = \frac{ds}{dx}\frac{dx}{dt}, \quad \text{and} \quad \sqrt{\left\{1+\left(\frac{dy}{dx}\right)^2\right\}} = \frac{1}{\left|\frac{dx}{dt}\right|}\sqrt{\left\{\left(\frac{dx}{dt}\right)^2+\left(\frac{dy}{dt}\right)^2\right\}};$$

thus

$$\left(\frac{ds}{dt}\right)^2 = \left(\frac{dx}{dt}\right)^2+\left(\frac{dy}{dt}\right)^2,$$

and

$$s(t) = \int_\alpha^t \sqrt{\left\{\left(\frac{dx}{du}\right)^2+\left(\frac{dy}{du}\right)^2\right\}}\,du, \quad \alpha \leqslant t \leqslant \beta.$$

Curve in polar form: $r = f(\theta)$

Here $\quad x = r\cos\theta = f(\theta)\cos\theta, \; y = r\sin\theta = f(\theta)\sin\theta,$

and

$$\frac{dx}{d\theta} = \frac{dr}{d\theta}\cos\theta - r\sin\theta, \quad \frac{dy}{d\theta} = \frac{dr}{d\theta}\sin\theta + r\cos\theta.$$

Hence $\left(\frac{ds}{d\theta}\right)^2 = \left(\frac{dx}{d\theta}\right)^2+\left(\frac{dy}{d\theta}\right)^2 = r^2+\left(\frac{dr}{d\theta}\right)^2 = (f(\theta))^2+(f'(\theta))^2.$

Example 1. Find the length of the curve $y = \cosh x$ between $x = 0$ and $x = \log 2$.

Here

$$\left(\frac{ds}{dx}\right)^2 = 1+\left(\frac{dy}{dx}\right)^2 = 1+\sinh^2 x = \cosh^2 x,$$

so that

$$\frac{ds}{dx} = \cosh x.$$

Thus the required arc length is

$$\int_0^{\log 2} \cosh x\,dx = [\sinh x]_0^{\log 2} = \sinh(\log 2)$$
$$= \tfrac{1}{2}(e^{\log 2} - e^{-\log 2}) = \tfrac{1}{2}(2-\tfrac{1}{2}) = \tfrac{3}{4}.$$

Example 2. Make a rough sketch of the curve $x = t^2+2t$, $y = t^2-2t$, $-2 \leqslant t \leqslant 2$, and find the length of the curve.

$$\frac{dx}{dt} = 2(t+1), \; \frac{dy}{dt} = 2(t-1); \; \frac{dy}{dx} = \frac{t-1}{t+1} \; (t \neq -1).$$

Hence

$$\frac{dy}{dx} = 0 \Leftrightarrow t = 1,$$

giving a critical point $(3, -1)$; check that this is a local minimum point.

The following table is useful in sketching the curve:

$t: -2$	$\rightarrow$	-1	$\rightarrow$	1	$\rightarrow$	2
$(x, y): (0, 8)$		$(-1, 3)$		$(3, -1)$		$(8, 0)$
$\dfrac{dy}{dx}: 3$	$+$	∞	$-$	0	$+$	$\frac{1}{3}$

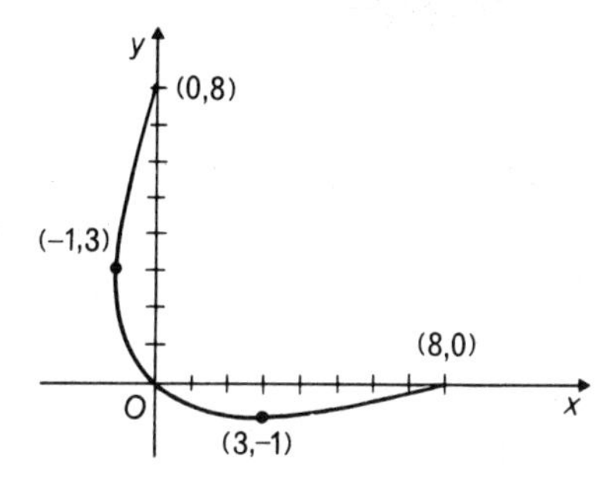

Now
$$\left(\frac{ds}{dt}\right)^2 = \left(\frac{dx}{dt}\right)^2 + \left(\frac{dy}{dt}\right)^2 = 8(1+t^2),$$
so that the arc length is
$$2\sqrt{2}\int_{-2}^{2} \sqrt{(1+t^2)}dt = 4\sqrt{2}\int_{0}^{2} \sqrt{(1+t^2)}dt,$$
since the integrand is even,
$$= 4\sqrt{2}\left[\tfrac{1}{2}t\sqrt{(1+t^2)}+\tfrac{1}{2}\log\{t+\sqrt{(1+t^2)}\}\right]_0^2 = 4\sqrt{10}+2\sqrt{2}\log(2+\sqrt{5}).$$

Example 3. Find the arc length of the cardioid $r = 1+\cos\theta$.

Here
$$\left(\frac{ds}{d\theta}\right)^2 = r^2 + \left(\frac{dr}{d\theta}\right)^2 = (1+\cos\theta)^2+\sin^2\theta = 2(1+\cos\theta) = 4\cos^2\tfrac{1}{2}\theta.$$

and so the arc length $= 2\displaystyle\int_0^{\pi} 2\cos\tfrac{1}{2}\theta\, d\theta = [8\sin\tfrac{1}{2}\theta]_0^{\pi} = 8.$

2. Areas

We have already met, in setting up the Riemann integral, the connection between definite integrals and areas of plane regions, and have only a few additional points to make here.

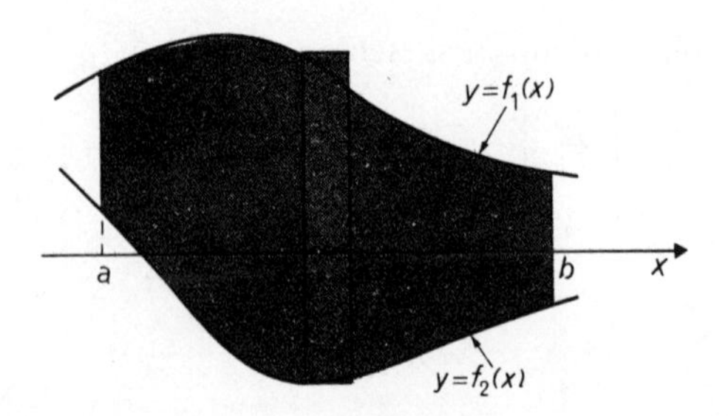

Areas between graphs

The area of the vertical rectangular strip in the diagram shown is $\{f_1(x)-f_2(x)\}dx$, and, in a simplified notation, a Riemann sum for the region bounded above by $y=f_1(x)$, below by $y=f_2(x)$, to left by $x=a$ and to right by $x=b$ is

$$\sum_{x=a}^{b}\{f_1(x)-f_2(x)\}dx.$$

Thus the region has area $\displaystyle\int_a^b \{f_1(x)-f_2(x)\}dx.$

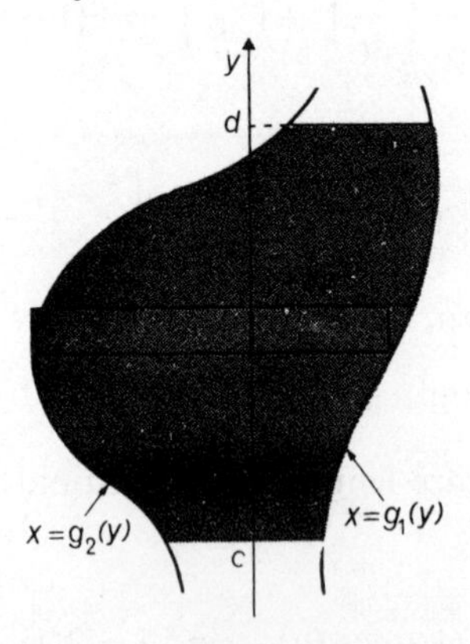

Similarly, the horizontal rectangular strip in the second diagram has area $\{g_1(y)-g_2(y)\}dy$ and the total shaded region has area

$$\int_c^d \{g_1(y)-g_2(y)\}dy.$$

Example 1. Find the area of the regions enclosed by the curve

$$y=\sin^2 x$$

and the line $$y = \frac{2}{\pi} x.$$

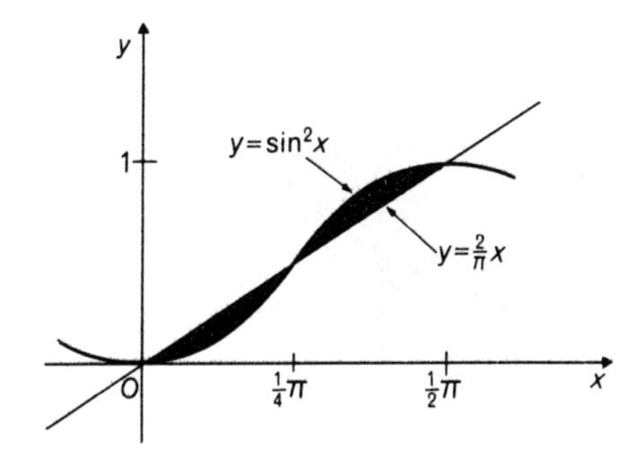

The curve and line meet at the points $(0, 0)$, $(\frac{1}{4}\pi, \frac{1}{2})$, $(\frac{1}{2}\pi, 1)$, and by symmetry the required area is twice the area of the region between $x = 0$ and $x = \frac{1}{4}\pi$.

$$\text{Thus the area} = 2\int_0^{\frac{1}{4}\pi} \left\{\frac{2}{\pi} x - \sin^2 x\right\} dx = \frac{2}{\pi}[x^2]_0^{\frac{1}{4}\pi} - \int_0^{\frac{1}{4}\pi} (1-\cos 2x)dx$$
$$= \tfrac{1}{8}\pi - [x - \tfrac{1}{2} \sin 2x]_0^{\frac{1}{4}\pi} = \tfrac{1}{2} - \tfrac{1}{8}\pi.$$

Areas associated with curves given by parametric equations

Example 2. Find the area of the region enclosed by the x-axis and the curve $x = t^2 + 2t$, $y = t^2 - 2t$, the curve of Example 2 in Section **1**.

$$\text{This area} = -\int_0^8 y\,dx = -\int_{t=0}^{t=2} y(t)\frac{dx}{dt}\,dt \quad (y(t) \leqslant 0 \text{ for } 0 \leqslant t \leqslant 2)$$
$$= \int_0^2 (2t - t^2)2(1+t)dt$$
$$= 2\int_0^2 (2t + t^2 - t^3)dt = 2[t^2 + \tfrac{1}{3}t^3 - \tfrac{1}{4}t^4]_0^2 = \tfrac{16}{3}.$$

Exercise. Check $\left(\text{by using } \int x\,dy\right)$ that the area enclosed by this curve and the y-axis is also $\frac{16}{3}$.

Polar areas (curve given by polar equation)

Consider the region bounded by the curve $r = f(\theta)$ and the lines OA, OB, where $\angle xOA = \alpha$ and $\angle xOB = \beta$. In this case we dissect $\angle AOB$

and obtain the area as the limit of the sum of the areas of approximating circular sectors such as POQ indicated. The area of sector

$$POQ = \frac{d\theta}{2\pi} \cdot \pi r^2 = \tfrac{1}{2} r^2 \, d\theta;$$

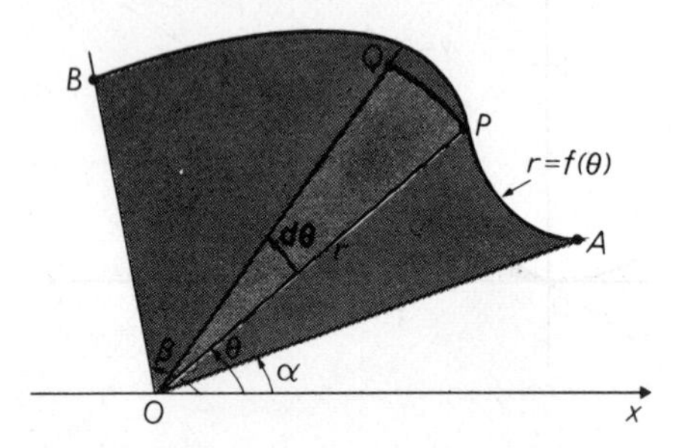

by forming the corresponding Riemann sum for the dissection it follows that the area AOB is

$$\int_{\alpha}^{\beta} \tfrac{1}{2} r^2 \, d\theta.$$

Example 3. Find the area of the region bounded by one loop of the curve $r^2 = 2a^2 \cos 2\theta$ $(a > 0)$.

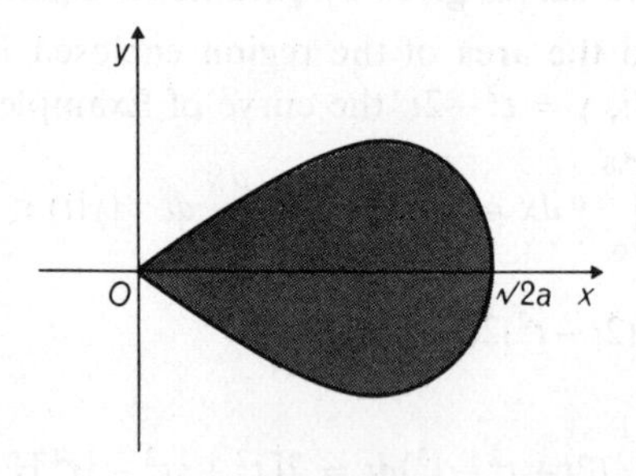

The loop given by $r = \sqrt{2}a\sqrt{\cos 2\theta}$, $-\frac{1}{4}\pi < \theta \leqslant \frac{1}{4}\pi$ is as shown (check the details). By symmetry, the area bounded by the loop

$$= 2 \int_0^{\pi/4} \tfrac{1}{2} r^2 \, d\theta = 2a^2 \int_0^{\pi/4} \cos 2\theta \, d\theta = a^2 [\sin 2\theta]_0^{\pi/4} = a^2.$$

3. Volumes of revolution

Suppose that the function f is continuous on $[a, b]$ and that $f(x) \geqslant 0$, $\forall x \in [a, b]$. The volume of the solid generated by rotating through one revolution about the x-axis the region bounded by the curve $y = f(x)$, the x-axis and the lines $x = a$, $x = b$ is defined as a Riemann integral using a dissection of $[a, b]$. The approximating volume generated by the upper half of the vertical rectangular strip shown is $\pi y^2 \, dx$, i.e. the volume of a circular cylinder of radius $y = f(x)$ and height dx. Hence the volume of revolution has measure

$$\int_a^b \pi y^2 \, dx = \int_a^b \pi (f(x))^2 \, dx.$$

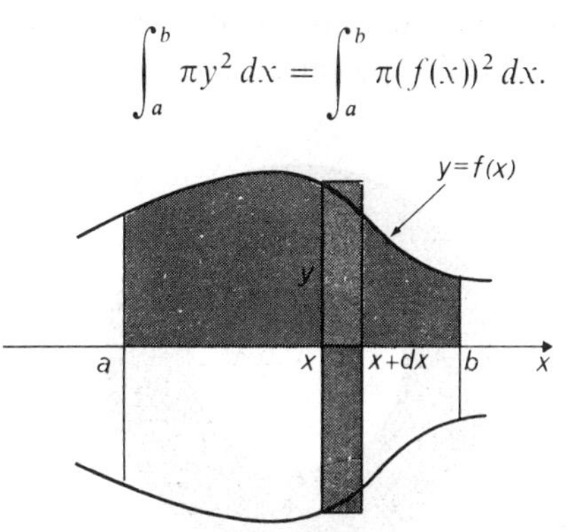

[Section of volume by x, y-plane.]

If the curve has parametric equations $x = x(t)$, $y = y(t)$, $\alpha \leqslant t \leqslant \beta$, then the volume is

$$\int_\alpha^\beta \pi (y(t))^2 \frac{dx}{dt} \, dt.$$

Similarly, if the curve $x = g(y)$, where g is continuous on $[c, d]$ and $g(y) \geqslant 0 \; \forall y \in [c, d]$, is rotated about the y-axis through one complete revolution, then the volume of the solid generated by the region bounded by $x = g(y)$, the y-axis and the lines $y = c$, $y = d$, is

$$\int_c^d \pi x^2 \, dy = \int_c^d \pi (g(y))^2 \, dy.$$

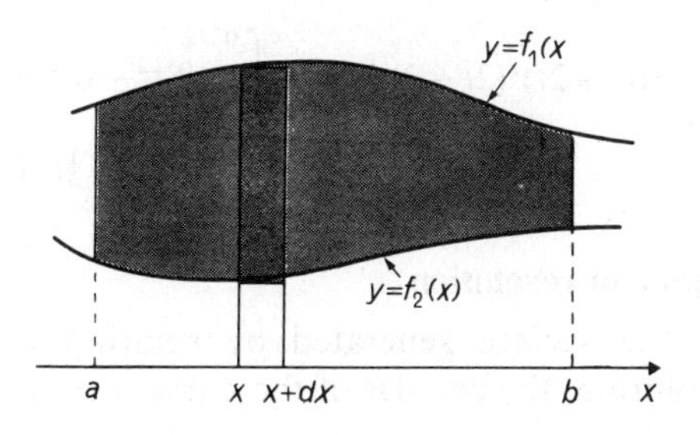

If $0 \leqslant f_2(x) \leqslant f_1(x)$, $\forall x \in [a, b]$, then the volume of the solid generated by rotating through one revolution about the x-axis the region bounded by the curves $y = f_1(x)$, $y = f_2(x)$ and the lines $x = a$, $x = b$ is

$$\int_a^b \pi\{(f_1(x))^2 - (f_2(x))^2\}\,dx;$$

for, the cross-section of the solid at x is the area of the region bounded by concentric circles of radii $f_1(x)$ and $f_2(x)$.

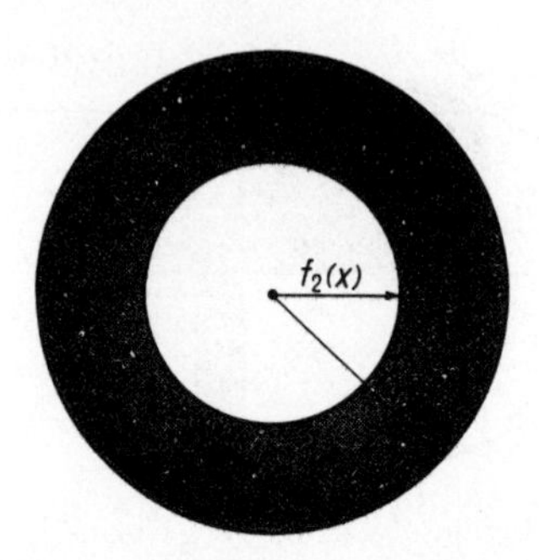

Example 1. If the region bounded by one arch of the curve $y = \sin^2 x$ and the x-axis is rotated through one revolution about the x-axis, find the volume of the solid generated.

$$\text{This volume} = \int_0^\pi \pi y^2\,dx = 2\pi \int_0^{\frac{1}{2}\pi} \sin^4 x\,dx = 2\pi \cdot \frac{3.1}{4.2} \cdot \frac{\pi}{2} = \tfrac{3}{8}\pi^2.$$

Example 2. The region bounded by the curve $x = t^2 + 2t$, $y = t^2 - 2t$, $-2 \leqslant t \leqslant 0$ and the y-axis is rotated through one revolution about the y-axis. Find the volume of the solid generated.

This curve is half of that described in Example 2 of Section **1**.

$$\text{The volume is} \quad -\int_{-2}^{0} \pi(x(t))^2 \frac{dy}{dt}\,dt \quad \left(\frac{dy}{dt} \text{ is } <0\right)$$

$$= -\int_{-2}^{0} \pi(t^2+2t)^2(2t-2)dt = \pi \int_{-2}^{0} (8t^2 - 6t^4 - 2t^5)dt$$

$$= \pi\left[\tfrac{8}{3}t^3 - \tfrac{6}{5}t^5 - \tfrac{1}{3}t^6\right]_{-2}^{0} = \tfrac{64}{15}\pi.$$

4. Area of a surface of revolution

We consider the surface generated by rotating about the x-axis, through one revolution, the arc AB of the curve $y = f(x)$ from $x = a$ to

$x = b$ (f having a continuous derivative on $[a, b]$). The area of the surface is defined as follows: we take a dissection

$$D = \{a = x_0 < x_1 < \cdots < x_n = b\}$$

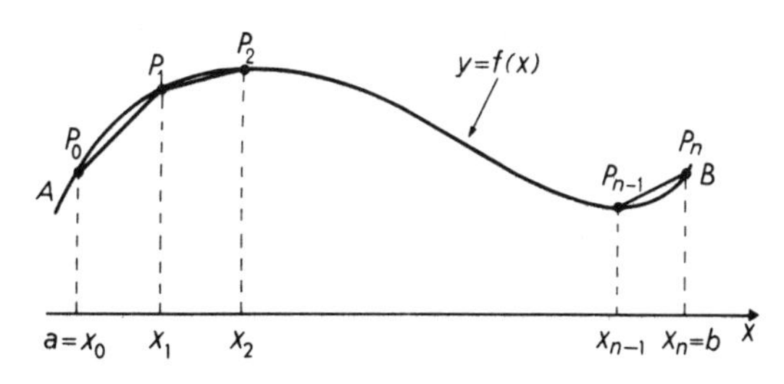

of $[a, b]$ and let P_i be the point $(x_i, f(x_i))$ $(i = 0, \cdots, n)$ on the curve $y = f(x)$; we form

$$\lim_{||D|| \to 0} \sum_{i=0}^{n-1} (\text{surface area generated by line-segment } \overrightarrow{P_i P_{i+1}}). \qquad (4.1)$$

If this limit exists (and it does when f' is continuous), it is defined to be the **surface area** of the surface generated by arc AB.

The surface area generated by $\overrightarrow{P_i P_{i+1}}$ is the area (shaded) of part of the surface of a right-circular cone cut off by planes perpendicular to the axis (i.e. the x-axis) of the cone; such a surface is called a **frustum** of a cone.

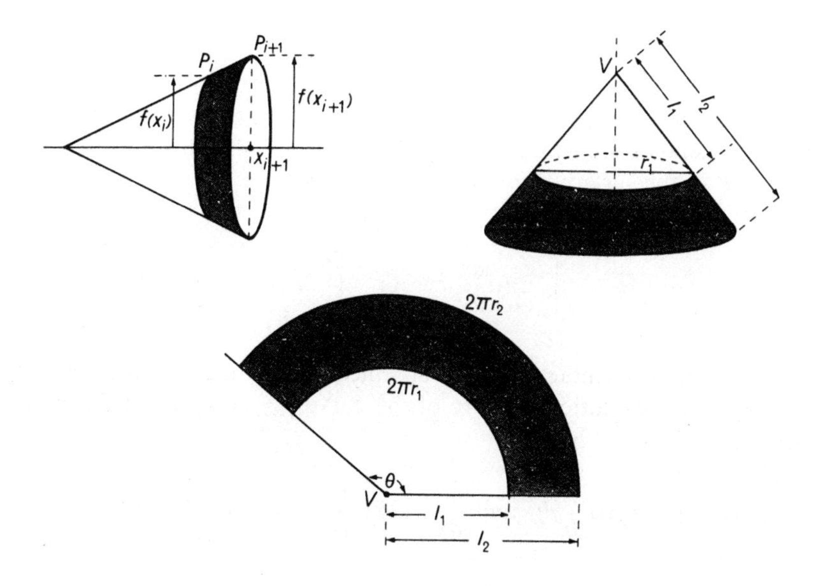

For a frustum determined by circular sections of radii r_1, r_2 and slant lengths l_1, l_2 from the vertex V, the area can be evaluated by cutting the cone along a generator and opening the area out onto a plane as shown. The area is bounded by arcs of circles of radii l_1, l_2 subtending an angle of θ radians at a common centre V, where $2\pi r_1 = l_1\theta$ and $2\pi r_2 = l_2\theta$. Thus the area of the frustum is

$$\tfrac{1}{2}l_2^2\theta - \tfrac{1}{2}l_1^2\theta = \tfrac{1}{2}(l_2 - l_1)(l_2\theta + l_1\theta) = \pi(r_1 + r_2)(l_2 - l_1). \qquad (4.2)$$

For S_i, the surface area generated by $\overrightarrow{P_iP_{i+1}}$, we have: $r_1 = f(x_i)$, $r_2 = f(x_{i+1})$ and $l_2 - l_1 = |P_iP_{i+1}|$. Consequently, from (4.2),

$$\begin{aligned} S_i &= \pi\{f(x_i) + f(x_{i+1})\}\,|P_iP_{i+1}| \quad (i = 0, \cdots, n-1), \\ &= \pi\{f(x_i) + f(x_{i+1})\}\sqrt{\{(x_{i+1} - x_i)^2 + (f(x_{i+1}) - f(x_i))^2\}}. \end{aligned}$$

Now, by the mean-value theorem,

$$\frac{f(x_{i+1}) - f(x_i)}{x_{i+1} - x_i} = f'(c_i), \quad \text{where} \quad x_i < c_i < x_{i+1},$$

and so

$$\begin{aligned} S_i &= \pi\{2f(x_i) + (x_{i+1} - x_i)f'(c_i)\}\sqrt{\{1 + (f'(c_i))^2\}}\,(x_{i+1} - x_i), \\ &\doteqdot 2\pi f(x_i)\sqrt{\{1 + (f'(x_i))^2\}}\,(x_{i+1} - x_i) \quad (i = 0, \cdots, n-1). \end{aligned}$$

It can be shown that, if f' is continuous on $[a, b]$, then

$$\lim_{||D|| \to 0} \sum_{i=0}^{n-1} S_i \text{ exists and equals } 2\pi \int_a^b f(x)\sqrt{\{1 + (f'(x))^2\}}\,dx,$$

i.e.
$$2\pi \int_a^b f(x)\frac{ds}{dx}\,dx,$$

where s denotes arc length along AB. Following (4.1), this integral gives the area of the surface of revolution described.

We usually use the notation

$$\int_a^b 2\pi y\frac{ds}{dx}\,dx \quad \text{or} \quad \int_a^b 2\pi y\,ds.$$

Note. If $S(x)$ denotes the area obtained by rotating about the x-axis, through one revolution, the arc of the curve $y = f(x)$ joining the point $A(a, f(a))$ to $P(x, f(x))$, then

$$S(x) = \int_a^x 2\pi y(t)\frac{ds}{dt}\,dt, \text{ and } \frac{dS}{dx} = 2\pi y\frac{ds}{dx} = 2\pi f(x)\sqrt{\{1 + (f'(x))^2\}}.$$

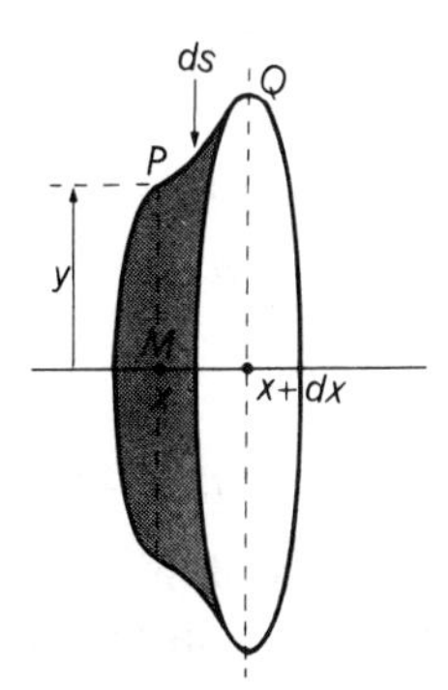

[In practice it is useful to see, from the diagram, that ΔS is approximately equal to $2\pi y\, ds$, where ΔS is the increment in $S(x)$ due to increment dx in x, and then to use $dS = 2\pi y\, ds$.]

In parametric form, $x = x(t)$, $y = y(t)$, we have: $\dfrac{dS}{dt} = 2\pi y(t)\dfrac{ds}{dt}$.

In polar form, $\dfrac{dS}{d\theta} = 2\pi y\dfrac{ds}{d\theta} = 2\pi r\sin\theta\dfrac{ds}{d\theta} = 2\pi r\sin\theta\sqrt{\left\{r^2+\left(\dfrac{dr}{d\theta}\right)^2\right\}}$.

Example 1. Find the area of the surface of revolution obtained by rotating through one revolution about the x-axis the ellipse $3x^2+4y^2 = 3$.

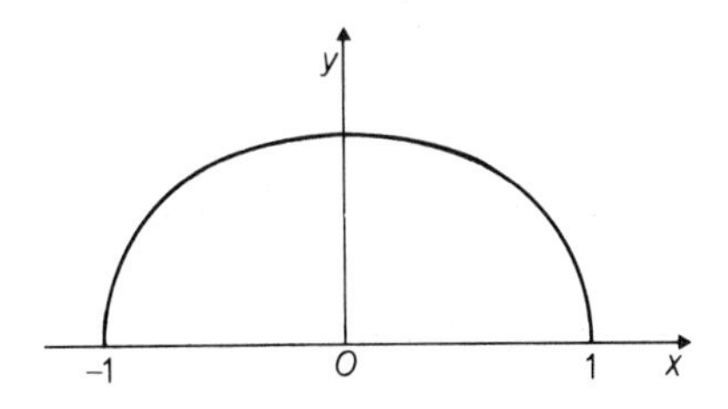

It is clearly enough to consider the upper half of the ellipse, i.e.

$$y = \frac{\sqrt{3}}{2}\sqrt{(1-x^2)}.$$

$$\frac{dy}{dx} = \frac{\sqrt{3}}{2}\frac{(-x)}{\sqrt{(1-x^2)}}, \text{ so that } \left(\frac{ds}{dx}\right)^2 = 1+\left(\frac{dy}{dx}\right)^2 = \frac{4-x^2}{4(1-x^2)}.$$

Hence
$$\frac{dS}{dx} = 2\pi y\frac{ds}{dx} = \pi\frac{\sqrt{3}}{2}\sqrt{(4-x^2)},$$

and the required area is, using symmetry,

$$2\pi\frac{\sqrt{3}}{2}\int_0^1 \sqrt{(4-x^2)}dx = \pi\sqrt{3}[\tfrac{1}{2}x\sqrt{(4-x^2)}+2\sin^{-1}\tfrac{1}{2}x]_0^1$$
$$= \pi\sqrt{3}(\tfrac{1}{2}\sqrt{3}+\tfrac{1}{3}\pi).$$

Example 2. Sketch the astroid

$$x = a\cos^3 t,\ y = a\sin^3 t,\ a > 0,\ 0 \leqslant t \leqslant 2\pi,$$

and find its arc length and the area of the surface generated by rotating through one revolution about the x-axis the arc given by $0 \leqslant t \leqslant \frac{1}{2}\pi$.

$$\dot{x} = -3a\cos^2 t\sin t,\ \dot{y} = 3a\sin^2 t\cos t,$$

and $$\frac{dy}{dx} = -\tan t;$$

$$\frac{dy}{dx} \to 0 \text{ as } t \to 0\ (t > 0)\ \text{(i.e. at point } (a, 0))$$

and $$\frac{dy}{dx} \to \infty \text{ as } t \to \tfrac{1}{2}\pi\ (t > 0)\ \text{(i.e. at point } (0, a)).$$

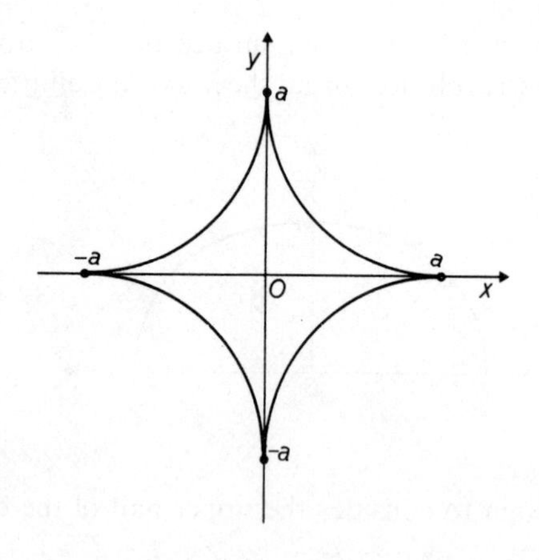

For $$0 < t < \tfrac{1}{2}\pi,\ \frac{dy}{dx} < 0$$

and curve in the first quadrant is a falling curve; also

$$\frac{d^2y}{dx^2} = \frac{1}{\dot{x}}\frac{d}{dt}\left(\frac{dy}{dx}\right) = \frac{1}{3a\cos^4 t\sin t} > 0 \text{ for } 0 < t < \tfrac{1}{2}\pi,$$

so that the curve is concave up in the first quadrant. It is easy to complete a rough sketch of the curve on noting that it is symmetrical about both axes and about the lines $y = \pm x$, and passes through the points $(\pm a, 0)$, $(0, \pm a)$, $(\pm\frac{1}{4}\sqrt{2}a, \pm\frac{1}{4}\sqrt{2}a)$.

$$\left(\frac{ds}{dt}\right)^2 = \dot{x}^2 + \dot{y}^2 = 9a^2 \cos^2 t \sin^2 t,$$

so that, for $0 \leqslant t \leqslant \frac{1}{2}\pi$,

$$\frac{ds}{dt} = 3a \cos t \sin t.$$

The curve has total arc length

$$4\int_0^{\frac{1}{2}\pi} 3a \cos t \sin t \, dt = 6a[\sin^2 t]_0^{\frac{1}{2}\pi} = 6a.$$

Also, $$\frac{dS}{dt} = 2\pi y \frac{ds}{dt} = 6\pi a^2 \sin^4 t \cos t, \; 0 \leqslant t \leqslant \tfrac{1}{2}\pi.$$

Hence the required surface area is

$$6\pi a^2 \int_0^{\frac{1}{2}\pi} \sin^4 t \cos t \, dt = 6\pi a^2[\tfrac{1}{5}\sin^5 t]_0^{\frac{1}{2}\pi} = \tfrac{6}{5}\pi a^2.$$

5. Circle, centre and radius of curvature at a point on a curve

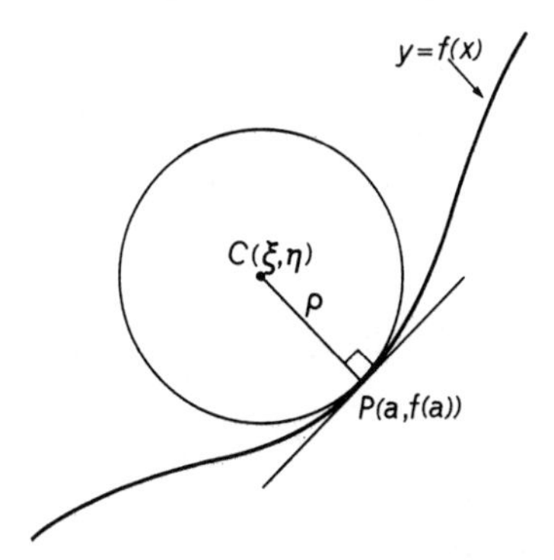

We consider a graph $y = f(x)$ and suppose that $P(a, f(a))$ is a point on the graph at which $f'(a)$ and $f''(a)$ exist and $f''(a) \neq 0$. We show that there is a unique circle through P which has the same values of

$$\frac{dy}{dx} \quad \text{and} \quad \frac{d^2y}{dx^2}$$

as the given curve at P, namely $f'(a)$ and $f''(a)$, and that its centre $C(\xi, \eta)$ lies on the normal at P to the given curve. If ρ is the radius of such a circle, its equation is

$$(x-\xi)^2+(y-\eta)^2 = \rho^2. \tag{5.1}$$

Differentiating (5.1) with respect to x,

$$2(x-\xi)+2(y-\eta)\frac{dy}{dx} = 0,$$

so that

$$x-\xi+(y-\eta)\frac{dy}{dx} = 0. \tag{5.2}$$

Differentiating (5.2) with respect to x,

$$1+\left(\frac{dy}{dx}\right)^2+(y-\eta)\frac{d^2y}{dx^2} = 0. \tag{5.3}$$

At P, $x = a$, $y = f(a)$,

$$\frac{dy}{dx} = f'(a) \quad \text{and} \quad \frac{d^2y}{dx^2} = f''(a).$$

Thus, from (5.3), (5.2) and (5.1) we have:

$$1+(f'(a))^2+(f(a)-\eta)f''(a) = 0,$$

and so

$$\eta = f(a)+\frac{1+(f'(a))^2}{f''(a)}, \tag{5.4}$$

$$a-\xi+(f(a)-\eta)f'(a) = 0,$$

and so

$$\xi = a-\frac{\{1+(f'(a))^2\}f'(a)}{f''(a)}, \tag{5.5}$$

$$\rho^2 = (\xi-a)^2+(\eta-f(a))^2 = \frac{\{1+(f'(a))^2\}^3}{(f''(a))^2},$$

and so

$$\rho = \frac{\{1+(f'(a))^2\}^{3/2}}{|f''(a)|}. \tag{5.6}$$

From this work the existence and uniqueness of the circle is ensured, its radius ρ being given by (5.6) and its centre $C(\xi, \eta)$ being given by (5.5) and (5.4). The circle is called the **circle of curvature** at P, its centre $C(\xi, \eta)$, the **centre of curvature** at P, and its radius ρ the **radius of curvature** at P. The circle is the circle with "closest contact" with the given curve at P. By definition, the circle has the same tangent at P as the given curve

$y = f(x)$, so that CP is perpendicular to this tangent and C lies on the normal at P.

The curve traced out by C as P traces out the given curve is called the **evolute** of the given curve. The given curve is often called an **involute** of this evolute.

The formulae for ξ, η and ρ are usually given for the point $P(x, y)$ on the curve and are

$$\xi = x - \frac{\left\{1 + \left(\dfrac{dy}{dx}\right)^2\right\}\dfrac{dy}{dx}}{\dfrac{d^2y}{dx^2}}, \quad \eta = y + \frac{1 + \left(\dfrac{dy}{dx}\right)^2}{\dfrac{d^2y}{dx^2}}, \quad \rho = \frac{\left\{1 + \left(\dfrac{dy}{dx}\right)^2\right\}^{3/2}}{\left|\dfrac{d^2y}{dx^2}\right|}, \tag{5.7}$$

where $\dfrac{dy}{dx}$ and $\dfrac{d^2y}{dx^2}$ $(\neq 0)$ are evaluated at $P(x, y)$.

Alternative expression for ρ

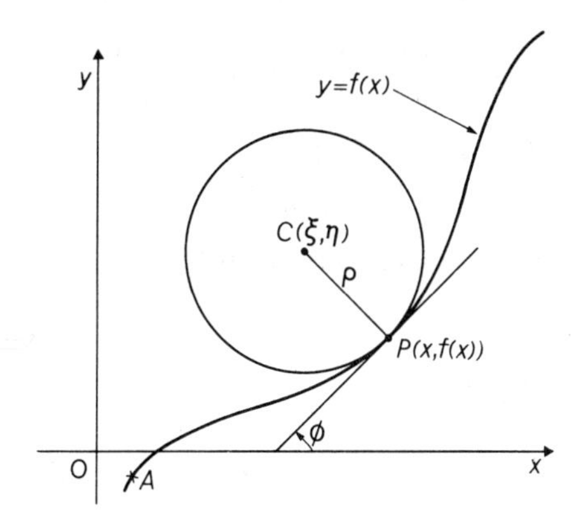

We denote by $s(x)$ the arc length along the curve $y = f(x)$ from some fixed point A on it to the point $P(x, y)$ and let ϕ be the radian measure of an angle which the tangent at P makes with Ox; we show that

$$\rho = \left|\frac{ds}{d\phi}\right|.$$

Now $\qquad \tan\phi = \dfrac{dy}{dx}$, and so $\sec^2\phi \, \dfrac{d\phi}{ds}\dfrac{ds}{dx} = \dfrac{d^2y}{dx^2}$.

Thus $$\frac{d\phi}{ds} = \frac{\dfrac{d^2y}{dx^2}}{(1+\tan^2\phi)\sqrt{\left\{1+\left(\dfrac{dy}{dx}\right)^2\right\}}} = \frac{\dfrac{d^2y}{dx^2}}{\left\{1+\left(\dfrac{dy}{dx}\right)^2\right\}^{3/2}},$$

so that, by (5.7),

$$\left|\frac{d\phi}{ds}\right| = \frac{1}{\rho}, \text{ and } \rho = \left|\frac{ds}{d\phi}\right|.$$

$\dfrac{d\phi}{ds}$ is often called the **curvature** at P of the curve $y = f(x)$; it describes the "rate of change of tangential direction" as a particle moves along the curve.

Example. Find the radius of curvature at the point $P(t)$ on the parabola $x = at^2$, $y = 2at$ $(a > 0)$. Find parametric equations for the evolute. Show that the normal at P to the parabola is the tangent at C to the evolute, where C is the centre of curvature at P of the parabola.

[*Note.* This last property holds for any curve and its evolute.]

$$\dot{x} = 2at,\ \dot{y} = 2a;\ \frac{dy}{dx} = \frac{1}{t}\ (t \neq 0) \text{ and } \frac{d^2y}{dx^2} = -\frac{1}{2at^3}.$$

$$\rho = \left\{1+\left(\frac{dy}{dx}\right)^2\right\}^{3/2} \Bigg/ \left|\frac{d^2y}{dx^2}\right| = 2a(t^2+1)^{3/2}.$$

The centre of curvature $C(\xi, \eta)$ is given by:

$$\xi = x - \frac{\left\{1+\left(\dfrac{dy}{dx}\right)^2\right\}\dfrac{dy}{dx}}{\dfrac{d^2y}{dx^2}} = a(3t^2+2),\ \eta = y + \frac{1+\left(\dfrac{dy}{dx}\right)^2}{\dfrac{d^2y}{dx^2}} = -2at^3,$$

so that the evolute has parametric equations

$$x = a(3t^2+2),\ y = -2at^3.$$

For the evolute,

$$\dot{x} = 6at,\ \dot{y} = -6at^2, \text{ and } \frac{dy}{dx} = -t = m_{CP},$$

the gradient of the normal at P to the parabola. Thus the normal at P is the tangent at C to the evolute.

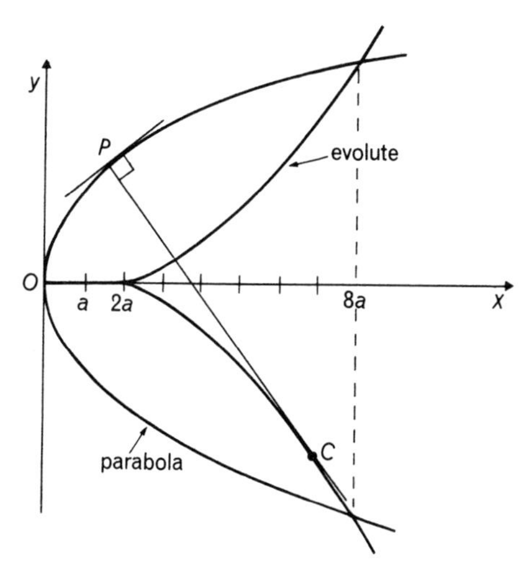

Exercise. Show that the evolute has x, y-equation $27ay^2 = 4(x-2a)^3$ and check that the curve is as indicated. It is called a **semicubical parabola**.

6. Polynomial approximations to functions, Taylor's and Maclaurin's theorems

One of the most important and useful techniques for dealing with real functions in mathematics and its applications is that of obtaining polynomial approximations to functions, for polynomials can easily be computed, differentiated and integrated. One of the basic results underlying this work can be stated as follows:

Theorem 7.1

If a function f has continuous derived functions $f^{(r)}$ $(r = 1, \cdots, n)$ on an interval I and if $a \in I$, then, $\forall x \in I$,

$$f(x) = f(a) + \frac{f'(a)}{1!}(x-a) + \frac{f''(a)}{2!}(x-a)^2 + \cdots + \frac{f^{(n-1)}(a)}{(n-1)!}(x-a)^{n-1} + R_n, \tag{6.1}$$

where the remainder R_n is given by

$$R_n = \frac{1}{(n-1)!}\int_a^x f^{(n)}(t)(x-t)^{n-1}\,dt. \tag{6.2}$$

Proof. We use induction on n. For $n = 1$, the right-hand side of (6.1) equals

$$f(a) + \int_a^x f'(t)dt = f(a) + \{f(x) - f(a)\} = f(x).$$

Thus the statement is true for $n = 1$.

Assume now that (6.1) is true for $n = k$, where $1 \leqslant k \leqslant n-1$. Then

$$f(x) = \sum_{r=0}^{k-1} \frac{f^{(r)}(a)}{r!}(x-a)^r + \frac{1}{(k-1)!}\int_a^x f^k(t)(x-t)^{k-1}\,dt$$

$$= \sum_{r=0}^{k-1} \frac{f^{(r)}(a)}{r!}(x-a)^r + \frac{1}{(k-1)!}\left[f^k(t)\left\{-\frac{(x-t)^k}{k}\right\}\right]_a^x + \frac{1}{k!}\int_a^x f^{(k+1)}(t)(x-t)^k\,dt,$$

using integration by parts,

$$= \sum_{r=0}^{k} \frac{f^{(r)}(a)}{r!}(x-a)^r + \frac{1}{k!}\int_a^x f^{k+1}(t)(x-t)^k\,dt.$$

Consequently the statement (6.1) is also true for $n = k+1$, and the required result now follows by induction.

Formula (6.1) is often called **Taylor's formula**. It expresses $f(x)$ as a polynomial of degree $n-1$ to an accuracy determined, for any given x, by the remainder R_n. A convenient formula for R_n is given by the following result.

$$R_n = \frac{f^{(n)}(c)}{n!}(x-a)^n, \tag{6.3}$$

for some number c in the interval determined by a and x.

Proof of (6.3). *Case* $x \geqslant a$. Since $f^{(n)}$ is continuous on $[a, x]$, it has a maximum value, $M = f^{(n)}(u)$ say, and a minimum value, $m = f^{(n)}(v)$ say, on $[a, x]$, so that

$$m \leqslant f^{(n)}(t) \leqslant M, \quad \forall t \in [a, x].$$

Multiplying these inequalities by $\dfrac{1}{(n-1)!}(x-t)^{n-1}$ ($\geqslant 0$) and integrating, we have, from (6.2),

$$\frac{m}{(n-1)!}\int_a^x (x-t)^{n-1}\,dt \leqslant R_n \leqslant \frac{M}{(n-1)!}\int_a^x (x-t)^{n-1}\,dt,$$

and so
$$\frac{m}{n!}(x-a)^n \leqslant R_n \leqslant \frac{M}{n!}(x-a)^n.$$

Now, by the intermediate-value theorem, $f^{(n)}(t)$ assumes on $[a, x]$ all values between m and M and so $f^{(n)}(t)(x-a)^n/n!$ assumes on $[a, x]$ all values between its minimum value $m(x-a)^n/n!$ and its maximum value

$M(x-a)^n/n!$. In particular it assumes the value R_n, so that $\exists c \in [a, x]$ such that $R_n = f^{(n)}(c)(x-a)^n/n!$.

Case $x < a$. In this case we can consider

$$(-1)^n R_n = \frac{1}{(n-1)!}\int_x^a f^n(t)(t-x)^{n-1}\,dt.$$

The details of the proof, which are similar to those for *Case* $x \geqslant a$ but a little more complicated, will be omitted.

Use of Taylor's formula for numerical approximations

The idea here is to obtain an approximation to $f(a+h)$ from $f(a)$ when $|h|$ is small. We take $a+h$ for x in (6.1) and (6.3) and obtain, under the assumptions made for Theorem **7.1**,

$$f(a+h) = f(a) + \frac{f'(a)}{1!}h + \frac{f''(a)}{2!}h^2 + \cdots + \frac{f^{(n-1)}(a)}{(n-1)!}h^{n-1} + R_n, \quad (6.4)$$

where $$R_n = \frac{f^{(n)}(a+c)}{n!}h^n,$$

and c lies between 0 and h. We can determine $f(a+h)$ up to a certain degree of accuracy by the polynomial on the right-hand side of (6.4), the remainder R_n giving the error.

Example 1. Use (6.4) with $n = 4$ to compute $\cos(\frac{1}{3}\pi + 0{\cdot}1)$ to five decimal places.

We take $f(x) = \cos x$ with $a = \frac{1}{3}\pi$ and $h = 0{\cdot}1$; then $f'(x) = -\sin x$, $f''(x) = -\cos x$, $f'''(x) = \sin x$ and $f^{(\mathrm{IV})}(x) = \cos x$. From (6.4),

$$\cos(\tfrac{1}{3}\pi + 0{\cdot}1) = \cos\tfrac{1}{3}\pi - \sin\tfrac{1}{3}\pi(0{\cdot}1) - \cos\tfrac{1}{3}\pi\frac{(0{\cdot}1)^2}{2} + \sin\tfrac{1}{3}\pi\frac{(0{\cdot}1)^3}{6} + R_4,$$

where $$R_4 = \cos(\tfrac{1}{3}\pi + c)\frac{(0{\cdot}1)^4}{24} \quad \text{and} \quad 0 \leqslant c \leqslant 0{\cdot}1.$$

Thus $$\cos(\tfrac{1}{3}\pi + 0{\cdot}1) = \tfrac{1}{2} - 0{\cdot}05\sqrt{3} - 0{\cdot}0025 + \frac{0{\cdot}001}{12}\sqrt{3} + R_4$$

$$= 0{\cdot}41104179\cdots + R_4.$$

Now $$0 < R_4 \leqslant \cos\tfrac{1}{3}\pi\frac{0{\cdot}0001}{24} < 0{\cdot}0000021.$$

Hence $\cos(\frac{1}{3}\pi + 0{\cdot}1) = 0{\cdot}41104$, rounded off to five decimal places.

Infinite-series expansions

Of special interest are the functions for which (6.1) holds for all positive integers n. If in such cases $R_n \to 0$ as $n \to \infty$, i.e. R_n can be made as small as we please by taking n sufficiently large (i.e. given $\varepsilon > 0$, $\exists n_0 \in \mathbf{N}$ such that $|R_n| < \varepsilon \ \forall n \geqslant n_0$), then we write

$$f(x) = \lim_{n\to\infty} \sum_{r=0}^{n-1} \frac{f^{(r)}(a)}{r!}(x-a)^r = \sum_{n=0}^{\infty} \frac{f^{(n)}(a)}{n!}(x-a)^n. \qquad (6.5)$$

Formula (6.5) is said to give the **Taylor series** or **expansion** for f about $x = a$. The special case with $a = 0$, namely

$$f(x) = \sum_{n=0}^{\infty} \frac{f^{(n)}(0)}{n!} x^n, \qquad (6.6)$$

is often called **Maclaurin's series** or **expansion** for f about $x = 0$.

More generally an infinite sum of numbers

$$\sum_{r=1}^{\infty} u_r$$

is called an **infinite series**. If

$$S_n = \sum_{r=1}^{n} u_r,$$

then the series is said to be **convergent** if $\exists L \in \mathbf{R}$ such that $|S_n - L|$ can be made as small as we please by taking n sufficiently large; then we write

$$\sum_{n=1}^{\infty} u_n = L,$$

and say that the series is convergent to L. A series is called *divergent* if it is not convergent.

A series of the form

$$\sum_{n=0}^{\infty} c_n(x-a)^n, \quad \text{where} \quad c_n(n = 0, 1, \cdots)$$

are given real numbers, is called a **power series** in $(x-a)$. It can be shown that, for such a series, one of the following statements is true: (i) the series is convergent $\forall x \in \mathbf{R}$, (ii) the series is convergent for $x = a$ only, (iii) $\exists R > 0$ such that the series is convergent for $|x-a| < R$ and divergent for $|x-a| > R$. [The end values given by $x-a = \pm R$ have to be considered separately.] The number R is called the **radius of convergence** of the power series; in case (i) we can say that $R = \infty$ and in case (ii) that

$R = 0$. R is given by the formula

$$R = \lim_{n\to\infty} \left| \frac{c_n}{c_{n+1}} \right|, \tag{6.7}$$

provided that the limit exists. A power series in $(x-a)$ with radius of convergence $R > 0$ is convergent on one of the intervals $[a-R, a+R]$, $[a-R, a+R)$, $(a-R, a+R]$, $(a-R, a+R)$, called the **interval of convergence** of the power series; it is convergent on $\mathbf{R}$ if $R = \infty$.

A power series can be differentiated and integrated on its open interval of convergence.

A Taylor series is a power series in $(x-a)$ and a Maclaurin series is a power series in x. In these cases we are interested not only in the interval of convergence of the series but also in the set of values of x for which the series is convergent to $f(x)$. In fact the series is convergent to $f(x)$ on its interval of convergence. Since at this stage in calculus we are interested merely in the formal appearance of the series for some of the elementary functions, we shall not embark on the long and demanding development of results on convergence for their own sake.

Maclaurin expansions of some elementary functions (with their intervals of validity)

(1) $e^x = 1 + \dfrac{x}{1!} + \dfrac{x^2}{2!} + \dfrac{x^3}{3!} + \cdots, \quad \forall x \in \mathbf{R};$

(2) $\sin x = x - \dfrac{x^3}{3!} + \dfrac{x^5}{5!} - \dfrac{x^7}{7!} + \cdots, \quad \forall x \in \mathbf{R};$

(3) $\cos x = 1 - \dfrac{x^2}{2!} + \dfrac{x^4}{4!} - \dfrac{x^6}{6!} + \cdots, \quad \forall x \in \mathbf{R};$

(4) $\sinh x = x + \dfrac{x^3}{3!} + \dfrac{x^5}{5!} + \dfrac{x^7}{7!} + \cdots, \quad \forall x \in \mathbf{R};$

(5) $\cosh x = 1 + \dfrac{x^2}{2!} + \dfrac{x^4}{4!} + \dfrac{x^6}{6!} + \cdots, \quad \forall x \in \mathbf{R};$

(6) $(1+x)^s = 1 + \dfrac{s}{1!}x + \dfrac{s(s-1)}{2!}x^2 + \cdots + \dfrac{s(s-1)\cdots(s-n+1)}{n!}x^n + \cdots,$

$-1 < x < 1;$

[This is the **binomial expansion**; it is *finite* if s is a non-negative integer and the expansion then holds $\forall x \in \mathbf{R}$.]

(7) $\log(1+x) = x - \dfrac{x^2}{2} + \dfrac{x^3}{3} - \dfrac{x^4}{4} + \cdots, \quad -1 < x \leqslant 1;$

(8) $\tan^{-1} x = x - \dfrac{x^3}{3} + \dfrac{x^5}{5} - \dfrac{x^7}{7} + \cdots, \quad -1 \leqslant x \leqslant 1.$

In discussing the radius of convergence R in each case we can either use R_n as given by (6.3) and find when $R_n \to 0$ as $n \to \infty$ or determine R assuming (6.7).

Proof of (1). Here $f(x) = e^x$ and $f^{(n)}(x) = e^x$ $(n = 1, 2, 3, \cdots)$. Using

$$f(x) = \sum_{r=0}^{n-1} \frac{f^{(r)}(0)}{r!} x^r + R_n, \quad \text{where} \quad R_n = \frac{f^{(n)}(c)}{n!} x^n, \tag{6.8}$$

we have: $\quad e^x = 1 + \dfrac{x}{1!} + \dfrac{x^2}{2!} + \cdots + \dfrac{x^{n-1}}{(n-1)!} + R_n,$

where $$R_n = \frac{e^c}{n!} x^n$$

and c is in the interval determined by 0 and x. We can show that, for each given $x \in \mathbf{R}$,

$$\frac{|x|^n}{n!} \to 0 \quad \text{as} \quad n \to \infty. \tag{6.9}$$

[We can choose an integer $k > 0$ such that $k > |x|$; then, for $n > k$,

$$\frac{|x|^n}{n!} = \frac{|x|^k}{k!} \frac{|x|^{n-k}}{(k+1)(k+2)\cdots n} < \frac{|x|^k}{k!} \left(\frac{|x|}{k}\right)^{n-k}.$$

Since $\quad \dfrac{|x|}{k} < 1, \; \left(\dfrac{|x|}{k}\right)^{n-k} = \left(\dfrac{|x|}{k}\right)^{n} \left(\dfrac{|x|}{k}\right)^{-k} \to 0 \quad \text{as} \quad n \to \infty,$

and from this (6.9) follows.]

From (6.9), $|R_n| \leqslant e^c \dfrac{|x|^n}{n!} \to 0 \quad \text{as} \quad n \to \infty \quad$ (for each $x \in \mathbf{R}$).

Hence $$e^x = \sum_{n=0}^{\infty} \frac{x^n}{n!}, \quad \forall x \in \mathbf{R}.$$

Note. From (1) we have

$$e^{-x} = 1 - \frac{x}{1!} + \frac{x^2}{2!} - \frac{x^3}{3!} + \cdots, \quad \forall x \in \mathbf{R}.$$

Then, using $\sinh x = \frac{1}{2}(e^x - e^{-x})$ and $\cosh x = \frac{1}{2}(e^x + e^{-x})$, the Maclaurin expansions (4) and (5) follow.

Proof of (2). Here $f(x) = \sin x$, $f(0) = 0$, $f^{(n)}(x) = \sin(x + \frac{1}{2}n\pi)$ for $n = 1, 2, 3, \cdots$ (by induction). Thus

$$f^{(n)}(0) = \sin \tfrac{1}{2}n\pi = \begin{cases} 0 & \text{when } n \text{ is even} \\ (-1)^{\frac{1}{2}(n-1)} & \text{when } n \text{ is odd,} \end{cases}$$

and, from (6.8),

$$\sin x = x - \frac{x^3}{3!} + \frac{x^5}{5!} - \frac{x^7}{7!} + \cdots + R_n,$$

where
$$R_n = \frac{\sin(c + \frac{1}{2}n\pi)}{n!} x^n.$$

In this case
$$|R_n| \leqslant \frac{|x|^n}{n!} \to 0 \quad \text{as} \quad n \to \infty,$$

and the result (2) follows.

Proof of (3). Here $f(x) = \cos x$, $f(0) = 1$, $f^{(n)}(x) = \cos(x + \frac{1}{2}n\pi)$ for $n = 1, 2, 3, \cdots$ (by induction), and the result can be established in the same way as (2).

Proof of (6). We can assume that s is not a non-negative integer; for, otherwise, the result is the usual finite binomial theorem.

$$f(x) = (1+x)^s,\ f(0) = 1,\ f^{(n)}(x) = s(s-1)\cdots(s-n+1)(1+x)^{s-n} \quad (n \in \mathbf{N}),$$

and the Maclaurin expansion is

$$1 + \frac{s}{1!}x + \frac{s(s-1)}{2!}x^2 + \cdots + \frac{s(s-1)\cdots(s-n+1)}{n!}x^n + \cdots.$$

In this case we can show that $R_n \to 0$ as $n \to \infty$ when $x \in (-1, 1)$, but the details are complicated; instead we find the radius of convergence R using (6.7). Here

$$\left|\frac{c_n}{c_{n+1}}\right| = \left|\frac{s(s-1)\cdots(s-n+1)}{n!} \cdot \frac{(n+1)!}{s(s-1)\cdots(s-n)}\right| = \left|\frac{1 + \frac{1}{n}}{1 - \frac{s}{n}}\right| \to 1 \quad \text{as} \quad n \to \infty.$$

Hence $R = 1$, and the result (6) follows.

Note. $$(1+x)^{-1} = \frac{1}{1+x} = 1-x+x^2-x^3+x^4-x^5+\cdots, \quad -1<x<1;$$

$$(1-x)^{-1} = \frac{1}{1-x} = 1+x+x^2+x^3+x^4+x^5+\cdots, \quad -1<x<1;$$

$$(1-x)^{-2} = \frac{1}{(1-x)^2} = 1+2x+3x^2+4x^3+5x^4+\cdots, \quad -1<x<1;$$

$$\frac{1}{\sqrt{(1-x)}} = (1-x)^{-\frac{1}{2}} = 1+\frac{(-\frac{1}{2})}{1!}(-x)+\frac{(-\frac{1}{2})(-\frac{3}{2})}{2!}(-x)^2+\cdots, \quad -1<x<1.$$

Proof of (7). For variety we shall use a proof involving integration. For each $n \in \mathbf{N}$ we have the identity

$$1 = (1+t)(1-t+t^2-\cdots+(-1)^{n-1}t^{n-1})+(-1)^n t^n,$$

so that $$\frac{1}{1+t} = 1-t+t^2-\cdots+(-1)^{n-1}t^{n-1}+\frac{(-1)^n t^n}{1+t}, \quad t \neq -1.$$

Hence

$$\log(1+x) = \int_0^x \frac{dt}{1+t} = x-\frac{x^2}{2}+\frac{x^3}{3}-\cdots+(-1)^{n-1}\frac{x^n}{n}+R_n(x), \quad (6.10)$$

where $$R_n(x) = (-1)^n \int_0^x \frac{t^n}{1+t}\,dt.$$

For $0 \leqslant x \leqslant 1$,

$$|R_n(x)| = \int_0^x \frac{t^n}{1+t}\,dt \leqslant \int_0^x t^n\,dt = \frac{x^{n+1}}{n+1} \to 0 \quad \text{as} \quad n \to \infty.$$

For $-1 < x < 0$,

$$|R_n(x)| \leqslant \int_x^0 \frac{|t|^n}{1+t}\,dt \leqslant \int_x^0 \frac{(-t)^n}{1+x}\,dt, \quad \text{since} \quad -1 < x \leqslant t \leqslant 0$$

implies $0 < 1+x \leqslant 1+t \leqslant 1$ and so $1 \leqslant 1/(1+t) \leqslant 1/(1+x)$; thus

$$|R_n(x)| \leqslant \frac{1}{1+x}\int_0^{|x|} u^n\,du \; (u=-t) = \frac{|x|^{n+1}}{(1+x)(n+1)} \to 0 \quad \text{as} \quad n \to \infty.$$

From (6.10) the required result now follows, namely that

$$\log(1+x) = x-\frac{x^2}{2}+\frac{x^3}{3}-\frac{x^4}{4}+\cdots, \quad -1 < x \leqslant 1.$$

Notes **1**. Taking $x = 1$ shows that the series $1-\frac{1}{2}+\frac{1}{3}-\frac{1}{4}+\cdots$ is convergent to $\log 2$.

2. $$\log(1-x) = -x-\frac{x^2}{2}-\frac{x^3}{3}-\frac{x^4}{4}-\cdots, \quad -1 \leqslant x < 1.$$

Proof of (8). We can proceed as for (7) using

$$\frac{1}{1+t^2} = 1-t^2+t^4-\cdots+(-1)^{n-1}t^{2n-2}+\frac{(-1)^n t^{2n}}{1+t^2}.$$

Hence $$\tan^{-1}x = \int_0^x \frac{dt}{1+t^2} = x-\frac{x^3}{3}+\frac{x^5}{5}-\cdots+(-1)^{n-1}\frac{x^{2n-1}}{2n-1}+R_n(x),$$

where $$R_n(x) = (-1)^n\int_0^x \frac{t^{2n}}{1+t^2}\,dt.$$

Here, if $0 \leqslant x \leqslant 1$,

$$|R_n(x)| \leqslant \int_0^x t^{2n}\,dt = \frac{x^{2n+1}}{2n+1} \to 0 \quad \text{as} \quad n \to \infty,$$

and, if $-1 \leqslant x \leqslant 0$,

$$|R_n(x)| \leqslant \int_0^{|x|} u^{2n}\,du \quad (u = -t)$$
$$= \frac{|x|^{2n+1}}{2n+1} \to 0 \quad \text{as} \quad n \to \infty.$$

The result (8) now follows. The particular value $x = 1$ gives the famous result

$$\tfrac{1}{4}\pi = \tfrac{1}{1}-\tfrac{1}{3}+\tfrac{1}{5}-\tfrac{1}{7}+\cdots.$$

Example 2. Show that the first four terms of the Maclaurin series for $\sin x$ gives $\sin 1$ to an accuracy of 10^{-4}.

$$\sin x = x-\frac{x^3}{3!}+\frac{x^5}{5!}-\frac{x^7}{7!}+\cdots+R_n,$$

where $$R_n = \frac{\sin(c+\frac{1}{2}n\pi)}{n!}x^n, \quad \text{so that} \quad |R_n| \leqslant \frac{|x|^n}{n!}.$$

Hence $$\sin 1 = 1-\frac{1}{3!}+\frac{1}{5!}-\frac{1}{7!}+R_8,$$

and $$|R_8| \leqslant \frac{1}{8!} = \frac{1}{40320} < \frac{1}{10^4}.$$

Example 3. Evaluate $\lim\limits_{x\to 0} \dfrac{\sin x - x}{x^3}$.

$$\frac{\sin x - x}{x^3} = \frac{\left(x - \dfrac{x^3}{3!} + R_4\right) - x}{x^3} = -\tfrac{1}{6} + \sin c \cdot \frac{x}{4!} \quad (x \neq 0)$$

$$\to -\tfrac{1}{6} \quad \text{as} \quad x \to 0.$$

[In practice we often present this as follows:

$$\frac{\sin x - x}{x^3} = \frac{1}{x^3}\left\{\left(x - \frac{x^3}{3!} + \frac{x^5}{5!} - \cdots\right) - x\right\} = -\tfrac{1}{6} + \frac{x^2}{5!} + \cdots \quad (x \neq 0)$$

$$\to -\tfrac{1}{6} \quad \text{as} \quad x \to 0.$$]

Example 4 (*illustrating composition of power series*). Find the first three non-zero terms in the expansion of $\log(2+\cos x)$ in ascending powers of x.

$$\log(2+\cos x) = \log\left(2 + 1 - \frac{x^2}{2} + \frac{x^4}{24} - \frac{x^6}{720} + \cdots\right)$$

$$= \log\left\{3\left[1 + \left(-\frac{x^2}{6} + \frac{x^4}{72} - \frac{x^6}{2160} + \cdots\right)\right]\right\}$$

$$= \log 3 + \log(1+t), \quad \text{where} \quad t = -\frac{x^2}{6} + \frac{x^4}{72} - \frac{x^6}{2160} + \cdots$$

$$= \log 3 + t - \frac{t^2}{2} + \frac{t^3}{3} - \cdots$$

$$= \log 3 + \left(-\frac{x^2}{6} + \frac{x^4}{72} - \frac{x^6}{2160} + \cdots\right) - \tfrac{1}{2}\left(\frac{x^4}{36} - \frac{x^6}{216} + \cdots\right)$$

$$+ \tfrac{1}{3}\left(-\frac{x^6}{216} + \cdots\right) + \cdots$$

$$= \log 3 - \tfrac{1}{6}x^2 + \tfrac{1}{3240}x^6 + \cdots.$$

Example 5. Show that when $\dfrac{1}{(x^2+1)(2-x)}$ is expanded as a power series in x, the coefficient of x^{2n-1} $(n = 1, 2, 3, \cdots)$ is $\frac{1}{5}(2^{-2n} + (-1)^{n-1})$, and find the coefficient of x^{2n}. What is the interval of convergence of the expansion?

Using partial fractions we can check that

$$\frac{1}{(x^2+1)(2-x)} = \frac{\frac{1}{5}}{2-x} + \frac{\frac{1}{5}(2+x)}{1+x^2}.$$

Hence

$$\frac{1}{(x^2+1)(2-x)} = \tfrac{1}{10}\left(1-\frac{x}{2}\right)^{-1} + \tfrac{1}{5}(2+x)(1+x^2)^{-1}$$

$$= \tfrac{1}{10}\left(1+\frac{x}{2}+\frac{x^2}{2^2}+\frac{x^3}{2^3}+\cdots+\frac{x^n}{2^n}+\cdots\right)$$

$$+\tfrac{1}{5}(2+x)(1-x^2+x^4-x^6+\cdots+(-1)^n x^{2n}+\cdots),$$

the expansions being valid for $-2 < x < 2$ and $-1 < x < 1$, respectively, so that the expansion of the given function is valid for $-1 < x < 1$. The coefficient of x^{2n-1} is

$$\tfrac{1}{10}\cdot\frac{1}{2^{2n-1}} + \tfrac{1}{5}(-1)^{n-1} = \tfrac{1}{5}(2^{-2n}+(-1)^{n-1}),$$

and the coefficient of x^{2n} is

$$\tfrac{1}{10}\cdot\frac{1}{2^{2n}} + \tfrac{2}{5}(-1)^n = \tfrac{1}{5}(2^{-2n-1}+2(-1)^n).$$

Example 6. Show that $\frac{1}{4}\pi = 4\tan^{-1}\frac{1}{5} - \tan^{-1}\frac{1}{239}$ and hence, using 6 terms of the series for $\tan^{-1}\frac{1}{5}$ and 2 terms of the series for $\tan^{-1}\frac{1}{239}$, show that $3{\cdot}14159262 < \pi < 3{\cdot}14159267$.

$$2\tan^{-1}\tfrac{1}{5} = \tan^{-1}\tfrac{1}{5}+\tan^{-1}\tfrac{1}{5} = \tan^{-1}\left(\frac{\frac{1}{5}+\frac{1}{5}}{1-\frac{1}{5}\cdot\frac{1}{5}}\right) = \tan^{-1}\tfrac{5}{12},$$

and so $$4\tan^{-1}\tfrac{1}{5} = \tan^{-1}\left(\frac{\frac{5}{12}+\frac{5}{12}}{1-\frac{5}{12}\cdot\frac{5}{12}}\right) = \tan^{-1}\tfrac{120}{119};$$

thus $$4\tan^{-1}\tfrac{1}{5} - \tan^{-1}\tfrac{1}{239} = \tan^{-1}\left(\frac{\frac{120}{119}-\frac{1}{239}}{1+\frac{120}{119}\cdot\frac{1}{239}}\right) = \tan^{-1}1 = \tfrac{1}{4}\pi.$$

The arithmetical details of the approximation are left to the reader.

Newton's approximation to a root of an equation

Suppose we know that there is a root of the equation $f(x) = 0$ near $x = a$ and that the actual root is $x = a+h$. Then

$$0 = f(a+h) = f(a) + \frac{f'(a)}{1!}h + \frac{f''(a)}{2!}h^2 + \cdots.$$

Hence, if h is small and $f'(a) \neq 0$, then

$$h \doteqdot -\frac{f(a)}{f'(a)} \quad \text{and the root is approximately} \quad a - \frac{f(a)}{f'(a)}.$$

This simple observation forms the basis of the Newton–Raphson method for numerical solution of equations, the original idea being usually attributed to Newton. In works on numerical methods details of the application of the technique are given.

Example 7. Prove that the equation $x^3+x-9=0$ has one real root. Find the nearest integer approximation to the root and a second approximation using Newton's method.

If $f(x) = x^3+x-9$, then $f'(x) = 3x^2+1 > 0 \;\; \forall x \in \mathbf{R}$, so that the graph is strictly rising from left to right; $f(1) = -7 < 0$, and $f(2) = 1 > 0$. Hence there is one real root close to $x = 2$ and in the interval $(1, 2)$. By Newton's method a second approximation is

$$2 - \left[\frac{f(x)}{f'(x)}\right]_{x=2} = 2 - \tfrac{1}{13} = \tfrac{25}{13} \doteqdot 1{\cdot}923.$$

[A third approximation is $\tfrac{25}{13} - \left[\dfrac{x^3+x-9}{3x^2+1}\right]_{x=\frac{25}{13}}$, and so on.]

7. Differential equations I, equations of first order

We start by noting the following results:

(1) If $y = c\,e^x$ where $c \in \mathbf{R}$, then $\dfrac{dy}{dx} = c\,e^x = y$, so that $y = c\,e^x$ for each real number c satisfies the equation

$$\frac{dy}{dx} - y = 0.$$

We say that equation

$$\frac{dy}{dx} - y = 0$$

has a solution $y = c\,e^x$ with c a parameter.

(2) If $y = c_1 \cos x + c_2 \sin x$ where $c_1, c_2 \in \mathbf{R}$, then

$$\frac{dy}{dx} = -c_1 \sin x + c_2 \cos x$$

and

$$\frac{d^2y}{dx^2} = -c_1 \cos x - c_2 \sin x = -y;$$

in this case the equation

$$\frac{d^2y}{dx^2}+y=0$$

has a solution $y=c_1\cos x+c_2\sin x$ with c_1, c_2 parameters.

(3) If $y=c_1+c_2e^x+c_3e^{-3x}$, where $c_1, c_2, c_3 \in \mathbf{R}$, then it is easy to check that

$$\frac{d^3y}{dx^3}+2\frac{d^2y}{dx^2}-3\frac{dy}{dx}=0;$$

thus this equation has a solution $y=c_1+c_2e^x+c_3e^{-3x}$ with c_1, c_2, c_3 parameters.

(4) If $y=c_0+c_1x+c_2x^2+\cdots+c_{n-1}x^{n-1}+e^{2x}$, where $c_0, \cdots, c_{n-1} \in \mathbf{R}$, then, by forming successive derivatives in order to eliminate the coefficients $c_0, \cdots, c_{n-1}$, we find that

$$\frac{d^ny}{dx^n}-2^n e^{2x}=0.$$

In this case the equation

$$\frac{d^ny}{dx^n}-2^n e^{2x}=0$$

has a solution with n parameters.

These examples illustrate the following general situation. A relation of the form

$$F\left(x, y, \frac{dy}{dx}, \frac{d^2y}{dx^2}, \cdots, \frac{d^ny}{dx^n}\right)=0, \tag{7.1}$$

where F is a given function, is called a **differential equation** of **order** n, the order of the derivative of highest order appearing. The main problem associated with such an equation is to find solutions y in terms of x which with

$$\frac{dy}{dx}, \cdots, \frac{d^ny}{dx^n}$$

satisfy (7.1). It can be proved that, if F satisfies certain conditions, then the differential equation (7.1) has a **unique general solution** involving n parameters. We shall assume this result. A solution given by a particular set of values of these n parameters is called a **particular solution** or **particular integral** of the given differential equation.

From examples (1), (2), (3), (4) we have, from the uniqueness of a general solution, the following list of equations and corresponding general solutions:

	differential equation	general solution
(1)	$\frac{dy}{dx} - y = 0$ (order 1)	$y = c\,e^x$ (one parameter c)
(2)	$\frac{d^2y}{dx^2} + y = 0$ (order 2)	$y = c_1 \cos x + c_2 \sin x$ (2 parameters c_1, c_2)
(3)	$\frac{d^3y}{dx^3} + 2\frac{d^2y}{dx^2} - 3\frac{dy}{dx} = 0$ (order 3)	$y = c_1 + c_2 e^x + c_3 e^{-3x}$ (3 parameters c_1, c_2, c_3)
(4)	$\frac{d^ny}{dx^n} - 2^n e^{2x} = 0$ (order n)	$y = c_0 + c_1 x + \cdots + c_{n-1}x^{n-1} + e^{2x}$ (n parameters $c_0, c_1, \cdots, c_{n-1}$)

Differential equations of first order (i.e. **of order one**)

Such an equation can be expressed in the form

$$\frac{dy}{dx} = f(x, y), \tag{7.2}$$

where f is a function of two variables. The differential equation (7.2) is of *first* order and so its general solution involves *one* parameter. We describe for three special types of function f methods of finding the general solution.

A. Separable first-order equations

The differential equation (7.2) is called **separable** if $f(x, y) = g(x)h(y)$, i.e. if $f(x, y)$ can be expressed as a product with the variables x and y separate (g and h being given functions). The equation is

$$\frac{1}{h(y)}\frac{dy}{dx} = g(x). \tag{7.3}$$

Its general solution is

$$\int \frac{1}{h(y)}\,dy = \int g(x)dx + C, \tag{7.4}$$

where C is a parameter; for, (7.4) involves *one* parameter and, on differentiating (7.4) with respect to x, we obtain

$$\frac{1}{h(y)}\frac{dy}{dx} = g(x),$$

i.e. the given differential equation (7.3).

Note. In practice we write (7.3) as

$$\frac{1}{h(y)}\,dy = g(x)dx$$

and formally obtain the general solution as

$$\int \frac{1}{h(y)}\,dy = \int g(x)dx + C.$$

Example 1. Find the general solution of the differential equation

$$\frac{dy}{dx} = e^{x+y}.$$

Since $e^{x+y} = e^x . e^y$, the equation is separable. It can be written as $e^{-y}\,dy = e^x\,dx$, and so has general solution

$$\int e^{-y}\,dy = \int e^x\,dx + C,$$

i.e. $-e^{-y} = e^x + C$, with C a parameter.

Example 2. Find the general solution of the differential equation

$$x\frac{dy}{dx} = (1+x)y^2,$$

and find the particular solution for which $y = 1$ when $x = 1$.

The equation can be written as

$$\frac{1}{y^2}\,dy = \left(1 + \frac{1}{x}\right)dx,$$

showing that it is separable. It has general solution

$$\int \frac{1}{y^2}\,dy = \int \left(1+\frac{1}{x}\right)dx + C, \quad \text{i.e.} \quad -\frac{1}{y} = x + \log|x| + C,$$

with C a parameter.

The particular solution for which $y = 1$ when $x = 1$ has parameter C given by $-1 = 1 + 0 + C$, so that $C = -2$. Consequently this particular solution is

$$-\frac{1}{y} = x + \log|x| - 2.$$

Example 3. The volume of a quantity of gas is expanding at a rate proportional to the volume present. If at the end of one hour the volume has doubled from its initial volume, determine the time by which the volume will have expanded to eight times its initial volume.

If $V(t)$ denotes the volume at time t (hours) and $V(0) = V_0$, then

$$\frac{dV(t)}{dt} = kV(t),$$

where k is a positive constant. Thus

$$\frac{1}{V(t)}\frac{dV(t)}{dt} = k,$$

so that $\log V(t) = kt + C$, C a constant. Since $V(t) = V_0$ when $t = 0$, it follows that $\log V_0 = C$. Hence $\log(V(t)/V_0) = kt$, and so $V(t) = V_0 e^{kt}$. But $V(t) = 2V_0$ when $t = 1$; thus $2V_0 = V_0 e^k$ and so $e^k = 2$. Consequently $V(t) = V_0 2^t$, so that $V(t) = 8V_0$ when $t = 3$, i.e. at the end of three hours.

B. Homogeneous first-order differential equations

The differential equation (7.2) is called **homogeneous** if $f(x, y)$ is such that $f(tx, ty) = f(x, y)$ for all (suitable) non-zero real numbers t. Examples of such functions are given by:

$$f(x, y) = \frac{x^2 - 3y^2}{2xy + y^2}, \ \sin\frac{x+y}{2x-3y}, \ \sqrt{\left(\frac{x^2+y^2}{x^2-y^2}\right)}, \ e^{\frac{x}{y}}, \text{ etc.}$$

Differential equations of this type can be transformed to separable equations by changing the variables from (x, y) to (x, v), where $v = y/x$, i.e. $y = vx$; for, then

$$\frac{dy}{dx} = x\frac{dv}{dx} + v \quad \text{and} \quad f(x, y) = f\left(\frac{1}{x}x, \frac{1}{x}y\right) = f(1, v),$$

using the homogeneous property of f, so that the equation (7.2) becomes

$$x\frac{dv}{dx} + v = f(1, v),$$

i.e. the separable equation

$$\frac{dv}{dx} = \frac{1}{x}\{f(1, v) - v\}.$$

Example 4. Find the general solution of the differential equation

$$x(2x - y)\frac{dy}{dx} = (x + y)^2, \tag{7.5}$$

and the particular solution for which $y = 0$ when $x = 1$.

Here
$$\frac{dy}{dx}=\frac{(x+y)^2}{x(2x-y)},$$

and the equation is homogeneous. We change the variables as above from (x, y) to (x, v) by the transformation $y = vx$. The equation becomes

$$x\frac{dv}{dx}+v=\frac{\left(1+\dfrac{y}{x}\right)^2}{2-\dfrac{y}{x}}=\frac{(1+v)^2}{2-v},$$

i.e.
$$x\frac{dv}{dx}=\frac{1+2v+v^2}{2-v}-v=\frac{1+2v^2}{2-v}.$$

This separable equation can be written in the form

$$\frac{2-v}{1+2v^2}\,dv=\frac{dx}{x},$$

i.e.
$$\left(\frac{1}{v^2+\frac{1}{2}}-\frac{v}{1+2v^2}\right)dv=\frac{dx}{x},$$

and has general solution

$$\sqrt{2}\tan^{-1}v\sqrt{2}-\tfrac{1}{4}\log(1+2v^2)=\log|x|+C.$$

Hence the given equation (7.5) has general solution

$$\sqrt{2}\tan^{-1}\left(\frac{y}{x}\sqrt{2}\right)-\tfrac{1}{4}\log\left(1+2\frac{y^2}{x^2}\right)=\log|x|+C.$$

The particular solution for which $y = 0$ when $x = 1$ has parameter C given by $0-0 = 0+C$, i.e. $C = 0$, and so is

$$\sqrt{2}\tan^{-1}\left(\frac{y}{x}\sqrt{2}\right)-\tfrac{1}{4}\log\left(1+2\frac{y^2}{x^2}\right)=\log|x|.$$

C. Linear first-order differential equations

In this case equation (7.2) takes the form

$$\frac{dy}{dx}+P(x)y=Q(x), \tag{7.6}$$

where $P(x)$ and $Q(x)$ are given expressions in x. Here $f(x, y)$ is the expression $Q(x)-P(x)y$, *linear* in y.

Our method of solution of (7.6) involves showing that we can find $\mu(x)$ such that (7.6), when multiplied by $\mu(x)$, becomes

$$\frac{d}{dx}\{\mu(x)y\} = \mu(x)Q(x), \tag{7.7}$$

and so has general solution

$$\mu(x)y = \int \mu(x)Q(x)dx + C, \tag{7.8}$$

with C a parameter.

Such a $\mu(x)$ is called an **integrating factor** of (7.6).

Now $\mu(x) \times (7.6)$ gives:

$$\mu(x)\frac{dy}{dx} + \mu(x)P(x)y = \mu(x)Q(x),$$

and (7.7) leads to:

$$\mu(x)\frac{dy}{dx} + \frac{d\mu(x)}{dx}y = \mu(x)Q(x),$$

so that these are identical provided $\mu(x)$ is chosen to satisfy the equation

$$\frac{d\mu(x)}{dx} = \mu(x)P(x);$$

thus $$\frac{1}{\mu(x)}\frac{d}{dx}\mu(x) = P(x), \ \log \mu(x) = \int P(x)dx + C_1$$

(assuming $\mu(x) > 0$),

$$\mu(x) = e^{\int P(x)dx + C_1} = a\, e^{\int P(x)dx},$$

where $a = e^{C_1}$. We can take $a = 1$ and so have, as an integrating factor of (7.6),

$$\mu(x) = e^{\int P(x)dx}$$

Then, the general solution of (7.6) is, as given by (7.8),

$$y = e^{-\int P(x)dx}\int e^{\int P(x)dx}Q(x)dx + C\, e^{-\int P(x)dx}.$$

Example 5. Find the general solution of the differential equation

$$x\frac{dy}{dx} + (x-2)y = x^3. \tag{7.9}$$

Since equation (7.9) can be written in the form

$$\frac{dy}{dx}+\left(1-\frac{2}{x}\right)y = x^2, \tag{7.10}$$

the equation is linear. It has an integrating factor

$$\mu(x) = e^{\int (1-2/x)dx} = e^{x-\log x^2} = e^x \,.\, e^{\log(1/x^2)} = \frac{1}{x^2}e^x.$$

On multiplication by $\mu(x)$, equation (7.10) becomes (as in (7.7))

$$\frac{d}{dx}\left(\frac{1}{x^2}e^x \,.\, y\right) = e^x,$$

and so has general solution

$$\frac{y}{x^2}e^x = e^x + C, \text{ with } C \text{ a parameter.}$$

Example 6. Find, by using the substitution $z = y^2$, the general solution of the differential equation

$$\frac{dy}{dx}+\frac{y}{x} = \frac{1}{y}. \tag{7.11}$$

Equation (7.11) can be written as

$$y\frac{dy}{dx}+\frac{1}{x}y^2 = 1;$$

putting $z = y^2$ and so

$$\frac{dz}{dx} = 2y\frac{dy}{dx},$$

this becomes the linear equation

$$\frac{dz}{dx}+\frac{2}{x}z = 2. \tag{7.12}$$

Equation (7.12) has an integrating factor

$$\mu(x) = e^{\int (2/x)dx} = e^{\log x^2} = x^2.$$

On multiplication by $\mu(x)$, equation (7.12) becomes

$$\frac{d}{dx}(x^2 z) = 2x^2,$$

and so has general solution $x^2 z = \frac{2}{3}x^3 + C$. Thus (7.11) has general solution $x^2 y^2 = \frac{2}{3}x^3 + C$.

Example 7. Find the general solution of the differential equation

$$(1-x^2)\frac{dy}{dx}-xy=1$$

(i) valid for $|x|<1$, (ii) valid for $|x|>1$.

The differential equation can be written as

$$\frac{dy}{dx}-\frac{x}{1-x^2}y=\frac{1}{1-x^2}, \tag{7.13}$$

showing that it is linear. It has an integrating factor

$$\mu(x)=e^{-\int\frac{x}{1-x^2}dx}.$$

Case (i), $|x|<1$. Here $\mu(x)=e^{\frac{1}{2}\log(1-x^2)}=e^{\log\sqrt{(1-x^2)}}=\sqrt{(1-x^2)}$.

On multiplication by $\mu(x)$, equation (7.13) becomes

$$\frac{d}{dx}\{y\sqrt{(1-x^2)}\}=\frac{1}{\sqrt{(1-x^2)}},$$

and its general solution is $y\sqrt{(1-x^2)}=\sin^{-1}x+C$, with C a parameter.

Case (ii), $|x|>1$. Here $\mu(x)=e^{\frac{1}{2}\log(x^2-1)}=e^{\log\sqrt{(x^2-1)}}=\sqrt{(x^2-1)}$.

On multiplication by $\mu(x)$, equation (7.13) becomes

$$\frac{d}{dx}\{y\sqrt{(x^2-1)}\}=-\frac{1}{\sqrt{(x^2-1)}},$$

and its general solution is $y\sqrt{(x^2-1)}=-\log|x+\sqrt{(x^2-1)}|+C$.

Example 8. The electric current i (amperes) flowing through a coil of inductance L (henrys) and a resistor of resistance R (ohms) due to an applied voltage E satisfies the differential equation

$$L\frac{di}{dt}+Ri=E,$$

where L, R, E are constants and t is time in seconds. If $i=0$ when $t=0$, determine i at time t.

The differential equation is

$$\frac{di}{dt}+\frac{R}{L}i=\frac{E}{L}.$$

Here $$\mu(t)=e^{\int(R/L)dt}=e^{(R/L)t}$$

and the equation, on multiplication by $\mu(t)$, becomes

$$\frac{d}{dt}(e^{(R/L)t}i) = \frac{E}{L}e^{(R/L)t}$$

This has general solution

$$e^{(R/L)t}i = \frac{E}{L}\cdot\frac{L}{R}e^{(R/L)t} + C, \ C \text{ a parameter,}$$

i.e.

$$i = \frac{E}{R} + C\,e^{-(R/L)t}.$$

But $i = 0$ when $t = 0$; so

$$0 = \frac{E}{R} + C \quad \text{and} \quad C = -\frac{E}{R}.$$

Hence

$$i = \frac{E}{R}(1 - e^{-(R/L)t}).$$

Note.

$$i \to \frac{E}{R} \quad \text{as} \quad t \to \infty.$$

8. Differential equations II, linear differential equations of second order with constant coefficients

These equations, which are of great importance in many applications, are of the form

$$a\frac{d^2y}{dx^2} + b\frac{dy}{dx} + cy = f(x), \tag{8.1}$$

where a, b, c are given real numbers, $a \neq 0$, and f is a given function. If f is not the zero function, equation (8.1) is said to be **non-homogeneous**; then the equation

$$a\frac{d^2y}{dx^2} + b\frac{dy}{dx} + cy = 0 \tag{8.2}$$

is called the **homogeneous** equation corresponding to the non-homogeneous equation (8.1). The two equations are connected by the following result.

Theorem 7.2

If $y = G(x)$ *is the general solution of* (8.2) *and* $y = y_1(x)$ *is a particular integral of* (8.1), *then* $y = G(x) + y_1(x)$ *is the general solution of* (8.1).

Proof. If $y = G(x)+y_1(x)$, then

$$a\frac{d^2y}{dx^2}+b\frac{dy}{dx}+cy = a\left(\frac{d^2G}{dx^2}+\frac{d^2y_1}{dx^2}\right)+b\left(\frac{dG}{dx}+\frac{dy_1}{dx}\right)+c(G(x)+y_1(x))$$

$$=\left(a\frac{d^2G}{dx^2}+b\frac{dG}{dx}+cG(x)\right)+\left(a\frac{d^2y_1}{dx^2}+b\frac{dy_1}{dx}+cy_1(x)\right)$$

$$= 0+f(x), \quad \text{since } G(x) \text{ satisfies (8.2) and } y_1(x) \text{ satisfies (8.1).}$$

Hence y is a solution of (8.1). Since (8.2) is of second order, its general solution $G(x)$ contains exactly two parameters. Thus $G(x)+y_1(x)$ contains two parameters and so is the unique general solution of the second-order differential equation (8.1).

Note. $G(x)$ is called the **complementary function** (C.F.) in the general solution of (8.1) and $y_1(x)$ a **particular integral** (P.I.). In order to solve (8.1) we have first to find the general solution of (8.2), and then to find *any one* particular solution of (8.1).

General solution of (8.2)

We look for solutions of the form $y = e^{mx}$, where m is a constant. If $y = e^{mx}$, then

$$\frac{dy}{dx} = m\,e^{mx} \quad \text{and} \quad \frac{d^2y}{dx^2} = m^2\,e^{mx}.$$

Hence $y = e^{mx}$ is a solution of (8.2) if and only if, for all suitable real x,

$$am^2\,e^{mx}+bm\,e^{mx}+c\,e^{mx} = 0,$$

i.e.

$$\Leftrightarrow am^2+bm+c = 0. \tag{8.3}$$

Equation (8.3) is called the **auxiliary equation** of (8.2) and (8.1). There are three possible cases.

Case 1. (8.3) *has distinct real roots,* $m = m_1, m_2$, say: In this case e^{m_1x} and e^{m_2x} are both solutions of (8.2) and so is $y = c_1\,e^{m_1x}+c_2\,e^{m_2x}$ for each pair of real numbers c_1, c_2. In fact, more generally, if $y_1(x)$ and $y_2(x)$ are both solutions of (8.2) so that

$$a\frac{d^2y_1}{dx^2}+b\frac{dy_1}{dx}+cy_1(x) = 0 \quad \text{and} \quad a\frac{d^2y_2}{dx^2}+b\frac{dy_2}{dx}+cy_2(x) = 0,$$

then

$$a \frac{d^2}{dx^2}(c_1 y_1(x)+c_2 y_2(x))+b \frac{d}{dx}(c_1 y_1(x)+c_2 y_2(x))+c(c_1 y_1(x)+c_2 y_2(x))$$

$$= c_1 \left\{ a \frac{d^2 y_1}{dx^2}+b \frac{dy_1}{dx}+c y_1(x) \right\} + c_2 \left\{ a \frac{d^2 y_2}{dx^2}+b \frac{dy_2}{dx}+c y_2(x) \right\}$$

$$= 0,$$

and so $$y = c_1 y_1(x)+c_2 y_2(x),$$

with c_1, c_2 real numbers, is also a solution of (8.2). (8.4)

It follows, from the above argument, that, with c_1 and c_2 parameters,

$$y = c_1 e^{m_1 x}+c_2 e^{m_2 x} \tag{8.5}$$

is the general solution of (8.2) and so the C.F. of (8.1).

Case 2. (8.3) *has one (repeated) real root*, m_1 *say*: In this case $e^{m_1 x}$ is one solution of (8.2). We show that $y = x e^{m_1 x}$ is also a solution of (8.2), *independent* of the solution $e^{m_1 x}$ in the sense that neither is a constant times the other.

Now $$a \frac{d^2}{dx^2}(x e^{m_1 x})+b \frac{d}{dx}(x e^{m_1 x})+c(x e^{m_1 x})$$

$$= a(m_1^2 x e^{m_1 x}+2m_1 e^{m_1 x})+b(m_1 x e^{m_1 x}+e^{m_1 x})+cx e^{m_1 x}$$

$$= (am_1^2+bm_1+c)x e^{m_1 x}+(2am_1+b)e^{m_1 x}$$

$$= 0+(2am_1+b)e^{m_1 x}, \quad \text{since } m_1 \text{ is a root of (8.3).}$$

But, since m_1, m_1 are the two roots of (8.3), we have:

$$2m_1 = \text{sum of roots of (8.3)} = -\frac{b}{a}, \quad \text{so that} \quad 2am_1+b = 0.$$

It follows that $x e^{m_1 x}$ is also a solution of (8.2) and, by the statement (8.4), that $c_1 e^{m_1 x}+c_2 x e^{m_1 x}$, for each pair of real numbers c_1, c_2, is a solution of (8.2). Hence

$$y = (c_1+c_2 x)e^{m_1 x}, \tag{8.6}$$

with c_1, c_2 parameters, is the general solution of (8.2) and so the C.F. of (8.1).

Case 3. (8.3) *has (distinct) non-real roots*, $\alpha \pm i\beta$, *with* α, β *real and* $\beta > 0$. Since $\alpha+i\beta$ is a root of (8.3),

$$a(\alpha+i\beta)^2+b(\alpha+i\beta)+c = 0,$$

$$a(\alpha^2-\beta^2)+b\alpha+c+i(2a\alpha+b)\beta = 0,$$

and so $$a(\alpha^2-\beta^2)+b\alpha+c=0 \quad \text{and} \quad 2a\alpha+b=0, \tag{8.7}$$

from the real and imaginary parts.

We show that $e^{\alpha x}\cos\beta x$ and $e^{\alpha x}\sin\beta x$ are independent solutions of (8.2).

$$a\frac{d^2}{dx^2}(e^{\alpha x}\cos\beta x)+b\frac{d}{dx}(e^{\alpha x}\cos\beta x)+c\,e^{\alpha x}\cos\beta x$$

$$= a\{(\alpha^2-\beta^2)e^{\alpha x}\cos\beta x-2\alpha\beta\, e^{\alpha x}\sin\beta x\}+b\{\alpha\, e^{\alpha x}\cos\beta x-\beta\, e^{\alpha x}\sin\beta x\}$$
$$+c\,e^{\alpha x}\cos\beta x$$

$$= \{a(\alpha^2-\beta^2)+b\alpha+c\}e^{\alpha x}\cos\beta x-(2a\alpha+b)\beta\, e^{\alpha x}\sin\beta x$$
$$= 0, \quad \text{from (8.7).}$$

Thus $e^{\alpha x}\cos\beta x$ is a solution of (8.2). Similarly $e^{\alpha x}\sin\beta x$ is also a solution and consequently

$$y = e^{\alpha x}(c_1\cos\beta x+c_2\sin\beta x), \tag{8.8}$$

with c_1, c_2 parameters, is the general solution of (8.2) and so the C.F. of (8.1).

Summing up, the general solution of (8.2) and so the C.F. of (8.1) is given by (8.5), (8.6) and (8.8) in each of the three possible cases arising from the nature of the roots of the auxiliary equation (8.3).

Example 1. Find the general solution of each of the following homogeneous differential equations of second order:

(i) $\dfrac{d^2y}{dx^2}-\dfrac{dy}{dx}-2y=0$; (ii) $\dfrac{d^2y}{dx^2}-a^2y=0$, a constant, $a\neq 0$;

(iii) $4\dfrac{d^2y}{dx^2}+4\dfrac{dy}{dx}+y=0$; (iv) $\dfrac{d^2y}{dx^2}+a^2y=0$, a constant, $a\neq 0$;

(v) $\dfrac{d^2y}{dx^2}+2\dfrac{dy}{dx}+4y=0$; (vi) $\dfrac{d^2y}{dx^2}-3\dfrac{dy}{dx}=0$.

We list in order in each case the auxiliary equation, its roots and the general solution with c_1, c_2 parameters.

(i) $m^2-m-2=0$; $m=-1, 2$; $y=c_1e^{-x}+c_2e^{2x}$;

(ii) $m^2-a^2=0$; $m=a, -a$; $y=c_1e^{ax}+c_2e^{-ax}$;

(iii) $4m^2+4m+1=0$; $m=-\frac{1}{2}, -\frac{1}{2}$; $y=(c_1+c_2x)e^{-\frac{1}{2}x}$;

(iv) $m^2+a^2=0$; $m=ia, -ia$; $y=c_1\cos ax+c_2\sin ax$;

(v) $m^2+2m+4=0$; $m=-1\pm i\sqrt{3}$; $y=e^{-x}(c_1\cos(\sqrt{3}x)$
$+c_2\sin(\sqrt{3}x))$;

(vi) $m^2-3m=0$; $m=0, 3$; $y=c_1+c_2e^{3x}$.

Particular integrals of (8.1), i.e. of

$$a\frac{d^2y}{dx^2}+b\frac{dy}{dx}+cy=f(x). \tag{8.1}$$

In most applications, f is a simple polynomial, an exponential, a sine or cosine, or a combination of these. We first show that, if

$$f(x)=f_1(x)+f_2(x),$$

and if $y_1(x)$ and $y_2(x)$ are P.I.s of the equations

$$a\frac{d^2y}{dx^2}+b\frac{dy}{dx}+cy=f_i(x) \quad (i=1,2), \tag{8.9}$$

then $y_1(x)+y_2(x)$ is a P.I. of (8.1). We have:

$$\begin{aligned} & a\frac{d^2}{dx^2}(y_1+y_2)+b\frac{d}{dx}(y_1+y_2)+c(y_1+y_2) \\ &= \left(a\frac{d^2y_1}{dx^2}+b\frac{dy_1}{dx}+cy_1\right)+\left(a\frac{d^2y_2}{dx^2}+b\frac{dy_2}{dx}+cy_2\right) \\ &= f_1(x)+f_2(x), \quad \text{from (8.9)}, \\ &= f(x), \quad \text{and so} \quad y_1(x)+y_2(x) \text{ is a P.I. of (8.1).} \end{aligned}$$

It follows that, if $f(x)$ is a sum of terms, we can deal with the individual terms separately and add the results together to obtain the required P.I.

In dealing with a given term our method will be to try for a P.I. of a suitable form, the exact expression being determined by ensuring that it satisfies (8.1). The following table lists the most important forms for $f(x)$ and the corresponding expressions to be tried as P.I.s. When $f(x)$ is contained within the C.F. of (8.1) (i.e. the general solution of (8.2)) we multiply the basic form for a P.I. by x or x^2 as indicated in the table.

$f(x)$	Form for P.I. of (8.1)
$e^{\alpha x}$	$y=Ae^{\alpha x}$, α not a root of (8.3) $y=Axe^{\alpha x}$, α *a* non-repeated root of (8.3) $y=Ax^2e^{\alpha x}$, α a repeated root of (8.3)
$xe^{\alpha x}$	$y=(Ax+B)e^{\alpha x}$, $(Ax^2+Bx)e^{\alpha x}$, $(Ax^3+Bx^2)e^{\alpha x}$, in the above three cases.
$H\cos\alpha x+K\sin\alpha x$	$y=A\cos\alpha x+B\sin\alpha x$, $i\alpha$ not a root of (8.3) $y=x(A\cos\alpha x+B\sin\alpha x)$, $i\alpha$ a root of (8.3)
$a_0+a_1x+\cdots+a_nx^n$	$y=A_0+A_1x+\cdots+A_nx^n$, $m=0$ not a root of (8.3) [The degree of y is increased by 1 or 2 according as $m=0$ is a non-repeated or repeated root of (8.3).]

We illustrate the methods by the following examples.

Example 2. Find the general solution of the differential equation

$$\frac{d^2y}{dx^2}+4\frac{dy}{dx}+4y=x^2. \tag{8.10}$$

The auxiliary equation is $m^2+4m+4=0$, with roots $m=-2,-2$. Hence the C.F. is $y=(c_1+c_2x)e^{-2x}$.

For a P.I. we try $y=Ax^2+Bx+C$, and determine the constants A, B, C by inserting this expression for y in (8.10). $y=Ax^2+Bx+C$ is a solution of (8.10).

$$\Leftrightarrow 2A+4(2Ax+B)+4(Ax^2+Bx+C)=x^2, \quad \forall x\in\mathbf{R}$$

$$\Leftrightarrow 4Ax^2+(8A+4B)x+(2A+4B+4C)=x^2, \quad \forall x\in\mathbf{R}$$

$$\Leftrightarrow \begin{cases} 4A=1 & \text{(equating coefficients of } x^2\text{)} \\ 8A+4B=0 & \text{(equating coefficients of } x\text{)} \\ 2A+4B+4C=0 & \text{(equating constant terms)} \end{cases}$$

$$\Leftrightarrow A=\tfrac{1}{4},\ B=-\tfrac{1}{2} \text{ and } C=\tfrac{3}{8};$$

thus

$$y=\tfrac{1}{4}x^2-\tfrac{1}{2}x+\tfrac{3}{8}$$

is a P.I. of (8.10). Hence the general solution of (8.10) is

$$y=(c_1+c_2x)e^{-2x}+\tfrac{1}{4}x^2-\tfrac{1}{2}x+\tfrac{3}{8},$$

with c_1, c_2 parameters.

Example 3. Find the general solution of the differential equation

$$\frac{d^2y}{dx^2}-2\frac{dy}{dx}-3y=e^{-x}, \tag{8.11}$$

and the particular solution for which

$$y=1 \quad\text{and}\quad \frac{dy}{dx}=-\tfrac{5}{4} \quad\text{when}\quad x=0.$$

The auxiliary equation is $m^2-2m-3=0$, with roots $m=-1,3$. Hence the C.F. is $y=c_1e^{-x}+c_2e^{3x}$.

For a P.I. we try $y=Ax\,e^{-x}$, since in this case $f(x)=e^{-x}$ appears in the C.F. ($m=-1$ is a root of the auxiliary equation). From $y=Ax\,e^{-x}$ we have

$$\frac{dy}{dx}=A(-x\,e^{-x}+e^{-x}) \quad\text{and}\quad \frac{d^2y}{dx^2}=A(x\,e^{-x}-2\,e^{-x}).$$

Hence $y = Ax\,e^{-x}$ is a solution of (8.11)

$$\Leftrightarrow A(x-2)e^{-x} - 2A(-x+1)e^{-x} - 3Ax\,e^{-x} = e^{-x}, \quad \forall x \in \mathbf{R}$$
$$\Leftrightarrow -4A = 1 \Leftrightarrow A = -\tfrac{1}{4}.$$

Thus $y = -\frac{1}{4}x\,e^{-x}$ is a P.I. of (8.11) and the general solution is

$$y = c_1 e^{-x} + c_2 e^{3x} - \tfrac{1}{4}x\,e^{-x},$$

with c_1, c_2 parameters.

Since $$\frac{dy}{dx} = -c_1 e^{-x} + 3c_2 e^{3x} + \tfrac{1}{4}x\,e^{-x} - \tfrac{1}{4}e^{-x},$$

the particular solution for which

$$y = 1 \quad \text{and} \quad \frac{dy}{dx} = -\tfrac{5}{4}$$

when $x = 0$ has parameters c_1, c_2 given by the equations:

$$c_1 + c_2 = 1, \quad -c_1 + 3c_2 - \tfrac{1}{4} = -\tfrac{5}{4};$$

on solving these equations, its parameters are $c_1 = 1$, $c_2 = 0$, and the required particular solution is $y = e^{-x} - \frac{1}{4}x\,e^{-x}$.

Example 4. Find the general solution of the differential equation

$$\frac{d^2y}{dx^2} + 2\frac{dy}{dx} + 5y = 5x + \cos 2x. \tag{8.12}$$

The auxiliary equation is $m^2 + 2m + 5 = 0$, with complex roots $m = -1 \pm 2i$. Hence the C.F. is $y = e^{-x}(c_1 \cos 2x + c_2 \sin 2x)$.

For a P.I., proceeding as described in the introductory discussion, we find P.I.s of the separate equations

$$\frac{d^2y}{dx^2} + 2\frac{dy}{dx} + 5y = 5x, \tag{8.13}$$

$$\frac{d^2y}{dx^2} + 2\frac{dy}{dx} + 5y = \cos 2x, \tag{8.14}$$

and from their sum obtain a P.I. of (8.12).

For a P.I. of (8.13) we try $y = Ax + B$; $y = Ax + B$ is a solution of (8.13)

$$\Leftrightarrow 0 + 2A + 5(Ax + B) = 5x, \quad \forall x \in \mathbf{R}$$
$$\Leftrightarrow 5A = 5 \quad \text{and} \quad 2A + 5B = 0$$
$$\Leftrightarrow A = 1 \quad \text{and} \quad B = -\tfrac{2}{5}.$$

Hence $$y = x - \tfrac{2}{5} \text{ is a P.I. of (8.13).} \tag{8.15}$$

For a P.I. of (8.14) we try $y = A\cos 2x + B\sin 2x$; this is a solution of (8.14)

$$\Leftrightarrow (-4A\cos 2x - 4B\sin 2x) + 2(-2A\sin 2x + 2B\cos 2x) + 5(A\cos 2x + B\sin 2x) = \cos 2x, \quad \forall x \in \mathbf{R}$$

$$\Leftrightarrow (A+4B)\cos 2x + (B-4A)\sin 2x = \cos 2x, \quad \forall x \in \mathbf{R}$$

$$\Leftrightarrow \begin{cases} A+4B = 1 & \text{(equating coefficients of } \cos 2x) \\ B-4A = 0 & \text{(equating coefficients of } \sin 2x) \end{cases}$$

$$\Leftrightarrow A = \tfrac{1}{17} \quad \text{and} \quad B = \tfrac{4}{17}.$$

Hence $$y = \tfrac{1}{17}(\cos 2x + 4\sin 2x) \text{ is a P.I. of (8.14).} \tag{8.16}$$

From (8.15) and (8.16) it follows that a P.I. of (8.12) is

$$y = x - \tfrac{2}{5} + \tfrac{1}{17}(\cos 2x + 4\sin 2x).$$

Hence the general solution of (8.12) is

$$y = e^{-x}(c_1\cos 2x + c_2\sin 2x) + x - \tfrac{2}{5} + \tfrac{1}{17}(\cos 2x + 4\sin 2x),$$

with c_1, c_2 parameters.

Example 5. The position $x(t)$, measured in metres from the origin O at time t seconds, of a particle moving on the x-axis satisfies the differential equation

$$2\frac{d^2x}{dt^2} + 3\omega\frac{dx}{dt} - 2\omega^2 x = \omega^2 e^{-\omega t}, \tag{8.17}$$

where ω is a positive constant. If the particle starts initially from the point $x = 1$ with velocity ω metres per second (i.e. in direction Ox), find $x(t)$.

Equation (8.17) has auxiliary equation $2m^2 + 3\omega m - 2\omega^2 = 0$, with roots $m = \tfrac{1}{2}\omega, -2\omega$; the C.F. is $x = c_1 e^{\frac{1}{2}\omega t} + c_2 e^{-2\omega t}$.

For P.I. we try $x = A e^{-\omega t}$; this is a solution of (8.17)

$$\Leftrightarrow 2A\omega^2 e^{-\omega t} + 3\omega A(-\omega) e^{-\omega t} - 2\omega^2 A e^{-\omega t} = \omega^2 e^{-\omega t}$$

$$\Leftrightarrow -3A = 1 \Leftrightarrow A = -\tfrac{1}{3}.$$

Thus $x = -\tfrac{1}{3}e^{-\omega t}$ is a P.I. of (8.17) and the general solution is

$$x = c_1 e^{\frac{1}{2}\omega t} + c_2 e^{-2\omega t} - \tfrac{1}{3}e^{-\omega t}.$$

Since $$\frac{dx}{dt} = \tfrac{1}{2}c_1\omega\, e^{\frac{1}{2}\omega t} - 2c_2\omega\, e^{-2\omega t} + \tfrac{1}{3}\omega\, e^{-\omega t},$$

the required particular solution, for which

$$x = 1 \quad \text{and} \quad \frac{dx}{dt} = \omega \quad \text{when} \quad t = 0,$$

has parameters c_1, c_2 satisfying the equations:

$$1 = c_1 + c_2 - \tfrac{1}{3}, \quad \omega = \tfrac{1}{2}c_1\omega - 2c_2\omega + \tfrac{1}{3}\omega,$$

i.e. $$c_1 + c_2 = \tfrac{4}{3}, \quad \tfrac{1}{2}c_1 - 2c_2 = \tfrac{2}{3}.$$

On solving these equations we obtain $c_1 = \frac{4}{3}$ and $c_2 = 0$; consequently

$$x(t) = \tfrac{4}{3}\, e^{\frac{1}{2}\omega t} - \tfrac{1}{3}\, e^{-\omega t}.$$

Example 6. Find the general solution of the differential equation

$$x^2 \frac{d^2y}{dx^2} + 3x\frac{dy}{dx} + y = \sin(\log x). \tag{8.18}$$

An equation of this type, linear in y, $x\dfrac{dy}{dx}$ and $x^2\dfrac{d^2y}{dx^2}$, can be transformed to an equation with constant coefficients by changing the variable from x to u where $x = e^u$ $(x > 0)$, and so $u = \log x$.

If $x = e^u$, then

$$\frac{dy}{du} = \frac{dy}{dx}\frac{dx}{du} = e^u \frac{dy}{dx} = x\frac{dy}{dx},$$

and $$\frac{d^2y}{du^2} = \frac{d}{dx}\left(x\frac{dy}{dx}\right)\frac{dx}{du} = \left(x\frac{d^2y}{dx^2} + \frac{dy}{dx}\right)x = x^2\frac{d^2y}{dx^2} + x\frac{dy}{dx},$$

so that $$x^2\frac{d^2y}{dx^2} = \frac{d^2y}{du^2} - \frac{dy}{du}.$$

In terms of u and y, equation (8.18) becomes

$$\left(\frac{d^2y}{du^2} - \frac{dy}{du}\right) + 3\frac{dy}{du} + y = \sin u,$$

i.e. $$\frac{d^2y}{du^2} + 2\frac{dy}{du} + y = \sin u. \tag{8.19}$$

We leave as an exercise to the reader to check that the general solution of (8.19) is

$$y = (c_1 + c_2 u)\, e^{-u} - \tfrac{1}{2}\cos u, \text{ with } c_1, c_2 \text{ parameters.}$$

Since $u = \log x$ and $e^{-u} = 1/x$, it follows that the general solution of (8.18) is

$$y = \frac{1}{x}(c_1 + c_2 \log x) - \tfrac{1}{2}\cos(\log x).$$

EXERCISE 7

1. Find the arc length of the curve $y = x^{3/2}$ from $x = 0$ to $x = 4$ and find the volume of the solid generated by rotation through one revolution about the x-axis of the region bounded by this arc, the x-axis and the line $x = 4$.

2. Find the length of the curve

$$y = \frac{2}{3\sqrt{3}}(x+1)^{3/2} \text{ from } x = 0 \text{ to } x = 5.$$

3. Find the arc length of the curve $x = at^2$, $y = at^3$ $(a > 0)$ from $t = 0$ to $t = 2$.

4. Find the arc length of the curve $y = \cosh x$ in the interval $[-1, 1]$. Find also the area of the surface obtained by rotating this arc through one revolution about the x-axis.

5. Express the arc length of the curve $y = e^{-x}$ in the interval $[0, \frac{3}{2}\log 2]$ as an integral, and find its value by using the substitution $u = \sqrt{(1+e^{-2x})}$.

6. Find the arc length of the curve $y = x^{1/2} - \frac{1}{3}x^{3/2}$ from $x = 1$ to $x = 3$.

7. Find the arc length of the curve $x = a(\theta - \sin\theta)$, $y = a(1-\cos\theta)$, $0 \leqslant \theta \leqslant 2\pi$ (one arch of a **cycloid**), a being a positive constant.

8. Show that the curve with polar equation $r = a(1+\cos\theta)$ $(a > 0)$ has arc length $8a$.

9. Find the arc length of the curve $r = \sec^2\frac{1}{2}\theta$ between $\theta = 0$ and $\theta = \frac{1}{3}\pi$.

10. Find the area of the finite region bounded by the parabolas $y = x^2 - 4x + 9$ and $y = 3 + 4x - x^2$.

11. Find the area of the region in the first quadrant enclosed by the circle $x^2 + y^2 = 4$ and the hyperbola $xy = \sqrt{3}$.

12. Find the area of the region in the first quadrant enclosed by the circle $x^2 + y^2 = 9$, the parabola $2x^2 = 9(2-y)$, and the line $y = 2$.

13. Sketch the curve $y = 9(x+1)/x(x-3)$. Show that the area of the region enclosed by the curve, the x-axis and the ordinates at $x = 4$ and $x = 8$ is $3\log(625/2)$.

14. Sketch the curve $y = x(1-x)^3$, and determine the area of the region bounded by the part of the curve above the x-axis and the x-axis.

15. Sketch the curve

$$y = \frac{x^3+1}{(x^2+1)^{3/2}},$$

and find the area of the region between the curve and the line $y = 1$ for $0 \leqslant x \leqslant 1$.

16. Sketch the curve $y = x^3 e^{-6x^2}$. Find the area of the region under the curve from $x = 0$ to $x = \infty$. Show that the ordinate which bisects this region into two regions of equal areas has equation $x = a$ where $6a^2 = \log(2 + 12a^2)$.

17. Sketch the curve $x = \cos 2t$, $y = \sin 3t$, $t \in [0, \frac{1}{3}\pi]$. Find the area of the region bounded by the curve and the x-axis.

18. Find the area of the region A bounded by the curve $x = t(t-1)$, $y = t(t+2)$ and the y-axis. Find also the volume of the solid generated when A is rotated through one revolution about the y-axis.

19. Find the area of the region enclosed by the loop of the curve $y^2 = x^2(1-x)$ and the volume of the solid generated when this loop is rotated through one revolution about the x-axis.

20. (i) Find the area of the region enclosed by the curve $r = a\sqrt{(\sin 2\theta)}$, $a > 0$.
(ii) Find the area of the region bounded by the curve $r = e^{\theta}$, $0 \leqslant \theta \leqslant \pi$, and the x-axis.

21. If the region bounded by $y = \cos \pi x$, the x-axis and $x = 0$, $x = \frac{1}{2}$ is rotated through one revolution about the x-axis, find the volume of the solid generated.

22. If the region in the first quadrant enclosed by the parabola $y = x^2$ and the lines $x = 1$, $y = 4$ is rotated through one revolution about the y-axis, find the volume of the solid generated.

23. By using integration, show that a sphere of radius a has volume $4\pi a^3/3$.

24. Sketch the curve $y = 1/(1+x^2)$. Find the area of the region bounded by the curve, the axes and the ordinate $x = 1$. Find also the volume of the solid formed when this region is rotated through one revolution about (i) the x-axis, (ii) the y-axis.

25. Sketch the curve $x^{\frac{1}{2}} + y^{\frac{1}{2}} = a^{\frac{1}{2}}$ for $0 \leqslant x \leqslant a$. Find the area of the region bounded by the curve and the axes, and the volume of the solid formed by rotation of this region through one revolution about the x-axis.

26. If the region in the first quadrant enclosed by the curve $y^4(1+x^2) = x^6$, the x-axis and the line $x = 1$ is rotated through one revolution about the x-axis, find the volume of the solid formed.

27. Sketch the curve $x = 1 - 3t^2$, $y = 3t - t^3$, $t \in \mathbf{R}$. Find (i) the arc length of the loop of the curve, (ii) the area of the region enclosed by the loop, (iii) the volume of the solid formed when this region is rotated through one revolution about the x-axis, (iv) the area of the surface of this solid.

28. For the curve

$$y = \tfrac{1}{6}\left(x^3 + \frac{3}{x}\right),$$

show that the length of the arc on $[1, 2]$ is $17/12$ and that the area of the surface formed by rotation of this arc through one revolution about the x-axis is $47\pi/16$.

29. The curve $y = \sqrt{(1-2x)}$ meets the x-axis at A and the y-axis at B. Sketch the arc AB. Find the area of the surface formed by rotating this arc through one revolution about the x-axis. Show that arc AB has length

$$s = \sqrt{2}\int_0^{\frac{1}{2}} \sqrt{\left(\frac{1-x}{1-2x}\right)}\, dx,$$

and evaluate s by using the substitution $u = \sqrt{(1-2x)}$, or otherwise.

30. Sketch the curve

$$y = \frac{x}{4}\sqrt{(2-x^2)}, \quad 0 \leqslant x \leqslant \sqrt{2}.$$

Find (i) the area enclosed by the curve and the x-axis, (ii) the arc length of the curve, (iii) the area of the surface formed by rotating the curve through one revolution about the x-axis.

31. Sketch the arc

$$x = 2\cos\theta - \cos 2\theta, \ y = 2\sin\theta - \sin 2\theta, \ 0 \leqslant \theta \leqslant \pi,$$

and find the area of the surface formed when the arc is rotated through one revolution about the x-axis.

32. Sketch the arc

$$x = \cos t(1+\cos t), \ y = \sin t(1+\cos t), \ 0 \leqslant t \leqslant \pi.$$

Find the length of the arc, and show that the area of the surface generated by rotating the arc through one revolution about the x-axis is $32\pi/5$.

33. Sketch the curve with parametric equations

$$x = 4\sqrt{2}\cos t, \ y = \sin 2t.$$

Find the total length of the curve, and the area of the surface formed by rotating the curve through one revolution about the x-axis.

34. An arc of a curve is defined by the parametric equations

$$x = a\log(\sec t + \tan t) - a\sin t, \ y = a\cos t, \ t \in [-\tfrac{1}{4}\pi, \tfrac{1}{4}\pi], \ a > 0.$$

Find the length of the arc, and the area of the surface formed by rotating this arc through one revolution about the x-axis.

35. (i) Find the area of the surface formed by rotating the curve $r = a\sqrt{(\sin 2\theta)}$, $a > 0$, through one revolution about the x-axis.
(ii) Find the area of the surface formed by rotating the curve $r = 1 - \cos\theta$ through one revolution about the x-axis.

36. Find the area of the surface generated by rotating the arc $y = \sin x$, $x \in [0, \pi]$, through one revolution about the x-axis.

37. Find the radius, centre and circle of curvature at the point $(a, 2a)$ on the parabola $y^2 = 4ax$, $a > 0$.

38. Find the radius and centre of curvature at the point $P(t)$ on the rectangular hyperbola with parametric equations $x = ct$, $y = c/t$ ($t \neq 0$, $c > 0$). Show that the evolute of the hyperbola has equation $(x+y)^{2/3} - (x-y)^{2/3} = (4c)^{2/3}$

39. If s is arc CP of the curve $y = c\cosh(x/c)$, where C is the point $(0, c)$ $(c > 0)$ and $P(x, y)$, and if ρ is the radius of curvature at P, prove that $c\rho = y^2 = c^2 + s^2$.

40. For the curve $x = a\cos^4 t$, $y = a\sin^4 t$ $(a > 0)$, show that

$$\rho = 2a(\cos^4 t + \sin^4 t)^{3/2}.$$

Find the coordinates of the centre of curvature at the point $(\frac{1}{4}a, \frac{1}{4}a)$.

41. For the curve

$$x = a(2\sin 2\theta + \sin 4\theta), \quad y = a(2\cos 2\theta - \cos 4\theta), \quad a > 0,$$

show that the radius ρ and centre of curvature $C(\xi, \eta)$ at the point $P(\theta)$ are given by $\rho = 8a|\cos 3\theta|$, $\xi = 3a(2\sin 2\theta - \sin 4\theta)$, $\eta = 3a(2\cos 2\theta + \cos 4\theta)$. Show that PC is the tangent at C to the evolute of the given curve.

42. Show that the radius of curvature at the point $P(\theta)$ $(\theta \neq \frac{1}{2}k\pi, k \in \mathbf{Z})$ on the astroid $x = a\cos^3\theta$, $y = a\sin^3\theta$ $(a > 0)$ is $3a|\sin\theta\cos\theta|$. Find parametric equations for the evolute.

43. For the ellipse $x = a\cos\theta$, $y = b\sin\theta$ $(a > b > 0)$, find the radius of curvature at the point $P(\theta)$. Show also that the evolute of the ellipse has parametric equations of the form $x = A\cos^3\theta$, $y = B\sin^3\theta$, determining the constants A and B.

44. For the curve $r = (\cos 3\theta)^{1/3}$, show that the radius of curvature at $P(\theta)$ is $\frac{1}{4}(\sec 3\theta)^{2/3}$ (taking $\cos 3\theta > 0$).

[*Hint.* Show that $\dfrac{dx}{d\theta} = -\sin 4\theta(\sec 3\theta)^{2/3}$, $\dfrac{dy}{d\theta} = \cos 4\theta(\sec 3\theta)^{2/3}$.]

45. Show that, by using the expansion of $(1+x)^{1/4}$ as far as the term in x^3, the decimal expansion for $\sqrt[4]{(1{\cdot}04)}$ can be obtained correct to five decimal places.

46. Find the number of decimal places to which $\log(1{\cdot}01)$ can be obtained correctly by using the expansion of $\log(1+x)$ up to the term in x^4.

47. By using Taylor's formula (6.4) with $f(x) = \sin x$, $a = \pi/6$, $h = \pi/180$, determine the number of terms needed to obtain $\sin(31\pi/180)$ correct to five decimal places.

48. Evaluate

(i) $\displaystyle\lim_{x\to 0}\frac{3\sin x - \sin 3x}{x - \sin x}$, (ii) $\displaystyle\lim_{x\to 0}\frac{(1+x)^3\log(1+x) - x}{x^2}$,

(iii) $\displaystyle\lim_{x\to 0}\frac{\log(1+x) - \log(1+\sin x)}{1 - e^{-x}}$, (iv) $\displaystyle\lim_{x\to 0}\frac{x\cos x - \sin x}{x^3}$.

49. If $\displaystyle\lim_{x\to 0}\frac{1}{x^2}(e^{ax} + e^{-ax} - 2e^{2ax^2}) = 60$, find the constant a.

50. Expand $\sqrt{\left(\dfrac{1+x}{1-x}\right)}$ as a power series in x up to the term in x^3. By taking $x = 1/5$, show that $\sqrt{6} \doteqdot 306/125$.

51. If $|x|$ is sufficiently small so that x^4 and higher powers of x may be neglected, show that

$$1-(1+x)^n e^{-nx} = px^2(1-\tfrac{2}{3}x),$$

and find p in terms of n.

Hence evaluate, to three decimal places, $(1{\cdot}06)^8 e^{-0{\cdot}48}$.

52. Find the quadratic polynomial approximations, for small $|x|$, to the following expressions

(i) $\dfrac{1}{(1+x)^3\sqrt{(2+3x)}}$, (ii) $\dfrac{(3-x)^{3/2}}{\sqrt{(1+x+x^2)}}$.

53. Obtain the power-series expansion in x for each of the following expressions up to the term indicated:

(i) $\log(1+\sin x)$ to x^4; (ii) $3\sin 2x - 2\sin 3x$ to x^5;
(iii) $e^{x^2}\sin 2x$ to x^5; (iv) $\cos\{\log(1+x)\}$ to x^4;
(v) $(2x/\sin 2x)^5$ to x^4; (vi) $\cos(\frac{1}{2}\pi\cos x)$ to x^6;
(vii) $\log(2\sec x - 1)$ to x^4; (viii) $e^{\cos x}$ to x^6.

54. Obtain the coefficient of x^n in the power-series expansion in x for each of the following expressions (use partial fractions for (i) and (ii)):

(i) $\dfrac{x^2+2}{(1-x)^2(1+2x)}$, (ii) $\dfrac{2(x-1)}{(x-2)(x-4)}$,

(iii) $\left(\dfrac{1+x}{1-x}\right)^3$, (iv) $\log(1-x-6x^2)$.

55. Show that, if $|x|$ is so large that $x^{-6}, x^{-7}, \cdots$ can be neglected, then

$$\frac{3x+1}{(x+2)(x^2+1)} = \frac{1}{x^5}(3x^3-5x^2+7x-15).$$

56. By using the power-series expansion in t for $1/\sqrt{(1-t^2)}$, and integrating, find the power-series expansion in x of $\sin^{-1}x$, showing that the coefficient of x^{2n+1} is $(2n)!/(2n+1)2^{2n}(n!)^2$.

57. Show that

$$\tan x = x + \tfrac{1}{3}x^3 + \tfrac{2}{15}x^5 + \cdots.$$

An arc AB of a circle subtends an acute angle of measure α radians at the centre O. A line through B, making an angle $\frac{1}{3}\alpha$ with OA meets the tangent at A in T. Show that $|AT|$ gives a close approximation to arc AB, the percentage error being approximately $5\alpha^4/81$.

58. Show that the perimeter s of the ellipse $x = a\cos\theta$, $y = b\sin\theta$ $(a > b > 0)$ is given by

$$s = 4a\int_0^{\frac{1}{2}\pi}\sqrt{(1-e^2\cos^2\theta)}d\theta,$$

where $e = \sqrt{\{(a^2-b^2)/a^2\}}$, the eccentricity of the ellipse.

If the ellipse is almost circular so that e is small and if e^6 and higher powers of e can be neglected in the expansion of $\sqrt{(1-e^2\cos^2\theta)}$ as a power series in e, evaluate s.

59. By using the power-series expansion in x of $(1-x)^{-3/2}$, evaluate

$$\sum_{r=0}^{\infty} \frac{(2r+1)!}{5^r(r!)^2}.$$

60. By putting $x = \sin^2 t$ in the power series in x of $\log\{(1+x)/(1-x)\}$, or otherwise, find the expansion in powers of t up to t^6 of $\log(\sec^2 t + \tan^2 t)$.

Show that $$\sum_{n=1}^{\infty} \frac{1}{2n-1}(\tfrac{1}{2})^{2n} = \tfrac{1}{4}\log 3.$$

61. Show that each of the following equations has one real root. In each case find the nearest integer approximation to the root and find another approximation by two successive applications of Newton's method.

(i) $x^5+x-35 = 0$, (ii) $x^3+6x^2+16x-121 = 0$.

62. Show that the equation $e^x = 1+2x$ has a root in the interval $(1, 2)$. By taking $x = 1$ as an approximation to this root, find another approximation by two successive applications of Newton's method.

63. Find the general solution of each of the following first-order differential equations, and any particular solutions mentioned.

(i) $(1+x)\dfrac{dy}{dx} = xy$, (ii) $\dfrac{dy}{dx} = x(1-y)^2$,

(iii) $(1+y)^2\dfrac{dy}{dx} = e^{x+y}$, (iv) $\cos^2 x\dfrac{dy}{dx} = xy^2$,

(v) $\dfrac{dy}{dx} = (1-y)\cos x$, and the particular solution for which $y = 2$ when $x = \frac{1}{2}\pi$,

(vi) $(x-y)\dfrac{dy}{dx} = y-4x$, (vii) $(x^2+y^2)\dfrac{dy}{dx} = xy$,

(viii) $\dfrac{dy}{dx} = \dfrac{y(x+y)}{x(y-x)}$, (ix) $(x^2-xy)\dfrac{dy}{dx}+2y^2 = 0$.

(x) $xy^3\dfrac{dy}{dx} = x^4+y^4$, (xi) $x\dfrac{dy}{dx}\tan\dfrac{y}{x}+x-y\tan\dfrac{y}{x} = 0$,

(xii) $(x+1)\dfrac{dy}{dx}-y = (x+1)^2$, (xiii) $\dfrac{dy}{dx}-y\tan x = \sin x\cos x$,

(xiv) $\tan x\dfrac{dy}{dx}+2y = x\operatorname{cosec} x$, (xv) $\dfrac{dy}{dx}+\dfrac{2y}{1-x^2} = 1-x$,

(xvi) $x(x+1)\dfrac{dy}{dx}+y = x(x+1)^2 e^{-x^2}$, and the particular solution for which $y \to 1$ as $x \to \infty$,

(xvii) $x(1+x)\frac{dy}{dx} - y = x^3 e^x$, (xviii) $(1+x^2)\frac{dy}{dx} + xy = 1$,

(xix) $\frac{dy}{dx} + \frac{x+1}{x} y = e^{-x}$, (xx) $(1-x)\frac{dy}{dx} + xy = (1-x)^2 e^{-x}$,

(xxi) $x\frac{dy}{dx} + y = y^2 \log x$ (put $z = 1/y$), and the particular solution for which $y = 1$ when $x = 2$,

(xxii) $x\frac{dy}{dx} + y = x^6 y^4$ (put $v = y^{-3}$),

(xxiii) $\frac{dy}{dx} - \frac{6x}{x^2+1} y = 2x^3\sqrt{y}$ (put $z = \sqrt{y}$), and the particular solution for which $y = 4$ when $x = 0$.

64. By putting $p = \frac{dy}{dx}$ $\left(\text{so that } \frac{d^2y}{dx^2} = \frac{dp}{dx} = p\frac{dp}{dy}\right)$, find the solution of the equation

$$y\frac{d^2y}{dx^2} + \left(\frac{dy}{dx}\right)^2 = 1$$

for which $y = 1$, $dy/dx = 0$ when $x = 0$.

65. The speed v of a car satisfies the equation $v\frac{dv}{dx} = F - kv^2$, where F, k are positive constants and x denotes distance. Show that the speed cannot exceed $\sqrt{(F/k)}$, and find the relation between speed and distance travelled from rest.

66. Find the general solution of each of the following linear second-order differential equations, and any particular solutions mentioned.

(i) $\frac{d^2y}{dx^2} + 3\frac{dy}{dx} + 2y = 2x^2 + 1$, (ii) $\frac{d^2y}{dx^2} + 5\frac{dy}{dx} + 6y = 3e^{-2x}$,

(iii) $\frac{d^2y}{dx^2} - 4\frac{dy}{dx} + 3y = 2e^x$, (iv) $\frac{d^2y}{dx^2} + \frac{dy}{dx} - 2y = x$,

(v) $\frac{d^2y}{dx^2} + 2\frac{dy}{dx} + 2y = \sin x$, and the particular solution for which $y = 0$, $dy/dx = 1$ when $x = 0$,

(vi) $\frac{d^2y}{dx^2} + 6\frac{dy}{dx} + 25y = 30 \sin 5x$, and the particular solution for which $y = 0$, $dy/dx = 1$ when $x = 0$,

(vii) $\frac{d^2y}{dx^2} - \frac{dy}{dx} - 6y = 5e^{3x}$, and the particular solution for which $y = 1$ and $dy/dx = -6$ when $x = 0$,

(viii) $\frac{d^2y}{dx^2} - 3\frac{dy}{dx} + 2y = 5 \sin x$, (ix) $\frac{d^2y}{dx^2} - 2\frac{dy}{dx} + 2y = x + \sin x$,

(x) $\dfrac{d^2y}{dx^2}+4\dfrac{dy}{dx}+4y = x^2+2e^{-2x}$, (xi) $\dfrac{d^2y}{dx^2}+2\dfrac{dy}{dx}+5y = x+\cos 2x$,

(xii) $\dfrac{d^2y}{dx^2}+4y = 8x\,e^{2x}+\sin 2x$, (xiii) $\dfrac{d^2y}{dx^2}-6\dfrac{dy}{dx}+8y = x+e^{2x}$,

(xiv) $\dfrac{d^2y}{dx^2}+\dfrac{dy}{dx}-6y = 4e^x-50\sin x$, and the particular solution for which $y = 0$, $dy/dx = 1$ when $x = 0$,

(xv) $x^2\dfrac{d^2y}{dx^2}+4x\dfrac{dy}{dx}+2y = \dfrac{1}{x}$ (put $x = e^u$),

(xvi) $x^2\dfrac{d^2y}{dx^2}+y = 4x$ (put $x = e^u$),

(xvii) $x^2\dfrac{d^2y}{dx^2}-2x\dfrac{dy}{dx}+2y = x+(\log x)^2$ (put $x = e^u$),

(xviii) $x^2\dfrac{d^2y}{dx^2}+x\dfrac{dy}{dx}-4y = x^2$ (put $x = e^u$), and the particular solution for which $y = -1/8$, $dy/dx = 0$ when $x = 1$.

67. The current i in a certain electrical circuit varies with time t in accordance with the relation

$$\frac{d^2i}{dt^2}+4\frac{di}{dt}+13i = 120\cos 3t.$$

Find the current at time t given that $i = 0$ and $di/dt = 0$ when $t = 0$.

68. A quantity x satisfies the equation

$$\frac{d^2x}{dt^2}+2k\frac{dx}{dt}+n^2x = E\sin\omega t,$$

where k, n, E, ω are positive constants, $k < n$. Show that as $t \to \infty$ the solution approaches $x = V\sin(\omega t+\alpha)$, where $V = E/\sqrt{\{(n^2-\omega^2)^2+4\omega^2k^2\}}$ and $\tan\alpha = -2\omega k/(n^2-\omega^2)$.

Answers

Answers

Exercise 1

1. (i) $\dfrac{-3}{(3x+1)^2}$; (ii) $\dfrac{-6}{(3x+1)^3}$.

2. (i) $f'(0)=0$; (ii) right derivative is 0, left derivative is 1; (iii) right derivative is 2, left derivative is 0; (iv) right derivative is 2, left derivative is $1-a$; $f'(0)$ exists when $a=-1$.

3. (i) $\dfrac{1-x}{(1+x)^3}$, (ii) $\dfrac{3-8x-3x^2}{(x^2+1)^2}$, (iii) $\dfrac{1-x^2}{(x^2+1)^2}$,

(iv) $-\dfrac{4x^3+3x^2+1}{x^2(x^2+1)^2}$, (v) $\dfrac{4+2x-5x^2}{(x^2-x+1)^2}$, (vi) $10\dfrac{(1+x)^4}{(1-x)^6}$,

(vii) $-\dfrac{3x^2(x^2+3)}{(x^2-3)^4}$, (viii) $\dfrac{1}{2(1-\sqrt{x})^2\sqrt{x}}$, (ix) $\dfrac{1}{(1-\sqrt{x})^2\sqrt{x}}$,

(x) $\dfrac{1}{(1+x^2)^{3/2}}$, (xi) $-\dfrac{3x+7}{2(2x^2+x-3)^{3/2}}$, (xii) $\dfrac{x^2(4x^2+3)}{\sqrt{(1+x^2)}}$,

(xiii) $\dfrac{(8x+10)(x+3)^{4/3}}{3(x+1)^{2/3}}$, (xiv) $x^2(8x^2+3a^2)(a^2+x^2)^{3/2}$,

(xv) $3\cos 3x-\sin 2x$, (xvi) $\dfrac{1+2\cos x}{(2+\cos x)^2}$, (xvii) $\dfrac{1}{(\sin x+\cos x)^2}$,

(xviii) $3\sin^2 x\cos 4x$, (xix) $-\left(\dfrac{1}{x^2}+\sin x\right)\cos\left(\dfrac{1}{x}+\cos x\right)$,

(xx) $-\dfrac{5\cos^4 x\cos 4x}{\sin^2 5x}$, (xxi) $-4\cos 4x\sin(\sin 4x)$,

(xxii) $\dfrac{5\cos x-2-2\cos^2 x}{(5-4\cos x)^{3/2}}$, (xxiii) $\dfrac{\cos 3x}{\sqrt{(\cos 2x)}}$,

(xxiv) $\tan 2x+2x\sec^2 2x$, (xxv) $\dfrac{x\sin x^2}{(\cos x^2)^{3/2}}$,

(xxvi) $-\dfrac{\cos(1-2x)}{\sqrt{\{\sin(1-2x)\}}}$, (xxvii) $-\dfrac{3\cos 5x}{\sin^4 x\sqrt{(\cos 6x)}}$, (xxviii) $\dfrac{3-8x}{3(1-2x)^{2/3}}\cos\{x(1-2x)^{1/3}\}$. (xxix) $\dfrac{-3(x^2-1)}{2\sqrt{(x^3-3x)}}\operatorname{cosec}^2\sqrt{(x^3-3x)}$.

(xxx) $\dfrac{3\sin 4x}{2(\cos^5 x\cos^3 3x)^{1/2}}$ (xxxi) $-\dfrac{\sin x^{1/3}}{3x^{2/3}\cos^2(\cos x^{1/3})}$,

(xxxii) $-\dfrac{5x^{1/4}\sec^2 x^{5/4}}{4\sin^2(\tan x^{5/4})}$.

4. (i) $8x-y=7$, (ii) $7x-y=16$, (iii) $x+3y=4$,
(iv) $x-8y=-1$, (v) $x-2y=-\sqrt{3}+\pi/3$, (vi) $4\pi x+y=\sqrt{3}+2\pi/3$.

5. (i) $\dfrac{(-1)^n 2^n n!}{(2x-1)^{n+1}}$, (ii) $(-1)^n 2^{n-1} n!\left\{\dfrac{1}{(2x-1)^{n+1}}-\dfrac{1}{(2x+1)^{n+1}}\right\}$,
(iii) $2^n\sin(2x+\frac{1}{2}n\pi)$.

6. $y=-\frac{1}{4}x-\frac{1}{2}$, point $(-3, 1/4)$.

7. $y=6-2x$, point $(-1, 8)$.

8. Tangent $x-t_1 y=-\frac{1}{2}t_1^2$, normal $t_1 x+y=\frac{1}{2}t_1^3+t_1$;
point $((t_1^2+2)^2/2t_1^2, -(t_1^2+2)/t_1)$.

9. Point of contact $(3, -3)$; other point $(0, 0)$.

10. $f''(x)=2(\cos x-\sin x)/(\sin x+\cos x)^3$; $x=\pi/4, 5\pi/4$.

11. (ii) $\dfrac{d^2y}{dx^2}+4y=0$.

12. $\dfrac{dy}{dx}=\{5-3(x+y)^2\}/\{1+3(x+y)^2\}$; $2x-4y+3=0$.

14. $4x-5y+12a=0$; point $(-16a/7, 4a/7)$.

15. $\dfrac{dy}{dx}=-(2x+3y)/(3x+4y)$.

16. $\dfrac{dy}{dx}=y/(y^3-x)$.

17. (i) the radius, (ii) half the radius.

18. $\dfrac{dr}{dt}=2$.

19. Velocity is 0 when $t=1/2$; acceleration is 30 metres/sec^2, and $x=-5/4$.

20. Point $(1, 5)$.

21. When $y=0$, $\dfrac{d\theta}{dt}=-\sqrt{(2ag)}/10$.

22. $25/9\pi$ metres/minute.

23. $\dfrac{\partial f}{\partial r}=\dfrac{(z^2-r^2)(2-\cos 2\theta)}{(r^2+z^2)^2}$, $\dfrac{\partial f}{\partial\theta}=\dfrac{2r\sin 2\theta}{r^2+z^2}$, $\dfrac{\partial f}{\partial z}=-\dfrac{2rz(2-\cos 2\theta)}{(r^2+z^2)^2}$.

Exercise 2

1. (i) incr. on $[-1, 1]$ and decr. on $(-\infty, -1]$, $[1, \infty)$;
(ii) incr. on $\mathbf{R}$; (iii) incr. on $(-\infty, -2]$, $[0, 2]$ and decr. on $[-2, 0]$, $[2, \infty)$;
(iv) incr. on $[-2, 0]$ and decr. on $(-\infty, -2]$, $[0, 1)$, $(1, \infty)$;
(v) decr. on $(-\infty, -2)$, $(-2, 1)$, $(1, \infty)$;
(vi) incr. on $[2/3, 2)$ and decr. on $(-\infty, 0)$, $(0, 2/3]$, $(2, \infty)$;
(vii) incr. on $[-1, 1]$ and decr. on $(-\infty, -1]$, $[1, \infty)$;
(viii) incr. on $(-1, \infty)$ and decr. on $(-\infty, -1)$; (ix) incr. on $\mathbf{R}$;
(x) incr. on $[-4, 0)$, $[1/4, 4)$ and decr. on $(-\infty, -4]$, $(0, 1/4]$, $(4, \infty)$;
(xi) incr. on $\mathbf{R}$; (xii) incr. on the intervals $[-2\pi/3 + 2n\pi, 2\pi/3 + 2n\pi]$ $(n \in \mathbf{Z})$ and decr. on the intervals $[2\pi/3 + 2n\pi, 4\pi/3 + 2n\pi]$ $(n \in \mathbf{Z})$.

2. (i) $f(1)$ local max. value, $f(-1)$ local min. value;
(ii) no critical values; (iii) $f(2)$, $f(-2)$ local max. values, $f(0)$ local min. value; (iv) $f(0)$ local max. value, $f(-2)$ local min. value; (v) no critical values; (vi) $f(2/3)$ local min. value;
(vii) $f(1)$ local max. value, $f(-1)$ local min. value;
(viii) $x = 1$ gives a H.P.I.; (ix) no critical values;
(x) $f(-4)$ local max. value, $f(1/4)$ local min. value;
(xi) no critical values;
(xii) $f(2\pi/3 + 2n\pi)$ local max. values $(n \in \mathbf{Z})$, $f(-2\pi/3 + 2n\pi)$ local min. values $(n \in \mathbf{Z})$.

3. (i) $(0, 0)$ H.P.I., $(-3, -27)$ local min. point;
(ii) $(-1, 4)$ local max. point, $(1, -4)$ local min. point;
(iii) $(0, 0)$ local min. point, $(1, 1)$ H.P.I.;
(iv) $(0, 0)$ local min. point, $(2, -4)$ local max. point;
(v) $(0, 0)$ H.P.I., $(-10/3, -6250/27)$ local max. point;
(vi) $(\sqrt{3}, \sqrt{3}/\sqrt[3]{2})$ local min. point, $(-\sqrt{3}, -\sqrt{3}/\sqrt[3]{2})$ local max. point;
(vii) $(-\pi/6, -\sqrt{3} - \pi/6)$ local min. point, $(-5\pi/6, \sqrt{3} - 5\pi/6)$ local max. point;
(viii) $(-\pi, 0)$, $(0, 0)$, $(\pi, 0)$ local min. points, $(-\pi/2, 1)$, $(\pi/2, 1)$ local max. points;
(ix) $(\pi/4, -1 + \pi/2)$ local max. point, $(-\pi/4, 1 - \pi/2)$ local min. point.

4. local max. points $(\pi/4, (3 + 4\sqrt{2})/6)$, $(3\pi/4, (4\sqrt{2} - 3)/6)$;
local min. point $(2\pi/3, (\sqrt{3})/2)$.

5. $a = 16$.

6. $a = -6, b = 9$; local max. point $(1, 4)$, local min. point $(3, 0)$.

11. (i) $f(x) = \begin{cases} 1, \frac{1}{2} < x < 1 \\ 0, 0 < x \leqslant \frac{1}{2} \end{cases}$, (ii) $f(x) = \begin{cases} \frac{1}{2}, \frac{1}{2} < x < 1 \\ x, 0 < x \leqslant \frac{1}{2} \end{cases}$

(iii) $f(x) = \begin{cases} x, \frac{1}{2} < x < 1 \\ \frac{1}{2}, 0 < x \leqslant \frac{1}{2} \end{cases}$, (iv) $f(x) = x, 0 < x < 1$.

12. (i) max. $f(-1) = 4$, min. $f(1) = 0$;
(ii) max. $f(5) = 54$, min. $f(-3) = -50$;
(iii) max. $f(1) = 53$, min. $f(-3) = -459$;
(iv) max. $f(1/3) = 9/2$, min. $f(-1) = 1/2$;
(v) max. $f(\pi/2) = 1$, min. $f(\pi) = -1$;
(vi) max. $f(\pi/8) = \sqrt{2}$, min. $f(5\pi/8) = -\sqrt{2}$.

13. max. $f(2) = 1/9$, no min. value.

14. $P(1, 1)$.

15. Normal $t_1x + y = t_1 + \frac{1}{2}t_1^3$, $t_1 = \pm\sqrt{2}$.
16. Taking A as the given area, (i) square of side $\sqrt{A}$. (ii) square of side $\sqrt{A}$.
17. max. perimeter for square of side $a\sqrt{2}$, min. perimeter for rectangle with edges of lengths 0 and $2a$.
18. Base radius 2 cm., height 4 cm.
20. Min. surface area is $3(2\pi V^2)^{1/3}$.
21. Length of side for min. surface area is 2 units; when side $\in [1, 3]$, max. surface area is $(17\sqrt{3})/2$, given by side = 1 unit.
22. Min. volume when $x = 10$ and $y = 5$.

Exercise 3

1. (i) Concave up for $x < 0$ and down for $x > 0$; $(0, 0)$ is a point of inflexion (P.I.): there $\dfrac{dy}{dx} = 3$ and concavity changes from up to down.
   (ii) Concave up for $x > 0$ or $x < -2$ and down for $-2 < x < 0$; at P.I. $(0, 0)$, $\dfrac{dy}{dx} = 0$ and concavity changes from down to up; at P.I. $(-2, -16)$, $\dfrac{dy}{dx} = 16$ and concavity changes from up to down.
   (iii) Concave up for $x > 0$ and down for $x < 0$; at P.I. $(0, 0)$, $\dfrac{dy}{dx} = 1$ and concavity changes from down to up.
   (iv) Concave up for $x > 1$ or $x < 1/3$ and down for $1/3 < x < 1$; at P.I. $(1, 1)$, $\dfrac{dy}{dx} = 0$ and concavity changes from down to up; at P.I. $(1/3, 11/27)$, $\dfrac{dy}{dx} = 16/9$ and concavity changes from up to down.
   (v) Concave up for $x < 1$ and down for $x > 1$; no P.I.
   (vi) Concave up for $-5^{1/4} < x < 0$ or $x > 5^{1/4}$ and down for $x < -5^{1/4}$ or $0 < x < 5^{1/4}$; at P.I. $(0, 0)$, $\dfrac{dy}{dx} = \frac{1}{3}$ and concavity changes from up to down; at P.I. $(5^{1/4}, 5^{1/4}/8)$, $\dfrac{dy}{dx} = -3/16$ and concavity changes from down to up; at P.I. $(-5^{1/4}, -5^{1/4}/8)$, $\dfrac{dy}{dx} = -3/16$ and concavity changes from down to up.
   (vii) Concave up for $-\pi \leqslant x < -\pi/2$ or $\pi/2 < x \leqslant \pi$ and down for $-\pi/2 < x < \pi/2$; at P.I. $(\pi/2, \pi)$, $\dfrac{dy}{dx} = 1$ and concavity changes from down to up; at P.I. $(-\pi/2, -\pi)$, $\dfrac{dy}{dx} = 3$ and concavity changes from up to down.

(viii) Concave up for $-\pi/2 \leqslant x < 0$ or $\pi < x \leqslant 3\pi/2$ and down for $0 < x < \pi$; at P.I. $(0,0)$, $\dfrac{dy}{dx} = 3$ and concavity changes from up to down; at P.I. (π, π), $\dfrac{dy}{dx} = -1$ and concavity changes from down to up.

(ix) Concave up for $-\pi/2 < x < 0$ and down for $0 < x < \pi/2$; at P.I. $(0,0)$, $\dfrac{dy}{dx} = 1$ and concavity changes from up to down.

2. (i) Local max. point $(1/\sqrt{3}, 2/\sqrt{3})$, local min. point $(-1/\sqrt{3}, -2/\sqrt{3})$; asymptote $y = 0$; P.I.s $(0,0)$, $(1,1)$, $(-1,-1)$.

(ii) Local max. point $(1, 1/4)$; asymptotes $x = -1$, $y = 0$; P.I. $(2, 2/9)$.

(iii) Horizontal P.I. $(0,0)$, local min. point $(3, 9/2)$, local max. point $(-3, -9/2)$; asymptotes $x = \sqrt{3}$, $x = -\sqrt{3}$, $y = x$.

(iv) Local min. point $(2, 3)$; asymptotes $x = 0$, $y = x$.

(v) Local min. point $(0,0)$, local max. point $(2^{1/3}, 2^{2/3}/3)$; asymptotes $x = -1$, $y = 0$.

(vi) Local min. point $(0, 2)$, local max. point $(-4, -6)$; asymptotes $x = -2$, $y = x$.

(vii) Local max. point $(2, 0)$, local min. point $(6, 8/9)$; asymptotes $x = 0$, $x = 3$, $y = 1$.

(viii) Local min. point $(2, 0)$, local max. points given by $x = \frac{1}{2}(3 \pm \sqrt{(21)})$; asymptote $x = 3$; $y \sim -x^2 - 2x + 2$ for large $|x|$.

(ix) Local max. point $(-2, 1/3)$, local min. points given by $x = -6 \pm \sqrt{(29)}$; asymptotes $x = 1$, $x = -1$, $y = 0$; $y = 0$ when $x = -5$ or $-3/2$.

3. Local min. point $(0, 2)$, local max. point $(-1, 25)$, horizontal P.I. $(1, 9)$; P.I.s given by $x = (-1 \pm \sqrt{(17)})/8$; $f(x) = 0$ has one real root, which lies in the interval $(-2, -1)$.

5. (i) The curve has the x-axis as an axis of symmetry; it exists for $x \leqslant -\sqrt{3}$ and for $0 \leqslant x \leqslant \sqrt{3}$; part $y = \sqrt{\{x(3 - x^2)\}}$ has a local max. point $(1, \sqrt{2})$; at the points $(0,0)$, $(\pm\sqrt{3}, 0)$, the tangent is parallel to the y-axis; the curve behaves like $y^2 = -x^3$ as $x \to -\infty$ [The curve has a loop and a separate infinite part.]

(ii) This is the image of curve (i) by reflection in the y-axis.

(iii) The curve has the x-axis as an axis of symmetry; it exists for $x \geqslant 0$; part $y = (3 - x)\sqrt{x}$ has a local max. point $(1, 2)$; at $(0,0)$ the tangent is parallel to the y-axis; at $(3, 0)$ there are two tangents of gradients $\mp\sqrt{3}$; the curve has a loop where $0 \leqslant x \leqslant 3$ and behaves like $y^2 = x^3$ as $x \to \infty$.

(iv) The curve has the y-axis as an axis of symmetry ($x \sin x$ is even); it touches the line $y = x$ where $x = (4k + 1)\pi/2$, $k \in \mathbf{Z}$, and touches $y = -x$ where $x = (4k - 1)\pi/2$, $k \in \mathbf{Z}$; it has local max. and min. points where $\tan x = -x$; it meets the x-axis where $x = k\pi$, $k \in \mathbf{Z}$.

(v) The curve has half-turn symmetry about the origin O ($x \cos x$ is odd); $|y| \leqslant |x|$; the curve touches $y = x$ where $x = 2k\pi$ ($k \in \mathbf{Z}$) and touches $y = -x$ where $x = (2k + 1)\pi$ ($k \in \mathbf{Z}$); it has a P.I. at $(0,0)$ and local max. and min. points where $\tan x = 1/x$; it crosses the x-axis where $x = 0$ or $x = (2k + 1)\pi/2$ ($k \in \mathbf{Z}$).

(vi) The curve is the union of (iv), i.e. $y = x \sin x$, and its image, $y = -x \sin x$, by reflection in the x-axis.

6. $(3/2, -3), (-3/2, 3)$.

7. $\dfrac{dy}{dx} = \cos x/(1+\sin y)$, $x = \pi/2$ gives a local max. point.

8. At P.I. $(-1/2, 1)$, $\dfrac{dy}{dx} = 2/3$ and concavity changes from up to down; at P.I. $(1/2, -1)$, $\dfrac{dy}{dx} = 2/3$ and concavity changes from up to down.

9. (i) $y = 4x - 26$, (ii) $x + y = 3$, (iii) $4x + 2y = 3$.

10. (a) $(1, 2)$; (b) $(0, -15)$ and the points given by $t = -1 \pm \sqrt{5}$; (c) $(-1/\sqrt{2}, 0)$.

11. (i) $x^4 = (y-1)^3$; (ii) $\{x - \sqrt{(1-y)}\}^2 = 4\sqrt{(1-y)}$; (iii) $y = 1 - 2x^2$, $-1 \leqslant x \leqslant 1$.

12. The points with parameters $\pm\sqrt{2}, \pm\sqrt{5}$.

13. $3x - 15y + 4 = 0$; $t = -1/4$.

14. $6x - 6t_0 y + 6t_0 + t_0^{\,3} = 0$, $t = -t_0/2$; $t = 0$ gives a cusp $(0, 1)$.

15. $\dfrac{dy}{dx} = \dfrac{2t}{3(t^2-1)}, \dfrac{d^2y}{dx^2} = \dfrac{2(t^2+1)}{9(t^2-1)^3}$; local max. point $(0, 1)$; $(\pm 2, 0)$, $(0, 1)$ and $(0, -2)$; y-axis is an axis of symmetry; curve behaves like $y = -x^{2/3}$ as $|x| \to \infty$; normal $3(t^2-1)x + 2ty = t(t^2-1)(7-3t^2)$; points given by $t = 0, \pm 1, \pm\sqrt{(7/3)}$.

16. $\dfrac{d^2y}{dx^2} = -4\cos^3\theta \sin 3\theta$; at P.I. $(-\sqrt{3}, -(\sqrt{3})/2)$, $\dfrac{dy}{dx} = -1/4$ and concavity changes from down to up; similarly at P.I. $(-\sqrt{3}, -(\sqrt{3})/2)$.

17. At P.I. $(0, 3)$, $\dfrac{dy}{dx} = 0$ and concavity changes from up to down; at P.I. $(0, 4)$, $\dfrac{dy}{dx} = 3$ and concavity changes from down to up; at $t = -1/2$, the tangent is parallel to the y-axis; $x \geqslant -\frac{1}{4}\ \forall t \in \mathbf{R}$; curve meets the x-axis where $t = 3^{1/3}$; curve behaves like $y^2 = x^3$ as $x \to \infty$.

18. The curve has both axes as axes of symmetry and half-turn symmetry about the origin; $-1 \leqslant x \leqslant 1$ and $-1 \leqslant y \leqslant 1$; the points $(\pm 1, 0)$ and $(0, \pm 1)$ are cusps.

19. (i) $r = a$; (ii) $\theta = 3\pi/4$; (iii) $r = -\sec\theta$, $\pi/2 < \theta < 3\pi/2$; (iv) $r = \cos\theta/\sin^2\theta$, $-\pi/2 < \theta \leqslant \pi/2, \theta \neq 0$; (v) $r^2 = \sin 2\theta$, (vi) $r^4 = \cos 2\theta$.

20. (i) $x^2 + y^2 = 9$; (ii) $x^2 + y^2 - 3x = 0$; (iii) $x = 3$; (iv) $x^2 + y^2 - 2y + \sqrt{(x^2+y^2)} = 0$; (v) $(x^2+y^2)^2 = a^2(x^2 - y^2)$; (vi) $x\sqrt{(x^2+y^2)} = 3y$.

Exercise 4

1. (i) $g(y)=\frac{1}{2}(y-1),\ y\in\mathbf{R}$; (ii) $g(y)=\sqrt{(y+1)},\ y\geqslant -1$;
(iii) $g(y)=-1+\sqrt{(4-y)},\ y\leqslant 4$; (iv) $g(y)=2-\sqrt{(y+1)},\ y\geqslant -1$;
(v) $g(y)=\sqrt{\{(2-y)/y\}},\ 0<y\leqslant 2$;

(vi) $g(y)=\begin{cases}\dfrac{1}{y}\{1-\sqrt{(1-y^2)}\}, & y\in[-1,1]-\{0\},\\ 0 & , y=0;\end{cases}$

(vii) $g(y)=\begin{cases}\dfrac{1}{2y}\{y+1-\sqrt{(1+2y-3y^2)}\}, & y\in[-1/3,1]-\{0\},\\ 0 & , y=0;\end{cases}$

(viii) $g(y)=\frac{1}{2}\{y-\sqrt{(y^2+4y-12)}\},\ y\geqslant 2$.

2. (i) $1/2$, (ii) $1/\sqrt{2}$, (iii) $-1/4$, (iv) $-1/8$, (v) $-25/3$, (vi) $25/24$, (vii) $49/72$, (viii) $-9/55$.

3. Inverse is $g:[-11,\infty)\to[2,\infty)$ where, for $y\in[-11,\infty)$, $g(y)=x$ with $y=f(x)$ and $x\geqslant 2$; $g'(-4)=1/15$.

4. (i) $-\pi/4$, (ii) 0, (iii) $\pi/2$, (iv) π, (v) $-\pi/3$, (vi) $\pi/4$, (vii) $\pi/4$, (viii) $\pi/3$.

5. (i) $x=1/\sqrt{2}$, (ii) $x=\sqrt{\{(-1+\sqrt{5})/2\}}$.

8. (i) $4\sqrt{2}x-4y=4-\pi$, (ii) $2\sqrt{3}x+3y=2\pi-3\sqrt{3}$, (iii) $2x+4y=\pi+2$.

9. (i) $\dfrac{-1}{\sqrt{(2x-x^2)}}$, (ii) $\dfrac{1}{(x+1)\sqrt{x}}$, (iii) $-\dfrac{x}{|x|\sqrt{(1-x^2)}}$,

(iv) $\sin^{-1}x^2+\dfrac{2x^2}{\sqrt{(1-x^4)}}$, (v) $-\dfrac{1}{(\sin^{-1}x)^2\sqrt{(1-x^2)}}$,

(vi) $\dfrac{2}{\sqrt{(1-4x^2)}\sin x}-\dfrac{\cos x}{\sin^2 x}\sin^{-1}2x$, (vii) $-\dfrac{3}{\sqrt{\{1-(3x+5)^2\}}}$,

(viii) $\dfrac{1}{2x\sqrt{(x-1)}}$, (ix) $\dfrac{1}{(1+x)\sqrt{\{2x(1-x)\}}}$, (x) $-\dfrac{1}{1+x^2}$,

(xi) $\dfrac{1}{2x-1-2x^2}$, (xii) $-\dfrac{1}{2(2-x)\sqrt{(1-x)}}$, (xiii) $\dfrac{6\cos 2x}{1+9\sin^2 2x}$,

(xiv) $\dfrac{1}{\sqrt{(1-x^2)}}$, (xv) $\dfrac{3}{1+x^2}$.

Exercise 5

1. (i) $-\sin x\, e^{\cos x}$, (ii) $(1+x-2x^2)e^{x-x^2}$,
(iii) $2x(1+x\sin x\cos x)e^{\sin^2 x}$, (iv) $\cot x$, (v) $-\tan x$,
(vi) $\sec x$, (vii) $-\operatorname{cosec} x$, (viii) $4\sin 2x/(1-2\cos 2x)$,
(ix) $1/\{2\tan^{-1}(\sqrt{x})(1+x)\sqrt{x}\}$, (x) $-3/\sqrt{(e^{6x}-1)}$,
(xi) $-1/\{x\sqrt{(1-(\log 2x)^2)}\}$, (xii) $(\sin x)^x(x\cot x+\log\sin x)$,
(xiii) $x^{x^2}(x+2x\log x)$, (xiv) $x2^x(2+x\log 2)$,

(xv) $(1+2x^2\log\pi)\pi^{x^2}$, (xvi) $\dfrac{1}{x}(\log x)^{\log x}(1+\log(\log x))$,

(xvii) $(\sqrt{2})^x x^{\sqrt{2}}\log\sqrt{2}+(\sqrt{2})^{x+1}x^{-1+\sqrt{2}}$, (xviii) $2\cosh x\cosh 3x$.

2. (i) $\dfrac{(-1)^{n-1}(n-1)!}{x^n}$, (ii) $(-1)^{n-1}(n-1)!\left\{\dfrac{1}{(x-1)^n}-\dfrac{1}{(x+1)^n}\right\}$,

(iii) $(x+n)e^x$, (iv) $(\sqrt{2})^n e^x\cos(x+\frac{1}{4}n\pi)$.

3. (i) x^4-2x^3+5x+C, (ii) $\dfrac{x^3}{3}-\dfrac{1}{x}+C$, (iii) $-\dfrac{1}{6(2x-1)^3}+C$,

(iv) $\dfrac{1}{4(3-2x)^2}+C$, (v) $-\frac{1}{2}\cos 2x+C$, (vi) $-\frac{1}{3}\sin(1-3x)+C$,

(vii) $\frac{1}{2}\tan(2x+1)+C$, (viii) $\log(\sin x)+C$ $(\sin x>0)$,
(ix) $-\log(\cos x)+C$ $(\cos x>0)$, (x) $\log(\sec x+\tan x)+C$
$(\sec x+\tan x>0)$,

(xi) $-\log(\operatorname{cosec} x+\cot x)+C$ $(\operatorname{cosec} x+\cot x>0)$,
(xii) $\frac{1}{2}x^2+2x+\log|x|+C$,

(xiii) $\dfrac{1}{x+1}+\log|x+1|+C$, (xiv) $\dfrac{1}{\sqrt{6}}\tan^{-1}(x\sqrt{\tfrac{2}{3}})+C$,

(xv) $\tan^{-1}(x-2)+C$, (xvi) $\frac{1}{3}\sin^{-1}(3x)+C$, (xvii) $\sin^{-1}\dfrac{x-1}{2}+C$,

(xviii) $x+3\log|x+2|+C$, (xix) $\dfrac{x}{3}-\frac{1}{9}\log|3x+1|+C$,

(xx) $\frac{1}{2}\log\{x+\sqrt{(x^2+\frac{1}{4})}\}+C$, (xxi) $\log|x+2+\sqrt{(x^2+4x+3)}|+C$,

(xxii) $\dfrac{3^x}{\log 3}+C$, (xxiii) $\frac{1}{2}\sinh 2x+C$, (xxiv) $\frac{1}{8}\sinh 4x-\frac{1}{2}x+C$.

4. (i) 36, (ii) 2, (iii) 8/81, (iv) $\frac{1}{4}$, (v) $\frac{1}{2}$, (vi) $\frac{1}{6}\sqrt{2}$,
(vii) $\frac{1}{2}$, (viii) $\log(1+\sqrt{2})$, (ix) $\frac{1}{2}\log 2$, (x) $\pi/24$, (xi) $\frac{1}{4}\pi$,
(xii) $\frac{1}{3}\pi$, (xiii) $\frac{1}{2}\pi$, (xiv) $1+\log 2$, (xv) $\frac{1}{2}-\frac{1}{4}\log 3$,
(xvi) $\log\{(2+\sqrt{(13)})/3\}$, (xvii) $\frac{1}{3}\log 2$, (xviii) $\log(1+\sqrt{2})$,
(xix) $1/\log 2$, (xx) 9/16, (xxi) $410/81+\frac{1}{2}\log 3$.

5. (i) $\frac{5}{2}+\log 3$, (ii) $\frac{1}{2}\pi+\log(\frac{3}{2})$.

6. (i) 2/3, (ii) 2/5, (iii) $\log 2$, (iv) $\frac{1}{2}\pi$.

7. (i) 32/3, (ii) 32/3, (iii) π, (iv) 19/30, 11/30, 19/30 (left to right).

8. $\frac{1}{2}\pi$.

9. Local max. point $(e, 1/e)$; P.I. $(e^{3/2}, \frac{3}{2}e^{-3/2})$;
$y\to 0$ as $x\to\infty$, $y\to-\infty$ as $x\to 0$ $(x>0)$.

10. Local max. point $(1, 1/e)$; P.I. $(2, 2/e^2)$; $y\to 0$ as $x\to\infty$,
$y\to-\infty$ as $x\to-\infty$.

11. Local max. point $(1/\sqrt{2}, 1/\sqrt{(2e)})$, local min. point $(-1/\sqrt{2}, -1/\sqrt{(2e)})$;
P.I.s $(0,0)$, $(\sqrt{(\frac{3}{2})}, \sqrt{(\frac{3}{2})}\,.\,e^{-3/2})$, $(-\sqrt{(\frac{3}{2})}, -\sqrt{(\frac{3}{2})}\,.\,e^{-3/2})$;
$y\to 0$ as $|x|\to\infty$.

12. Local min. point $(1/e, e^{-1/e})$; $y\to\infty$ as $x\to\infty$.

13. (ii), (iii), (v), (vii), (viii) are convergent; (i), (iv), (vi), (ix) are not.

14. (i) 1, (ii) 1, (iii) $\log 3$, (iv) 1.

15. (i) $\dfrac{1}{4+x^4}$, (ii) $\dfrac{1}{\sqrt{(1-x^3)}}-\dfrac{2x}{\sqrt{(1-x^6)}}$, (iii) $2^{4x^2+1}-2^{x^2}$.

16. $\dfrac{3}{x}-2x+2\cot x$.

18. $\dfrac{x}{a}\cosh t_1-\dfrac{y}{b}\sinh t_1=1$; $x=-a\cosh t$, $y=b\sinh t$ $(t\in\mathbf{R})$.

19. $t=\frac{1}{2}\log 2$; particle $\to O$.

20. (i) $t=60\log(5/2)/\log 2$, (ii) 25 .

Exercise 6

1. (1) $\frac{1}{4}\log(1+x^4)+C$, (2) $\sqrt{(2+x^2)}+C$, (3) $-\dfrac{2}{5\sqrt{(x^5-4)}}+C$,

(4) $\frac{1}{5}\log|x^5+\sqrt{(x^{10}-4)}|+C$, (5) $\frac{1}{3}\sin^{-1}\left(\dfrac{x^3}{\sqrt{2}}\right)+C$,

(6) $\frac{1}{12}\tan^{-1}\left(\dfrac{2x^2}{3}\right)+C$, (7) $-\frac{1}{4}e^{-x^4}+C$, (8) $e^{x^2-x}+C$,

(9) $-\frac{1}{2}\cos x^2+C$, (10) $\frac{1}{5512}(52x^2-a^2)(x^2+a^2)^{52}+C$,
(11) $\log(\cosh x)+C$, (12) $\frac{1}{2}(\log x)^2+C$, (13) $\frac{1}{4}\{\log(2x+1)\}^2+C$,
(14) $-\frac{1}{2}x\cos 2x+\frac{1}{4}\sin 2x+C$, (15) $x^2\sin x+2x\cos x-2\sin x+C$,
(16) $-(x^2+2x+2)e^{-x}+C$, (17) $-\frac{1}{5}e^{-2x}(2\sin x+\cos x)+C$,
(18) $\frac{1}{2}e^x+\frac{1}{10}e^x(\cos 2x+2\sin 2x)+C$,
(19) $\frac{1}{2}x\{\cos(\log x)+\sin(\log x)\}+C$, (20) $\frac{1}{2}x\{\sin(\log x)-\cos(\log x)\}+C$,

(21) $\frac{1}{3}x^3\log x-\frac{1}{9}x^3+C$, (22) $-\dfrac{1}{2x}\{\sin(\log x)+\cos(\log x)\}+C$,

(23) $\frac{1}{2}(x^2+1)\tan^{-1}x-\frac{1}{2}x+C$, (24) $\frac{1}{2}(x^2+1)\log(x^2+1)-\frac{1}{2}x^2+C$,
(25) $(\sin x)\log(\sin x)-\sin x+C$, (26) $x\cosh x-\sinh x+C$,

(27) $x\dfrac{2^x}{\log 2}-\dfrac{2^x}{(\log 2)^2}+C$, (28) $\frac{1}{2}x\,e^x(\sin x-\cos x)+\frac{1}{2}e^x\cos x+C$,

(29) $\frac{1}{4}\cos 2x-\frac{1}{12}\cos 6x+C$, (30) $\frac{1}{4}\sin 2x-\frac{1}{8}\sin 4x+C$,
(31) $-\frac{1}{3}\cos^3 x+\frac{1}{5}\cos^5 x+C$, (32) $\frac{1}{5}\sin^5 x-\frac{2}{7}\sin^7 x+\frac{1}{9}\sin^9 x+C$,
(33) $\frac{1}{16}x+\frac{1}{64}\sin 2x-\frac{1}{64}\sin 4x-\frac{1}{192}\sin 6x+C$,
(34) $\frac{3}{128}x-\frac{1}{128}\sin 4x+\frac{1}{1024}\sin 8x+C$,
(35) $\frac{1}{3}\tan^3 x-\tan x+x+C$, (36) $-\cot x-\frac{1}{3}\cot^3 x+C$,
(37) $\frac{1}{3}\tan^3 x+C$, (38) $-2/(1+\tan\frac{1}{2}x)+C$,

(39) $\dfrac{1}{\sqrt{5}}\tan^{-1}\left(\dfrac{1+2\tan\frac{1}{2}x}{\sqrt{5}}\right)+C$, (40) $\frac{1}{2}\tan^{-1}(2\tan x)+C$,

(41) $\dfrac{x}{\sqrt{(1+x^2)}}-\frac{1}{3}\dfrac{x^3}{(1+x^2)^{3/2}}+C$, (42) $\dfrac{1}{a^4}\left\{\dfrac{x}{\sqrt{(a^2-x^2)}}+\frac{1}{3}\dfrac{x^3}{(a^2-x^2)^{3/2}}\right\}+C$,

(43) $\sqrt{(1+x^2)}+\log\{x+\sqrt{(1+x^2)}\}+C$, (44) $\log\{x+1+\sqrt{(x^2+2x+3)}\}+C$,

(45) $\sqrt{(2+x-2x^2)}+\dfrac{1}{2\sqrt{2}}\sin^{-1}\left(\dfrac{4x-1}{\sqrt{17}}\right)+C.$

(46) $x-2\sqrt{(x-1)}+\log\{x+\sqrt{(x-1)}\}+\dfrac{2}{\sqrt{3}}\tan^{-1}\left(\dfrac{1+2\sqrt{(x-1)}}{\sqrt{3}}\right)+C.$

(47) $-\dfrac{1}{\sqrt{2}}\log\left|\dfrac{1}{x}+\dfrac{1}{x}\sqrt{(1-\frac{1}{2}x^2)}\right|+C.$ (48) $-\log\{e^{-x}+\sqrt{(1+e^{-2x})}\}+C.$

(49) $\dfrac{1}{\sqrt{2}}\tan^{-1}\left(\dfrac{x\sqrt{2}}{\sqrt{(1-x^2)}}\right)+C.$ (50) $\sin^{-1}\left(\dfrac{2x-a-b}{b-a}\right)+C.$

(51) $\frac{1}{4}\log|(2+x)/(2-x)|+C.$ (52) $\log\{(e^x-1)/(e^x+1)\}+C.$

(53) $x+\frac{1}{2}\log(x^2+1)-\tan^{-1}x+C.$

(54) $\frac{1}{2}\log(x^2+2x+3)-\dfrac{1}{\sqrt{2}}\tan^{-1}\left(\dfrac{x+1}{\sqrt{2}}\right)+C.$

(55) $\frac{1}{2}x^2+\frac{9}{2}\log|x^2-4|+C.$

(56) $\frac{1}{2}x^2+\log|x|-2\log|x+1|+3\log|x-2|+C.$

(57) $\frac{1}{3}\log|x+1|-\frac{1}{6}\log(x^2-x+1)+\dfrac{1}{\sqrt{3}}\tan^{-1}\left(\dfrac{2x-1}{\sqrt{3}}\right)+C.$

(58) $2\log|x+1|-\frac{1}{2}\log(x^2+1)+C.$

(59) $\log|x|+\frac{1}{2}\log(x^2+1)-\frac{1}{2}\tan^{-1}x-\dfrac{x}{2(x^2+1)}+C.$

(60) $x+\log|x+2|+\dfrac{2}{\sqrt{3}}\tan^{-1}\left(\dfrac{2x+1}{\sqrt{3}}\right)-\dfrac{2}{\sqrt{3}}\tan^{-1}\left(\dfrac{2x-1}{\sqrt{3}}\right)+C.$

2. (1) $\frac{1}{3}\log 2.$ (2) $2-\sqrt{3}.$ (3) $\pi/12.$ (4) $\pi/16.$ (5) $\frac{1}{2}.$
(6) $(\sqrt{2}-1)/\sqrt{2}.$ (7) $(e-2)/e.$ (8) 6. (9) $\frac{1}{5}.$
(10) $\frac{1}{4}\pi-\frac{1}{2}\log 2.$ (11) $\frac{7}{48}\pi-\frac{1}{16}\sqrt{3}.$ (12) $\frac{1}{2}\pi.$
(13) $\frac{1}{2}\sqrt{3}+\log\{(1+\sqrt{3})/\sqrt{2}\}.$ (14) $(e-2)/(\log 3)^3.$ (15) $\frac{1}{3}.$
(16) $\frac{3}{64}\sqrt{3}-\frac{1}{48}\pi.$ (17) 2/35. (18) $3\pi/512.$ (19) $\frac{1}{64}\pi+\frac{1}{48}.$
(20) $\frac{1}{2}-\frac{1}{2}\log 2.$ (21) $\frac{1}{2}\sqrt{2}+\frac{1}{2}\log(1+\sqrt{2}).$ (22) $\pi/3.$

(23) $\dfrac{1}{\sqrt{2}}\tan^{-1}\dfrac{1}{\sqrt{2}}.$ (24) $\frac{1}{8}\pi-\frac{1}{4}\log 2.$ (25) $\sqrt{2}-\frac{2}{3}\sqrt{3}.$

(26) $\frac{1}{3}\sqrt{3}-\frac{1}{6}\pi.$ (27) $\frac{1}{6}\pi-\frac{1}{2}\sqrt{3}+1.$ (28) $\sqrt{2}-1+2\log(1+\sqrt{2}).$
(29) $2\sqrt{2}-2\log(1+\sqrt{2}).$ (30) $\pi/8.$ (31) $\sqrt{2}\log(1+\sqrt{2}).$
(32) $1-\frac{1}{4}\pi+\log 2.$ (33) $\log(3/2).$ (34) $\log(2/\sqrt{3})+\frac{1}{6}\pi\sqrt{3}.$

(35) $\log\left(1+\dfrac{1}{\sqrt{2}}\right)+\frac{1}{8}\pi\sqrt{2}.$ (36) $1-\frac{1}{3}\sqrt{3}+\log(\sqrt{2}/\sqrt{3})+\frac{1}{12}\pi.$

3. $(e^2+3)/8.$
4. 8/105.
5. $-\frac{17}{72}+\frac{5}{128}\pi^2.$
6. (i) $\frac{1}{2}\pi(\pi-2),$ (ii) $\frac{1}{4}(\pi-1),$ (iii) $\frac{1}{4},$ (iv) $\frac{1}{4}\pi\sqrt{2}\log(1+\sqrt{2}),$
(v) 0, (vi) $\frac{1}{8}\pi\log 2.$
7. 1·311.
8. 0·506.

9. Exact value of integral: $4\log 3-4$.
10. Exact value of integral: $\pi/6$.

Exercise 7

1. $\frac{8}{27}(10^{3/2}-1)$, 64π.
2. $\frac{38}{9}\sqrt{3}$.
3. $\frac{8}{27}(10^{3/2}-1)a$.
4. $2\sinh 1$, $\pi(2+\sinh 2)$.
5. $\frac{1}{4}\sqrt{2}+\log\left(\dfrac{4+3\sqrt{2}}{1+\sqrt{2}}\right)-\frac{1}{2}\log 2$.
6. $2\sqrt{3}-\frac{4}{3}$.
7. $8a$.
9. $\frac{2}{3}+\frac{1}{2}\log 3$.
10. $8/3$.
11. $\frac{1}{3}\pi-\frac{1}{2}\sqrt{3}\log 3$.
12. $\sqrt{5}+\frac{9}{2}\sin^{-1}\frac{2}{3}-4$.
14. $1/20$.
15. $3-2\sqrt{2}$.
16. $1/72$.
17. $\frac{3}{5}\sqrt{3}$.
18. $\frac{1}{2}$, $\pi/10$.
19. $8/15$, $\pi/12$.
20. (i) a^2, (ii) $\frac{1}{4}(e^{2\pi}-1)$.
21. $\frac{1}{4}\pi$.
22. $\frac{9}{2}\pi$.
24. $\frac{1}{4}\pi$; (i) $\frac{1}{8}\pi(\pi+2)$, (ii) $\pi\log 2$.
25. $\frac{1}{6}a^2$, $\frac{1}{15}\pi a^3$.
26. $\frac{1}{3}\pi(2-\sqrt{2})$.
27. (i) $12\sqrt{3}$, (ii) $\frac{72}{5}\sqrt{3}$, (iii) $\frac{81}{4}\pi$, (iv) 27π.
29. $\frac{2}{3}\pi(2\sqrt{2}-1)$, $\frac{1}{2}\sqrt{2}+\frac{1}{2}\log(1+\sqrt{2})$.
30. (i) $\frac{1}{6}\sqrt{2}$, (ii) $\frac{1}{2}\pi$, (iii) $\frac{1}{2}\pi$.
31. $\frac{128}{5}\pi$.
32. 4.
33. 8π, 16π.
34. $a\log 2$, $4\pi a^2(1-\frac{1}{2}\sqrt{2})$.
35. (i) $4\pi a^2$, (ii) $\frac{32}{5}\pi$.
36. $2\pi\sqrt{2}+2\pi\log(1+\sqrt{2})$.
37. $4a\sqrt{2}$; $(5a, -2a)$; $(x-5a)^2+(y+2a)^2=32a^2$.
38. $c(1+t^4)^{3/2}/2|t|^3$; $\left(\frac{1}{2}c\left(3t+\dfrac{1}{t^3}\right), \frac{1}{2}c\left(\dfrac{3}{t}+t^3\right)\right)$.
40. $(\frac{3}{4}a, \frac{3}{4}a)$.
42. $x=a(\cos^3\theta+3\cos\theta\sin^2\theta)$, $y=a(\sin^3\theta+3\sin\theta\cos^2\theta)$.
43. $\dfrac{1}{ab}(a^2\sin^2\theta+b^2\cos^2\theta)^{3/2}$; $A=\dfrac{a^2-b^2}{a}$, $B=-\dfrac{a^2-b^2}{b}$.
46. 9 places.
47. 4 terms.

48. (i) 24, (ii) 5/2, (iii) 0, (iv) $-1/3$.

49. $a = 10$ or -6.

50. $1+x+\frac{1}{2}x^2+\frac{1}{2}x^3+\cdots$.

51. $p = \frac{1}{2}n$, 0·986.

52. (i) $\frac{1}{\sqrt{2}}(1-\frac{15}{4}x+\frac{291}{32}x^2)$, (ii) $3\sqrt{3}(1-x+\frac{1}{6}x^2)$.

53. (i) $x-\frac{1}{2}x^2+\frac{1}{5}x^3-\frac{1}{12}x^4$, (ii) $5x^3-\frac{13}{4}x^5$,
(iii) $2x+\frac{2}{3}x^3-\frac{1}{15}x^5$, (iv) $1-\frac{1}{2}x^2+\frac{1}{2}x^3-\frac{5}{12}x^4$,
(v) $1+\frac{10}{3}x^2+6x^4$, (vi) $\frac{\pi}{4}x^2-\frac{\pi}{48}x^4+(\frac{\pi}{1440}-\frac{\pi^3}{384})x^6$,
(vii) $x^2-\frac{1}{12}x^4$, (viii) $e(1-\frac{1}{2}x^2+\frac{1}{6}x^4-\frac{31}{720}x^6)$.

54. (i) $n+1+(-1)^n 2^n$ $(n \geqslant 0)$, (ii) $\dfrac{1}{2^{n+1}}-\dfrac{3}{4^{n+1}}$ $(n \geqslant 0)$,
(iii) 1 $(n = 0)$, $4n^2+2$ $(n \geqslant 1)$, (iv) $\dfrac{1}{n}((-1)^{n-1}2^n-3^n)$ $(n \geqslant 1)$.

58. $2\pi a(1-\frac{1}{4}e^2-\frac{3}{64}e^4)$.

59. $5\sqrt{5}$.

60. $2t^2-\frac{2}{3}t^4+\frac{34}{45}t^6$.

61. (i) $(4a^5+35)/(5a^4+1)$, $a = 163/81$;
(ii) $(2a^3+6a^2+121)/(3a^2+12a+16)$, $a = 229/79$.

62. $(a e^a-e^a+1)/(e^a-2)$, $a = 1/(e-2)$.

63. (i) $\log|y| = x-\log|1+x|+C$, (ii) $\dfrac{1}{1-y} = \frac{1}{2}x^2+C$,
(iii) $(y^2+4y+5)e^{-y}+e^x = C$, (iv) $\dfrac{1}{y}+x\tan x+\log|\cos x| = C$,
(v) $\log|1-y|+\sin x = C$; $\log|1-y|+\sin x = 1$,
(vi) $(y-2x)(y+2x)^3 = C$, (vii) $-\dfrac{x^2}{2y^2}+\log|y| = C$,
(viii) $\dfrac{y}{x}-\log|y| = \log|x|+C$, (ix) $x^2y/(x+y)^2 = C$,
(x) $y^4/4x^4 = \log|x|+C$, (xi) $x\sec\dfrac{y}{x} = C$,
(xii) $y = (x+1)(x+C)$, (xiii) $y\cos x = -\frac{1}{3}\cos^3 x+C$,
(xiv) $y\sin^2 x = x\sin x+\cos x+C$,
(xv) $(1+x)y = (1-x)(x+\frac{1}{2}x^2+C)$,
(xvi) $y = \left(1+\dfrac{1}{x}\right)(-\frac{1}{2}e^{-x^2}+C)$; $y = \left(1+\dfrac{1}{x}\right)(1-\frac{1}{2}e^{-x^2})$,
(xvii) $(1+x)y = x(x e^x-e^x+C)$,
(xviii) $y\sqrt{(1+x^2)} = \log\{x+\sqrt{(1+x^2)}\}+C$,
(xix) $xye^x = \frac{1}{2}x^2+C$, (xx) $y = (1-x)(-\frac{1}{2}e^{-x}+Ce^x)$,
(xxi) $1/xy = \dfrac{1}{x}\log x+\dfrac{1}{x}+C$; $1/xy = \dfrac{1}{x}\log x+\dfrac{1}{x}-\frac{1}{2}\log 2$,

(xxii) $1/x^3y^3 = -x^3+C$,
(xxiii) $\sqrt{y} = x^4+3x^2+2+C(x^2+1)^{3/2}$; $\sqrt{y} = x^4+3x^2+2$.

64. $y = \sqrt{(1+x^2)}$.

65. $v = \sqrt{\left(\frac{F}{k}\right)}\sqrt{(1-e^{-2kX})}$, where X is the distance travelled from the initial point at which $v = 0$.

66. (i) $y = c_1e^{-x}+c_2e^{-2x}+x^2-3x+4$,
(ii) $y = c_1e^{-2x}+c_2e^{-3x}+3xe^{-2x}$,
(iii) $y = c_1e^x+c_2e^{3x}-xe^x$,
(iv) $y = c_1e^x+c_2e^{-2x}-\frac{1}{2}x-\frac{1}{4}$,
(v) $y = e^{-x}(c_1\cos x+c_2\sin x)+\frac{1}{5}(\sin x-2\cos x)$;
$y = \frac{1}{5}e^{-x}(2\cos x+6\sin x)+\frac{1}{5}(\sin x-2\cos x)$,
(vi) $y = e^{-3x}(c_1\cos 4x+c_2\sin 4x)-\cos 5x$;
$y = e^{-3x}(\cos 4x+\sin 4x)-\cos 5x$,
(vii) $y = c_1e^{3x}+c_2e^{-2x}+xe^{3x}$; $y = (x-1)e^{3x}+2e^{-2x}$,
(viii) $y = c_1e^x+c_2e^{2x}+\frac{1}{2}(\sin x+3\cos x)$,
(ix) $y = e^x(c_1\cos x+c_2\sin x)+\frac{1}{2}(x+1)+\frac{1}{5}(\sin x+2\cos x)$,
(x) $y = (c_1+c_2x)e^{-2x}+\frac{1}{4}x^2-\frac{1}{2}x+\frac{3}{8}+x^2e^{-2x}$,
(xi) $y = e^{-x}(c_1\cos 2x+c_2\sin 2x)+\frac{1}{5}x-\frac{2}{25}+\frac{1}{17}(\cos 2x+4\sin 2x)$,
(xii) $y = c_1\cos 2x+c_2\sin 2x+e^{2x}(x-\frac{1}{2})-\frac{1}{4}x\cos 2x$,
(xiii) $y = c_1e^{2x}+c_2e^{4x}+\frac{1}{8}x+\frac{3}{32}-\frac{1}{2}xe^{2x}$,
(xiv) $y = c_1e^{2x}+c_2e^{-3x}-e^x+\cos x+7\sin x$;
$y = -e^{2x}+e^{-3x}-e^x+\cos x+7\sin x$,
(xv) $y = \frac{c_1}{x}+\frac{c_2}{x^2}+\frac{1}{x}\log x$,
(xvi) $y = \sqrt{x}\{c_1\cos(\frac{1}{2}\sqrt{3}\log x)+c_2\sin(\frac{1}{2}\sqrt{3}\log x)\}+4x$,
(xvii) $y = c_1x+c_2x^2-x\log x+\frac{1}{2}(\log x)^2+\frac{3}{2}\log x+\frac{7}{4}$,
(xviii) $y = c_1x^2+\frac{c_2}{x^2}+\frac{1}{4}x^2\log x$; $y = -\frac{1}{8}x^2+\frac{1}{4}x^2\log x$.

67. $i = -e^{-2t}(3\cos 3t+11\sin 3t)+3\cos 3t+9\sin 3t$.

Index